Special Printing Instr

***FOLD OUTS

Title: Narrative of an Excursion to the Mou
in the Year MDCCCXXIII
Author: Gilly, William Stephen
ISBN: 2546

FOLD OUTS!!!
Map before Chapter 1: Narrative
Letter before Map, prior to Appendix
Map before Appendix

NARRATIVE

OF AN EXCURSION TO THE

MOUNTAINS OF PIEMONT,

IN THE YEAR MDCCCXXIII.

AND

RESEARCHES AMONG THE

VAUDOIS, OR WALDENSES,

PROTESTANT INHABITANTS OF THE COTTIAN ALPS:

WITH MAPS,

And an Appendix,

CONTAINING COPIES OF ANCIENT MANUSCRIPTS, AND OTHER INTERESTING DOCUMENTS, IN ILLUSTRATION OF THE HISTORY AND MANNERS OF THAT EXTRAORDINARY PEOPLE.

BY

WILLIAM STEPHEN GILLY, M.A.

RECTOR OF NORTH FAMBRIDGE, ESSEX.

" Qui non palazzi, non teatro, o loggia,
Ma 'n lor vece un' abete, un faggio, un pino
Tra l'erba verde e' l bel monte vicino
* * * * *
Levan di terra al Ciel nostr' intelletto."

Petrarch, Son. 10.

THIRD EDITION.

Eugene, Oregon

Wipf and Stock Publishers
199 W 8th Ave, Suite 3
Eugene, OR 97401

Narrative of an Excursion to the Mountains of Piemont,
in the Year MDCCCXXIII
And Researches among the Vaudois, or Waldenses
By Gilly, William Stephen
ISBN: 1-59752-254-6
Publication date 6/10/2005
Previously published by C. and J. Rivington, 1826

DEDICATED,

BY EXPRESS PERMISSION,

TO HIS MOST GRACIOUS MAJESTY,

GEORGE THE FOURTH,

KING OF GREAT BRITAIN AND IRELAND,

&c. &c. &c.

TO THE

KING'S MOST EXCELLENT MAJESTY.

SIRE,

HAVING been honoured with Your Majesty's gracious permission to lay before You this Narrative, which is principally occupied in detailing researches made into the present condition and ancient history of the VAUDOIS, or WALDENSES, I embrace, with sincere satisfaction, the hope that a community, which has often found relief and protection from Your August Predecessors, may engage some portion of Your Royal regard.

Such favour has this extraordinary race of people found in the sight of those Monarchs, who have successively swayed the sceptre of these dominions, that for the last two hundred years scarcely has there reigned a Sovereign who has not espoused their cause. To whom, indeed, could the DEFENDERS OF THE FAITH be more consistently expected to extend their regards than to the descendants of those primitive confessors, who had transmitted to them the Faith they so strenuously upheld ?

I cannot but express my humble conviction, that should circumstances ever render Your Benevolent Interposition necessary, this interesting people would not need to have recourse to precedents to move Your Majesty in their behalf. In such an event they would find their most sure and earnest advocate in Your Majesty's own breast.

Sensible as I am of the high distinction of being admitted to approach Your August Presence with this volume, I am still more gratefully impressed with the feeling of the prospect it opens to the Vaudois, of obtaining a large share of Your Sympathy; conscious that a just and righteous cause will never reach Your Majesty's ears without exciting a proportionate interest, and securing a corresponding support.

I have the honour to be,

SIRE,

with profound Respect,

Your Majesty's most dutiful Subject,

and most devoted Servant,

WILLIAM STEPHEN GILLY.

May 20, 1824.

PREFACE

TO THE FIRST EDITION.

In the course of the last and present century, the press has teemed with accounts of excursions made to almost every part of the known world: but the picturesque valleys at the eastern foot of the Cottian Alps, with the magnificent mountains which surround them, and the extraordinary race of people who inhabit this romantic region, would seem, from the little notice that has been taken of them, to have escaped the researches of the tourist. Independent of the unrivalled attractions of the scenery, there are higher considerations, which might have induced travellers, and particularly those from Protestant states, to visit these Alpine fastnesses, which nature seems to have reserved for the theatre of uncommon events. It was here that the Reformed Religion had its birth, and that its martyrs and champions made the first effectual resistance to Papal tyranny; and here too may yet be found that primitive Christianity, those simple manners, and noble traits of character which must have distinguished the ancient natives of a district, where the corruptions, introduced elsewhere by the Roman hierarchy, were never tolerated.

I am not aware of any publication, that has anticipated this attempt to call the attention of readers to the scenes described in the following pages, nor do I know of any volume in which the present condition of the Vaudois, and their former interesting history is brought under review in the form which I have here adopted. The list of books, inserted in the Appendix, No. I. contains the principal authorities, which have been consulted for the purpose of giving a correct sketch of the ancient Waldensian churches: these books are, for the most part, very rare, and if they were not so, the distance of time at which they were printed, and the periods of history that they comprise, would shew, that the writer of a narrative, who brings the relation down to the last year, is taking up ground that has not yet been occupied, unless indeed by an occasional pamphlet.

My principal object is to make the singular community, which forms the leading subject of this volume, more known to the world, than it has lately been[a]; and to re-announce, what seems to be almost forgotten, that the race of the old Waldenses, of whom such extraordinary tales have been told by crusaders, inquisitors, troubadours, romancers, and historians, still exists in the Vaudois, still occupies the strong holds of rock and mountain, from which their fathers never could be driven, and still resembles the ancient stock in every thing that constitutes "A PEOPLE OF GOD." I have therefore chosen to throw a great part of my materials into the more attractive form of a traveller's narrative, interwoven with incidents, anecdotes, and observations, in order that I may catch the attention of such readers, as would not engage with a work professedly ecclesiastical.

The weightier matter, and such as could not conveniently be introduced in the Narrative, but which is indispensable towards an illustration of

[a] Those who take an interest in the Vaudois must regret, that they have not found a more conspicuous place in Mr. Southey's admirable work, "The Book of the Church."

the subject is added in an Appendix, which has been adopted in preference to notes, as the latter are sometimes thought to interrupt the continuity of a relation, and are often overlooked entirely.

The documents contained in the Appendix will not be thought cumbersome or unessential to the work, by those who love to grapple with the subject. They will assist the researches of such as are inclined to investigate the opinions and conduct of the Waldenses, as opposed to the Romanists; and will enable them to trace the former, with the interruption of very short intervals, from the primitive, through the dark and middle ages, to the present enlightened times; and to recognize their political existence from century to century, either in the writings of their barbes, in the bulls of popes, or in the edicts of princes.

One of the maps, that of "part of Savoy and Piemont," is delineated upon a larger scale, and in a more accurate style, than could have been otherwise accomplished, if I had not been fortunate enough to obtain the assistance of a grand topographical chart of Piemont, which was lately made, under the direction of scientific persons, employed by the Sardinian government. The other, that of the "three valleys of Luzerna, San Martino, and Perosa," is taken from an old map, drawn by Valerius Crassus, in the year 1640.

I am proud to acknowledge how much I am obliged to my friend, the Rev. John Lamb, the present Vice-Chancellor of the University of Cambridge, and Master of Corpus Christi College, for facilitating my access to the valuable Vaudois manuscripts, deposited in the University Library, and for furnishing me with the fac-similes that front pages 214, 234, and in the Appendix, p. x.

To the Honourable Mrs. Fortescue I am also more indebted, than I know how to express in adequate terms, for permitting me to embellish my volume with Mr. Nicholson's six lithographic drawings[b], from her faithful and beautiful sketches of the scenery in the valley of Luzerna. I employed an artist of Turin, to go from that city to the Vaudois villages, for the purpose of taking views both of the landscape and buildings; but when they were finished and transmitted to me, in England, I had the mortification of finding

[b] In the Quarto, but not in the Octavo Edition.

that most of them proved such indifferent performances, that it would be useless to have them engraved. The views[c] of the churches of San Giovanni, Villaro, and La Torre, and of the interior of the latter, drawn on stone by Mr. King, from the originals by the Piemontese daughtsman, are the only four which I could venture to retain out of the whole collection, and these are merely inserted to give an idea of the construction of the Vaudois churches.

In this dilemma, Mrs. Fortescue most kindly made me an offer of a selection from her valuable portfeuille, and expressed her regret, that from several untoward circumstances, she was not able to make more than five sketches in the Vaudois country. The letter in which this gratifying proffer was communicated, contained an observation, which I cannot but transcribe, as it offers so strong a confirmation of the account which this volume is meant to give of the Vaudois, and the transcendant beauties and sublimities of nature, by which they are environed.

" I do not know any part of the continent that

[c] In the Quarto Edition.

we more lamented not being able to explore than this: the scenery promised a rich harvest for the pencil, and the inhabitants, particularly the pastors, are a most interesting people. I assure you we are not a little pleased, that their sufferings, which they bear with Christian resignation, will now be made known."

This leads me again to advert to the principal object which I have in view in the publication of this work, viz. that of bringing the Vaudois under notice; because it has been the occasion of my hurrying the following pages through the press with greater rapidity, than perhaps is strictly consistent with an author's reputation [d]. It is of importance to the interests of the Vaudois, to bring their claims, and distressed condition, before those, with whom the decision, with regard to the proposed relief, will rest, *at this particular period;* and I have not suffered any thing else to interfere with this paramount consideration.

[d] The author has endeavoured to correct the errors and inaccuracies of the First Edition.

PREFACE

TO THE SECOND EDITION.

To reduce the price and bulk of the work, the engravings and much of the appendix have been omitted in the Second, or Octavo Edition; but nothing has been taken away which was necessary to an illustration of the past or present condition of the Vaudois. The omissions consist principally in the Latin, Italian, or French copies of documents, while the English translations have been retained. This has enabled the author to give some very material additions, and has left room for the insertion of matter, which it is hoped will be considered both important and interesting.

June 15, 1825.

CONTENTS.

CHAPTER I.

CHAPTER II.

CHAPTER III.

CHAPTER IV.

CHAPTER V.

CHAPTER VI.

CHAPTER VII.

CHAPTER VIII.

CHAPTER IX.

CHAPTER XII.

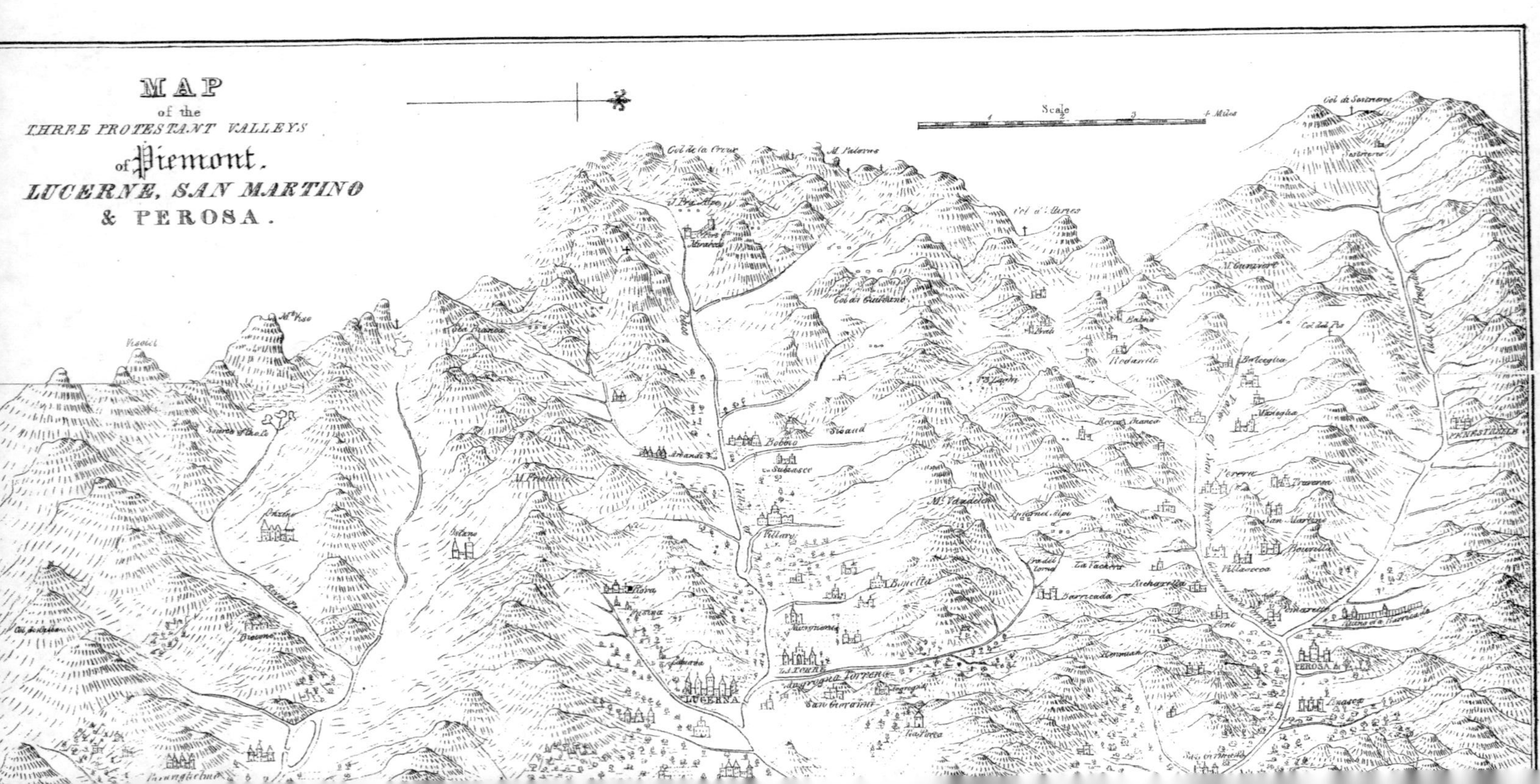
MAP
of the
THREE PROTESTANT VALLEYS
of Piemont.
LUCERNE, SAN MARTINO
& PEROSA.
Scale
4 Miles
Col de la Croix
M. Palevas
Col di Sestriere
Col d' Abries
Col di Giuliano
M. Viso
Source of the Po
River Po
Bobbio
Villar
M. Vandelin
LUCERNA
Angrogna Torrent
San Giovanni
Bonetta
La Vachera
Barricada
PEROSA
Rodaretto
Bovile
Traverse
San Martino
Villasecca
Pomaretto
Valley of Pragela
The Clusone River

NARRATIVE,

&c. &c.

CHAPTER I.

Secluded situation of the Vaudois—Derivation of their name—Inducements to make the excursion—Peyrani's letter—Romantic accounts of Waldensian heroism—Passage across the Channel from Dover to Calais—Fog at sea—Dull journey from Calais to Paris—French equestrians and sportsmen—Awkward machinery—Frightful-looking crucifix—State of religion in Paris—Chapel of British ambassador—English Liturgy—Leave Paris—Journey towards the South of France—Forest of Fontainbleau—Nemours—Moonlight scenery—Old Châteaus—Sabbath in France—Sabbath day in England—Its effect on the character of the nation—Nevers—Anecdote—Moulins—Inscription in the cathedral—Votive tablets—Sterne—Poor Maria—Village near Moulins—Landscape—Appearance of Plenty—Palisse—French traveller—Road from Palisse to Lyons—Lyons—Rousseau—Les Etroits—Library of Lyons—Caligula's edict—Charitable Institutions at Lyons—Hôtel Dieu—Veterinary school—Magnificence of Lyons—Alarm of fire at night—Peter Waldo, the reformer of Lyons—Waldo's translation of the Scriptures—Waldo persecuted—Flies from Lyons—Death of Waldo—Waldo, not the founder of the Waldensian church—Antiquity of the Vaudois—Rainerus, the inquisitor—The Vaudois reformers anterior to those of Lyons—Attend Protestant chapel—Extempore preaching—Communion service in Protestant chapel—Organ—Sacred Music.

Amidst the wildest and most secluded of those Alpine fastnesses, which lie between the Clusone and the Pelice, two mountain torrents that fall into the river Po, there is a small community of hardy and resolute men, who have continued to maintain their religious independence against the supremacy of the Roman Church, for more than a thousand years. Subjects of the present King of Sardinia, and of the ancient Dukes of Piemont and Savoy, and inhabitants of that part of the Province of Pinerolo (Pignerol), which is nearest to the frontiers of France, they do not entirely assimilate either with the Italians, or the French, in manners, customs, religion, or language. Their situation in the heart of the valleys, which extend along the eastern foot of the Cottian Alps, between Mount Viso and the Col de Sestrieres, first gave them the name of Vallenses, Waldenses, or Vaudois[a], a name which has since been employed to distinguish them as a primitive and episcopal Church.

[a] " Les premiers qui nommoient les Vallées *Vaux*, en nommoient les habitans *Vaudois*, n'entendans purement par le nom de *Vaudois* que les habitans des *Vaux*, comme les autres les appelloient Valdesi ou Valdenses, ayant égard au mot de *Val*, ou même, si vous voulez, aux mots Latin et Italien de *Vallis* ou *Valle :* comme en effét le nom de *Valdesi* en Italien, et de *Valdenses* en Latin, ne leur a été donné que de ceux qui parloient ces langues, au lieu que parmi eux ils se nommoient *Vaudés* en leur langue, ou *Vaudois* par ceux qui vouloient mieux parler François, mais toûjours soit *Vaudés*, soit Vaudois du nom de *Vaux*, par ce qu'ils habitoient les Vaux, à raison de quoy les anciens Latins les nommoient *Vallenses*, et quelques fois comme Thuanus, *Convallenses*, eû égard à l'assemblage de ces Vallées.—Pourquoy non donc les *Vaudés* ou *Vaudois* de leur *Vaux*, comme *Montagnards* de leur *Montagnes*, et *Alpinois* de leur Alpes, et *Cisalpins*, *Transalpins*, ou *Inalpins*, selon qu'ils demeurent deçà, de la, ou dans les Alpes? D'où il soit arrivé en suite que ce nom de *Vaudois* ait passé pour le nom de leur Religion, ou comme il plait à Messieurs de Rome, pour une sect, certainement il n'est guères mal-aisé de le diviner, puisque c'est une méthode dont les exemples sont sans nombre, d'entendre par le nom des habitans d'un lieu la Religion qu'ils professent.—Genéralment châcun entend par un Albigeois une personne qui suit la doctrine que les Vaudois des Vallées introduisirent en Albi de Languedoc. De cette même façon dès que les habitans des Vaux se sont ouvertement opposés au Pape, parler d'un Vaudois, ou parler d'un hérétique, a toûjours été la même chose chez Messieurs de Rome." *Leger*, p. 17.

" Les habitans de nos Vallées qui n'avoient jamais été infectés de ces opinions (les opinions de la cour de Rome) furent aussi les seuls qui conservèrent le nom de VAUDOIS, comme le pays qu'ils habitent conserve le nom de VALLEES par excellence." *Histoire des Vaudois*, p. 40.

There are few spots which present more attractions to the eye or to the imagination than these picturesque retreats of the Vaudois, which I was induced to visit by one of those accidental circumstances, to which we sometimes owe the most agreeable events of our life.

I happened to attend a meeting of the Society for Promoting Christian Knowledge, on the day when a very affecting letter [b] was read to the board by the Rev. Dr. Gaskin, the late Secretary, which was signed "Ferdinand Peyrani, Minister of Pramol," and requested that some aid might be sent in books or money to the ancient protestant congregation in the mountains of Piemont, who were struggling hard against poverty and oppression. Of these Vaudois at the time I had but an imperfect knowledge, but from

[b] "A communication has likewise been received from M. Peyrani, one of the Pastors of the ancient Protestant Church of the Waldenses. He states that the numbers who now remain in the valleys of Piemont amount to 18,000; that they are divided into thirteen parishes, with an equal number of pastors, and are the subjects of their lawful sovereign the King of Sardinia. He enters at some length into a description of their past and present state, and represents the difficulties which they have now to encounter as very serious. The stipends of the Clergy are low; provisions are at a high price; and they have no private fortunes. Some of them are reduced to the greatest distress, and the expence of bringing up their children to succeed them in the ministry is greater than they are able to bear. Since peace has been restored on the Continent, they have also been exposed to fresh injuries from the Roman Catholics. The principal object, however, of M. Peyrani was to request the assistance of the Society in furnishing books for their churches.

"It was resolved, in consequence of this letter, that the sum of forty pounds should be granted to M. Peyrani; and be laid out partly in the French works on the Society's list, and partly in the purchase of copies of a book of Psalms and Hymns, which is in use among the Vaudois, and of which the Society's correspondent stated them to be particularly in want. The resolution was communicated to M. Peyrani; and in acknowledging the receipt of the Secretary's letter, and the kindness of the Society, he takes occasion to regret the misfortunes which have deprived the Waldensian Church of the benefit of an episcopal government." See Report of the Society for Promoting Christian Knowledge, p. 115, for the year 1820.

The Society has since made the Vaudois a grant of several thousand Copies of Books and Tracts in the French Language.

the moment my attention was thus directed to the subject, it took complete possession of me; and the books to which I now applied for farther information, confirmed me in my purpose of visiting this people in their native valleys.

Some of the narratives that I read seemed to give quite a romantic, and even fabulous air, to the conflicts which this little community (never exceeding twenty thousand souls) had the courage to hold with their powerful neighbours; and my expectations were raised by several of the descriptions to see a region, which would appear more like fairy land, than the theatre of real achievements. Every vale and glen is represented in these relations as sacred ground, from having been ennobled by some exploit in defence of liberty or religion, or consecrated to the memory of a hero who had bled, or a martyr who had suffered there. One writer calls the valleys of these Vaudois, "an holy asylum which God has wonderfully and even miraculously fortified [c];" and a popish author who wrote against the Vaudois, bears this remarkable testimony to their successful resistance of aggression. "Toutes sortes de gens en divers temps, par un très-grand effort, ont en vain essayé de les arracher, car contre l'opinion de tout le monde ils sont toûjours demeurez vanquers, et du tout invincibles [d]." But highly coloured as such accounts may be thought to be, an investigation into the history of these mountaineers, and a survey of their country, will clearly prove, that neither the extraordinary events in the one, nor the beauty or sublimity of the other have been exaggerated.

It was on the 11th of December, 1822, that I crossed the Channel from Dover to Calais, on my way to Piemont, in search of these secluded valleys and their patriarchal inhabitants. Three young friends, Mr. Colville Coverly Jackson, Mr. John Saville Hallifax, and Mr. Robert Dampier Hallifax, were the companions of my journey; and we flattered

[c] Leger. [d] Claude Seyssel.

ourselves that the mildness with which the month had set in, promised a favourable season for the excursion. It was our intention to make the tour of Italy after our visit to the Vaudois, and that we might have the whole year before us, we improvidently made our arrangements so as to begin where, with better judgment, we should have ended; but there are so many things which occur to control the movements of the traveller, that it is in vain to argue upon regrets when the journey is concluded. Mountain scenery will no doubt be seen to most advantage in the summer; but if those, who have a few months only at their disposal, are resolved to make the most of that time, they must regulate their movements less by choice than necessity.

The deceitfulness of a winter's sun was never felt more truly than on the day we sailed for the coast of France. It was a clear, bright, and warm morning when we left Dover: the vessel made her way calmly, yet rapidly, through the waves, and in three hours we expected to land on the opposite shores; but in mid-channel the atmosphere began to thicken, and at half past one a dense fog came on. We knew that we were nearing Calais; but, instead of the cheerful salutations of the French boatmen, we had the melancholy notes of the leads-man, and the portentous warning of quarter-less-three proclaimed the necessity of keeping off the land, lest we should get a-ground upon the sand-banks. Not an object could be seen from the packet, but the faint sounds of a bell, which were borne on the air from one of the churches in the town, gave us notice to cast anchor, and to wait till it should clear up. It was evening before we landed. A cold frost commenced at night; and, in a thick mist, we started for Paris the next morning.

Our more experienced travellers, however, comforted us with the assurance, that there was not much beauty of scenery between Calais and Paris, and that we had now proof positive that fogs and vapours were not confined to

England. The same weather continued nearly all the way to the capital: great part of the journey was performed at night, and we arrived at Meurice's hotel, having seen but little, and consequently much disposed to criticise. It is, besides, at all times difficult to divest ourselves of the prejudices arising from the habits of years; and, I must frankly confess, that in our first view of things, we were inclined to look at them only in comparison with the superiority we had left behind in England. Of course there was no lack of objects for spleen to feed upon; for where indeed would not spleen find something to gratify its appetite? It is, in one respect, like Shakspeare's jealousy, and may be said to make the meat it feeds on. The French equestrians and sportsmen were peculiarly ridiculous to untravelled Englishmen; the former on sorry beasts, in a stiff jog trot, with large ill-made saddles, and trappings of the last century; the latter, with curs for pointers, and old muskets for fowling-pieces, in pursuit of blackbirds and green-finches, objects worthy of such an equipment.

Then, too, the awkward and inconvenient vehicles, from the diligence to the travelling carriages, and the coarse harness and rope traces of the horses, contrasted with the gay attire of some of the postillions, were also subjects of derision; and not less so the imperfect condition of machinery in general. But, viewed in connexion with the advancement of the mind, there were other things which we noticed with feelings very different to those of merriment. For example, the hideous-looking crucifixes, erected at intervals on the road-side, which seem more like a mockery, than a record, of the most important event in Christian history. Can a clumsy representation of our Lord's sufferings on the cross, with an image, whose features are frightfully distorted, surrounded with all the implements that are supposed to have been used at the crucifixion, and the whole carved in petty detail, and presenting a combination of objects which is any thing but reverend;—can such a sight raise the thoughts from earth to heaven?

A Sunday in Paris, (December 15) with the sight of open shops, and hundreds of busy tradesmen, did not help to satisfy my mind as to the efficacy of what the Romanists consider the external helps and adjuncts of religion. Processions of priests, and an ostentatious display of popish emblems, are again to be seen in the metropolis of France; but the spirit of devotion does not seem to be much moved by these outward signs of it. Considering, however, what this country was a few years back, we have cause to congratulate her even upon the slightest symptoms of religious observances. There is a tale in the Arabian Nights' Entertainments, where it is told, that the holy word, Alla, God, accidentally pronounced, broke the enchantment over a whole city of idolaters, and restored its inhabitants, who had been changed into stone, to their human form. The transformation of hearts of stone to hearts of flesh, may not be far distant even in France.

It was delightful to turn out of streets, where the Sabbath presents no appearance of being a day of rest or holiness, into the court-yard of the British Ambassador, and to find our way into his chapel; for there, at least, there was some evidence, that a reverential esteem of things sacred was not quite effaced from every heart in this gay and noisy capital. The congregation consisted of about six hundred: and a devout air prevailed among all present. It is not easy to believe, that when persons are in a strange land, they can go into a place of worship, where the language of prayer and praise is heard in the well-known terms of our beautiful Liturgy, without being seriously affected. Many of those who were assembled upon this occasion were absentees from their native soil, whom illness, or afflicting events, had sent abroad in search of health, or composure of mind. Others had left behind them objects most dear to their affections, and had brought away regrets, which neither amusements, nor society, nor change of scene, nor time itself, could soften. To each of these the formulary of our Church spoke something so applicable to their immediate condition, that many of the passages might almost appear to have been composed for their particular cases, and could not have been heard with indifference.

Our stay in Paris was but very short, and, during the greater part of the time, I was confined to my room with a cold upon my lungs. The weather was intolerable. Fortunately, on the first day of our departure for the South, (the 21st of December) we had a clear bright sky to add to the interest of a journey perfectly new to us. The sun shone brilliantly for several hours, and the glittering of his rays on the frozen waters of the streams and canals, imparted a degree of cheerfulness to the landscape, which scarcely allowed us to regret that we were travelling in the winter. We entered the forest of Fontainbleau at twilight, and the increasing shades of the evening fell timely enough to throw a sombre colouring over every object, which accorded well with the gloomy character of the scenery. The forest of Fontainbleau possesses all the romantic and poetical features of a forest: the picturesque, the dreary, the solitary, and the magnificent. Its dismal thickets, masses of rock and stunted shrubs, intermixed with venerable and branching timber trees, present a scene altogether of uncommon grandeur.

Without making any stop in the town, we journeyed through the night; and just as we left Nemours, the moon shone forth in all her splendour, and upon a scene that cannot be described without losing some portion of its beauty. A broad stream runs for several miles to the right of the road, and a ridge of hills enclose it on the left, whose fantastically-shaped rocks and crags assumed a variety of forms, as the moon-beams played among them. The châteaus, which we passed, looked as if they had been standing for centuries; and as we gazed at some of their antiquated roofs and gables, we amused ourselves with the idea, that the flower of the ages that are gone, the Chevalier Bayard, or Henri le Grand himself, might have taken up his abode in these habitations of olden times.

Early in the morning of the 22d, we descended the steep declivity that leads to Briare; and here what Reichard calls "a new soil, and a new sky," really burst upon our sight. A boldly expanding country, abounding in vineyards, was spread before us, while the Loire rolled along with a magnificence that it can have in the wintry season only, and carried with it huge masses of ice, that reflected a thousand colours under the rising sun. In summer, the volume of its waters is considerably diminished, and in many places it is then a mere current, bordered by a bed of sand.

At Pouilly, a town which is said to have 2500 inhabitants, though it is no easy matter to determine how the few houses which it contains can find room for them, we had an opportunity of observing the influence of the Sabbath upon the rustics of France. They appeared to be absolutely indifferent to the holiness of the day: they were buying and selling, treating and exchanging, and pursuing their several occupations. Strings of carts, herds of swine, and droves of cattle, were passing and repassing as if it were a market day. Even the few females, whom we saw directing their steps to Church, had none of that decent appearance, and Sabbath-day preparation, which we observe in England. How the inseparable connexion between revealed religion and human happiness, displays itself at every view! We are commanded to sanctify the Sabbath; but "the Sabbath was made for man;" that is, it is subordinate to, and intended for his good. Its proper observance imparts enjoyment and gladness of heart, as well as seriousness to the disposition: and there can be no doubt that the solemnity, the decency, the cheerfulness, and the independent leisure of an English Sabbath, contribute largely to form the steady and manly character of the nation. When we neglect this day as much as our Roman Catholic neighbours do, we shall probably become like some of them, degraded in condition, as well as debased in sentiment and principle: and those who would make the Tiber or the Seine to flow into the Thames, and introduce continental usages and amusements, to the interruption of our present quiet mode of spending the Sunday, are either inimical or indifferent to that spirit of rational independence, which prevails among the middling and lower orders of the community; or they do not know upon what the national character depends.

In our way through Nevers we met with a much more striking instance of what has been called "interesting confidence," and "affecting sensibility," than that of throwing fruit or flowers into a travelling carriage as it rolls along the road: an experiment in which there may be as much policy as simplicity, for it is almost sure of making a purchaser. It was dusk when we entered Nevers, but girls of all ages followed our vehicle; and when it stopped, they thrust into it baskets of bead necklaces and bracelets, beautifully worked. Handsome features do not distinguish the females of the Nivernois, but there was light enough to perceive that one of these girls had the sweetest expression in her face that can be imagined. It was one of those lovely countenances, so exquisitely indicative of amiability and goodness, as to rivet the attention, and to force you to become a convert to Lavater. We read the character of the wearer at a glance; and a little incident gave manifest proof that the favourable impression was not raised without reason. One of her companions, whilst importuning us to buy her trinkets, spoke of a sick and infirm mother, upon which this interesting girl withdrew her own basket, and intimated that the claims of the other were more urgent. Who could refuse to purchase a few articles of both under such an appeal?

We stopped at Moulins for one day. In the church of Nôtre Dame there is a tomb which attracted our attention. It represents a body in a state of corruption, sculptured with hideous fidelity. Under it is the following inscription, dated 1557.

> Olim. formoso. fueram. qui. corpore. putri.
> Nunc. sum. Tu. simili. corpore. Lector. eris.

"My body, which was once beautiful, is now in a state of putrefaction. Reader, yours will be the same."

One person only was in the Church, and that a middle-aged woman. She was reading her missal before a shrine with such earnestness, as not to be disturbed by, or take the slightest notice of the strangers, whose curiosity had drawn them to the scene of her devotion.

It was here, for the first time, I noticed a vestige of the old Pagan custom of hanging up a votive tablet in a temple, after some signal preservation[e]. The little side chapels and shrines were decorated with small images of saints, wreaths and chaplets of flowers, and tinsel hearts. There were also several painted representations of cures and deliverances ascribed to the Virgin, or to the interposition of patron saints. Some were such as might excite a smile, either by their performance or superstitious tendency; but one was extremely affecting. It was a small picture, not badly executed, representing an infant in its cradle, and at the point of death; its parents kneeling by it, and praying for its recovery. The child was restored, and this was the memorial of their gratitude. We could have wished that the praise had been given where alone it was due; but even though it was the votive offering of a superstitious adoration of saints, it was superstition too pious and amiable to be sneered at.

[e] "Me tabulâ sacer
Votivâ paries indicat uvida
Suspendisse potenti
Vestimenta maris Deo." *Hor. Od. Lib. i. Od. 5.*

Moulins has not much to amuse a stranger; and to have an object for a walk it was proposed to go in search of the spot, which Sterne has assigned as the scene of his interview with poor Maria. There are so many localities in Sterne's tale of Maria, that my young companions thought it a fair field of research, and away we went to follow him through his descriptions. "When we had got within half a league of Moulins," says the story, which every body remembers, "at a little opening in the road leading to a thicket, I discovered poor Maria sitting under a poplar,—a small brook ran at the foot of the tree." The distance from Moulins, the opening in the road, the thicket and the brook, were so many realities it was thought, even if there were no love-lorn and melancholy Maria, to render this classic ground; and at about two miles from Moulins, we reached a spot which answered to the description plainly enough. Several aged poplars shaded the road, a small stream crossed it, and pursued its course through ground, which had evidently been once a thicket. It was now cleared, for the most part, of its bushes and brambles; but a few remain, and with them an abundance of those old pollards, which are generally allowed to stand, and to point out a spot which was once consecrated to the Dryads. At the foot of one old tree, the brook ran so closely, that we should have gone away satisfied that this was the very tree, and perhaps we should have searched its bark to find if the names of Maria and Sterne were cut upon it, if it had not unfortunately been an *elm* instead of a *poplar*.

We did not return to Moulins by the high way, but struck into a cross road which took us through a scene that amply compensated for the fatigue of a ramble of several hours. It led to a green lane, bordered on each side by some of those pretty little enclosures of corn and meadow land, which are much less common in France than in England. Soon afterwards we came to a village, where every cottage had its own orchard or vineyard: the vines, unlike those low stunted plants, which render most of the vineyards in France, Switzerland, and Germany, so uninteresting to the eye, were trained to fruit trees, that the fruit and foliage might fall in those clusters and festoons, which add so much to the scenery in Italy. Each cottage had also its scores of poultry before the door,—fowls, turkeys, and geese; and adjoining to most of the farm-houses, were large stacks of every kind of corn. This aspect of plenty struck me the more forcibly, from my having observed this same season a very different appearance in England, where few corn-stacks were standing, the pressure of the times having unhappily obliged most of the farmers to thresh out the greater part of their crops, as quickly as they could, to carry the grain to market for an immediate supply of money.

We were at Palisse on Christmas-day, a dull country town, which would have left nothing in our recollection, if the festival of our Lord's nativity had not been celebrated there with all the solemnity, which Popish rites can put forth, even in such a place, upon such an occasion. A military band, and a large body of conscripts, who were marching through the town, added to the gaiety of the day. We had some conversation with two agreeable young Frenchmen at Palisse, from whom we endeavoured to gain some information as to our route; but although one of them had been in Italy, and had made some stay in Turin, he knew nothing of the Protestant valleys of Piemont. What surprised us still more was, that he had been educated in the Polytecnic school at Paris, talked of algebra, geometry, and trigonometry, and quoted Virgil and Horace, but yet appeared to be lost when we spoke of Hannibal's passage over the Alps. I question very much if he recollected any part of the Carthaginian general's history, or had ever heard of his march along the banks of the Rhone, although he was a native of Vienne. The other young man had just purchased his discharge from a dragoon regiment, in which he had served as a private. It cost him 1800 francs, or about 70*l.* to procure a substitute.

After leaving Palisse, on our road to Lyons, we began to have some fine views of the mountains of Auvergne, and the bridge which is thrown across a torrent, at the distance of about six miles from Palisse, was the most magnificent object we had seen since we left Paris. If the season had been favourable, we should have enjoyed the first distinct view of the Alps from the heights above Lyons; but, unluckily, the weather was so thick, that during the four days we remained in that city, where we arrived on the 26th of December, we saw nothing of the fine prospects which are so much its boast. Lyons is said to have been founded by Lucius Munatius Plancus, and they give a curious derivation of its name: Lucii Dunum, Luc-dunum, Lug-dunum, Lyons. The etymology of Mount Fourvieres is equally forced, that it may have the honour of a Roman origin: Forum vetus, Forum-viel, Fort-viel, Four-vieres. The tower upon its summit commands, upon a clear day, as fine a panoramic view as can be conceived: but we were obliged to be satisfied with being told this was the case, and to confine our attention to what is contained within the city. Rousseau, who was always extravagant, (but perhaps less so in this instance than in many others,) was such an enthusiastic admirer of some of the environs of Lyons, that he professes to have passed a whole night on the banks of the Saone, at a spot called "Les Etroits," and gives the following description of his midnight ramble. "The evening was serene, the air was fresh without being too cold; the setting sun had left some crimson clouds, whose reflection added a rosy tint to the waters below, and the trees upon the terrace were full of nightingales, who were singing to each other. I proceeded in a sort of ecstasy; and, surrendering up my whole soul and every sense to the enjoyment of the scenery, I pursued my walk far into the night without experiencing the least fatigue. At last I lay down in voluptuous repose, in a sort of grotto upon the terrace. The trees were the canopy of my bed, a nightingale was directly above me; I fell asleep in the middle of his song. My slumber was delightful, and my waking was still more so. It was a brilliant morning. My opening eyes were fixed now upon the waters, and then upon the green verdure and the lovely landscape." The same writer, in his endeavours to describe the munificent affluence of the merchants of Lyons, has condescended to borrow a thought from the volume, whose creed he affected to hold in contempt. " Et son peuple opulent semble un peuple de rois."—" The crowning city, whose merchants are princes, whose traffickers are the honourable of the earth." Isaiah xxiii. 8.

The opulence and munificence of the merchants of this city may still be the same; but, to judge from our visit to the public library, their literary taste must be on the decline. It is a fine building, and is said to contain 100,000 volumes; but it does not appear that they are frequently visited; and we indeed did not meet with a single student: nor was there any accommodation for visitors, either chairs, fire, pens, ink, or paper: a reproach, by the bye, from which certain great libraries in our own country are not more exempt than that of which I am complaining. It seemed as if this former seat of the Muses was one of the most deserted places in the world, and that the edict of Caligula had been again proclaimed, who is said to have established a lyceum of elocution at Lugdunum, and to have enacted that if any body should produce a bad composition, he should be compelled to efface the writing with his tongue, that is, to lick it out, or be thrown into the Rhone. The filth which was accumulated at the entrance of the library, was even more appalling than the air of desertion which reigned within. Nuisance of every sort lay on the stairs, and in the corridor. After witnessing such proofs of the estimation in which the Lyonese held their public library, we were not a little amused with the following sentimental and philosophical description, which a French guide book gives of the terrace leading out of the library. "Une grande terrasse de soixante dix pas de longueur joint la grande salle de la bibliothêque, et procure à l'homme studieux la faculté de se promener, de respirer un air pur, de méditer tranquillement sur l'objet de ses travaux, ou de s'entretenir avec un ami sur ce qui peut les perfectionner et en assurer le succès."

But, for the honour of Lyons, it should be recorded, that if works of literature are neglected, those of humanity are not; and that few cities in Europe can shew more useful or more charitable establishments. At the head of these stands L'Hôtel Dieu, the noblest institution of the kind in all France, perhaps in all the world. It receives under its care the sick, the lame, the wounded and the insane, *les femmes en couche*, and the foundling. Even the victims of crime and vice, as well as those of accident or malady, find admission here; and, after the example of our blessed Lord, who, when he fed the seven thousand, did not enquire who were sinners, and who were not, its doors are open to all who require assistance. For each description of sufferers, as well for male as female, there is a separate compartment: and upon so large a scale is this establishment, that four thousand five hundred unfortunates may be relieved at the same time. It is supported in part by settled funds, and in part by voluntary contributions. I cannot describe the effect which the spacious rooms, the airy halls, and the ample provision for the comfort and convalescence, as well as the cure of the patients, had upon my mind. All the beds are furnished with iron posts and frames, and nothing can exceed the cleanliness, the regularity, and the good and tender management, which prevail in this glorious institution. Among other things, it is so arranged, that the position of the altar, and the space allotted for the daily administration of divine service, enable every person in the hospital, whether in his bed or not, to hear the voice of the officiating minister, the whole building being in the form of a cross, and the chapel in the centre thus

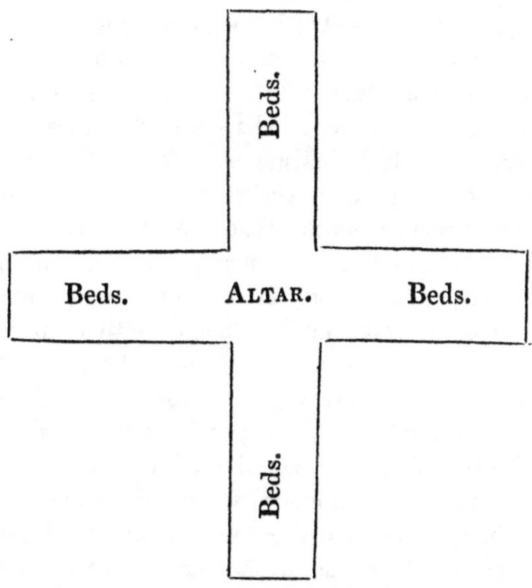

Among other excellent institutions at Lyons, I was much interested by that of the Veterinary School. In England, much as the breed of horses is cultivated, and the animal itself valued and petted, the profession of veterinary surgeon is by no means encouraged as it should be; but here the hippiatrique art is so patronized, that "L'ecôle Royale Vetérinaire" has its own pharmacy, its cabinet of natural history, its botanical garden, its spacious laboratory, and every thing else which is necessary for the improvement of the student.

There are few cities in France to be compared with Lyons, either in situation, antiquities, or splendour; but it is too much of a manufacturing and trading town, the prejudices of its inhabitants against the English are too deep-rooted, and its revolutionary atrocities are too recent, to make it a desirable residence for a stranger. Its two magnificent rivers, the Rhone and the Saone, its hill-begirt site, its charming promenades, its Museum, and its antique-looking edifices, are noble objects; but who would willingly remain long in a place where he knows that a strong national antipathy prevails against him? We were disturbed at midnight by alarming cries of fire: bells sounded, drums beat, and voices called loudly for assistance. We rose from our beds, and hastened to the spot, where we lent our aid in passing the hand buckets from the Rhone to the burning houses. When we thought the fire was nearly extinguished, and that we had performed our part in the labour, we endeavoured to return to our hotel, but for a length of time the soldiers on duty would not permit us to depart, but obliged us to continue the exercise, very much to the delight of the mob, who were pleased to see the predicament in which four Englishmen had placed themselves. The Gazette of Lyons afterwards did us the honour to mention our names, and to talk of the services we had rendered upon the occasion.

One of the objects of my stay at Lyons was connected with the history of the extraordinary people, who will form the principal subject of this volume. I was anxious to learn whether there were still existing any remains of the sect of Peter Waldo, who has often been mistaken as the founder of the Vaudois Church; whereas, in fact, he derived his doctrine from it[f]. There have been so many religious changes in the South of France, and the revolutionary spirit was so active and successful in this city, that it is difficult

[f] "Ce qui a donné juste sujet au grand et judicieux de Beze de nous assurer, dans son livre des Hommes Illustres, pag. 985, que bien loin que les Vaudois des Vallées eussent pris leur nom de *Valdo* de Lyon, que luy tout au contraire a premièrement été nommé *Valdo*, parce qu'il avoit reçeu la Doctrine des Vaudois."—*Leger*, p. 16.

"Il est vrai que plusieurs auteurs, et même de ceux qui ont écrit notre histoire, tels que Perrin et Gilles, donnent une toute autre origine au nom de Vaudois. Ils prétendent qu'il vient de Pierre Waldo de Lyon. Mais rien n'est moins fondé."—*Histoire des Vaudois*, p. 41.

to prove that any opinions have been steadily maintained from one age to another. At all events the Protestants here have no pretensions whatever to consider themselves upon a footing with the Vaudois, either in antiquity, perseverance, sound doctrine, or simplicity of life and manners.

The reformer of Lyons, Peter Waldo, has, in one respect, acquired a degree of celebrity, to which, whatever were his real merits, he certainly had no claim. As the great patron and supporter of a sect, who boldly resisted the corrupt innovations of the Church of Rome, he demands our admiration: but nothing can be collected from his history, which could warrant our ascribing to him the superior character of the founder of a Protestant Church. Happily for the cause of truth, the courage, zeal, and piety of Waldo were most conspicuous at a period, when the Papal Hierarchy began to put its threats in execution against all who questioned its infallibility. But even these great qualities would not have been sufficient to raise the spirits of the reformers of the twelfth century, if the means of this great and good man had not been equal to his strength of mind. His extensive mercantile engagements gave him opportunities of conversing with strangers, and of learning what were the general sentiments upon those practices of idolatry, which accompanied the doctrine of transubstantiation; and his riches and influence enabled him to assert his own opinions the more boldly, and to countenance those who were friends to the same doctrines. It was about the year 1160 that Waldo first began to take a decided part with those, who refused submission to the continued encroachments of the See of Rome. All his wealth was employed in their service; and at length he resorted to a measure, which put the seal upon their undertaking, that of diffusing the Scriptures [g] among

[g] It must not be understood that Waldo made a complete translation of the Holy Scriptures; *parts* only of the sacred volume were rendered into French upon this occasion. The first *entire Bible* in the French language was translated and

his countrymen in their own tongue. This, in my opinion, is the greatest praise of Peter of Lyons. Latin had, for several centuries, continued to be the language of the southern part of Christendom. The Bible, and books of devotion were all written in this language; and when it ceased to be spoken in its purity, there was no provision for those who could not understand it. Waldo's opulence, and perhaps his learning, gave him the power of having translations of the Scripture executed and distributed in the vulgar tongue, and of dispersing also such collections of passages from the ancient fathers, as accorded with his own doctrines. He also maintained, at his own expence, several persons, who were employed to recite and expound these translations to the people; and hence, most probably, proceeded the name of the disciples of Waldo, and the opinion that he was the preacher and apostle of a new faith: an opinion which the Roman Catholics were glad to encourage; for it has ever been their object to represent the Waldenses as a sect of late date, and to vindicate the antiquity and universal recognition of their own dogmas.

The enemies of popery, being thus provided with copies of the Scriptures in their own tongue, were encouraged to declare themselves with the greater confidence, because they were now able to explain to the people that they were not advancing doctrines of their own, but a pure faith, as it really existed in the Bible. They were able to argue effectually, that the tenets of their adversaries were in direct opposition to the divine oracles; and they boldly defied the Papists to justify themselves by any reference to the canons of the New Testament. As long as Waldo and his friends confined themselves to the grounds which had already been taken up, the Hierarchy of Rome suspended its thunders;

printed by Robert Olivetan, a native of the Valleys, at Neufchatel, in the year 1535 or 1537. Beza, as quoted by Leger, speaking of this, says, "Il faut avouer que c'est par le moyen des Vaudois des Vallées, que la France a aujourhuy la Bible en son langage."

but as soon as they employed that invincible engine, the Scriptures in the Vulgar tongue, they were immediately anathematized and excommunicated. For three years after his first condemnation by the Archbishop of Lyons, which took place in 1172, Waldo contrived to remain concealed in the city or its environs: but at length Pope Alexander the Third fulminated his threats and terrors so effectually against all, who should dare to hold the slightest communication with the reformer, that, for his friends' sake, he fled from Lyons, and became a wanderer for the rest of his life. At first he took refuge in Dauphiné, with an intention possibly of finding his way to the secluded valleys of Pragela, or Angrogna, among the Vaudois Protestants of Piemont. But the persecution was too fierce on this side of France, and he was obliged to make his escape towards the western provinces. For a short time he was sheltered in Picardy; but there was no resting-place in the dominions of Philip Augustus for any of his subjects, who presumed to question the papal prerogative. Germany was his next asylum, and it is supposed that he finally escaped into Bohemia, and there died previous to the year 1179. Such are the outlines of Waldo's history; from no part of which can it be gathered, or even presumed, that the Protestant Church of Piemont is to ascribe its origin to him. We can find no trace of him whatever in Italy; and while his name never occurs prior to the year 1160, we can adduce incontrovertible evidence that the Vaudois had existence as a church, and were recorded as separatists from Rome, long before that period.

In the library of the University of Geneva, there is an old manuscript[h] in old Gothic characters, of the date 1100, which speaks of the Vaudois by name. There is also another at Cambridge[i], dated 1120, forty years anterior to any

[h] See Appendix, No. 2.

[i] This was one of the Waldensian manuscripts presented by Sir Samuel Morland to the public library of the University of Cambridge, upon his return

mention of Waldo, containing several sermons of the pastors of the Vaudois, or Valdenses of the Alpine valleys, and a treatise on Antichrist, in which there is the following passage—"These things are a cloak, in which Antichrist hides his wickedness, that he may not be rejected as a pagan. Knowing these things, *we depart from Antichrist*, according to express scriptural directions [k]."

from his mission to Piemont, in 1658. This valuable collection of manuscripts, which formed a record of Waldensian History from the twelfth century, was comprised in twenty-one volumes, each marked with a letter of the alphabet from A to W.

The author regrets to state that the seven first volumes, from A to G, have been stolen from the University Library, and, as he believes, within the last fifty years, but, fortunately, transcripts of *La Nobla Leyçon*, and some others of the more valuable papers and parchments, are preserved in Morland's and Leger's History.

k Rainerus, the inquisitor of the middle of the thirteenth century, and a renegade Waldensian, whose business it was to ascertain and report the origin of the opinions of the heretics of Lyons, is so far from attributing their rise to Peter Waldo, that he declares the heresy to be of long establishment, and to have taken deep root.

"The heresy of the Vaudois, or poor people of Lyons, is of great antiquity. Among all sects that either are, or have been, there is none more dangerous to the Church, than that of the Leonists, and that for three reasons: the first is, because it is the sect of the longest standing of any; for some say that it hath been continued down ever since the time of Pope Sylvester; and others, ever since that of the Apostles. The second is, because it is the most general of all sects; for scarcely is there any country to be found where this sect hath not spread itself. And the third, because it has the greatest appearance of piety; because, in the sight of all, these men are just and honest in their transactions, believe of God what ought to be believed, receive all the articles of the Apostles' creed, and only profess to hate the Church of Rome."

The opinion of Seyssel, Archbishop of Turin, in his book dated 1547, is equally against the notion of Waldo's being the founder of the sect, and even goes to attach a different origin to the Leonists, or Lyonists, themselves. "La sect des Vaudois a prise son commencement d'un certain Leon homme très-religieux du temps de Constantin le Grand, qui ayant deteste l'avarice de Silvestre," &c. &c.

Another book of the date of 1608, printed at Paris with the approbation of the clergy, contains the answer of the theologian Dungald *, to the Treatise of

* Dungald wrote about 828. This book is entitled "Liber responsionum adversus Claudii Taurinensis sententias." See Appendix, No. 3.

There is a numerous Protestant congregation at Lyons; but it is by no means so distinct a community as that, which drew my attention to the valleys on the other side of the Alps. The Protestants are intermixed with other Lyonese families, occupy no separate district, and have not that ecclesiastical discipline to keep them together as effectually, as the church government and pastoral authority, which prevail among the Vaudois.

It was on the last Sunday of the year 1822, a sacrament day, that I attended service at the chapel, which was ori-

Claude, Bishop of Turin, in the ninth century, wherein he charges Claude with having occasioned the separation and apostacy of his flock from the Church of Rome. Now the inhabitants of the three Valleys were then part of his flock, and are the only people who have persevered from that early date in their separation from the Roman See *.

I trust that while I am upon the subject of Lyons, I have said enough to prove, that although the Churches of the Vaudois in Piemont may have reason to thank Peter Waldo for the first translation of part of the Scriptures into the vulgar tongue, and for spreading their doctrines, he has not the least claim to be considered as their founder.

An additional and very strong argument might be drawn from a comparison between the irregularity of Waldo's followers, and the scrupulous adherence to the forms of church government, which has always distinguished the Vaudois. Waldo himself is acknowledged by his historians to have assumed the pastoral functions and character, and to have persuaded others to do the same. The persecutions, and the extraordinary crisis at which he began to preach, and to expose the errors of the Church of Rome, and the necessity of his taking upon himself the office, which he could not regularly obtain by the imposition of hands, have justified him, according to the opinion of most persons, in this assumption. An ecclesiastical writer, Milner, has made a very judicious observation upon Waldo's conduct as a self-ordained pastor. "Let not such extraordinary cases give a sanction to many self-created teachers, who disturb rather than strengthen the hands of faithful pastors, by their irregular proceedings." But the Vaudois, whose zeal has always been tempered by discretion, have never allowed any circumstances, however trying, to warrant an usurpation of the clerical character: the holy functions have been uniformly confined to such as have been canonically admitted to them; and the power of administering the sacraments, from the earliest to the latest period of their history, has been most scrupulously withheld from unordained persons.

* See Appendix, No. 3. Allix endeavours to shew that the churches of the north of Italy were all independent of Rome at this period.

ginally the "Loge du Change," and still exhibits its former inscription, "*Virtute duce, comite fortunâ.*" Many of the edifices in Lyons have changed their destination, and this among the rest. The Palais des Arts was an abbey belonging to the Benedictines; the Theâtre des Celestins was an abbey of the Celestines; most of the barracks were monasteries; and the House of Correction was anciently occupied by the Jesuits.

We were rather late, and lost the beginning of the service, which consisted of the reading of some chapters from the Old and New Testament, and the decalogue. When we entered, the minister was offering up his petitions to heaven from a form of prayer. The three first verses of a canticle, called the Canticle of Zachariah, were then sung, by the whole congregation, to the solemn notes of the organ.

Béni soit à jamais le grand Dieu d'Israel;
L'auteur de tous les biens, tout-puissant, éternel,
Qui, touché de nos cris et de notre misère,
Dans nos pressans besoins s'est montré notre Père.

Dans ses compassions il nous a visités;
Par son bras invincible il nous a rachetés;
Et malgré nos péchés, ce Dieu tendre et propice,
A fait lever sur nous le soleil de justice.

La maison de David, ce grand Roi des Hébreux,
Nous donne ce jour un Sauveur glorieux,
Qui vient nous affranchir d'un funeste esclavage,
Et nous faire obtenir un céleste héritage.

The sermon followed; it was delivered extempore, or from memory, with much animation, fluency, and action: but, at the same time, with a propriety of manner, and an absence of all extravagance, which it would be better if we could notice in many of those English preachers, who venture to give their exhortations without having them written out. Long pauses were made during the sermon, of which the congregation seemed to take advantage, for the purpose of coughing, sneezing, &c.: there was so much of this, that it was pretty clear, colds are almost as general here as in England at the same season: and though Lyons is represented as being extremely favoured by mildness of air in the winter, we did not find it so; but, on the contrary, the cold was intense, and the atmosphere very thick. Another prayer was read, from the formulary, after the sermon; then the Lord's Prayer, and the Apostles' Creed. Next was sung the Canticle of Simeon, and three short benedictions concluded this part of the service.

The minister next began the Communion service, by reading, from his book of prayers, an explanation of the institution. He then addressed a prayer to God, that the communicants might participate in faith, humility, and charity: one sentence was extremely like part of our own supplication; "Vivement touchés de ce don précieux, nous nous consacrons entièrement à toi; nous te présentons nos corps et nos esprits en sacrifice vivant et saint." This was succeeded by two invitations to the people, to approach the holy table. The minister then quitted the pulpit, from which he had delivered the whole of his prayers, sermon, and exhortations, and stood at the table with another clergyman to assist him. He dispensed first to his colleague, and then to himself. After this the communicants, who consisted of two-thirds of a very large congregation, approached the table in two bodies, of which the men formed one, and the women the other. They passed the table in solemn order; and, as they passed, received the bread from one minister, and the cup from the other. The form of consecration and distribution was as follows: "The bread which we break, is the communion of the body of Jesus Christ our Lord."—"The cup of benediction, which we bless, is the communion of the blood of Jesus Christ our Lord." These words, or some sentences from Scripture, were repeated to each person, as he received the bread or the wine. Nothing could be more touching, more imposing, than this simple ceremony, which appealed to the heart, and its best affections. During the whole time of the solemnity, the organ continued to play in its softest tones, and they harmonized with the voice of the ministers, and the calm devotion of the communicants, in a way which must be felt, to be rightly understood.

CHAPTER II.

Leave Lyons—Severe winter—Scenery in France—compared with landscapes in England—French and English villages—Gaul and Britain on ancient medals—Hannibal's passage of the Alps—Discovery of a silver votive Buckler—Pont de Beauvoisin—Letters examined—Enter Savoy—The river Guiers—Melancholy condition of the peasantry of Savoy—Sterne's Sentimental Journey—Addison's remarks on several parts of Italy—Tremendous pass—La Chaille—Les Echelles—Montagna della Grotta—Charles Emanuel II.—The persecutor of the Vaudois—Enter the defile of Aiguebelle—The river Arc—A French disputant—Description of the passage of the Alps—The various features of the mountain—Cultivation—Vines—View of sun-rise among the Alps—Cascades—Torrents—Masses of ice—Alpine sublimity—Fortress on the mountain—Lans-le-bourg—Mount Cenis—Cross the mountain on a sledge—Description of the grand route over Mount Cenis—Attack of the French upon Mount Cenis—Hospice—Plain of St. Nicholas—Murat—Traineaus—Mountain prospects—View of Italy from the Alps—Hannibal—Polybius—Livy—Route of the Carthaginian army.

On Monday evening, December 30, we left Lyons, and commenced our journey to the Alps with all those feelings of expectation, which the name of these tremendous barriers of Italy is calculated to inspire. Livy's fine wintry descriptions, and Eustace's glorious picture of the eternal snows, and frightful passes, which we were going to encounter at the most trying period of an inclement winter, were fresh in our recollection; and we were delighted even with the unusual inhospitality of the season, because it would afford us a better opportunity of ascertaining how far their accounts are correct. We had seen too little of the boasted landscapes of *La belle France*, to regret that we were not travelling in the summer, or to be convinced that they are of such superior order of beauty, as to bear any comparison with the rich landscapes of merry England. When we are speaking of a mountainous region, it is at once understood what is meant by fine scenery; but perhaps it is not easy to agree upon the essentials which are to constitute beautiful scenery in a flat country. Most people, however, concur in filling up the prospect with groves and streams, gentle undulations of hill and dale, vineyards or hop-grounds, a gay intermixture of corn and meadow land, hedge rows and groups of timber trees, and frequent enclosures of various forms and sizes. But, to complete the picture in an Englishman's eyes, there must be the village spire and green, the snug cottage and neat garden, and the substantial farm-house; and he must be occasionally greeted with the sight of a park and mansion-house, and with that general aspect of cheerful comfort, which the residence of the nobility and gentry of a nation, at the hospitable seats of their ancestors, never fails to impart. Every tourist knows that ornamental gardening, the art of laying out grounds to advantage, and the taste for a country life, do not prevail among the French; that the châteaus of the noblesse are formal, and often melancholy-looking buildings; and that pretty hamlets or villages are rarely to be seen. I do not remember passing through one which had attractions sufficient to make me say, what I have so often thought in England, "Here I could pitch my tent; I could take up my abode in this sweet place, and never desire a lovelier spot." These observations are made with all due allowance for the season of the year in which I was travelling.

"Where are the cattle upon a thousand hills?" is a question which every body puts, who looks for flocks and herds to adorn the landscape. These are not to be seen in

France at any time of the year, in that abundance which we should presume from the fertility of the country. In former days, Gaul was so famous for her cattle, that, in old medals, she is often represented with a sheep at her side to signify the multitude of her flocks, and the richness of her pastures; but now, for one flock of sheep, or one field with cattle grazing in it which you see in France, you may see ten in England. The wealth of Gaul[l] was anciently so proverbial in this respect, that Horace mentions it among the most enviable productions of the world:

> " Quanquam nec Calabræ mella ferunt apes,
> Nec Læstrigoniâ Bacchus in amphorâ
> Languescit mihi, *nec pinguia Gallicis*
> *Crescunt vellera Pascuis*——." B. iii. O. 16.

We took no interest in our journey from Lyons till we arrived at Bourgoin, the ancient Bergusium. Here we flattered ourselves, that we were following pretty nearly the same route which Hannibal took in his passage over the Alps. An able dissertation[m] on this subject was published about three years ago, by a member of the University of Oxford; and I am inclined to follow the line of march which this writer has traced, in preference to any other that has been laid down. He conducts the Carthaginian army along the banks of the Rhone to Vienne, the Vienna of the Allobroges; and proceeds to argue, with a great deal of in-

l Speaking of Gaul, and ancient medals, reminds me, that the representation of Britain on some of the Roman coins, was not unlike that which appears on our present copper coins. The reverse of an Antoninus Pius has Britain sitting on a globe placed in the water. Addison's interpretation of this figure is rather too conjectural: he says it meant to denote that Britain was *mistress of a world*, separated from the Roman empire by the interposition of the sea. The Romans were too fond of speaking of Britain in terms of contempt, to pay her this compliment; but, at all events, the present condition of the British empire is more conformable to its ancient emblem, than that of France to hers.

m See " A Dissertation on the Passage of Hannibal over the Alps." Oxford, 1820.

genuity and probability, that it must have taken an easterly direction from thence, passed over the Mont du Chat, into the plains of Chamberry, followed the course of the river Isere from Montmeillan to Moutier and Scez, crossed over the Graian Alps, or Little St. Bernard, pursued the banks of the Doire[n] through Aoste (Augusta Prætoria,) and Ivree (Eporedia,) and so to Turin, the capital of the Taurini.

A curious discovery, which was made about a hundred years ago at Le Passage, a village very near the road by which we were travelling, makes it more than a dream of the imagination to suppose, that we were, for a few miles at least, in the track of the most enterprising soldier who ever dared encounter the Roman arms. A peasant ploughed up a large stone which attracted his notice: he dug under it, and found a round silver plate, of twenty-seven inches in diameter, and weighing 344 ounces. The engraving in the centre of this relic of antiquity, argues strongly in favour of its being Carthaginian: it represents a lion and a palm tree, and under them, in a sort of *exergue*, the torn limbs of some animal. The French Academy pronounced the plate to be a votive buckler, and the lion and the palm tree to be the ordinary emblems of Carthage. It is still to be seen in the King's Library at Paris. Tradition says, what is not unlikely, that the Village of Passage derives its name from the celebrated march of Hannibal; and its position renders it extremely probable that here, if any where, he would offer up his vows for a safe passage over the mountains, and deposit a votive offering, as a memorial of the hazardous expedition. It is at Passage that the flat and more fertile country is left behind; and here the traveller not only begins to mount a chain of hills, which rise higher and higher, until they are succeeded by the formidable Alps themselves;

[n] The Doire, Dora, or Duria, rises on Mount Blanc, and falls into the River Po, between Crescentino and Brusaco; and another river of the same name flows from the Cottian Alps, by Susa and Pianezza, and joins the waters of the Po near Turin. The former was anciently called the Duria Major.

but it is here also that he meets the first acclivity, from which he has a good view of those snow-topped mountains, that threaten to arrest his progress.

At Pont de Beauvoisin we crossed the Guiers, a river that forms the boundary between France and Savoy; and, on the French side, I met with a detention that might have been followed with more disagreeable consequences. The very strict search to which we were exposed at the Custom-house, revealed a packet of introductory letters, which I had about my person. The discovery appeared to be of a most important nature; and caused such consternation and suspicion among the Douaniers, that they made no hesitation in telling me, that some of these letters might contain treasonable correspondence. I was marched off under the escort of a soldier to the post-office, to have the matter examined by the post-master; and my busy imagination conjured up pains and penalties, such as Mr. Bowring had not long before suffered in the prison at Boulogne. At the post-office my letters were examined, and myself questioned. The illegality of my being the bearer of a packet of eight or ten letters, some of which were sealed, was strongly urged against me; and a fine of 300 francs for each, and even imprisonment, were thundered in my ears, as the punishment of my transgression. I pleaded the necessity of taking charge of the letters myself, as they were all introductory, and begged they would open those addressed to the British ministers at Florence and Naples, Lord Burghersh, and Mr. Hamilton, in proof of my being a true man, and no spy. After some consultation, it was determined that I might go my way in peace; but the letters were demanded, in order that they might be transmitted by the post. This I strenuously resisted; and having succeeded in convincing the gentlemen in office, that letters of introduction could be of little use, unless presented in person, I was permitted to carry away my despatches. It is due to the post-master to add, that I was treated with as much civility as the case would allow; and that it was in his power to put me to a great deal of embarrasment.

The aspect of the country became more attractive to the eye, as soon as we got into Savoy. The villages are well situated, and well grouped. Many of them in the midst of stately trees, with streams running through them; others upon the edge of precipices, and embosomed by mountains. The river Guiers runs for many miles by the side of the road, or within sight of it; and the sound of its noisy waters harmonises well with the scenery. But though Savoy is one of the most picturesque countries in Europe, and has all the charms and ever-varying features of mountain beauty, yet the traveller cannot be said to carry away with him any of those recollections, which will make him think of it in future as a region, whose inhabitants are to be envied. I formed the same opinion in my first and second journey through it, and even in an excursion to the romantic vale of Chamouny, and upon the banks of the lake of Geneva, in the Chablais, where nature has done so much to favour man; and where the difference between the happiness of the Swiss, and the wretchedness of the Savoyards, is so strikingly visible. Scarcely can the limits between Geneva, or the Valais, and the Chablais, be crossed, before want and beggary appear at every step. Romance and poetry may assign joy and gaiety to what they call the happy valleys of Savoy, and may speak of it as another Arcadia, where gladsome shepherds, and lovely shepherdesses, make the hills resound with their music; but as far as my observations went, neither in the winter, nor afterwards in the summer, did rustic dance or song enliven morning or evening; no sound of pipe or tabor greeted my ears, nor did the voice of merriment proceed from cabin or cottage, to invite my stay. In the journey that I am now describing, it was certainly too cold for any out-of-door amusements; but if cheerfulness be the character of a people, it will surely display itself, under some form, at every season. As the snow lay deep upon the ground, and the wind blew keenly and dismally from the mountains, we could not but pity the condition of a peasantry, whose huts are exposed to all the bitterness of cold, wind, frost, and rain, with unglazed windows, and holes in the walls or roofs, for the exit of the smoke. Their clothing was as bad as their shelter; and their general dirty and squalid appearance, the goitres which disfigured their necks, and the vacant stare of idiotcy, which haunted us in every hamlet, the swarms of beggars, and the eagerness and gratitude with which the poor creatures snatched at the smallest alms, left the most painful impressions upon our minds.

Sublime as the scenery may be, it is impossible to enjoy it, where the occupiers of the soil are as miserable as they are here; and no person of any feeling can witness their condition, and return home to talk of the happy Savoyard. Things must be sadly changed, or Sterne, whose "Sentimental Journey" was by the same route which we followed, must have seen them with a very different eye. "Poor, quiet, patient, honest people!" is his language, "fear not! your poverty, the treasury of your simple virtues, will not be envied you by the world, nor will your valleys be invaded by it. *Sweet are the dwellings which stand so sheltered!*" It is insulting poverty to talk of the happiness which does not enter its dwelling, or of the simplicity which is not its protection. The poor Savoyard is as little sheltered from the invasion of the world, as from the rough visitings of storms and weather; and the experience of the last thirty years proves, that he has derived no more safety in his scanty means, and secluded situation, than in former times. The tender mercies of French invaders have always been cruel; and when Addison passed through this country more than a hundred years ago, he made an observation which was enough, of itself, to turn the current of Sterne's reveries, if he had ever seen it. "The common people of this state," says Addison, "are more exasperated against the French, than even the rest of the Italians. For the great mischiefs they have suffered from them, are still fresh upon their memories; and notwithstanding this interval of peace, one may easily trace out the several marches, which the French armies have made through their country, by the ruin and desolation they have left behind them. I passed through Piemont and Savoy at a time when the Duke was forced, by the necessity of his affairs, to be in alliance with the French."

I cannot help observing here how strangely the Vaudois were overlooked, even by such an inquisitive and intelligent traveller as Addison. He was contemporary with some of their most celebrated worthies, lived at the very time when the great struggles were taking place for Protestant and Popish ascendency, and visited Turin, soon after the most striking part of an eventful drama° had been performed in the Protestant valleys of Piemont: yet he leaves even the very name of the Vaudois unnoticed. It has been the same with all the principal tourists of the last and present century.

The further we proceeded on our road, the wilder it became. We kept ascending and ascending, as if we meant to reach the very summit of the rocks that soared above us. At length we arrived at the tremendous passage of La Chaille. This struck me as being more formidable than any of those at which we afterwards arrived; but perhaps we are more reconciled to such terrors the more we see. To our right, the river Guiers rolled beneath us at the depth of several hundred feet, foaming and thundering as it dashed along, and forcing its way between two ridges of mountains, which seemed to separate to leave a channel for its course. To our left, lofty and perpendicular ramparts of rock reared their heads to the clouds; and though we were so many fathoms above the bed of the torrent, yet this wall of cliffs appeared to be, at places, as much elevated above us, as we were above

° The failure of the attempt to exterminate the Vaudois in 1686, and their triumphant return to their valleys in 1690.

the river. Two carriages could with difficulty pass each other on this frightful road, stretching, as it were, along a ledge of the rock, or dug, like a gallery, out of it. It wound its way among the cliffs, looking as if it would sink under the weight upon it, and having nothing but a slight parapet, to render it secure on the side of the chasms that yawned in view. Should any sudden swing of a heavy carriage dash it against the parapet, it would inevitably give way. But this is not the only apprehension: the projecting crags, which frown above the traveller's head, retain their place by so slight a hold, that the wonder is, why they do not oftener fall. In fact, enormous fragments are often detached from the heights, and lie in masses by the road side, to justify any fears that may be entertained on the score of personal danger. But a certain degree of peril adds to the interest of an excursion, and every thing combines to render the pass of La Chaille one of the most magnificent and awful on the journey.

The next grand sight, which was reserved for our lowland eyes, was the Montagna della Grotta, or mountain and gallery of Les Echelles. After crossing a plain, and surmounting several heights, which the industry and ingenuity of man had rendered practicable for carriages, we arrived before a line of rocks, which seemed to say, "Here you must stop; you cannot climb this barrier." They stood directly at right angles with the road, and rose like a screen so perpendicularly and abruptly, that no means of ascent offered themselves. The effect is grand in the extreme, to discover that this gigantic pile has been pierced, and a way hollowed out through its very bowels. The magnificent design was achieved by Charles Emanuel II. Duke of Savoy, in 1666. But the most splendid monuments of art ought not to throw a veil over acts of moral turpitude, and public works are not to divert our attention from the misgovernment of a sovereign. Napoleon, *that imperial road-maker*, as he has been called by a lively writer, is lauded to the skies for the facility with which he has enabled travellers to pass into Italy; and as they roll over those celebrated roads which run across Mount Cenis and the Simplon, made not for their accomodation, but for the passage of his own artillery and desolating armies, they forget the great good he has left undone, in the little that he has done.

Charles Emanuel II. was one of the most cruel persecutors that his faithful Vaudois subjects ever had: their three valleys were bedewed with tears and blood during his reign; and tortures of so hideous a description were inflicted upon persons of all ages, from the infant of six months old, to the superannuated of fourscore, that I am unwilling to sully my pages with a detail of his atrocities [p].

On the first day of January, 1823, we began to cross the Alps; for the passage of these celebrated mountains can hardly be said to commence, before the traveller arrives at the foot of those immense heights, which close in upon the Arc, about twenty miles from Chamberry, and a little before that river falls into the Isere, near Freterive. I will here attempt to explain the appearance of the route over Mount Cenis, which has often been spoken of in general terms, but seldom minutely described. Between its junction with the Isere, and its source on Mount Iseran, a few miles beyond Lans-le-bourg, the river Arc winds its way between two chains of Alps, and literally assumes the form of a bow, as its name denotes. The northern chain is called La Grande Montagne, of which the Glacier, and Mont de la Venoise compose the most formidable ridges. The southern is divided into several branches, of which the Col de la Batie, the Col de la Rou, the Col d'Albin, and Mount Cenis, are conspicuous above the rest. Along the banks of the Arc,

[p] As considerable doubt has been thrown upon the truth of statements which record these monstrous cruelties, I have inserted in the Appendix some copies of vouchers, the originals of which are to found among the invaluable Vaudois MSS. that are still preserved in the public library of the University of Cambridge. See Appendix, No. 4.

crossing and recrossing it at several points, and never at any great distance from its brink, the grand road into Italy bends its way.

At Aiguebelle, a town which is quite locked in among the mountains, we had a magnificent specimen of the sort of scenery, which we expected would improve upon us as we advanced: it was real Alpine sublimity. The inn, where we took some refreshments, happened to be crowded at the time with a very motley party; three French gentlemen, four or five Piemontese officers, and ourselves. The Piemontese kept aloof, but the Frenchmen were very communicative; and the subject turned upon religion. An ex-prefect, a merchant of Lyons, and a captain of dragoons, were the principal interlocutors. The prefect was curious and inquisitive; and after a great many close questions, obtained the information that I was a clergyman of the Church of England. Upon this he began to address me in Latin; and, in spite of my reluctance, forced me into a discussion, in which he affected to have the advantage upon every point, and kept exultingly appealing to his countrymen, and translating our conversation, so as to suit his own purpose. The polemic did not, however, succeed in forming an alliance with the captain or the merchant: the former boldly avowed his opinion, that it was all unnecessary disputation between Papists and Protestants, and that it mattered not which party was right. The merchant declared against the mummery of the Roman Catholic priesthood, and professed his ignorance as to what it could all mean. By way of ending the debate, I told them, I hoped there were two roads to heaven, one for the Roman Catholics, and the other for the Protestants. "Yes, yes," replied the ex-prefect, "there are two roads, but one goes up, and the other goes down; and the latter is the path you take."

But although the French party did not agree upon theological subjects, they cordially joined forces against the *amateurs of nature,* as they styled us; and laughed heartily at, what they considered, our extravagant admiration of mountain scenery. Not one of them seemed to take the least interest in a journey over the Alps, or to have any taste for picturesque beauty.

Upon leaving Aiguebelle, we entered a narrow defile, the road through which rises upon a gentle ascent, which is perceptible rather from the slow pace at which you are travelling, than from any visible elevation. For several leagues this continues, and you are scarcely sensible that you are climbing a mountain. The most obvious mark of our progress was in the changing character of the Arc, which ran in a contrary direction to the course we were following. When first we saw this river, it was flowing along in a broad, shallow, transparent sheet of water; but the further we advanced, the more impetuous was the current. At St. Jean de Maurienne, it was no longer gliding " in aquas tenues;" and at St. Michel, it was a frightful torrent. The river and the mountain may be said to vary in the same degree: where the one is only a lively stream, the sides of the other are cheerful-looking slopes, smiling under the influence of human industry; and, in many places, cottages are seen up to the very ridges, peeping from among vines and trellice-work, or half-concealed in the midst of chesnut and walnut trees. But where the Arc is a mighty rushing water, there you see " montes concurrere montibus altos," and huge heaps of rocks thrown together in the most appalling confusion.

Between St. Jean de Maurienne and St. Michel, the sides of the mountain become more and more bare, the cascades increase in power and number, and those insecure Alpine bridges of firs, thrown across the torrents, strike the eye more frequently, and add to the picturesque beauties of the pass. It is here that one begins to wonder how cultivation can succeed, and more especially how the vines can find nourishment among the almost bare crags, upon which they are trained. Upon a close inspection it is found, that the strata consist of a soft kind of stone, which yields to the action of the weather upon it, and pulverises into a soil, which is sufficiently nutritious to the trees and shrubs that find root there.

On the 2d of January, the day on which we were to cross Mount Cenis, we set out from St. Michel at three o'clock in the morning. Our expectations were raised to the highest pitch. We were all impatience; and whenever any salutation passed upon the road, Mount Cenis was sure to be introduced. "In what condition is the mountain? Is it passable? Have any carriages crossed within the last day or two? Is the snow deep?" The rising sun this morning afforded us a most glorious sight: there was not a colour which his rays did not throw upon the mountains. It was at one time like a vast mantle of crimson, which gradually changed from one hue to another, until it mellowed down to the softest purple: it then brightened again, and irradiated the snow-clad tops of the extreme heights, till every crag looked like a flame of fire. No words can describe the ever-varying splendour accasioned by the glorious orb, while he was slowly climbing the heavens, and pouring his streams of light first upon one ridge, and then upon another. I have since beheld that magnificent spectacle, the sun-rise from the summit of Mount Vesuvius, a sight which is said to be unrivalled; but to my eyes, never did any thing equal the lustre which the same object displayed this morning, while wc were in the midst of some of the most sublime and stupendous scenery, which this passage of the Alps affords. The hard, bright, glittering beds of snow, that lay upon the peaks, receiving and transmitting the rays of light; the frozen sides of the cascades, and channels of the torrent, that sparkled under every ray that fell upon them; the pendent icicles of a thousand forms and sizes; the crisp and fringy flakes of snow that hung from the pines; the enormous masses of ice, clear as chrystal or diamond, and reflecting as many colours; the foaming Arc in the abysses below; the shining roofs of a village, which was more than a hundred yards beneath us; all these objects, contrasting with the black and gloomy bank of firs in the shade, presented a coup d'œil surpassing the wildest dreams of the imagination. To add to the glory of this morning view, we had the fortress which the King of Sardinia has been constructing to guard the defile, and which kept breaking in detached masses upon our sight, till at last the entire building stood revealed before us. It is erected on one of the wildest and most inaccessible spots that could be chosen, amidst larches, firs, and mountain pines; some clothed in their darkest drapery, and others bare, or cleft and riven by the irresistible convulsions of nature.

Just before we arrived at Lans-le-bourg, the road stretched across a branch of, what I should suppose to be, Mount Iseran, from which is caught the first sight of Mount Cenis, and its snows of a thousand years.

> "Cuncta gelu canâque æternum grandine tecta,
> Atque ævi glacies."——*Sil. It.* b. 3.

Our eyes were fixed upon the stupendous object before us, and our thoughts upon the *traineaus* on which we were to cross the mountain. We took two of these at Lans-le-bourg, one drawn by a horse, and the other by a mule, and set off from the town at a gallop, at eleven o'clock. The first line of the zig-zag ascent, was mounted at a brisk trot; but after we had gained about a quarter of it, we were glad to stop, and look down upon the vale below, where every object was soon reduced to the most diminutive proportions. The day was peculiarly bright and clear, and so far from being cold, that we dispensed with part of the thick clothing, which we had provided against the expected severity of the wind and frost. Nothing could be more lively or amusing than this sledge expedition. The conductors managed their *traineaus* with admirable skill, and with a dexterity that, to our unpractised eyes, seemed really wonderful, varying their position with the occasion, and sometimes getting out of the vehicle to assist in dragging it over the more difficult parts of the ascent.

The snow had fallen deep upon the mountain; but by the exertions of the men, who were stationed at intervals for that purpose, it was cleared away sufficiently to enable us to pass without any real difficulty. The passage, even at this season of an unusually severe year, was so far from being impracticable, that we met two carriages on their journey, and we almost began to be disappointed in finding Mount Cenis so accessible. The ancient route, however, must have been dangerous as well as difficult; though the present offers an easy ascent, which requires of the traveller nothing but time and patience. The road winds gradually up the mountain, sometimes forming a sort of terrace, with parapets of immense strength, composed of enormous blocks of stone, and lofty posts of wood, to mark the track, in case of any unusual drift of snow. In many places, the road looks as if it were suspended among the clouds; and at every turn or traverse, you necessarily take a direction which is nearly the reverse of what you were following a minute before. In fact the lines of your course form something like alternate angles, by which means all abruptness and steepness of way is entirely prevented, and the summit of the pass is reached by an ascent that has been regularly graduated. Travellers up and down the mountains were seen in various directions, and of various occupations; some at a prodigious height above our heads, and others as far below us; while parties of muleteers were descending by the old route, forming a dark outline with the shining banks of snow, and adding not a little to the general effect of the scene, by the sense of peril connected with their situation.

We were about three hours in gaining the highest point of the pass, which was, as I should judge, about 250 feet below the peak of the mountain. Our guides pointed out to us a very steep and projecting ridge, on which two hundred Savoyard peasants stationed themselves, to oppose some French troops at the beginning of the Revolutionary war, but they were soon driven from their position, though the first attack, which was made upon Mount Cenis by the French, completely failed. It was attempted to be executed by 1500 men, who advanced in three columns, from Lans-le-Villars, Le Monfrey, and by the grand route. The second attack succeeded, which was also made in three columns, under the command of General Dumas, in May, 1794. The left column, consisting of 400 men, took the battery of Villaret, at the point of the bayonet: the right column, of 900 strong, made itself master of the battery of Rivet, in the same gallant style; and the centre, of 600 men, charged along the main pass, and carried every thing before it, until it arrived at the summit of the position, which was the object of the attack.

After reaching the most elevated part of the road, the traveller proceeds across, what is called, the plain of Mount Cenis, which is of considerable extent; and here he finds the well known Hospice, founded originally by Charlemagne, and re-established by Napoleon. During the whole passage of the Alps, Mount Cenis itself was the least dreary-looking part of our journey. Its hamlets and Hospice, its houses of refuge, twenty-five in number, each occupied by a cantonnier, and built for the reception of those who might otherwise be lost in the snow storms, and the concourse of travellers through the passes, take away from the mind all idea of desolation, notwithstanding the wild character of the scenery. Indeed we met with more traffic on the mountain, than on any other part of our road within an equal distance; and we could hardly believe that we had really passed that dreaded barrier, which had for so many centuries been the terror of those who were obliged to cross it. The most magnificent section of the mountain is that which overhangs the plain of St. Nicholas: the rocks rise so perpendicularly, and with such aspiring loftiness, that in the clearest day, the clouds hang about the peaks, and the very chamois avoid them.

Here you look down upon the road, which appears at some places hollowed out of the rock, at others, supported by arches, crossing over bridges, bordered by precipices, protected by walls, and shewing at every yard that there had been an arduous conflict, before the perseverance of man had been able to overcome the obstinacy of nature. We were about two hours in accomplishing the descent into Susa; and towards the afternoon, (although we had none of those violent gusts which generally blow from Piemont) the sharpness of the air together with the wilfulness of our conductors, who seemed to delight in shaking our nerves, and shewing us how near they could take the *traineaus* to the edge of the precipices, made us glad that this part of our journey was over. The descent into Lans-le-bourg may be performed in a sledge in seven minutes; and Murat is said to have done it in six; but it must be by one of the old routes, and attended with extreme hazard.

The general appearance of Mount Cenis, when seen from a distance, is more striking from the side of Turin, than from that of Chamberry, because it rises more abruptly from its base in Piemont than in Savoy: the view of the valleys is also more interesting from the Piemontese side. But the traveller must not expect to see an unbounded horizon, or any thing like a panoramic view: it is quite fabulous to talk of any of the passes, as commanding a general prospect of the plains of Lombardy. Much may probably be seen in a clear day if a person be enterprising enough to ascend one of the summits; but a passage across mountain scenery rarely presents that extensive and distant view which is imagined; and it is difficult to determine where Polybius and Livy could have placed Hannibal, to give him and his army that sight of the plains of the Po, which had the effect of animating their sinking spirits: the direction is all that could possibly have been pointed out, from whatever spot the Carthaginian harangued his troops; for wherever there is a pass that conducts across mountains, there must be intersections, and chains and ridges flanking and crossing each other, and effectually intercepting any distant prospect.

I have crossed the Alps by the Simplon, Mount St. Gothard, and the great St. Bernard, as well as by Mount Cenis; but I do not remember seeing, or hearing any body speak of, those boundless views, which Hannibal's historians had in their imagination. The general accuracy of Polybius's account of that great general's march over the Alps, must make us loth to deny all credit to his statements; but Livy's descriptions are the dreams of a poet, rather than the details of an historian. Nothing can be more beautiful than the dreary and wintry picture which he has drawn; his scenery is truly Alpine; and the sufferings and embarrassments of the Carthaginian army are those which they must really have encountered, had they actually been exposed to the situations in which he has placed them. But it is more than exaggeration, it is mere fable, to talk of an experienced soldier attempting to lead an armament, consisting of certainly not less than 26,000[q] men, with cavalry, elephants, and baggage, over the Alps, and through hostile tribes, under the conduct of guides, whose fidelity[r] or knowledge of the passes was questionable; and to march troops by mountain paths, which were so slippery[s], that they could not move without falling, beyond the power of recovering themselves; and where man and beast kept rolling over one another in endless confusion. His other accounts are even still more preposterous. For instance,

[q] "Minimum, viginti millia peditum, sex equitum," &c.

[r] "Nono die in jugum Alpium perventum est, per invia pleraque, et errores, quos aut ducentium fraus, aut ubi fides iis non esset, temerè initæ valles a conjectantibus iter faciebant."

[s] "Omnis enim ferme via præceps, angusta, lubrica erat, ut neque sustinere se a lapsu possent, nec si paullulum titubassent, hærere afflicti vestigio suo: aliique super alios, et jumenta et homines occiderent."

the romantic dilemma of arriving at a spot, where an army, which had passed through so many real obstacles, was at last stopped by a precipice of a thousand [t] feet deep, and obliged to spend four days in digging, and burning, and melting a passage through the rock. The fact is, that Hannibal was a general of two much experience, to think of a random expedition in the face of such mountain obstacles as Livy has represented: on the contrary, he must have supplied himself with able and trust-worthy guides, who knew and described the passes which the army was to take: he must have ascertained his route and resources before he set out, and have taken that line of march where his troops would have the means of subsistence, and the least fatigue. The plains of Chamberry, the valleys of the Isere and the Aouste, and the passes which were traced by following the courses of the Isere and the Doire, offered Hannibal a practicable route; which, though it was not without its perils and difficulties, yet did not expose his forces to the certainty of being starved to death, or lost amidst precipices.

[t] "Ventum deinde ad multo angustiorem rupem, atque ita rectis saxis, ut ægre expeditus miles tentabundus, manibusque retinens virgulta ac stirpes circa eminentes, demittere se posset——in pedum mille altitudinem——tantum nivis fodiendum atque egerendum fuit——struem ingentem lignorum faciunt: eamque succendunt, ardentiaque saxa infuso aceto putrefaciunt——quatriduum circa rupem consumptum."—*Livy*, l. 21. c. 35, 36, 37.

CHAPTER III.

Arrive at Turin—Priests and officers—Monks—Penitents—Popish cathedral service—Its effect on the imagination—Chapel of the British minister—A Vaudois pastor—Eloquent appeal—The Superga—Retrospect—Victor Amadeus II.—Prince Eugene—Meeting of Eugene and Amadeus—Persecutions of the Vaudois—France and Savoy attack the Protestants—Henri Arnaud—Imprisonment of the whole Protestant Population—Thousands perish in the Jails—Flight of the Vaudois to Switzerland—Restored to their country—Reconciled to their sovereign—Victor Amadeus and the Duke of Marlborough—M. Vertu—Distressed English lady—Bigotry—Opera at Turin—King of Sardinia—Revolutionary movements in Roman Catholic countries.

We arrived at Turin on Friday, January 3; and never, since we left England, had we been gratified with the sight of so many cheerful-looking houses and gardens, as between Rivoli, and the capital of Piemont. The city itself is much more imposing at first entrance, than either Paris or Lyons, from the breadth and cleanliness of the streets, and the uniformity of the houses. There was something also in the appearance of the population, which told us we were in a new region, and added to the general effect; but the most striking objects were priests and soldiers, both of whom swarm in Turin. The dress and figures of the Piemontese officers were equally handsome; and the long flowing cassocks and cloaks, the large flapped hats, and confident air of the priests, told that they are by no means the despised and neglected order that they are in France. Once only, on my journey through France, did I see any mark of respect paid to the clergy, and that was at Lyons, where an aged priest, not in the full garb of his profession, passed a boy, who bowed to him; and the visible delight of the old man sufficiently proved the attention to be neither usual nor expected. At Moulins we happened to follow a priest for some distance, arrayed in all his canonicals; but "none cried, God bless him." The influence of the Roman hierarchy is sensibly felt in the metropolis of his Sardinian majesty; we noticed, on the outside of Churches, innumerable such inscriptions as, "*Plenary indulgence*," and "*Pray for the soul of Filippo Costani*;" and saw votaries offering up their supplications before pictures of the Virgin, at the corners of the streets, penitents kneeling on the steps of churches, and mendicant monks with their cowls and rosaries. The whole scene is not only strikingly new, but even romantic, to a Protestant, who is accustomed to think of such things as divided from him by centuries.

One of my young friends went into a church the first day of our arrival, and came out amazed at what he had seen: he could talk of nothing but the crossings, and bowings, and genuflexions, and ringing and tingling, and placing and displacing and replacing the sacred utensils upon the altar, as if the worship of the ministers consisted in a sort of manual exercise, and gymnastic exhibition, in theatrical prostrations, and prescribed and studied obeisances. He was as much inclined to turn all that he saw into ridicule, as another of my companions was disposed to set an undue value upon some of the more impressive ceremonials of the Catholic service. We went together to the cathedral upon a festival day, in which high mass was performed, in presence of the bishop and chapter, and a large body of troops, who filled the nave. Certainly the appeal to the imagination was strong, but it was only to the imagination: a dim mysterious light fell through the stained glass of the arched windows, and mingled strangely with the blaze of the numberless tapers upon the altar: the cross, and the sacred vessels, were magnificent in the extreme; long trains of priests and choristers gave a solemn animation to the scene; and even the incense had its share in bewildering the senses; the brain was all but intoxicated with the overwhelming sweetness of the odour. But the effect of the music, inexpressibly fine in itself, thus favoured by every concomitant circumstance, had an influence beyond the power of language to describe; the soft breathings of the organ, and the wind-instruments, seemed to linger upon every column and upon every monument, till at last there was a rush of sound that reached the remotest parts of the cathedral, and, for the moment, filled the breast with unusual emotions; but, it was only for the moment, and could be only for the moment. Religious feeling that is called forth by appeals to the senses, must pass away with the existing cause; it should well from the heart itself, or we can hardly hope that it will be lasting. We may go to a Catholic cathedral to gratify our taste for music and splendour, but not for sentiments of pure devotion. The choir and the chaunting, the military band and the opera singers, the banners and trophied monuments, the decorated altars and splendid paintings, the voluptuous portraits of beautiful Magdalenes and handsome St. Sebastians, these are all "of the earth earthy," far removed from the true "image of the heavenly."

At the British minister's chapel, on the following Sunday, I had the good fortune to fall in with a merchant (M. Vertu), who is a native Vaudois, but settled as a resident at Turin; and from him I gathered all the particulars which were necessary for my excursion to the valleys of the Pelice and Clusone. Some of his family were living at La Torre (La Tour), the principal village of the community, and to them he most kindly offered to give me a letter of introduction. To my great surprize, I also learnt that the minister, who officiated, was one of the Vaudois clergy, the pastor of La Torre, the learned and excellent

M. Bert. This was unexpected pleasure; I found myself at once enjoying the advantage of being introduced to a distinguished member of that church, which was the cradle of the Protestant faith. Upon this occasion our conversation was short, but I had the prospect before me of gathering all the information I desired, and from the best source. The service at the British chapel is not performed in English, nor according to the English Liturgy; but in French, and after the ritual of the Church of Geneva or Neufchatel, for the accommodation of the numerous Protestants in Turin, who, not being permitted to have any place of worship of their own, petitioned to have the use of the privileged chapel of the British Ambassador. All the seats in two large rooms were full, and the service not unlike that which we attended at Lyons. The sermon was delivered with considerable earnestness. M. Bert preached on the subject of the new year; and some of his sentences were uncommonly energetic, but without the least rant or extravagance. I wrote down from memory a few of those which were the most striking; but I fear I shall do them injustice in the translation.

"Oh thou omnipotent, most gracious and adorable Father of all, great and good and just as thou art, with what displeasure must thou behold thine erring children! Thou givest them time and opportunity for improvement, but they embrace it not. Thou grantest unto them a new year, but they renew not their hearts." * * * * *

"My brethren, I know your pleas and excuses; I can recount to you every pretext upon which you think to justify your culpable negligence. I know, too, the foundation of sand upon which you build your hopes." * * * *

"You are in health and vigour, you are young and strong; and many years of life and enjoyment are yet before you: time enough, you say, for reformation. I look around me with melancholy regret. How many youthful, blooming countenances do I miss! How many vigorous frames are now returning to dust; how many of the robust and healthy, upon whom I used to gaze with interest from this very pulpit, not more than twelve months since, are in their graves. To them, alas, time is no more!"

" Others among you say, that they have engagements and occupations, which distract their minds, and prevent their performing their Christian duty as strictly as they know they ought to do. Engagements! What! are all your engagements then for man, and none for God? Oh! the sublimity, the boundless extent of God's mercy and indulgence! He suffers you to break engagements with him, which you would not dare to violate with your fellow-creatures. He still continues to say to you, come unto me, faithless and sinful children; come unto me, and I will receive you. Repent, reform, and I will forget the past; I will pardon, love, and bless you."

The weather remained for several days too severe, and the atmosphere too thick, to permit our making our excursion to the mountains of the Vaudois; and part of the intervening time was spent in visiting objects in and near Turin. The Superga is the principal. This magnificent edifice was erected by Victor Amadeus II. on the elevated spot from which Prince Eugene, in 1706, reconnoitred the position of the French army, then besieging the capital, and in memory of the successful campaign which delivered the Ducal states from the invading enemy. Nothing can surpass the grandeur of the design or execution; and pages might be filled with a description of the treasures, which have been exhausted in completing this *reale basilica*, and in producing the dazzling effect caused by its marble columns and pavement. As an object of curiosity to the traveller, it is beyond all praise; but as I rambled through the superb cloisters and terraces, and the proud arcades of this glorious cathedral, as aspiring in its magnificence as it is towering in its situation, I could not help reproaching the ostentatious devotion of its founder, who might have made thousands and thousands happy by a better application of his treasures. Had he built an asylum for the reception of the widows and children of those, who fell in his service; or an hospital for the brave men, whose blood sprinkled the laurels which he won, it might still have been the Superga, and commanded the admiration, as well as the wonder, of those who visit it.

The bones of Victor Amadeus rest in a royal sepulchre, certainly the most costly in Europe; and his ashes repose under a cupola, from whose lofty top the rich plains of Piemont, the Alps, those eternal barricades of Italy, and the Po, king of floods, may be seen in all their pride and glory. The memorial of his gratitude to the Virgin, is beheld for many leagues before that capital can be approached, which his valiant legions saved by their devoted heroism; and none can ascend the Superga without thinking and speaking of Victor Amadeus the Second! But had he founded an institution like that of the Hôtel Dieu at Lyons, or the College at Chelsea, or the Hospital at Greenwich, his name would have been blessed by hundreds of thousands; it is now only mentioned among the number of those many vain-glorious sovereigns, who knew how to conquer their enemies, but not to make their subjects happy. Man may try to outdo the works of nature; he may erect the most stupendous and costly monuments; but, in most cases, they expose him to censure or reproach. The hill, on which the Superga stands, would have commanded the same extensive prospect without the aid of that aspiring dome. Its bold elevation would of itself have reminded posterity, that upon that height stood Eugene, by the side of the warlike Duke of Savoy, when his great mind comprehended at a glance the blunders of the French army, and formed a plan for their defeat: but the basilica of Victor Amadeus ought never to be seen without raising emotions unfavourable to its founder. It was cemented with the blood, and washed with the tears of his people. He kept his vow to the Virgin; and thousands must have been wrung from his subjects, to enable him to do so: but he knew not how to abide by his promises of protection to his faithful Vaudois, although they were drawn from him by services and sacrifices, which deserved the amplest recompence.

In the annals of Europe, if the register of provincial cruelties can be kept out of sight, and his private character suppressed, Victor Amadeus will always make a conspicuous figure, and interest the reader. The romantic events of his military career, his martial spirit, and the personal disasters which he had to encounter, render his name dear to history. Recorded with those of Eugene and Marlborough, it will go down to posterity with more than its just share of glory. Eugene and the Duke of Savoy first met in a meadow near Carmagnola. The one had effected the interview by descending from the Tyrolese Alps, and traversing the plains of Lombardy with his victorious troops; and the other, by stealing a march from the recesses at the foot of Mount Viso, where he had been concealed and protected by the Vaudois. They ascended the heights of the Superga together; and the transport of the royal fugitive was so great at hearing Eugene's plan for the relief of his capital, that when he was asked where he would dine, "At Turin, at Turin!" was his exulting reply.

There is still extant in one of the Vaudois families, a letter of the Duke of Savoy, dated September 2, 1684; in which the fidelity of his Vaudois subjects, and their inviolable attachment to their sovereigns, is acknowledged in the very strongest terms. There are also among the archives of the state, copies of no less than ten edicts, issued between the years 1561 and 1686; in which concessions are granted to the Protestants, and the free exercise of their religion confirmed to them. One of these concessions, viz. that of 1620, was purchased at the expence of six thousand crowns, by the poor inhabitants of the three valleys [u]. Notwithstanding, in the face of these solemn instruments, the last of which was signed in 1679, Victor Amadeus published a decree on the 31st of January, 1686, in which it was declared, that every Protestant church and chapel should be razed to the ground; and that every person professing the Protestant faith, should publicly renounce his errors within fifteen days from the date of the proclamation, under penalty of banishment.

Every sort of remonstrance was made against so horrible an edict, not only on the part of the Vaudois themselves, but also in the names of Protestant governments in alliance with the sovereign of Piemont. But Victor Amadeus was deaf to prayers and expostulations, and proceeded to put his decree into execution. The whole population of the Protestant valleys at that time did not exceed 15,000 souls: of these, 2500 only were capable of bearing arms, and even they were unprepared, and indifferently provided with supplies of any sort to defend themselves against an attack. But what will not men do, who are driven to desperation? "Death rather than the mass," was shouted from mountain to mountain; the vales re-echoed with the cry; and it was determined to defy the threats of the persecutors. The King of France, who had urged on the Duke of Savoy to carry fire and sword into the Protestant villages, assailed these poor people with his troops from the French frontier, while an armed force marched against them from Turin. Hostilities commenced in April, 1686, and enemies from all quarters poured in upon their prey. The French General, Catinat, wrote to the Duke of Savoy, that he would have *the honour of striking the first blow at the heretics*. He did so: but, says Henri Arnaud, who has written a history of this sanguinary invasion, *he had the honour of being well beat:* "ils eurent aussi l'honneur d'être bien battus." The

[u] See Appendix, No. 5.

Vaudois gallantly withstood the first shock of war; and, for three days, were victorious in every engagement. At length they were compelled, by the overwhelming numbers of their invaders, to submit; but not before such horrible devastation had been carried into every hamlet, and such unheard-of barbarities committed upon all ages, even upon women and infants, that it would be outraging human nature to recount them[x].

The survivors were given to understand, that they would experience their sovereign's clemency, if they would submit unconditionally. They did submit; and Victor Amadeus, *in his mercy*, commanded a seizure to be made of their houses, land, and property, and divided them among his troops, and the most zealous of the Catholic persecutors. He then committed the whole of the Protestant population to prison; " and the jails in his dominions were so full of these wretched people, that they perished by hundreds, of hunger, thirst, and infectious diseases. It would be a hard

[x] In Mr. Acland's most interesting " Sketch of the History and present Condition of the Vaudois, 1826," 2d Edition, there is an account of the termination of this short conflict, translated from Arnaud's History. " One would have thought that two such glorious days would have raised the courage of the victors; but unhappily, and by a fatality altogether unaccountable, these people, who at first appeared so intrepid in the support of this war, after the example of their forefathers who had surmounted thirty-two wars for the sake of the same religion, became suddenly enervated, and with frozen hearts laid down their arms on the third day, surrendering themselves meanly to the discretion of the Duke of Savoy, who in triumph over this meanness did them the favour to shut them up in thirteen prisons in Piemont, and thus extinguished at one blow the flames of this war, not by the blood of the Vaudois, but by their unhoped-for submission."

I am glad to have it in my power to vindicate the conduct of the Vaudois on this occasion, and to shew that it was not owing to " enervation," " frozen hearts," or " meanness." The mystery of this extraordinary submission, is solved in a very rare tract, a copy of which may be seen in the British Museum. It is entitled, " Histoire de la Negociation des Ambassadeurs envoyés au duc de Savoy, par les Cantons Evangeliques, 1686. Geneva 1690," and explains that the Swiss Ambassadors persuaded the too-confiding Vaudois to throw themselves upon the generosity of their sovereign, and to lay down their arms. They did so, and the treatment which they experienced was such as Arnaud stated. *Note to Third Edition.*

matter to represent all the miseries and calamities they suffered during their captivity; and they were more or less ill treated, according to the humours of those who had the command of their prisons. They had nothing but bread and water for their ordinary food: the one without substance, and the other from the kennels in the streets. In some places they gave them water only at certain set times, and that in such small quantities, that many perished. They slept on the bare bricks; or, if they were allowed straw, it was rotten, and full of vermin; while the dungeons were so thronged, they were crowded to suffocation. The place of the dead, numbers of them dying every day, was constantly supplied with fresh prisoners, that the dungeons might always be equally thronged; and the intense heat of the summer, and the corruption with which the chambers were infected, by reason of the great number of the sick, engendered evils too horrible for recital[y]." In six months, three thousand only of the sufferers were alive: and for these the Protestant ambassadors at the court of Turin made such urgent intercession, that the Duke of Savoy was again constrained to exercise his clemency. He was pleased to pardon and release them, upon condition of their banishing themselves for ever from their homes and habitations.

The poor wanderers set out upon their melancholy journey destitute, after having, in many instances, had their children forcibly taken from them, that they might be brought up in the Catholic religion. Their pastors were separated from the people, and in this condition they were obliged to make their way across the mountains, and bend their steps towards Switzerland. The weather was uncommonly severe, and hundreds perished on the road, of cold and hunger. But a remnant providentially escaped; and at the expiration of three years, an intrepid band of 800 of

[y] See the History of the Vaudois, p. 200, by Peter Boyer. London. 1692.

these exiles put themselves under the command of one of their pastors, Henri Arnaud, determined to regain their valleys at the point of the sword, or die upon their native soil. They were miraculously supported by the arm of Providence; and maintained their position among the fastnesses of Angrogna, until the alliance was dissolved between the King of France and the Duke of Savoy, and the latter engaged to recal their brethren in exile, and to re-instate them all in their former possessions, upon condition of their putting themselves under his banners, against Louis XIV. Henry Arnaud's account of this glorious return to their valleys, (*La glorieuse rentrée des Vaudois dans leur vallées*) will be further noticed in the course of this work. I had the gratification of visiting some of the spots, where they successfully maintained their ground against a frightful superiority of forces: but I cannot resist the pleasure of noticing in this place the Christian manner in which that brave soldier, Arnaud, speaks of the remorseless tyrant, who had exposed him, and his people, to such unmerited sufferings. "The French," said he, "artfully insinuated, that his Serene Highness the Duke of Savoy ought to imitate the zeal of Louis XIV, in destroying the churches of the Vaudois, and forcing them to embrace the Catholic religion. That prince, although he was then quite a youth, was for a time unwilling to come to such extremities with subjects, who had always served him faithfully; and generously, and with a Christian spirit, refused to comply with their pernicious counsels; but at length he was over-persuaded," &c. &c. The Duke himself when he received the first deputation of the Vaudois, after their restoration to favour and protection, acknowledged that it was no fault of theirs, but the evil counsel of others, which had been the occasion of their misfortunes. "Jusqu'à présent," was his language, "Nous avons été ennemis; désormais il nous faut être bons amis: d'autres ont été la cause de vôtre malheur."

The sequel of the history is worthy of the beginning.

Victor Amadeus had so much reason to be satisfied with the loyalty and extraordinary valour of his Vaudois troops, that he would not suffer them to be intermixed with other regiments. They were brigaded by themselves, commanded by their own officers, and invariably occupied a distinguished post in every action. But their fidelity did not end here. Successive reverses obliged the duke to retreat before the French. He even became a fugitive; and where did he take refuge? In the valleys of the Vaudois! The persecutor fled to the persecuted for safety; and behind the Pelice, in a secluded spot in the village of Rora, Victor Amadeus found a safe asylum among the very people, whom he had denounced, proscribed, and hunted down even to torture and death. Such was the fidelity and loyalty of the Vaudois; and how did the sovereign testify his sense of their services? To the family indeed, in whose house he had found shelter, he granted the *invaluable* privilege of having an enclosed burial-place! But the Vaudois, as a community, were forgotten. At the return of peace, and upon his re-instatement in power, the grateful Victor Amadeus added one more to the edicts in force against his Protestant subjects, and built the Superga!!!

"I do not only esteem, but I really love that prince," wrote the Duke of Marlborough to his Duchess, in 1706; but great generals and great statesmen are too apt to love and hate, according to the temperature of the political atmosphere. And in the following year, when the Duke of Savoy, with his natural treachery of character, began to transfer his jealousy of the French to his allies and deliverers, the English commander entertained very different sentiments [y].

[y] "Your highness sees how the duke acts: and if our allies will let him go on, and will continue their confidence in him, to our exclusion, they will repent of it another day."—*Letter from Count Wratislaw to Marlborough.*

"The Duke of Savoy, with his usual policy, seeing the great difficulties, not to say impossibilities, of this operation, throws it entirely on me. He does it with

Our new Vaudois friend, M. Vertu, was unremitting in his kindness and attention to us; he invited us to his house, made a party to meet us, introduced us to several of his Italian acquaintances, and contributed much towards making our time pass agreeably in Turin. One of the gentlemen, whom we met at his house, was a Piemontese officer, the son of a colonel, who was assassinated in his own chamber. The assassin has escaped justice, and is now at large. Among other things we were doubly obliged to M. Vertu, for giving us an opportunity of receiving some Italian lessons from a countrywoman, who is reduced to the necessity of giving instruction, and of recommending her to English families, who may have better means of serving her than we had. Perhaps it will be more delicate not to mention her name. Those who may chance to read these pages, and feel an inclination to do her a kindness, will easily find a way to do so.

Madame ——— is of a most respectable family, I believe from the west of England; but was unfortunately taken to the continent at too early an age to know how to estimate the English character. Her education and accomplishments were of the first order, and so must have been her beauty; but the latter has been cruelly impaired by the sorrow and drudgery which she has since undergone. The

the more cunning, because he praises me on my capacity, and says I can do what I will."—*Prince Eugene to Marlborough.*

" I have long entreated your highness that such approbation and facility should not be given in England to the projects of the Duke of Savoy. He insinuates, &c. This poison, however subtle and insinuating, is too apparent to deceive persons so enlightened as you, and who reflect on the conduct of the Duke of Savoy at all times. I do not affirm that we ought not to conciliate him, and must grant what we have promised; but at the same time distrust his personal conduct and advice; and not be the dupes of his suggestions. Far from placing the same confidence in him as we have lately done," &c. &c.—*Letter from Count Wratislaw.*

" The enclosed is a copy of a letter I have received from Count Wratislaw, and all in Cypher. I am afraid his characters are very just."—*Marlborough to Godolphin.*—See Coxe's Memoirs of Marlborough, vol. ii. chap. 61.

flattery, and persevering gallantries of a foreigner, were too much to be withstood by a young and inexperienced girl, who had hitherto been accustomed to nothing more than the honest and sober attention of her own countrymen; and in an evil hour she consented to unite her destiny to his. The man's mind and endowments, his condition and situation in life, were all considerably beneath her. She was discarded by her family, and obliged to take her chance with his. If her connexions were aware of the trials to which she has been exposed, how meekly she has submitted to them, and how well she has acquitted herself under the duties of a wife and mother of three children, their hearts would relent, and she would again be received into the bosom of her kindred. She has been more than the nurse, the only servant to her children; and her time is so occupied between her pupils and her domestic toils, as to leave not a moment even for necessary relaxation. When she was confined with her first child, she was reduced to a state of the extremest indigence: her husband was away; she had not a soul near her to whom she could look for comfort: and after eight days of the most critical danger, at the moment when she most wanted assistance, the woman who was to attend her, left her bed-side to go to mass!

In addition to deprivations and sufferings such as these, which are inseparable from her present condition in life, she has had to encounter all those vexatious and harassing proceedings, to which the Protestant wife of a Romanist is subject in this country. Her father-in-law has instituted several suits to annul her marriage, and to prove the illegitimacy of her children; happily, without success: but her husband has so far entered into the bigoted feelings of his father, as to oblige her to receive the visits of priests, who have resorted to every expedient to effect her conversion. He has even treated her at times so harshly, because she would not be an apostate from her faith, that, to use her own words, she has literally been "without food, clothes, or shelter." But, in spite of such ill treatment, she is so dutifully attached to her husband, that, to my own knowledge, she refused to accept an invitation from her kind friend, Madame Vertu, when he was not asked to be of the party; and I never heard her speak of him but in terms of tenderness and affection. Those who know the importunities of the Roman Catholic priesthood, and the never ceasing perplexities to which a Protestant wife is exposed, will know how to estimate the firmness of this unfortunate lady.

Before I left Turin, I had several times the means of gratifying my curiosity by a sight of the royal family. They move about with very little parade or ostentation, and appear to have no apprehensions of an unfavourable reception from the people. At the opera, a stranger may have a full gaze at them almost every evening: they are constant in their attendance there, and sit in full view of the audience. The queen has not a very prepossessing countenance: hers is the long, uninteresting Spanish-Bourbon face, in which we can discover nothing attractive. The king is a mild, good-humoured looking man, with nothing, but this indication of a kindly disposition, particularly striking either in his aspect, or deportment; and to judge from several favourable traits of character, which have discovered themselves, when he has acted for himself, I should be inclined to believe, that the grievances, of which his Protestant subjects, the Vaudois, complain, are to be attributed to others, rather than to himself[z]. The Vaudois themselves are decidedly of this opinion; and never speak of the king personally, but in the language of respect and affection. On

[z] I have lately received a letter from a Protestant gentleman in Piemont, dated the 28th of March, 1825, in which he complains of permission having been refused to a young surgeon to exercise his profession in Turin, for no other reason, but that he adheres to the religious tenets of the Vaudois. "BUT I DARE SAY," continues my correspondent, "THE KING HIMSELF HAS NO KNOWLEDGE OF SUCH REFUSAL, OTHERWISE HE IS TOO GOOD AND TOO JUST TO SANCTION IT." *Note to the second Edition.*

the nights that I visited the opera at Turin, I observed that there was but little notice taken of the royal party, which may be owing, in part, to their showing themselves so frequently in places of public resort. Every body rose at their entrance, but there was nothing expressive of a cordial or joyous reception; and perhaps this struck me the more forcibly, from the recollection of what I had witnessed the year before, at our own opera in London, when the King of England presented himself before a hearty English audience, who had been waiting with impatient anxiety for his appearance. I thought the magnificent chandelier, suspended over the pit, must have been shaken from its hold, under the acclamations with which the house rang, when George the Fourth made his first entrée in the royal box. How enviable must be the feelings of the sovereign, who listens to the honest applauses of his people; and who knows that he has merited them.

When kings reign by virtue of a constitution, and in the spirit of it, they cannot fail of reigning in the hearts of their people. It is by Roman Catholic courtiers, that the divine right of Kings has been principally asserted, and yet it cannot but have been noticed, that almost all the late revolutionary movements have been in Roman Catholic countries. Protestant subjects are generally less lavish of adulation, but not less faithful in the hour of trial; the truth of which has often been experienced by the kings of Sardinia. The late king of Sardinia was reminded of this, and requested by a British minister to ameliorate the condition of the Vaudois. He gave a quibbling answer: "Do you emancipate the Irish Catholics, and I will emancipate the Vaudois." It was rejoined, "We only beg of your Majesty to concede as much to the Protestants of the valleys, as has been conceded to the Roman Catholics of Ireland." The king was silent, but inexorable.

CHAPTER IV.

Leave Turin—The Po—Face of the country—Irrigation—Pinerolo—Popish hospital—Infant stealing—Edict of Victor Amadeus—Defile between Pinerolo and Fenestrelle—Valley of the Clusone—Inn at Perosa—Excellent fare—Pomaretto—Mountain torrents—A Vaudois village—Presbytery of Pomaretto—Rodolphe Peyrani—Moderator of the Vaudois—His extreme poverty, and sufferings—Erudition of Peyrani—Interesting conversation—Pattern of Christian mildness—The moderator's library—Sold to purchase the necessaries of life—Episcopacy among the Vaudois—Reduced numbers of the Vaudois—Innovations—Waldensian Church—Church of England—Persecutions—The Protestant valleys of Piemont, the cradle of the Reformation—Wickliffe—Lollards—Doctrines of the Vaudois not Calvinistic—Peyrani and Napoleon—Anecdote—Napoleon's pension to the Vaudois—The Pastor Rostain—His extreme poverty—Toilsome duties of the Vaudois Clergy—British pension to the pastors of the Vaudois—The Count Truchsess—Emperor Alexander—New hospital at La Torre—Letters from the valleys—Suspension of the royal pension—Collection for the Vaudois during the Protectorate—Oliver Cromwell establishes a fund for the Vaudois—King William III.—Noble character of Peyrani—Lord William Bentinck—Victor Emanuel, the late king—Anecdote—Ferdinand Peyrani, pastor of Pramol—Parting with Peyrani—Reduced condition of the Waldensian Church—Death of Peyrani—The moderator's son in poverty at Lausanne—Peyrani's admirable pamphlet—Anecdote.

On Saturday, January 11, we set out from Turin on our journey to the mountains. Our excellent friend, M. Vertu, had not only provided us with letters of introduction to some Vaudois families, but had the kindness to allow his son to accompany us, a most amiable and intelligent young man of about twenty years of age, whose knowledge of the English language, and of the country to which we were directing our steps, promised us every assistance and facility of intercourse. We proceeded through the borgo of Monviso, out of the Porta Nuova, passed the citadel, and then followed the high road to Pinerolo, in a south-westerly direction from the capital. The Po was in view for a few miles upon our left; but from this part of the river at least the swans [a] were fled, which once used to haunt its banks. It ran now swiftly but calmly, and without any indications of that raging violence, which it shews when swelled by the floods of spring; at such times it not unfrequently happens, that it overflows its banks for many miles, and rushes along in one broad impetuous torrent, that sweeps away every thing before it, fully justifying the character it has obtained from the Roman poet [b].

There was nothing strikingly interesting in the first sixteen or eighteen miles, but Sterne had said, "If I were in a desert, I would find out wherewithal to call forth my attention," and so it was with us. The scenery was new, though not particularly picturesque, and the division of the lands, the costume of the peasants, and the novel form of the buildings furnished materials enough for curiosity and conversation. Nona was the only town through which we passed before we arrived at Pinerolo (Pignerol,) but the population of this part of the province appeared to be as great as its fertility, and the meadows, vineyards, and corn-fields bore ample proof of the industry of its inhabitants. The method

[a] ——————— Piscosove amne Padusæ
Dant sonitum rauci per stagna loquacia cygni.
Æn. xi. 457.

[b] Proluit insano contorquens vortice sylvas
Fluviorum rex Eridanus, camposque per omnes
Cum stabulis armenta tulit.
Geor. i. 481.

of irrigation used here is as ingenious as it is effectual; it did not indeed present the exact image to our eyes, which the poet[c] has given to the imagination; we neither saw the brow of the hill from which the streamlets are conducted, nor heard the sound of their murmuring course, yet the cleverness, with which the little sluices and channels were contrived, made ample amends for the absence of more poetical objects.

At Pinerolo, we left behind us that rich and extensive plain, which spreads from the foot of the Cottian Alps, and stretches away to the shores of the Adriatic; and reached the first swell of those mountains, behind which lay the villages of our research. The city has nothing to detain a traveller, nor any thing worth mentioning, but that it is the see of a Prelate, who enjoys the rent of lands which were assigned by Buonaparte to the maintenance of the Protestant clergy, and boasts of a hospital, where children of the Vaudois used to be immured, that they might be compelled to embrace the Popish faith. Till within a very few years an edict was in force, which permitted any zealot to decoy or carry off a Protestant child, and to place him in this asylum, for the purpose of being instructed in the principles of the Roman church. Many have been the poor infants so stolen away, and committed to the management of strangers, whose first lessons were, that they should renounce the ties, and abjure the faith of their parents; and neither the tears of the little victims, nor the expostulations of their distracted mothers, ever succeeded in restoring a child to the bosom of its family. It could scarcely be believed that such abominable practices continued to be resorted to in the present age, if a royal ordinance, of the following curious tenor, did not confirm the truth of the com-

[c] Ecce supercilio clivosi tramitis undam
Elicit: illa cadens raucum per lævia murmur
Saxa ciet.

Geor. i. 108.

plaints that have been made upon the subject. "We renew our orders to prevent the taking away of children, with the view of obliging them to embrace the Catholic religion; and that those children who have been taken away may be restored. Those, who at the prescribed age (girls at ten, and boys at twelve) enter voluntarily into the hospital of Pinerolo, must be under the direction of the ecclesiastical judges: but no difficulty will be made in permitting the parents to see their children, provided that proper precautions be taken." This *indulgent* edict, wrung from the government, dated June 4th, 1794, and signed "Victor Amadeus," at a time, when the invasion of the French rendered it necessary for the King to conciliate his Protestant subjects, speaks volumes, and proves that abuses of the most horrible nature were tolerated, that the Vaudois might be the victims of them. Even now, melancholy enough is the condition of a child who can be persuaded to enter this asylum, either in sickness or destitution. The clause for the discreet admission of parents to see their children, under certain precautions, is virtually a bar to all that freedom of intercourse, without which there can be no true reciprocity of parental and filial affection.

From Pinerolo we took the Fenestrelle road, it being our first object to visit Pomarre, Pomaret, or Pomaretto, the parish of Rodolphe Peyrani, the venerable moderator or primate of the ancient Church of the Waldenses. After bearing to the west for two or three miles, the road takes a northerly direction, and follows the Clusone through the defile which is called the valley of Perosa. The contrast was striking between the fertile and champaign country on the other side of Pinerolo, and the bleak and rugged district through which we were travelling to Pomaretto. The rocks to our right were bare and black; and their fantastic shapes, and the rude huts which were built at their base, for several miles, offered but little variety to the melancholy sameness of our drive. Some few groves of chesnuts, and pasturages were seen at intervals. All were Roman Catholics on this side of the river. The Protestant villages were concealed from our view by the natural barriers, which rise in terrible and forbidding aspect on the western bank of the Clusone, and in many places serve to keep the valley in almost perpetual shade. So cold and so repulsive appeared the tract of country, through which lies one of the most practicable passes that conducts from Piemont to France. The black mud of the road added to the general gloom of this savage defile, and made us consider it the most dismal of the valleys we had yet seen. In others, the mountains breaking into precipices, and the abruptness with which the topographical features change from one aspect to another, varied the scene enough to make even horrors not unpleasing; but here all was melancholy uniformity, and the slow pace at which we were obliged to move, rendered the stage of ten miles from Pinerolo to Perosa as tedious, as if it had been three times the distance.

At Perosa, where there are the ruins of a strong castle, which formerly commanded the valleys of the Clusone and San Martino, we stopped for about an hour, and called for refreshments at an inn, whose cheerless appearance promised us fare corresponding with the journey. We were shewn into a cold bed-room, and had to wait some time before any fire was prepared to warm us: but when at length the cloth was laid, as good entertainment was put before us as we could desire. It consisted of two ducks, mutton chops, omelets, and a dish of small birds roasted, in themselves a meal for an epicure. Two or three bottles of rich muscat wine finished the banquet, and a moderate charge sent us away well satisfied with the culinary accommodation of our hostess at Perosa. Her kind-heartedness and Christian charity pleased us even more than her good fare. When we enquired after the pastor, Rodolphe Peyrani, she spoke of him in terms of the highest respect, and regretted that so good a man should have to contend with poverty and illness at his advanced period of life. Her own priest, she said, could not display more Christian resignation than he had done.

We were obliged to leave our carriage at Perosa, and to proceed on foot to Pomaretto; with a young peasant as our guide, we set out, all impatience, to visit the first Vaudois village in the valley of Perosa. This valley extends to that of Pragela, which was formerly one of the Protestant valleys, is intersected by the valleys of San Martino, and is inserted in most of the old maps as La Valle di Clusone, because it is divided along its whole length by that river. The Protestants are confined to the western side of the Clusone. At the point where we crossed it, near the confluence of the Germanasca, it is an impetuous body of water which divides itself into a variety of channels, and rushes over masses of rock that are brought down by the torrents from the mountains, and lie in strange confusion in every part of its bed. We could not have passed over less than half a dozen wooden bridges, in the space of about three hundred yards: some of them intended for the use of foot passengers only, and others thrown over the stream for mules and cattle.

After walking half an hour or more, the village of Pomaretto discovered itself, and seen as it was, in its wintry aspect, never did a more dreary spot burst upon the view. It is built upon a declivity, just where the mountains begin to encrease in height and number, with rocks above, and torrents below. There is such a scene of savage disorder in the immediate vicinity of Pomaretto, that one would imagine it had been effected by the most violent convulsions of nature; huge fragments of rock encumber the ground on all sides, and it seems as if the mountains must have been rent asunder to produce so much nakedness and desolation. The street which we slowly ascended was narrow and dirty, the houses, or rather cabins, small and inconvenient, and poverty, in the strictest sense of the word, stared us in the face at every step we took. In vain did we cast our eyes about, in search of some better-looking corner, in which we might descry an habitation fit for the reception of the supreme Pastor of the Churches of the Waldenses. The street was every where no better than a confined lane. At length we stood before the *Presbytery* of M. Peyrani, for by this name the dwellings of the ministers are known. But in external appearance, how inferior to the most indifferent parsonages in England, or to the humblest manse in Scotland. Neither garden nor bower enlivened its appearance, and scarcely did it differ in construction or dimension from the humble cottages by which it was surrounded. The interior was not much better calculated to give us an idea of the *otium cum dignitate,* which usually appertains to the condition of dignitaries in the church ; and had we not known it before, we should soon have discovered, that additional labour only distinguishes the appointment of moderator of the Vaudois.

We were received at the door by a mild, sensible, and modest-looking young man dressed in faded black, to whom we communicated our wish of being introduced to M. Peyrani. He replied, that his father was very unwell, but would be happy to see any English gentlemen, who did him the honour of a visit. We were afraid that we might disturb the invalid, and therefore hesitated to intrude, until we had begged M. Vertu to see M. Peyrani first, and ascertain whether the sight of strangers would be agreeable. The answer was in our favour, and we were now conducted up a narrow stair-case, through a very small bed-room, the size of which was still further contracted by several book-cases. This led into another bed-room, more amply provided still with shelves and books. The apartment was about fourteen feet square, low, and without any kind of decoration of paint or paper hanging. It was thick with dust; and the only attention to those *munditiæ vitæ,* to which we were in the habit of looking, were the sheets of the bed, than which nothing could be cleaner. At a small fire, where the fuel was supplied in too scanty a portion to impart warmth to the room, and by the side of a table covered with books, parchments, and manuscripts, sat a slender, feeble-looking old man, whose whole frame was bowed down by infirmity. A night-cap was on his head, and at first sight we supposed he had a long white beard hanging down upon his neck; but, upon his rising to welcome us, we perceived that it was no beard, but whiskers of a length which is not often seen, and which had a very singular effect. His dress consisted of a shabby, time-worn, black suit, and white worsted stockings, so darned and patched, that it is difficult to say, whether any portion of the original hose remained. Over his shoulder was thrown what once had been a cloak, but now a shred only, and more like the remains of a horse-cloth, than part of a clerical dress. This cloak, in the animation of his discourse, frequently fell from his shoulders, and was replaced by his son with a degree of filial tenderness and attention extremely prepossessing.

The sickly-looking sufferer, in this humble costume, in this garb of indigence, was the moderator of the Vaudois; the successor of a line of prelates, whom tradition would extend to the apostles themselves; the high-priest of a church, which is, beyond all shadow of doubt, the parent church of every Protestant community in Europe, and which centuries of persecution have not been able to destroy. It is indeed a vine, "which has stretched her branches to the sea, and her boughs unto the river:" but while her branches are flourishing, "the wild boar out of the wood doth root up the stem, and the wild beasts of the field devour it." And unless the same Providence which first planted this vine, and made room for it, shall turn again, and look down from heaven, and visit it, it must, it is feared, perish; for nothing short of the divine succours can enable men to bear up against the poverty, humiliation, and deprivations, to which most of the Vaudois clergy are exposed to this hour.

M. Peyrani was upwards of seventy-one years of age at the time we saw him; the whole of his income did not exceed 1000 francs, or about forty pounds a-year; and with this pittance he had been obliged to meet the demands of a family, the calls of charity, the incidental expences of his situation as moderator, and the additional wants of age, sickness, and infirmity. An accident, occasioned by the kick of a mule, had added to the ills of his condition. A large and prominent rupture, and an incurable weakness, were increased by his inability to procure surgical aid, as often as he required it. For two years he underwent excruciating pain: and had his means enabled him to obtain the medical assistance, which his case demanded, the malady might have been materially, if not effectually, alleviated.

The welcome, which we received from our venerable host, was expressed with all the warmth and sincerity of one, whose kindly feelings had not yet been chilled by years or sufferings: and the manner in which it was delivered, displayed a knowledge of the world, and a fine tact of good breeding, which are not looked for in Alpine solitudes, or in the dusty study of a recluse. We were pre-disposed to respect his virtues and piety, and had been given to understand that he was a man of the first literary acquirements; but we did not expect to find the tone and manners of one, whose brows would do honour to the mitre of any diocese in Europe: nor did we know that he, who was now drooping in a state of the veriest penury, had been, during the French domination, one of the twenty-five[c] members of the provisional government of Piemont. Such a reverse could never have been discovered from his complaints, for there was nothing of querulousness in any of his observations, nor did

c The author has been informed of an error in this passage, and has learnt that it was M. Geymet, the predecessor of Peyrani in the office of moderator, who was so employed by the French Government. M. Peyrani never filled any civil office.—*Note to Second Edition.*

he once express himself with the least degree of bitterness upon the subject of his own grievances, or those of his community. That, which we gathered from him upon these topics, was related more in the form of historical detail, than as matters which so materially concerned himself and connexions.

Our conversation was held generally in French; sometimes we addressed him in English, which he understood, but did not speak; but when I engrossed his discourse to myself, we spoke in Latin, as being the language in which we could not mistake each other, and affording the most certain medium of communication upon ecclesiastical subjects, where I was anxious to ascertain facts with precision. Nothing could be more choice or classical than his selection of words; and I was not more surprised by his fluency of diction, than by the extraordinary felicity with which he applied whole sentences from ancient poets, and even prose authors, to convey his sentiments. One or two of these I remember. In reply to an observation made by me, that if the state of the Vaudois church were sufficiently known, the English government might probably be induced to restore the pensions which were formerly given to the clergy, and withheld since the year 1797, he clasped his hands together, and thus expressed his hope that he might live long enough to see it:

> Oh mihi tam longæ maneat pars ultima vitæ,
> Spiritus, et quantum sat erit tua dicere facta [d] !

When I asked some question upon the subject of the lands, which were appropriated by the late imperial government to the Protestant clergy, but have since been sequestered in favour of the Bishop of Pinerolo: he said it was true, that he and his brethren had been reduced to extreme

[d] Virg. Ecl. iv. 53.

poverty by this arrangement, which was totally unexpected, because it was hoped that the acts of the late government would not have been rescinded, in so far as they regarded such equitable provisions. He spoke without any asperity, and mildly added:

——— Vivi pervenimus, advena nostri,
Quod nunquam veriti sumus, ut possessor agelli
Diceret: hæc mea sunt; veteres migrate coloni.
Nunc victi, tristes, quoniam Fors omnia versat[e].

The manner in which he pronounced the last words was particularly moving; he dwelt upon the words *veteres* and *tristes,* as being peculiarly applicable to his own case, deprived, as he had been in his old age, of what would have constituted his maintenance and comfort.

M. Peyrani spoke with so much rapidity, and his thoughts followed each other in such quick succession, that he never suffered himself to be at a loss for words. If the Latin term did not immediately occur to him, he made no pause, but instantly supplied its place by a French or Italian phrase. This animation of manner had such an effect upon his whole frame, that very soon after we began to converse with him, the wrinkles seemed to fall from his brow, a hectic colour succeeded to the pallidness of his countenance, and the feeble and stooping figure, which first stood before us, elevated itself by degrees, and acquired new strength and energy. In fact, while he was favouring me with a short history of himself, I might have forgotten that he had exceeded the usual limits of man's short span; and I must repeat, that it is impossible to admire sufficiently the Christian character of the individual, or of the church which he represented, when I recollect the meek resignation with which he submitted to his hard fate, and the forbearance he exhibited, whenever his remarks led him to talk of the vex-

[e] Virg. Ecl. ix. 2.

atious and oppressive proceedings, which have never ceased to mark the line of conduct pursued by the Sardinian government, in regard to the churches of the Waldenses.

M. Peyrani's book-shelves were loaded with more than they could well bear; and when I noticed the number of volumes which lay scattered about the room, or were disposed in order, wherever a place could be found for them, he told me, that if he were now in possession of all that once were his, the whole of his own, and the adjoining house, would be insufficient to contain them. He said, he had bought a great many himself; but the principal portion of his library was the accumulation of his father and grandfather, and of more distant ancestors; and expressed much regret that he could no longer display the folios, and curious old manuscripts that had been handed down to him. I asked what had become of them. "They have been sold," he replied, with considerable emotion: for he had been compelled to part with them from time to time, to purchase clothes, and even food, for himself and family!!!

Upon my enquiring, whether there had not been formerly bishops in the Vaudois church, properly so called, he answered, "Yes; and I should now be styled bishop, for my office is virtually episcopal; but it would be absurd to retain the empty title, when we are too poor to support the dignity, and have little jurisdiction, but that which is voluntarily submitted to among ourselves: the term moderator [f] is therefore now in use with us, as being more con-

[f] However inferior the title of Moderator may now be to that of Bishop, it was anciently considered of higher consequence and authority. When a synod or convocation of Bishops, Presbyters, and Deacons was assembled together to regulate ecclesiastical matters, a Moderator or Prolocutor was elected in the person of one of the senior or most respected Bishops, to preside over this council. Cyprian was Moderator of the Council of Carthage; Palmas, Bishop of Amastris, was Moderator of a Synod of Pontus; Polycrates, Bishop of Ephesus, was Moderator of a Synod of Asia Minor; and Theophilus, Bishop of Cæsarea, and Narcissus, Bishop of Jerusalem, presided at a Synod in Palestine, under the same name. See Eusebius, lib. v. c. 23, 24.

sistent with our humiliation[g]." He immediately afterwards declared, that he did not desire a large income, and would not wish for more than 3000 francs a-year; but that, in the best times which he had enjoyed, his means were inadequate to his situation; and that, among other contingent expences, his correspondence with foreign Protestants was a heavy tax upon his purse.

M. Peyrani added another remark to his reasons why the title of bishop is dropped, and substituted by that of mode-

[g] The episcopal succession and character were retained in such acknowledged purity, for centuries after the establishment of the Vaudois church, as independent of Rome, that Commenius, the Bohemian Bishop, who wrote in 1644, states, that the Bohemian Separatists, in their anxiety to have their pastors ordained by prelates in regular succession from the Apostles, sent three of their preachers to "a certain Stephen, Bishop of the Vaudois; and this Stephen, with others officiating, conferred the vocation and ordination upon the three pastors, by the imposition of hands." This took place about 1450, and a century afterwards there were still Bishops in the Waldensian church; for in a confession of faith, presented to Francis I. King of France, in 1544, we find the following article: "Nous tenons cecy pour résolu parmi nous, que les *Evêques* et les pasteurs doivent être irreprehensibles dans leur doctrine et en leur meurs," &c.

Morland, in his "History of the Evangelical Churches of Piemont," has given (p. 72) a long chapter on their ancient discipline, the materials of which he professes to have extracted from "divers authentic manuscripts, written in their own language several hundred of years before either Luther or Calvin." The following passages will be found applicable to the question of regular ordination.

Article II. concerning Pastors or Ministers. "Having good testimonials, and being approved, they are received with imposition, or laying on of hands. He that is received last ought to do nothing without the permission of him that was received before him, and in like manner the former ought to do nothing without the consent of his associate, that so all things may be done amongst us in good order.—Amongst other privileges which God hath given to his servants, he hath given them this, to choose their Leaders, and to constitute Elders in their charges, according to the diversity of the work in the unity of Christ, which is clear by that saying of the Apostle in the Epistle to Titus, i. 5."

The original, in the language of the ancient Vaudois, stands thus, "Eslegislan Regidors del poble, et Preires en li lors officis," and Morland, who had no great affection for prelatical institutions, appears to have put an interpretation which is less favourable to my hypothesis than the words admit. *Preires* ought to have been rendered more literally, by the term *Priests*, and *Regidors* should have been taken in the sense of church officers superior to Priests.

rator; the Vaudois, or Protestants of the valleys, were formerly much more numerous than they are now; the persecutions of centuries have contributed to reduce their numbers and limitations in a most alarming degree; and whereas they once extended into the provinces of Susa[h] and Saluzzo, and occupied all the mountainous regions of that of Pinerolo, they are now confined to three valleys, and thirteen parishes, in the latter province. So small a flock, he said, can hardly confer the *title of Bishop*, in its generally received sense, although the episcopal functions may be retained. It was evident that M. Peyrani was sincerely attached to the episcopal forms of church government; and I believe he spoke the sentiments of his brethren, as well as his own; but it must be confessed that his predilections led him to assign more importance to his own office, than his real jurisdiction, and the relaxed discipline of the churches of the valleys, would strictly warrant. Many circumstances have concurred to cause this relaxation, and more especially the necessity which has thrown the Vaudois upon Switzerland, for the education of such of their youth as are intended for holy orders. Formerly there was a college at Angrogna, where the candidates for ordination received their instruction; but since its demolition by the Catholics, and the sequestration of its funds, they are obliged to have recourse to Geneva and Lausanne. To judge from the sentiments of their clergy, there would be no difficulty in restoring the ancient discipline, if this college could be re-established: but while their principal support is derived from Switzerland, it is not surprising, if some of the leaven of that country has found its way among them.

At present, orders conferred at Lausanne or Geneva, are

[h] There were six Protestant Churches in the valley of Pragela until the year 1727, when Victor Amadeus, with his usual perfidy, and in violation of the treaties of Turin and Utrecht, and of his promise to Queen Anne, given under his own hand, put an end to the free exercise of the Protestant Religion in that valley, and banished the ministers of the reformed faith.

held good, after some confirmation on the part of their own moderator; but before the dreadful persecution of 1685, when the whole Protestant population were driven out of the country, the holy office was committed to none, except in one instance, which I shall presently state, but to those who had gone through all the examinations and necessary forms at home. The candidates were severely examined in Latin, Italian, and French; their lives and conversation were strictly scrutinized; and if the result was satisfactory, the moderator then proceeded to the ceremony of ordination in full synod. He first delivered an exhortation, next exacted the usual vows, and directing the pastor elect *to kneel before him, he laid his hands upon his head,* and implored the blessing and gifts of the Holy Spirit. He then raised him up; and, giving him the hand of fellowship, presented him as a minister of the church.

Two great changes had previously taken place in the Valleys in the year 1630. The one was in consequence of a terrible plague, which swept off three-fourths, or certainly not less than two-thirds, of the inhabitants; and spared two only, out of their thirteen pastors. Upon the venerable ministers, Gilles and Gros, who were already worn down by years and infirmities, devolved the care of all the churches of the Vaudois. They were obliged to have recourse to France and Geneva for a supply of Protestant clergy, but none could be found who were able to administer divine service in the Italian tongue, which had hitherto been the language of their Liturgy, although the patois of the country still continued to be spoken. It was necessary, then, either to be without pastors, or to have the service performed in French; and as the ancient language of the Vaudois is a sort of dialect between French and Italian, the people soon became accustomed to the new formulary. This accounts for the first adoption of the Liturgy of Geneva.

The other change was the annexation of the Valleys to

the crown of France in the same year. The new government and the new clergy produced many innovations, contrary to the spirit of the former discipline of the Church, and among others was the neglect of the moderator's annual visitation. "La discipline," says Leger, "ne s'y exerça plus avec la même vigueur et rigueur qu' aupavarant: Messieurs les nouveaux Pasteurs accoûtumés à une conduite plus indulgente, la trouvans encore trop sévère, sur tout ne voulurent-ils plus souffrir que le modérateur des Eglises des Vallées, qui avec son adjoint, et un ancien à ce député, alloit toûjours visiter une fois l' année toutes les Eglises, donnant, ou luy même ou son adjoint, à châcune un préche, et luy faisant les remonstrances qu'il jugeoit nécessaires, selon les deffaus qu'il y avoit remarqué, et s'informant exactement, et de la doctrine, et des déportemens du Pasteur du lieu[i]."

After we had been some little time with M. Peyrani, he produced a packet of papers and parchments, which he opened in a sort of fidgetty haste, and appeared anxious to submit to our inspection. Dust, damp, and mould, had discoloured, and almost obliterated the characters in many of them, but they proved to be family memorials, and he at length succeeded in selecting those which he was most solicitous to lay before us. One paper contained the letters of orders of his maternal grandfather, who was ordained by Dr. Robinson, Bishop of London, in the year 1707, or 1717, I forget which, and licensed by the same prelate as tutor in a nobleman's family. The others, were some letters from a mercantile family of the first distinction in London, to whom he thought himself distantly related. He was interested, he said, in these documents, not on his own account, because time was advancing rapidly with an old man like himself,

[i] Leger, p. 207.

but for his children's sake; they were what they might carry into the world, as proofs of their connection with England.

I cannot forget, nor must I omit to notice, the evident satisfaction M. Peyrani felt in explaining, how closely the doctrines of the Vaudois Church assimilate to those of the Church of England. He pointed to the works of Tillotson, Barrow, and Taylor, which still enriched his book-case, and declared that every time he read them, he was more and more gratified by the light which these English divines had thrown upon truths, for their adherence to which, his poor brethren had been so often obliged to conceal themselves in their mountain fastnesses. "But remember," said the old man, with conscious and becoming pride, "remember that you are indebted to us for your emancipation from papal thraldom. We led the way. We stood in the front rank, and against us the first thunderbolts of Rome were fulminated. The baying of the blood-hounds of the inquisition was heard in our valleys, before you knew its name. They hunted down some of our ancestors, and pursued others from glen to glen, and over rock and mountain, till they obliged them to take refuge in foreign countries. A few of these wanderers penetrated as far as Provence and Languedoc, and from them were derived the Albigenses, or heretics of Albi. The province of Guienne afforded shelter to the persecuted Albigenses. Guienne was then in your possession. From an English province our doctrines found their way into England itself, and your Wickliffe [k] preached nothing more than what had been advanced by the ministers of our valleys, four hundred years before his time." "Whence," continued my aged informant, with increased

[k] Thomas Walden, who wrote against the doctrine of Wickliffe, says, "C'est la doctrine des Vaudois, qui s'étoit glissée des quartiers de France," &c.

Cardinal Bellarmine bears the same testimony; "Wickliffe n'a pas pu enrichir la doctrine des Vaudois."—*Leger*, p. 176.

animation, "came your term *Lollards* [l], but from a Waldensian Pastor, Walter Lollard, who flourished about the middle of the thirteenth century? And the Walloons of the Low Countries were nothing more than a sect, whose name is easily found in the corruption of our own. As for ourselves, we have been called heretics, and Arians, and Manicheans, and Cathari, but we are like yourselves, a Church built up in Christ, a Church with the discipline and regular administration of divine service which constitute a Church [m]. We have adhered to the pure tenets of the Apostolic age, and the Roman Catholics have separated from us. Ours is the Apostolical succession, from which the Roman hierarchy has departed rather than ourselves. We are not only a Church by name and outward forms, but a Church actually interested by faith in Jesus Christ the corner stone."

M. Peyrani then went to his book-shelves, and produced the evidence of Leger to prove the correctness of his assertions, and turned to the chapter in which the author having devoted five long folio pages to the discussion, thus sums up his arguments. "Cette doctrine Vaudoise se trouvant donc suffisamment justifiée par les Lutheriens, aussi bien que par les Calvinistes, et même par les Papistes, et par eus tous, reconnue si éloignée des sentimens Hérétiques,

l Dr. Southey in his "Book of the Church" has followed erroneous authority in his observations upon the Lollards, as far as the derivation of their name goes. Speaking of Wickliffe, he says, "His proselytes became very numerous, and obtained the name of Lollards, which had been given in the Low Countries to the persecuted Franciscans, and other enthusiasts, from their practice of singing hymns, *lollen*, or *lullen*, in one of the old German dialects, signifying to sing, as a mother sings when she lulls her babe." Vol I. p. 344. In the Appendix, No. 10, the name of Lollard will be found among the distinguished Waldensian *Barbes* or Pastors.

m See ancient Catechism of the Waldenses, given by Morland, p. 79.

"Q. Whereby dost thou know the Church of Christ?

"A. By the Ministers lawfully called, and by the people participating in the truth of the Ministry."

et des Manichéens, et des Ariens, et des Cathares, il ne sera necessaire que je m'y estende d' avantage [n]."

I ventured to ask M. Peyrani if the Vaudois clergy urged the doctrine of absolute predestination and election. He replied that these nice points of controversy were not often discussed in their pulpits, and that for his own part he had never given his assent to the belief in absolute predestination. "If God infallibly saves some, and as infallibly rejects others, I do not see what is the use of his laws," was one of his remarks.

I mentioned Calvin. "Calvin," said he, "was a good man, I am inclined to think, though I cannot account for his judicial murder of Servetus. He desired to be thought a faithful servant of God, but many of his tenets convey a strange notion of the Almighty's attributes."

I also took the liberty of observing to M. Peyrani, that the close intercourse between the Vaudois students and candidates for holy orders, and the ministers of the Genevan Church, rendered it an object of apprehension, lest they might become tainted with the Socinian infection of Geneva. He rejected the idea with considerable energy, assured me that the doctrine of the Trinity [o] was still preserved in all its purity by the whole of his community, and shewed me an old Catechism, which he trusted would always form the basis of their belief. Some few of the questions and answers on this head are very simple.

"You say that you believe God the Father, God the Son, and God the Holy Ghost to be three persons. You have three Gods then?

"No, I have not three.

[n] Leger, p. 131.

[o] "It deserves to be noticed that in their exposition of the Apostles' Creed, the Waldensian reformers give us that well known text in 1 John v. 7., as a proof of the doctrine of the Trinity. They were, it seems, perfectly satisfied of its authenticity, and most probably at that time had never heard of any suggestion to the contrary."—*Milner*.

"But you have named three."

"Yes as far as relates to the distinction of the persons, but not in regard to the essence of the Divinity."—"Ma non per rason de la essentia de la Divinità," are the words in the ancient language of the Vaudois.

Upon a question as to the learning and acquirements of the Vaudois clergy, M. Peyrani lamented that, not being able to finish their education at home, the youth, who were intended for holy orders, were obliged to submit to the inconvenience and expence of going to Switzerland, but said that they returned in general well stored with scholastic and useful information. His own son, he said, would shortly go there, if he could raise the funds necessary to support the charges of so distant a journey.

Talking of the present and late government of Piemont, the good old moderator drew no comparisons to the disadvantage of the former, but only remarked that Napoleon had done the poor Protestants good and harm; good, in that he had placed them upon a footing with the Romanists, and equalized their condition in the state with the rest of the subjects of the empire; and harm, in that the privileges, then extended to them, only served now to make them more sensible of their present grievances. This subject led to a mention of the audience which M. Peyrani had with the late Emperor of France, when he formed part of a deputation who were charged with an address to him.

Buonaparte noticed M. Peyrani immediately, and accosted him in a style of unusual condescension, and even respect.

N. You are one of the Protestant Clergy?

P. Yes, Sire, and the moderator of the Vaudois Church.

N. You are schismatics from the Roman Church?

P. Not schismatics, I hope, but separatists from scruples of conscience, on grounds that we consider to be Scriptural.

N. You have had some brave men among you. But your mountains are the best ramparts you can have. Cæsar found some trouble in passing your defiles with five legions. Is Arnaud's La Rentrée Glorieuse correct?

P. Yes, Sire, believing our people to have been assisted by Providence.

N. How long have you formed an independent Church?

P. Since the time of Claude, Bishop of Turin, about the year 820.

N. What stipends have your Clergy?

P. We cannot be said to have any fixed stipend at present.

N. You used to have a pension from England?

P. Yes, Sire, the Kings of Great Britain were always our benefactors and protectors till lately. The royal pension is now withheld, because we are your majesty's subjects.

N. Are you organized?

P. No, Sire.

N. Draw out a memorial, and send it to Paris. You shall be organized immediately.

In consequence of the Emperor's order, the Vaudois clergy were enrolled with the clergy of the empire, and lands were allotted for their provision, which yielded 1000 francs yearly to each of the parochial pastors; and in addition to this maintenance, 200 francs [p] a-year were paid to them from the treasury, for forwarding annually to the government certain copies of registers, and population returns. At the restoration of his Sardinian Majesty they were deprived of both these payments, and in failure of these resources, the families of several of the pastors were reduced for a time to such extreme necessity, as to depend upon the charity of their neighbours for subsistence. The sufferings of one of the Clergy and his seven children, were such as

[p] The author has been since informed that this was not an allowance made to the Pastors as Pastors, but to such only as occasionally undertook the charge of making out the registers, when there was no regular Secretary of the Commune, whose business it was to do it. *Note to Second Edition.*

the veriest pauper in England does not experience, and to every stranger who visits the valleys, the name of Alexander Rostaing, Pastor of Ville-seche, or Villa-secca, in the Valley of San Martino, is mentioned as that of a Minister, who has faithfully discharged his duty as a parochial Clergyman, and Secretary of the Synod, in spite of trials severe enough to bend the firmest mind.

M. Rostaing's parish consists of the two villages of Ville-seche or Villa-secca and San Martino, and the hamlets of Faetto, Riclaretto, Bovilla, and Traversa. He has more Romanists in his parish than in any other, which not only exposes him to more vexatious proceedings of every sort, but renders the number of those who would contribute to his occasional assistance still less. The principal villages within his cure are on the north side of the Germanasca torrent; but Faetto and Riclaretto are situated on the southern side: all are detached from each other, and many of the cottages are perched upon the brows of the mountains. This will give a pretty good idea of the arduous duties this exemplary pastor has to perform, of his difficulty in visiting the greater proportion of his flock during the inclement seasons, and the fatigue of moving from one hamlet to another, when his poverty, and the nature of the country, oblige him to go on foot. In the winter he is often in danger of perishing of cold, of being lost in the snow, or carried away by those terrible avalanches and inundations, which are not uncommon in this mountainous region; and in the summer his labours are almost endless, from having to preach upon the mountains to part of his flock, who leave the valleys and take up their residence in the châlets, as long as they can find pasturage for their cattle. In fact, none but those who have been among them, can imagine what are the toils and deprivations of the Vaudois clergy; not one of whom has a population to attend to of less than seven or eight hundred; and these, from the sterility of the soil, spread over a great extent of mountain and valley not easy of access.

In consequence of the urgent application of the Prussian and Belgian ministers, the king was, after a while, persuaded to take into consideration the very distressed state of these exemplary men, and to allow them a pension of 500 francs each[q]. There is also a small charge upon each commune, varying from 100 francs to 140 francs, towards their maintenance; the Dutch government allows 100 francs yearly to each of the two senior pastors, and 75 francs each to three who are next in age, and the pension of about 300[r] francs annually to every one of the thirteen clergy, from the national grant[s] of 1768, is now regularly received from England. Thus 1040 francs a-year, with the use of the presbytery, or parsonage-house, is the utmost fixed and certain income, upon which any of these poor ministers have to depend. They have no fees for burials, baptisms, or marriages.

[q] This sum is raised by a tax laid upon the Vaudois exclusively.

[r] The Author has had great pleasure in learning, that the allowance made to each of the Clergy of the Vaudois, by the Society for the Propagation of the Gospel in Foreign Parts, amounts at present to twenty pounds, or about 500 francs, a-year. *Note to Second Edition.*

[s] "VAUDOIS CLERGY.

"In the year 1768, His Majesty was graciously pleased to grant his Royal Letters Patent, in favour of the Protestants of the Vaudois Churches, in the valleys of Piemont, to empower them to solicit the contributions of well-disposed persons, 'to enable them to maintain the Ministers, Churches, Schools, and Poor, which they were not able to support in any tolerable manner.' His Majesty was also pleased to direct, that the amount of this charitable collection should be paid into the hands of the Incorporated Society for the Propagation of the Gospel in Foreign Parts, and be by them invested in government securities, the interest of which should be appropriated to the religious uses of the Protestant inhabitants of the valleys of Piemont. In obedience to these directions, the Treasurer was empowered to receive the contributions, and carry into effect the gracious designs of His Majesty; since which period, annual stipends have been regularly paid to the thirteen Pastors of the valleys of Piemont, independently of certain small allowances to the widows of the deceased Ministers. By the accumulation of the excess of interest, and other gratuities, the capital sum has been raised to 10,000*l.* 3 per cent. bank annuities, which has enabled the Society to extend the gross amount of the salaries to 292*l.* per annum, for which sum the thirteen Pastors draw upon the Treasurer."—*See Abstract of the Proceedings of the Incorporated Society for the Propagation of the Gospel in Foreign Parts.*

If it were not for the occasional bounty which they receive from Switzerland, Prussia, and the Netherlands, it would be impossible for the ministerial office to be supplied. The former contributes 600 francs towards the annual support of four students at Lausanne; and in 1820, the sum of 4650 francs was remitted from Holland in aid of the schools, and widows of the clergy. The king of Prussia is said to have presented 10,000 francs towards the general support of the schools, clergy, and widows of clergy; and the Emperor of Russia [t] has given the same sum in aid of a new hospital, which is to be built at La Torre.

Of all their benefactors, the Vaudois are most indebted to the Prussian Ambassador at Turin, the Count Waldbourg de Truchsess [u] who is incessant in his endeavours to serve them; and whenever importunity and zeal can avail, he is sure to succeed. I was informed of one kind office which

[t] The Emperor of Russia's donation was 12,000 francs, of which 4000 were bestowed in aid of a new Hospital, 6000 towards the construction of a new church at Pomaret, and 2000 for general purposes of relief. *Note to Second Edition.*

[u] In a letter, which I have lately received from one of my Vaudois correspondents, I found the following grateful acknowledgment of this excellent nobleman's attention to the interests of a people, who stand so much in need of protection. "The very worthy count, General de Truchsess, the Prussian Ambassador, employs all his great influence in favour of the Vaudois, who, since the Stewarts and Trevors have never had so powerful a protector. He has obtained a very liberal subscription from the Emperor of Russia, for an hospital for the Vaudois, which is forwarding rapidly. The ground for the house, the garden, and vigne, are already purchased, at the distance of about half a mile from La Torre, on the road to the church. If you can insert in your book the gratitude of the Vaudois to this generous protector, and to the Emperor of Russia, you will greatly oblige us."

It is a melancholy task to have to add, that serious doubts are entertained whether this excellent work can be brought to a completion. The funds for the erection and support of the hospital must be materially encreased by liberal contributions from abroad, or the design will fail *.

* A subscription for the Vaudois, which will be further noticed at the conclusion of this Narrative, has been opened at the Banking Houses of Messrs. Glynn, Mills, Hallifax and Co. Messrs. Bosanquet, Pitt, Anderdon, Franks and Co. Messrs. Masterman, Peters, Mildred and Co. and Messrs. Hoare and Co. Fleet Street. *Note to Second Edition.*

he did, which will not soon be effaced from the memory of the individual whom he relieved from his embarrassment; or of the little flock, whose minister he restored to them. Among other laws in their favour, enacted by the French government, which the King of Sardinia repealed at his restoration in 1814, was that which rendered the Protestants capable of enjoying public employment, and of rising to rank in the army. The royal edict of May 21, 1814, reduced them to all the degradations to which they had been obliged to submit in former times. They cannot rise in civil employment; they cannot practise in the learned professions; and they cannot be promoted to the rank of commissioned officers; but all are liable to serve as common soldiers and none are exempt from military conscription; not even the clergy. M. Peyrot, the pastor of Rora, was drawn in the conscription of 1821: in vain he urged his sacred character, and pastoral duties. His remonstrances were of no use; he was too poor to purchase a substitute, and orders of a most peremptory nature arrived for his joining his regiment, as a private soldier, immediately. The interposition of Count Truchsess was prayed for, and obtained. M. Peyrot was released, not as a clergyman, but with a pretended understanding, on the part of the war-office, that he was beyond the age prescribed for military service.

M. Peyrani himself, and afterwards M. Bert, the pastor of La Torre, searched all their accounts in my presence, to see what succours had been rendered to the Vaudois on the part of England, independent of the pension arising from the national grant. Every benefaction and service is carefully recorded in books kept by the moderator, the moderator adjoint, and the secretary; but some Bibles from the Bible Society, some books from a few generous individuals, and two hundred pounds from the Baptist Society, were all that appeared under the head of British bounty.

Of the royal pension, to which Napoleon alluded in his conference with M. Peyrani, no part whatever has been received since the year 1797: it was suppressed by the British government when Piemont became subject to France, and has not been restored with the legitimate dynasty. This pension proceeded, if I have been rightly informed, from a grant of William and Mary, encreased by a bequest of Queen Mary.

The hardship of being deprived of a pension, amounting to 400 francs [*] a-year, which had been enjoyed for more than a hundred years, is rendered the more insupportable, because it is considered a right rather than a benefaction, and claimable upon every principle of equity. I was shewn, by M. Peyrani, a copy of an order in council, held at Westminster, under the protectorate of Oliver Cromwell, a transcript of which is in the hands of almost every pastor in the three valleys; and, upon the strength of which, they partly found their claim to the pension in question. The collection alluded to, amounted to more than 38,000*l.* of which upwards of 16,000*l.* was put out to interest.

"Rapport ayant esté fait à Monsieur le Commissaire par le comité des affaires des pauvres Eglises des Vallées de Piemont, qu'ils avoient esté bien informés par Monsieur Morland de l'état des dites Vallées, &c. il a esté arresté que l'argent qui reste de la collecte faite pour elles, sera employé comme s'ensuit pour un establissement ferme et ordinaire à l'avenir.

"A Monsieur Jean Leger, Modérateur, qui a toûjours agi des Vallées, 100 livres sterlins.

"A huit Ministres demeurans sur les terres du Duc de Savoy, 320 livres sterlins.

"A trois Ministres demeurans sur terre de France en val Peyrouse, 30 livres sterlins.

"Au Maître d'Ecole génerale, 20 livres sterlins.

"A dix Maîtres d'Ecoles particulieres, 60 livres sterlins.

"A trois Maîtres d'Ecole en Val Peyrouse, 9 livres sterlins.

[*] Eighteen pounds a-year.—*See Note to the Conclusion.*

"A quatre Etudians en Theologie, ou en Médecine, 40 livres sterlins.

"Au Médecin, 20 livres sterlins.

"Au Chirurgien, 10 livres sterlins.

"En tout annuellement, 609 livres sterlins.

"Signé. SCOBELL. CLERC DU CONSEIL[y]."

According to Morland's account, the collection amounted to 38,241*l.* 10*s.* 6*d.*; and of this, 9501*l.* 16*s.* 3*d.* was immediately disposed of in remitting sums of money, bedding, linen, and provisions, to the distressed sufferers, in the course of the year 1655. A commission was appointed

[y] According to the original instrument preserved in the State Paper Office, to which the author has been favoured with permission to have access, the distribution of pensions arising out of the collection of 1655, as settled by the Council of State on the 18th of May, 1658, was to be as follows:

Copy.	Annual Pensions. £.	s.	d.
"To Mr. John Leger, their chiefe minister, who has been eminently active from the beginning, and whose expenses are very great by reason of his daily entertaynments of all sorts of people, who come to him about business	100	0	0
"Item, to each of the other eight ministers under the Duke's dominions, an annual pension of 40*l.*, which, for all the eight, amounts yearly to	320	0	0
"Item, to each of the three ministers of Val Perosa, under the King of France his dominions, an annual pension of 10*l.* which is in all	30	0	0
"Item, to the chief school Mr. of the valleys 20*l.* per ann.: as also to 10 under school Mrs. 6*l.* a man pr an:—to 3 under school Mrs. in the valley of Perosa, 3*l.* a man pr an: in all amounts to	89	0	0
"Item, for the maintaining 4 schollers, students in Divinitie & Physick, an annual pension of 10*l.* to each amounts to	40	0	0
"Item, for a Physitian 25*l.* pr an, & a Chirurgien 10*l.* pr an: in all	35	0	0
	614	0	0
	Present Gratuities.		
"Item, for a recompence to those who have lost their estates, beyond the Pelice, merely because they would not sell them to the Papists against their ancient right	500	0	0
"Item, among the chief commanders 100*l.* whereof 40*l.* may be to Cap[n] Gianavel	100	0	0

Note to Second Edition.

for the management of the rest: and, in the course of the two following years, 12,550*l.* was distributed in the three valleys. There then remained upwards of 16,000*l.*; of which Morland, who was himself the principal commissioner, speaks thus, (p. 596.) "As for the monies that yet remain in the hands of the treasurers, the good people of this nation are desired to believe, that it hath hitherto been his highness's exceeding great care, that no part of the collected monies might be distributed or delivered, but by the advice, and through the hands, of persons of known honour and fidelity: so likewise it shall be his constant endeavour, that what yet remains, shall be improved for the best advantage of those for whom it was solely intended. For which end and purpose his highness, after mature consultation with his commissioners at home, and his public ministers abroad, hath already caused some part thereof to be put out to interest in sure hands, (but so that it may be called in upon urgent occasion); and for the future will take such resolutions, as the necessities of these poor people, and the circumstances of their condition, shall require [z]."

It is manifest from the agreement of these two accounts, the one of which is to be found in Leger's, and the other in Morland's History, that a permanent fund was raised, during the Protectorate, for the annual relief of the Vaudois.

It is little to the credit of Charles the Second, that he sequestrated, or rather abolished this fund; and that all the pathetic appeals, and pressing remonstrances, of the poor Vaudois, could not persuade him to restore it. His only answer was, "that he did not consider himself bound by any of the engagements of an usurper and tyrant, nor responsible for his debts [a]."

[z] Documents in the State Paper Office, shew in what manner a part, at least, of this 16,000*l.* was put out to interest. Sir Thomas Vyner had 5000*l.* at four per cent. The Chamberlain of London 4000*l.* and Mr. Bakewell 2000*l.* also at four per cent. The capital to be paid in, if required, at a month's notice. *Note to Second Edition.*

[a] There are authentic vouchers in the State Paper Office to prove, that the

James the Second could not be expected to pay any attention to the claims of the Protestants; but William and Mary restored the Pension, or at least established a new one, and were the constant friends of this oppressed community. King William gave the celebrated Henri Arnaud the commission of colonel in one of his own regiments. The commission itself, dated May 14, 1691, signed "William," and counter-signed "Nottingham," is still preserved in the family of Appia, at La Torre.

It was with extreme regret we witnessed the approach of the hour, which told us we must take leave of the venerable Peyrani. The good-humour, cheerfulness, and resignation of the old man, his perfect recollection of events and conversations which took place years ago, his profound erudition and general information, lent a deep and peculiar interest to his discourse. My young companions were rivetted with attention. He appeared to them like a being of a different order to what they had been used to see: all that they heard and saw had more the air of romance than reality. The little window of the room opened upon the

money collected for the Vaudois was fairly disposed of, and the pension regularly paid during the Protectorate.

The minutes of "the Committee for the affairs of the poor people in the valleys of Piemont" state, that at the sitting of a Committee on the 12th of October 1658, it was resolved, that the same half-yearly sum of 307*l.* be paid in pensions, due December 24, 1658, which "His late Highness and Council did by their order, bearing date, May 18th 1658, settle upon the ministers, school-masters, and several others among the said Protestants, and by another order, of the 27th of May 1658, did appoynt the actual remission of the said pensions, that is to say for one half year, ending the 24th of June, amounting to the summe of 307*l.*"

By this minute then it appears, that the first half yearly pension was paid as soon as it was fixed during Oliver Cromwell's life—and that the second was paid when it became due, during the protectorate of Richard Cromwell. Charles the Second seized the fund, or refused to see justice done to the poor Vaudois, upon the plea, that he was not responsible for the debts of an usurper. It is clear from the above that the Cromwells did not misapply the proceeds of the collection. *Note to Second Edition.*

wild mountain scenery of Pomaretto; the roar of the distant torrents was heard through the casement; and the impression left by the whole scene was so much the greater, from the contrast between the elevated character of the noble old man, and the circumstances in which he was placed. Poverty within, and desolation without, formed a dark and striking back-ground to the portrait of the philosophic minister, whose lips teemed with eloquence, and whose mind was stored with all the riches of the most intellectual society. The looks of my friends as they wandered from the window to the moderator, sufficiently told me what was passing within their breasts; and they did not escape the notice of M. Vertu, who watched with an enquiring eye, to observe what impression the aged moderator of his church would make upon the strangers. Holding him in the utmost reverence himself, he was all anxiety that we should do the same; and could not disguise his feelings of delight at every mark of respect, which we paid to the sacred representative of this primitive Christian community.

Before we parted, I looked several times earnestly round the room, that I might carry away with me every possible recollection of the chamber, in which Rodolphe Peyrani was likely to finish his days. The ordinary and antique furniture, and the prints which hung upon the walls, were all objects of interest; and some of them illustrated the character of the man. In the centre, and directly over the fire-place, was the moderator's diploma, presented to him by the Royal Academy of Turin. On one side of the diploma was George the Fourth, taken when he was Prince of Wales: on the other the King of Sardinia; for no sufferings or injustice done to him could efface the loyal principles of M. Peyrani. Several kings of Prussia, Isaac Newton, Luther, and Calvin, occupied another place; and the Duke of Wellington, and Lord William Bentinck, were in a very conspicuous situation. The good man pointed to the latter, and spoke of him with much gratitude. "If any thing could have been done for the Vaudois, Lord William would have effected it," he said; "but the restored king was deaf to his intercessions."

The British general naturally conceived that he, who had been instrumental in replacing his Majesty upon the throne of his ancestors, had some pretensions to be heard in favour of subjects, who professed the same religion as his own sovereign and himself. He took the earliest opportunity of urging their suit; and at Genoa, before the king could even set foot in the hereditary dominions to which the British arms had restored him, and while he was yet under the protection of a British escort, Lord William Bentinck most earnestly pleaded for the oppressed churches of the valleys. The king listened to the eloquent and feeling appeal with worse than indifference. His determination, most probably, was already made; for in four days afterwards, and on the morning after he had taken possession of his palace at Turin, the ungrateful monarch issued an edict, by which he dispossessed the Vaudois of all that they had enjoyed during his dethronement; and put many vexatious decrees in force, which had been proclaimed against them by his bigotted and intolerant predecessors.

Victor Emanuel, the late king, is but just gathered to his fathers. The Vaudois never speak with any bitterness even of those, who have used them the most unfairly; and his death was announced to me by one of my friends in the valleys, with an observation which does honour to the kindness of his heart. "On ne lui a connu d'autre defaut, que d'être trop bon et trop crédule, de sorte que tous avoient raison, mais plus particulièrement le dernier venu."

As M. Peyrani followed us feebly down stairs, he shewed us the door of an apartment, which had never been opened, he told us, since the day on which his brother had been carried out of it to be consigned to the grave. I asked what brother, and the answer was a momentary shock. It was Ferdinand Peyrani, the pastor of Pramol. It was like hearing the knell of a dear friend. Ferdinand Peyrani was the first person who interested me in the history of the Vaudois. It was his letter, addressed to the Society for promoting Christian Knowledge, which directed my attention to them, and occasioned this excursion to their Alpine retreats. He was one of the pastors to whom I felt so anxious to be introduced, and this was the first news of his being no more. His death was hastened by the scurvy, a disorder increased by poverty and want.

At the door of his humble presbytery the aged moderator wrung our hands, and said farewell, with every symptom of regret at parting. He stood at the threshold, watching our departing steps, and the last sight that I had of his long grey locks, floating in the wind, left an impression that will not soon be removed. I am sure nobody could take leave, as we did, of M. Peyrani, with the certainty of seeing him no more, without being sensibly affected. His son accompanied us to the edge of the torrent, and there we said adieu to him.

Such was our visit to the successor of the bishops of the purest church in Italy, whose necessities were such, that we felt bound, by a sacred sense of duty, to run the hazard of wounding those feelings of pride, which every man of sensibility must retain, even amid the most urgent poverty, by pressing upon his acceptance a heart offering for the purchase of a few of those comforts, which his age and infirmities required. I have had many struggles, before I could make up my mind as to the propriety of stating this circumstance, and nothing could have induced me to do it, but the persuasion that it will put the case in the strongest light, and shew at once the deplorable situation to which many of these excellent pastors are reduced. We could not have presumed to proffer, nor would the venerable moderator have condescended to accept the assistance of private individuals like ourselves, if it had not been a very timely succour: and certainly the circumstance never could have appeared in print, but with the object of drawing attention to the wants of a people, who have been too much overlooked by those who have the means of aiding them.

Who knows but, as the flood of time rolls on, some successor of the primate of England may be reduced to the same condition; that the archiepiscopal chair of Canterbury may no longer be filled by a mitred prelate, that the functions and arduous duties may outlive the well appointed dignity of the sacred office, and that some humble pastor, like Rodolphe Peyrani, with the empty title of Bishop, may be obliged to the compassion of strangers for temporary relief. I am only imagining a fatal recurrence of what may happen again. The visible and Episcopal Church of England was once dwindled down to a few faithful adherents of Charles the Second, who formed his little court, and more than shared his need. May heaven avert a second such blow, and may the honoured members of the English hierarchy continue to exert themselves, as some of them have hitherto done, to preserve the remnant of a Church, from which their own pure Establishment derives most of its doctrines!

* * * * * * * *

Reader, the sufferings of Rodolphe Peyrani are at an end. He died about three months after our interview with him. His spirit could no longer bear up against a complication of maladies and sorrows, and now, all that I remember of him is literally like a dream that is past, or a tale that is told. His death was communicated to me in a letter from one of my Vaudois friends, M. Bert, the pastor of La Torre. Its simple eulogy does honour both to the writer, and to him of whom it was written.

“Dans la supposition que vous n'avez pas entretenir de relation avec d'autres personnes de ce pays, c'est à moi un triste devoir de vous annoncer que nous avons perdu M. Peyrani, Modérateur, depuis le fin d'Avril. C'est dans son genre une perte irréparable."

The father is happily gone to his rest, but it is painful to speak of his son, of that excellent young man whom we were all so disposed to esteem. He is now studying, preparatory to taking orders, at Lausanne, and existing upon a pittance which is not enough for the necessaries of life. I heard of him lately. He was invited to the house of an English family, but his garb was so indifferent that he could not accept the invitation, until a fellow-student had the kindness to lend him his clothes for the day [b].

[b] The author is most happy in having the opportunity of reporting, that several unsolicited donations have been remitted to him, to enable this good young man to pursue his studies more comfortably at Lausanne. He has written his acknowledgements of this succour, which, however, is only temporary, in a strain of piety worthy of his venerable father. "Je me bornerai donc à vous assurer, que je regard mes nouveaux Bienfaiteurs, comme des moyens dont la bonne Providence se sert pour me tirer de la situation pénible où je me trouve. Cette grande considération sera pour moi un nouveau motif de la bénir sans cesse, et de m'attacher de plus en plus au service de notre bon Sauveur." Until he received this assistance, the poor youth was indebted to the charity of the benevolent M. Monastier, a professor of the University, for his daily dinner. M. Monastier himself has but a very contracted income, and a large family. *Note to Second Edition.*

The following ample and correct detail, testified by several respectable Vaudois Ministers and elders, of the embarrassed state in which the late moderator Peyrani, left his children, was transmitted to the author at the close of the year 1825.

"Monsieur Jean Louis Samuel Rodolphe Peyrani, après avoir tenu l'Ecole Latine deux ans et desservi seize les Eglises montueuses et penibles de Maneille, de Praly, et de Ville-Seche, fut transferé dans celle de Pomaret (et constitué Moderateur des Vallées Evangeliques du Piemont) en 1791, qu'il a occupé trentdeux ans jusqu'au 26 Avril, 1823, époque de son decés. Il herita de son père un patrimoine de 160 à 200 Louis au plus: il l'augmenta pendant les premières années de son ministère de quelques acquisitions de peu de consequence; mais le rang de *Moderateur adjoint*, celui de *Moderateur en chef*, et les *circonstances critiques dans lesquelles* et *luimême*, et sa *Paroisse*, et sa *Patrie* se trouvèrent plongés lors de l'entrée des *François en Piemont*, et surtout à l'approche des armées *Austro-Russes*, l'ont forcé de contracter des dettes auxquelles il faut attribuer la perte de son heritage pour ses enfans, au nombre de trois, savoir, une fille qui s'est mariée et qui a cinq enfans;—et deux fils dont un est Etudiant en Theologie à Lausanne, et l'autre sans vocation decidée.

"D'abord l'un de ses debiteurs, saisissant l'epoque où les billets monnoyés, qui

An anecdote, in illustration of the talents of the late Moderator Peyrani, of his useful application of them, and the obscurity in which they were buried, must conclude my melancholy narrative.

avaient cours ici, allaient tomber, lui fit un payement de 96 Louis. La loi l'obligeoit de les recevoir, et la conscience l'empecha de les donner à ses creanciers.

" Le passage des troupes de France en Piemont, lui occasionna des frais de logement considerables et pendant un grand nombre d'années. Lorsque les Allemands prirent possession de nos vallées, il essuya un pillage de linge, meubles, betail, montre en or, et avec peril imminent de la vie. Les voisins avaient fui;—seul, il demeure pour s'opposer à un pillage et incendie générale dont sa paroisse etait menacée.

" Aussi long temps qu'il géra le Moderateur, et même, lorsq'il fut depouillé, son savoir et son credit le mirent en etat de rendre des services de divers genres à ses compatriotes; sa table était ouverte à tout le monde, suivant ses foibles moyens;—et la modicité de ses ressources pecuniaires ne fut jamais pour lui un motif legitime de refus, quand il s'agissoit de secourir un malheureux. Celui qui se rendait auprès de lui pour implorer ses bons offices, était assuré qu'il tendroit la main à l'indigence, et qu'il n'epargneroit rien pour lui obtenir une faveur, un emploi, ou pour le tirer d'embarras et de prison.

" Telles sont les principales occasions dans lesquelles cet indefatigable Bienfaiteur de sa Patrie contracta des dettes;—tel est l'usage qu'il fit des sommes empruntées:—nous passons sous silence ses demarches auprès du Gouvernement pour les interêts de la Patrie.

" Les deux fils, pour faire honneur à la memoire de leur respectable père, ont abandonné complètement les biens meubles et immeubles qu'ils tenaient de lui, à ses creanciers, avec reserve de les racheter s'ils se trouvoient un jour en etat de le faire: ils ont été evalués à près 300 Louis. Avec ce sacrifice qu'il nous est penible de l'avouer, il reste encore des dettes legitimes pour près 150 Louis. Les deux fils ont fait esperer aux creanciers qu'il consacreraient leur premiers épargnes à s'acquitter envers eux.

" Telle est la declaration que nous avons cru devoir leur accorder, parceque nous avons une parfaite connoissance de son contenu: puisse-t-elle être de quelque utilité à eux.

" *Pomaret*, 19 *Août*, 1825.

" JUILLET JEAN, *Ancien Syndic.*
JEAN COMBE, *Consilier.*
JACQUES BERTALOT, *Conseiller et Diacre.*
JACQUES JAYER, *Ancien.*
JEAN BERTALOT, *Ancien.*
JEAN BAR, *Ancien.*
RIBET DAVID, *Vice Syndic à Pomaret.*
JACQUES GAUDIN, *Ancien.*
JEAN JAQUES DE JALLA, *Pasteur.*
ALEX. ROSTAING, *Pasteur à Ville-Secche et Moderateur Adjoint.*

" Vu pour legalisation des signatures de Messrs. Rostaing et Jalla.

" P. BERT, *Moderateur.*

" *La Tour, le* 25 *Août* 1825."

Haud facile emergunt, quorum virtutibus obstat
Res angusta domi.

A few years ago a Roman Catholic Curè of Geneva, wrote a pamphlet in defence of the adoration of saints, and image worship. It was much admired, had a great sale, and was thought by the friends of the Curè to be unanswerable. The Protestants of Geneva were burning to see a reply to this able tract, but none appeared, to the disappointment and mortification of every good Lutheran and Calvinist. Just at the crisis of its popularity, Mr. Lowther, the author of "Brief Observations on the present State of the Waldenses," happened to be on his visit to the Valleys, and in an interview with M. Peyrani, expressed his regret that no answer had been made to this redoubtable pamphlet. The moderator drew some papers [d] from his desk, and shewed Mr. Lowther that he himself had drawn up a reply.

a The Rev. Thomas Sims has lately circulated the following Prospectus, relative to the MSS. of M. Peyrani, which have been entrusted to his charge, and the admirers of the late venerated Minister will, it is hoped, soon have an opportunity of judging of his merits as a scholar and a divine.

"The MSS. left by M. Peyrani consist of Dissertations and Letters on a variety of Theological, Philological, Philosophical, and Historical Subjects; many of which, it is probable, will be found worthy of being made public at a future time. For the present, it is deemed expedient to publish a single Volume in the original, containing pieces of an argumentative nature against the errors of the Church of Rome.

"The first part of the Volume will consist of *Four Letters addressed to Cardinal Pacca,* a Prelate who, during the time of Napoleon's usurpation, was a state-prisoner in the fortress of Fenestrelles, in the immediate neighbourhood of the Waldenses. These Letters furnish a very able historical defence of the antiquity and purity of the Waldensian Church. The importance of the Author's arguments to all the *Protestant Churches,* will be at once seen, when it is remarked that the Author undertakes to prove the following points, from the testimony of even Roman Catholic Writers:—

"I. That, although stigmatized as Arians and Manichees, the Waldenses opposed the errors of those heretics more successfully than the Church of Rome did.

"II. That, to ascertain the origin of the Waldenses, we must recur not only to an age prior to that of Peter Waldo, but to the first ages of the Christian Church.

"III. That the Waldenses have both steadfastly adhered to true doctrines

"But why have you not published it?" it was asked.

"Because I have not the means. I cannot print it at my own expence, and know of nobody who will undertake it."

Mr. Lowther begged, and obtained consent to take charge of the MS. and to send it to the press.

from age to age, and opposed the *novelties* that Rome superadded from time to time to the Christian faith.

"IV. That, with the exception of the Primitive Church, founded by Christ and his first Disciples, no Christian people have been more distinguished for rare virtues and irreproachable morals.

"V. That, since the Apostolic Age, no Christian Church has shewn more zeal for the propagation of the Gospel, or greater fortitude and constancy under long and severe trials and afflictions.

"Next to these Letters, the Volume will contain M. Peyrani's *Reply to the Roman Catholic Bishop of Pignerol,* who, in his Pastoral Addresses, had animadverted on the religious opinions of the Waldenses, and endeavoured to persuade them to embrace the tenets of the Church of Rome. This Reply may be considered a specimen of M. Peyrani's great skill and temperate spirit as a controversialist, and is characterized by a train of reasoning that undermines at once the very foundations of the Church of Rome, and justifies the Protestant Churches in their separation from that apostate Church.

"The next piece, which it is proposed to include in the Volume, is a masterly *Reply to M. Ferrary, a Roman Catholic Priest near Geneva,* who had attempted to defend the use of images in the Christian Church, and the invocation of saints; and this will probably be followed by a *Treatise on the Adoration of the Virgin Mary,* an error both prominent and pernicious in the Church of Rome, but which the Author, in the most conclusive manner, shews to be entirely unscriptural.

"It is hoped that the publication of this Volume will not only be the means of affording pecuniary relief to the immediate descendants of M. Peyrani, (two sons and a daughter;) but be found also a valuable acquisition, at a period like the present, when the Church of Rome is making new and strenuous efforts to recover her former influence; re-asserts, with more than ordinary vehemence, her pretensions to supreme authority; and employs the most effective and most artful of her emissaries, the revived order of Jesuists, to regain her ancient ascendancy, if possible, in several of the nations of Europe.

"The French language being now very generally understood, it is thought desirable to publish the work in that language, in which the Author originally wrote.

"It is believed that the price of the Volume will not exceed 10*s*.

"The profits arising from the publication will be appropriated to the exclusive benefit of Peyrani's family." *Note to Third Edition.*

It was printed, had a rapid run, and was so admirably well written, was so convincing, so keen and cutting, that the Popish polemic bought up all the remaining unsold pamphlets of his own, out of shame. Mr. Lowther assured me that he was unable to buy a single impression, though he offered a louis for one, when he wanted to have it inserted in a volume of miscellaneous articles, and that he was obliged to borrow one, and to have it *written* out in the place of a printed copy [e].

e "Lettre de Ferrari à M. Cellerier," was the title of the first pamphlet, and "Réponse à la Lettre de M. Ferrari, Curè du Grand Sacconex, par un Protestant," was the title of the second.

CHAPTER V.

Leave Pomaretto—Alpine scenery—Pinerolo—Ancient inn—Excursion to the valley of Luzerna—Mount Viso—Intolerance—Anecdote—Vaudois Heroism—Anecdote—Patriarchal Simplicity—Church of San Giovanni—Ludicrous Bigotry—Lovely vale of San Giovanni—Beautiful Landscape—La Torre—Too frequent intermarriages—Church of La Torre—Its romantic situation—M. Bert—Attend service in the Church—Monumental inscriptions—Peasantry—Village inn and accommodation—Murderous plot against the Protestants—M. Odetti—The plot—Fanaticism—Rendezvous of conspirators—General Godin—March of the Vaudois soldiers for the preservation of their families—Threatened by the Torrents—Vespers bell, signal of destruction—Work of assassination—The assassins—Retribution—Injustice—General Zimmerman—Immunities and privileges granted to Vaudois—Grievances of the Vaudois—Absurd restrictions—Imposts—Disqualifications—Agriculture—Trade—Laughable mistake.

After our most interesting visit to Pomaretto, we returned to Perosa in that serious and meditative mood, which the nature of our inquiries was calculated to produce. The obscurity of evening was increased by the masses of rock that projected above and around, and every object corresponded with the dreariness of the scenery, and the gloom that affected us.

* * * "At every step,
Solemn and slow, the shadows blacker fell,
And all was awful listening gloom around."

As we passed one of the insecure bridges that are thrown across the torrent, we met a string of mules, whose cautious steps reminded us, that it is not inconvenience only, which attends a traveller in this wild and rugged region, but that perils also wait upon his path, and that nature is too sparing of her bounty, in the valley of the Clusone, to suffer its inhabitants to provide against more than the absolute necessities of the hour. A few loose planks formed the largest of the bridges which connect Pomaretto and Perosa. Before next winter they will most likely be washed away. The furnace of a smelting house was blazing as we passed it: its strong glare in the darkness of the night served to discover, and to set off some of the savage features of this rude glen, and seeing them, as we did, to perfection, we could not feel surprised that the Alps should furnish materials for so many tales and romances, when they present such outlines to the eye, which the imagination may fill up with all that can inspire wonder or terror.

We returned to and slept at Pinerolo, in an inn or hotel which must once have been the residence of some bold baron, but has been long since converted into one of an humbler designation. A large court-yard serves now for the receptacle of carts and other vehicles, a gallery runs round the building, and opens into several corridors, which communicate with large and dreary apartments; some gilded wainscoting, and the remains of what were once ornamental cornices, proclaim the departed grandeur of other days. The kitchen is an immense and vaulted chamber, the ceiling and walls of which have not been whitened for years; it resounded when we walked across it, as if it were constructed over a range of subterraneous passages. We had a capital supper, and among other things a large dish of the very small fish, a minute species of eel, which is considered so delicious in Piemont, and some of the Muscat wine, which pleased us so much at Perosa; but this good cheer did not reconcile us to what followed. Upon asking for our bed rooms, we were told that we were to sleep where we had supped. There were but two beds, and these, it was thought, afforded ample accommodation for *five* gentlemen. For a length of time we were scarcely believed, when we refused to be so accommodated, and it was not till after a great deal of discussion, that they made up a third bed in this room, and put two of us into a cold straggling apartment, where we found what we demanded.

The morning, on which we left Pinerolo for the Valley of Luzerna, was so bright and beautiful, that the air was fresh rather than cold, and for the first time since we were upon Italian soil, we enjoyed the sight of an Italian sky. There was all that clear blueness, and appearance of wider expanse in the firmament, which make one fancy that the vault of Heaven is loftier in this region than in our own. The country too, that we passed over, wore a very different aspect to that which we visited the previous evening, it was more open and productive, and did not so soon shrink into glens and defiles. The silvery tops of the distant mountains shone with uncommon splendour, and the whole drive to La Torre (La Tour) was one of the most cheerful that we had enjoyed. The first view of Mount Viso was imposing in the extreme. It is below the level of eternal snow, but its sides and brow were now covered, and the dazzling whiteness of its peaks burst upon us at a sudden turn in the road, and called forth a general exclamation of delight. No pencil can do justice to the bright tints of a mountain's snowy top sparkling in the sun.

On leaving Pinerolo we followed the fine broad road that leads to Saluzzo, in a due southerly direction for about two miles, crossed the Clusone over an ill-built and crazy bridge, and at the hamlet of Osasco turned into a cross-road to the right, and continued our route towards the west. Bricherasio was the last Popish commune through which we passed: it is well situated, but though it is within the Pelice and the Clusone, the boundary rivers of the Protestant limits, yet, like the other two or three villages in the plain, its lands are considered too productive to be suffered to remain under the cultivation of heretics; and Protestant families are not permitted to make any purchases or settlements within its limitations. The laws on this subject are so severe, that a Vaudois pastor is not permitted to sleep in any of the villages, which are immediately adjoining to those of his own community, and a minister was exposed here to a curious dilemma upon this very edict of exclusion. He had been to visit one of his flock who was taken ill at Bricherasio, and a snow-storm at night was so violent that he was unable to return to his own habitation. The poor man dare not go to bed, for fear of exposing himself to the penalties of the law, and actually sat up all night to evade it, and to be able to swear that he did not *sleep* at Bricherasio.

The nearer we approached the boundaries of San Giovanni, or St. Jean, the first Protestant village, the greater interest M. Vertu took in the country; and when he crossed the limits, he seemed to breathe a new air, and to enjoy a new existence. He was all delight to be upon the soil of his own native valley, kept pointing out to us every well-known spot, recounting anecdotes of the days of persecution, and assigning a tale to every hamlet within view. The grove upon the slope of the hill, and by the road-side, just as we got within the confines, was an object of particular regard. "It had been an out-post," he said, "in many a bloody skirmish between the Popish and the Protestant borderers."

He pointed to the banks of the Pelice, near Luzerna. "At that bend of the river," he told us, "tradition had consecrated the spot to the recollection of an exploit more memorable than the achievement of Leander himself. A Romanist had paid great attention to the lessons of a Vaudois friend, and gave such proof of his heart being touched, that the latter thought no opportunity ought to be lost of pressing his conversion while he appeared to be in a favourable mood. His visits used to be nocturnal. On the night when he flattered himself that his arguments would prevail, the floods had cut off the usual means of access. It was winter, and the torrent was alarmingly broad and rapid; but the Christian hero was not to be interrupted or daunted in his holy enterprize: he boldly plunged into the waters, swam across, and reaped his reward in the conversion of his friend from Popery."

The new church of San Giovanni, and that of La Torre, or La Tour, just distinguishable under the frowning crag, that serves as a land-mark for many miles before it is approached, were spots to which M. Vertu particularly directed our eyes, and where he fixed his own with looks of reverential admiration; but when we were once fairly among the houses and inhabitants of San Giovanni, he could no longer contain his satisfaction. It was a burst of youthful ecstacy, of undisguised and irrepressible joy, which communicated itself to us, and encreased the esteem which we already entertained for our amiable companion. He had not been for many months in the valley which gave him birth, and where every string that was touched beat in unison with those of his own heart.

The mountains and vales of the Vaudois are retreats of hospitable kindness and confidence, where patriarchal simplicity and unaffected manners prevail to an extent, which is seldom seen elsewhere; and when a young man like M. Vertu finds himself transported from a capital, where all is constraint and suspicion, to such a scene, his heart cannot but surrender itself to the enthusiasm of the moment.

It was a Sabbath morning when we passed through San Giovanni, and the peasants were going to church. As groupes, or individuals, met us, our friend from Turin nodded to one, and spoke to another; seemed to know every body, and told us who were Roman Catholics, and who Protestants: in fact, we soon distinguished them ourselves; for it is notorious that the Protestant peasantry may be recognized by the superior cleanliness of their appearance.

The new church of San Giovanni is a large brick building, which stands nobly upon rising ground, and may be seen at some distance. Nearly opposite to it is the Roman Catholic church. Before the great door of the former, I was surprised to see a lofty screen, or palisade; and concluded that the front of the edifice had never been finished. But this unsightly wood-work was erected, that the pious Romanists of San Giovanni might not be shocked, at seeing their heretical neighbours enter their place of worship, or house of abomination. The number of the latter amounts to seventeen hundred, and more; that of the former does not exceed forty! The old Protestant Church was destroyed above a hundred years ago, in one of the persecutions, and never suffered to be rebuilt till the French occupied Piemont. It has been the policy of the government not to allow a dilapidated church or presbytery of the Waldenses to be restored: and to this hour the pastor of San Giovanni has not been permitted to have a house appropriated to his office, as the ministers of the other twelve parishes have. When the French put the Vaudois upon the same footing as the other inhabitants of the province, they took advantage of their privileges, and built a new church. But what was the consternation of the Protestant population of San Giovanni, when the edict of May, 1814, commanded them to shut up the sacred edifice! Their supplications were unnoticed; the court paid no attention to its heretical subjects, and the interdict would have continued, but for the repeated intervention of the Protestant ambassadors; among whom the Prussian minister exerted himself with his wonted ardour. The church was reopened, but only upon the humiliating condition of raising this hideous screen, this deformity, so disgraceful to the Papists who insisted upon its erection, and so mortifying to the professors of the other creed, who are obliged to submit to it.

The scruples of the Romanists of La Torre were indulged

in another matter, equally at the expence of the Protestants of that village. The new school gave offence: the Papists were scandalised as they passed it, to hear the infant heretics repeating their wicked lessons! Their remonstrances were respected by the minister of the interior, who, when he found he could not shut up the school, removed the scandal, as far as he could, by commanding a partition to be made on the outside, so that the ears of the faithful might no longer be offended. Such are the pitiful and vexatious proceedings, which are still in force against the innocent and harmless Waldenses. The opinions of the age will no longer allow of corporal punishment for religious differences, and bigotry therefore is obliged to content itself with this wretched mode of shewing its disappointment. As it cannot be cruel, it is ridiculous.

After leaving the village of San Giovanni, we entered a lovely vale. The Pelice flowed in the middle: on the other side of the river stood Luzerna, which is seen to great advantage from the road. La Torre was directly before us, and the heights of Angrogna rose magnificently to the right. This is by far the richest spot which is left in possession of the Protestants. In the sweet language of Italy it is indeed "una pianura fertile e graziosa, e l'amenità della campagna rende questo viaggio sommamente delizioso." Gardens and vineyards, orchards and groves, corn land and pastures, mulberry trees and the stateliest chesnuts, are intermingled in the most picturesque confusion; and the variety of hill and dale, before the acclivities swell into mountains, complete one of the loveliest landscapes in Piemont.

The descriptions of Leger, the historian of the Vaudois, are generally plain matter-of-fact statements, where the style is uniform; but the beauties of San Giovanni, for once, called forth a more animated strain. "It would be a little earthly paradise," said he, "if it were not besieged by Roman Catholics on the east and on the south. It is a beautiful vale, embroidered on the south by verdant meadows, which are watered by the river Pelice: the rest of the vale does not merely consist of corn fields, but of fields, vineyards, and orchards intermixed. The vines are trained up to the very tops of lofty trees; and the tendrils, twining together, and forming graceful festoons, stretch from branch to branch, and *ferment des ravissantes treilles,* under which the peasants are seen plowing with their oxen, or reaping the finest wheat in the world. All the roads, the walks, and the hedges, which separate different farms, are agreeably bordered with different sorts of fruit trees, and particularly with mulberries, which the inhabitants cultivate for their silk-worms, and which help them to raise the money to pay their rents and taxes. This vale is environed and adorned, on the north and west, by the most superb *costiere,* as they call it, in the world, and the prettiest hills imaginable, which look like one continued vineyard, or bower of vines, under which they sow all kinds of grain; while the soil is refreshed by means of a conduit of water brought from the torrent of Angrogna."

When we arrived at the torrent of Angrogna, the smiling features of San Giovanni were immediately succeeded by the more grand and imposing scenery of La Torre. We were now again in the midst of mountains, and had hastened on, that we might be in time for the church service, when the sound of the steeple bell, pouring its music on the breeze, greeted us with the welcome information that we were not too late. The clatter of the wheels, and the unusual sight of a carriage in this secluded village brought but few people to the doors; for almost all were gone, or hurrying forward, to the house of God. We alighted at the little inn, and joined those who had not yet reached the sacred spot, to which they were bending their steps; and the greetings and salutations, which passed between M. Vertu and the cheerful-looking groupes whom we overtook, were even more affecting than what we witnessed at San

Giovanni; for here he was in his native parish, and in the midst of relations. Almost every one whom he accosted was an uncle or an aunt, or a cousin of near or distant branch. But however interesting at the moment it may be to see the hearty shake of the hand, and the kind salute of kindred and clanship, it must be considered as one of the evils to which they are exposed, that the little community of the Waldenses must be for ever intermarrying, family with family. Romanists and Protestants cannot wed, under the risk of being subjected to a variety of vexatious suits; and the consequence is, that there is no end to the connexions, which are perpetually forming between very near relatives.

The first appearance of La Torre gives a more favourable idea of this village, than a closer inspection will permit the traveller to form. The two bridges that are built over the torrent at its entrance, the water-mill and the Popish church, that are seen to the right, with the ruins of the old castle that peep from among the trees by which they are surrounded, on a hill that rises sufficiently high to command the village, are picturesque objects, which cheat the imagination into the belief, that La Torre itself must be a most enviable spot. But the street is narrow and ugly, and the houses are poorly constructed, and stand close together. The broadest part is dignified by the name of the Square, or Place de la Tour; and the principal building in it is a long heavy-looking edifice, which is still called the palace, although no longer the residence of the ancient Counts of La Torre. The family is extinct, and the house is now the property of one of the Vertus, who occupies a part, and lets the rest.

After passing through a long line of street, we came to a hamlet which is called the Borgo of S. Marguerita, from whence the church of La Torre, overhung by the tremendous crag of Castaluzzo, is seen to great advantage. In passing through La Torre, every thing that I saw reminded me of what I had been accustomed to in England on a Sabbath-day, so unlike the usual appearance of towns on the continent. Silence and decency prevailed in the streets, smartness in the dress, and cleanliness in the countenance of the rustics. Even the clean close caps of the female peasantry resembled those of my own native parish in Suffolk; and when we reached the church-yard the comparison was still more striking; for the villagers were assembled before the church-door, waiting for the clergyman, who had not yet come, and enjoying the fineness of the weather. The sunshine of the heart seemed to harmonize with the brightness of the day. I employed the short interval before we entered the sacred walls, in taking a view of the objects around me. The Church of La Torre is rather a large building, and stands upon a very picturesque eminence, surrounded by trees and vineyards, and at the distance of about a mile from the village. The rising ground on which it is built bursts abruptly towards the north and west, into rocky eminences, and these into lofty crags and towering mountains; some of which protrude so far from their base, that they look as if they would inevitably fall, and overwhelm every thing below them. The church-yard might be rendered still more pleasing to the eye, if the graves and turf were kept in better order; but I have never seen any consecrated spot on the other side of the channel, which in this respect can compare with those of our own. The front of the church not only commands a prospect of the village, and the winding road conducting from it, but also a very extensive view of the vale through which the Pelice flows, on the San Giovanni side: and the heights above are said to present the magnificent sight of the plains of the Po, spreading like a map before the eye.

M. Bert, the exemplary pastor of La Torre, soon arrived in his gown and band, and received the affectionate attentions of his flock, before he preceded them into church. The service commenced with reading two chapters from the

Gospels, (second and third of St. Matthew) by the schoolmaster; and after the chapter, an explanation of it. The practice of permitting a layman to read the lessons, is not at all unusual in some of our own country places, and therefore did not strike me as being irregular. After the chapter, a psalm was sung (Psalm v. 3, 4), accompanied by an organ, the only one in the Protestant valleys; and M. Bert then delivered an exhortation to prayer, from a printed form. A kind of state prayer followed; and, if I remember right, an extempore supplication. Next the Lord's prayer; afterwards the sermon; and then a long petition, or collect, from the book; the Lord's prayer again; the belief; a psalm sung (Psalm ciii. 1, 2); another exhortation from the Liturgy; and a blessing concluded the service.

The inside of the church was perfectly plain; and, with the assistance of a gallery, calculated to hold a very large congregation. I did not observe any division, to answer the description of a chancel: the communion table stands directly in front of the pulpit; and the pulpit is placed near the centre of the church. The men sit on one side, and the women on the other; not in pews, but on benches; and the whole congregation join in the singing. There were several monumental inscriptions in the church, both on the pavement, and on mural tablets: one of the latter excited my attention so much that I took an opportunity of copying it. It was erected in memory of an English lady [f], who died at Turin, in 1817.

[f] The Sister of ELIZABETH SMITH. Among numerous unsolicited contributions, which the author has received towards a Fund for the relief of the Vaudois, one came accompanied with a note, intimating that it was the donation of the Mother of the Lady, whose memorial he had seen in the Church of La Torre. "I beg leave to trouble you with the enclosed trifling acknowledgement of a Mother's gratitude for the grave afforded to the remains of a beloved daughter, and whose feelings are soothed by their being deposited in that sacred retreat of persecuted virtue."

The Author hopes he shall be pardoned for transcribing this passage from a

HIC JACET QUOD RELIQUUM EST CHRISTINÆ,
THOMÆ ALLAN ARMIGERI, EDINBURGENSIS,
DILECTISSIMÆ CONJUGIS,
NECNON GEORGII SMITH, ARMIGERI DE MONK-CONISTON
IN COMITATU LANCASTRIÆ APUD ANGLOS
FILIÆ PIISSIMÆ.
OBIIT AUGUSTÆ TAURINORUM. MAIÆ DIE 14, 1817.

"Here lie the remains of Christina, the beloved wife of Thomas Allan, Esquire, of Edinburgh, and the affectionate daughter of George Smith, Esquire, of Monk-Coniston, in the County of Lancaster, in England. She died at Turin, on the 14th day of May, 1817."

I observed that neither in the church of La Torre, nor in any of the other churches that I examined, was there any appearance of armorial bearing to be discovered, among the inscriptions that recorded the names and family of native Vaudois. In fact, these simple people have no distinctions of birth or rank; and if any of them are descended from the nobles of Piemont, or any other country, they do not, as far as I could gather, keep up the honours of such ancestry. It would be happy for them if they had some kindred and friends among the great and powerful.

The countenances and figures of the rustics, whom we saw assembled together upon this occasion, were not, upon the whole, particularly striking for beauty or symmetry; some of the young women were pretty, but there were only two whom we noticed above the rest. One had a very sweet face, lovely in health and innocence: the other was a charming girl, whose manner and appearance were much superior to the others'. Her fair complexion, light hair, and

Letter which was perhaps written confidentially, though addressed to him by a stranger; there is something so irresistibly affecting in it, as relating to a people like the Vaudois, and coming from the bereaved Mother of two such daughters as Elizabeth and Christina Smith, now no more, that it was impossible to withhold it. *Note to second Edition.*

blue eyes, would have distinguished her amidst the darker features of her companions, even if her blushes, when she met M. Vertu, had not told a tale. We learnt that a mutual attachment existed between them, and that the belle of the valley is as amiable as she is handsome.

Upon our return to the village, I renewed my acquaintance with M. Bert, and received the kindest assurances from him, that every accommodation which his house could furnish, should be at our service. The uncles of M. Vertu did the same; but we considered ourselves too large a party to press upon their hospitality, and established ourselves at the very comfortable inn in the centre of La Torre, where we were surprised, and gratified to find that nothing was wanting to make it an agreeable residence, for as many days as a traveller may choose to stay. We had been told at Turin, and by persons, whose official situation rendered it a duty to make themselves better acquainted with the condition of the inhabitants of this Protestant district, that it would be necessary to carry provisions with us, if we thought of remaining any time in either of the three valleys: and the same informants added, that there was nothing in the scenery to make a journey of thirty miles from the capital worth the trouble; so little are these interesting people, and their picturesque country, known by the world. They are certainly poor, and unprovided with what contributes to the luxuries of life; but none, whose object is research, and for whom the sublime beauties of nature have charms, need fear that their habits will be too much intrenched upon even in these secluded spots.

Our visit to one of the houses of La Torre had a degree of intense interest communicated to it, by receiving a confirmation of the horrible plot against the Vaudois, in 1794, which Mr. Lowther[g] has detailed in his little memoir with

[g] See also "Notice sur l'etat actuel des Eglises Vaudoises, Paris, 1822," for a confirmation of this plot.

so much feeling. We were shewn the very spot, on which the generous Odetti communicated the nature of the conspiracy to the father of the present possessor of the house, and it was explained to us how the windows and entrances were to have been barricaded, and the feeble means of defence prepared against the treacherous assault. M. Odetti was a captain of the Piemontese militia, then embodied, and acting against the French invaders, and a little before the fatal blow was to have been struck, he had been invited to join the conspirators in a general massacre of the Vaudois. M. Odetti was a rigid Romanist, and it was expected, that the well-known severity of his principles would have induced him to sanction any measure for the destruction of heresy. The Curè of Luzerna, M. Brianza, was also admitted into the secret, but these two worthy men had too much of the real spirit of Christianity even to conceal, and much less to join in the plot. Brianza sent a private message to La Torre, to apprize the inhabitants of their danger, but did not succeed in putting them sufficiently upon their guard. Odetti, knowing that the hour of action was so near, that nothing but very prompt measures could frustrate the sanguinary design, set out from Cavour himself, which is on the other side of the Pelice, and at some distance from La Torre, and hastened to his friend, to give him the alarming information. "I am afraid," said he, "that I am too late to prevent bloodshed.—There is a conspiracy against you. The assassins are even now on foot, but if I cannot save you, I will perish with you. The honour of my religion is at stake, I must justify it by sharing your danger."

The consternation in La Torre was beyond all description at the horrible intelligence, which was now spread from house to house, and every habitation soon assumed the appearance of hopeless terror. The windows were closed and barred, and piles of stone were collected to hurl down upon the heads of the assailants, but aged men, and women and children, were the only persons left to use them. The strength and flower of the population were eight or nine miles off, and occupied in defending the mountain passes against the French. Scarcely a man who could bear arms was away from this loyal duty, and yet this was the moment, at which no less than eight hundred bigoted monsters had sworn to exterminate all the Protestants of the valley of Luzerna, and to spread murder and devastation from San Giovanni to Bobbio.

But even assassins like these must have some false motive to disguise their real object. Piemont was at this period the scene of operations between the French and the allied armies. The plan of the campaign on the part of the republicans was, to penetrate into the country with a vast superiority of forces, to extend their line from the Valais to the sources of the Stura, and to seize the first favourable opportunity to march upon the capital. The invading army had a division of 25,000 men preparing to move upon the provinces of Pinerolo and Saluzzo only, and keeping up a line of communication with 50,000 more, who were waiting to strike a blow against Turin. The French troops had met with such effectual resistance, in attempting to enter the valleys of the Vaudois by the other passes, that they determined to try what could be done in a quarter, where they were not so much expected to make an attack. A detachment crossed the mountains between Mount Viso and the Col d'Aliries, or Abries, and suddenly appeared before the fort of Mirabouc, which stands at no great distance from the source of the Pelice, and at the very extremity of the valley of Luzerna. Not a Vaudois was in the fort when it surrendered, but the fanatical party thought it a good opportunity to inflame the public mind against the Protestants, and it was pretended that they had betrayed the fortress. The cry of "revenge, revenge," passed from mouth to mouth; the night of the 14th of May was appointed for the execution of it, and the house and garden of the Roman Catholic Curè of La Torre were the head quarters, or rendezvous, from which the conspirators were to rush upon their defenceless prey.

Not an instant was to be lost; the day was already arrived when Captain Odetti gave the information, and at sunset the murderers were to begin to assemble.

The only chance of safety consisted in sending notice of the plot to General Godin, a Swiss officer, who commanded the Piemontese troops on the nearest frontier. That brave man turned a deaf ear to the messenger, because he could not believe in the existence of so base a conspiracy. Another and another messenger arrived, but with no better success. At length several fugitives made their appearance from La Torre; the dreadful news reached the Vaudois soldiers themselves, and in a state of the utmost apprehension for the lives of their families, they insisted upon being despatched to their succour. The general became sensible of his error, but not in time to give him hopes of being able to preserve the innocent victims. The day was wearing away, the fatal hour was named in which the work of blood was to commence, and nothing but extraordinary speed could possibly enable a detachment to reach the spot before it began. To repair his unfortunate error the general commanded the brigade of Vaudois to march instantly, and followed himself with another division.

The wretched husbands and fathers pursued their way in almost frantic desperation. The imminent danger of their wives and children rendered any regularity of march out of the question: they precipitated themselves down steeps, which they would have shuddered to encounter upon any other occasion, urged each other on with wild shouts, and prayed aloud to heaven to give them additional speed. As they advanced on the road, they were repeatedly met by parties of distracted women, and frightened children, sent forward from La Torre to hasten their pace. Many of these, in their terror and despair, assured them that they were too late: that the business of death was even then proceeding.

With breathless haste, and in a state of excruciating suspense, they hurried on. The shades of the evening fell with encreasing darkness, and with them a storm of rain that brought the torrents down the mountains, and threatened to impede their further advance. They began to accuse Providence of being leagued against them. The waters poured down from the heights in such accumulated violence, that it was almost madness to prosecute their march: nothing but desperation could have prompted them to go on. The last torrent that they had to pass was rushing with unusual impetuosity, but they dashed through it in safety, and in a few minutes after arrived within sight of La Torre. At the same moment they heard the tolling of the vespers bell of the convent of the Récollets: this, they had been told, was to be the fatal signal for the assassins to sally forth.

The unhappy men felt that they were too late. "We will revenge," they cried, "if we cannot prevent"—and their speed was not abated. They rushed into the street of the village; the tramp of their feet, and the clangor of their arms were heard within the houses, and to the unutterable joy of these gallant deliverers, hundreds of voices were raised to welcome and bless their appearance.

The arm of God had done that which man's could not do: the time was not enough to allow of the arrival of the Vaudois, before the signal was to have been given for the conspirators to put themselves in action, but the rain-storm, and violence of the torrents, which had no terrors for men advancing in a good cause, had alarmed and stopped the murderers. Many of those, who should have arrived at the rendezvous, had not reached it, and those, who were there, dared not move forward upon this sanguinary enterprize, until their numbers were increased.

Considering the violent state of excitement to which the passions of the Vaudois soldiery were raised, it is natural to suppose, that surrendering themselves up to the feelings of the moment, they wreaked their vengeance upon the most criminal, at least, of their enemies. But no, not a drop of blood was spilt; satisfied with the preservation of their friends, they were guilty of no violence upon the persons or property of any of the Papists, who were accomplices in the plot. The assassins escaped in the darkness of the night, and the Vaudois took no other steps towards their chastisement, than to forward a list of the conspirators to the government, who made no enquiry into the matter, and suffered them to go unpunished.

The guilty escaped, but the innocent were disgraced. General Godin was tried by a military commission for suffering his detachment to quit the frontiers. Upon that charge he was acquitted, but he had excited the jealousy of the court by favouring the Protestants, and was first removed from the command of the troops in the valley of Luzerna to the Valley of San Martino, and afterwards was dismissed from the service, without receiving any mark of the royal approbation. His successor, General Zimmerman was a Romanist, but his sense of equity would not allow him to bear hard upon the Vaudois: on the contrary, he made repeated representations to the king in their favour, and at last succeeded in obtaining certain privileges, which were never before conceded to them. It is almost like a fable to record what these concessions were, in return for "the constant and distinguished proofs of their attachment and fidelity" to the royal cause. But they appear among the state papers of the day, and were, first, "*permission to practise medicine* among themselves;" secondly, "an investigation into the choice of municipal officers, placed at the head of Protestant communes, many of whom were ineligible to the office from their general want of qualification;" thirdly, "an amendment of the law by which the Protestant children might be forcibly taken from their parents, and educated in the Roman Catholic religion," and fourthly, a promise, that "if any charge should be brought against the Vaudois, from which Roman Catholics are exempt, we shall see that justice is administered."

These magnificent concessions were headed with the following preamble, and dated 4th June, 1794, a convincing proof that there could be no foundation for accusing the Vaudois of betraying Fort Mirabouc, or of any other treason against the state.

"We have read the memorial presented to us from you, by General Zimmerman, respecting the desires expressed by our dear and faithful subjects the Vaudois, relating to their actual political existence. In consideration of the constant and distinguished proofs, which they have ever given to our royal predecessors, of their attachment and fidelity, and the zeal which they have shewn *in pressing into the army for the defeat of our enemies;* we are disposed to receive their memorial favourably, and to make them feel, from the present moment, the effects of our special protection; making only some reservation as to some articles which require more explanation; granting them, after the war, such concessions as may be compatible with the constitution of the state, and which may assure them of the *value we entertain for their services,* and the interest which we take in their existence and their happiness.

(Signed) "VICTOR AMADEUS[h]."

It is difficult to reconcile these and similar royal acknowledgements of the services, which the Vaudois have never ceased to render to their sovereigns, in times of emergency, with the grievances and humiliations to which they are exposed. The nineteenth century is disgraced by the barbarous edicts in force against them; and if they

[h] In the year 1821 an enemy of the Waldensian Church having endeavoured to insinuate something to the disadvantage of the Vaudois, the king of Sardinia nobly expressed himself to the following effect. "I know I have faithful subjects in the Vaudois. During the war, I was engaged in their Valleys, and passed my time pleasantly among them. They will never dishonour their character."

could not be authenticated by the most indisputable evidence, it would appear incredible that the following complaints should be but a few among the numberless, which they have to urge. Some of the restrictions would be quite ludicrous, if their effects were not felt too keenly to be matter for a smile.

" No Protestant can inherit or purchase land beyond the limitations of the Clusone and Pelice."—It is hoped that puchases made before the restoration, will not be disturbed; but no petitions have succeeded in obtaining a repeal of the obnoxious law. A Protestant lately applied to the government for permission to buy a house, and a small piece of ground contiguous to it in Turin. It was answered by an intimation, that the enactments on this subject must remain untouched; but that no interruption to the transaction would be offered by the legal authorities. Of course, land upon such a tenure is scarcely worth having.

" No books of instruction or devotion, for the use of the Protestants may be printed in Piemont;" and the duty upon the importation of such books is enormous.

" No Vaudois may practise as a physician, surgeon, apothecary, attorney, or advocate, except among his own community, and within the limits."

Even in the syndicates of the communes of the three valleys, there may not be a majority of Protestants. For example; of the five syndics, three must be Roman Catholics. This is a crying evil in such places as Bobbio and San Giovanni, where the Protestants are as 1700 to 40, and the Roman Catholic population of the lowest order. It frequently happens that a duly qualified Romanist cannot be found in the commune to complete the number; and that the very refuse of the people have been nominated, to keep within the letter of the law.

The Protestants are obliged to observe the festivals of the Papists, and to abstain from work on those days. This is another excessive hardship. There is one holiday at least every week, and sometimes two or three: so that the Protestant peasant has never more than five days in the week for labour, and sometimes only three. The Sabbath day he keeps with scrupulous observance, while the Roman Catholic cares not for violating it. A poor Vaudois peasant was accused of irrigating his little meadow upon a festival day, and condemned to pay a fine for not observing the sanctity of a saint's day.

Fifteen sous a day in the winter, and twenty in the summer, is the utmost a peasant can earn: take away two or three days from his weekly earnings, and what a pittance is left! Roasted chesnuts, potatoes, and bread, if any, of the blackest and most ordinary sort, are the principal food they can obtain.

The Protestants have to pay a land-tax of 20½ per cent.; while the Roman Catholics pay but 13 per cent.

It will be seen from this statement, how very few are the resources of the Vaudois. From the military and civil employments, and from the learned professions, they are excluded. The valley of Luzerna is the only one which can be called productive; and, even there, agricultural pursuits cannot be prosecuted to much advantage, where the duties are high, and the restrictions so burdensome. A small trade is carried on in charcoal; and the silk-worm is reared in some of the hamlets; but there can scarcely be said to be any manufactures, when one woollen manufactory, and two tan-yards, are principally what come within this designation. The looms employ about thirty men, and forty women and children, and make about eight hundred pieces of cloth annually, of about forty yards to the piece. The tan-yard at Bobbio finds occupation for four men; and that at La Torre, for about five.

I did not ascertain what business is done in the few smelting-houses that I observed: the hands at work were not numerous.

This will not be an improper place to mention, that

although La Torre is the principal village or town of the Vaudois, and contains a population of two thousand inhabitants, yet it offers not the least appearance of trade. Few shops are to be seen, and those are of a very humble character. My surprise at this want of shops, led me into a laughable mistake; and it was the more ludicrous, considering the simple character of the people.

" You have no shops at all," I said to M. Vertu; " not even that of a *bourreau.*" I meant to say, *boucher*. "*Bourreau!*" he exclaimed, " what do we want with an *executioner?* Why we have had but one capital conviction among us for a hundred years!"

CHAPTER VI.

Angrogna—La Barricade—Cultivation—Cheerful landscape—Sabbath on the mountains—Religious and moral character of mountaineers—Village pastor's house—M. Paul Goante—Alpine cottages—Thuanus—Want of religious books—Peasant of Angrogna—Mode of tillage—Mountain fastnesses—La Vechera—Pre du Tour—Obstinate and gallant conflicts there—Sublime mountain scenery—The Bouquetin—The Jumarre—Beautiful vale—Comparison between solitary and busy life—The fortress of La Torre.

M. VERTU, of La Torre, brother to our friend at Turin, was many years in England during the early part of his life; and his intimate knowledge of the English language, rendered him of great service to us, when we wished to make enquiries connected with local and technical explanations. He had the kindness to accompany us to Angrogna, acting as our interpreter in several conversations which he had with the peasantry, who spoke the patois[1] only of the country; and to him I was indebted for much of the immediate information I picked up, as to the condition of agriculture, and the few manufactures of the Vaudois.

Angrogna lies to the north of La Torre, at the distance of about a mile and a half from the latter, and in the midst of some of the finest mountain scenery of which the Alps can boast. The mountain stream, which is called the Torrent of Angrogna, gives its name to a cluster of valleys which branch out like the boughs of a tree, and runs into the Pelice, just below La Torre. It is supplied by innumerable springs of

[1] See Appendix, No. 9.

water, which gush from the rocks, and by following its course from the vale, the tourist will be conducted to the village itself, and higher up, to such a succession of picturesque spots, and secluded glens, as no description can do justice to. The natural beauties of the scenery of Angrogna, and the sublime objects of crag rising above crag, of enormous masses of rock debouching into the glens beneath, and of abysses, the depths of which the eye cannot penetrate, are rendered still more interesting by their being consecrated to the memory of heroes and martyrs, whose histories are in the mouth of every peasant.

There are few of these Alpine recesses occupied by the Vaudois, which have not legends of their own to amuse the stranger, independent of their local attractions; but no commune is more distinguished in this respect than that of Angrogna. "L'éternel nostre Dieu," says Leger, "qui avoit destiné ce Paiis-là pour en faire particulièrement le Theatre des ses merveilles, et l'Asyle de son Arche, l'a naturellement et merveilleusement fortifié." According to the same historian there were formerly two strong forts, or barriers, which defended the entrance of the passes to Angrogna, on the side of Luzerna and Bricherasio, capable of being held for a long time by a very few troops, who, if these were forced, might easily fall back upon a place called La Barricade, about half a league higher up, among the mountains. A reference to the map will shew that La Barricade is a narrow defile, upon the side of the torrent: it is fenced in by steep rocks, and at the spot where the rocks were supposed to leave too wide a passage, a strong wall of flints was thrown up, to add to the natural strength of the position, and so contrived, that one opening only was left, by which the retreating party might escape to the fastnesses behind it.

Angrogna was formerly so often the retreat of the Vaudois, when they were forced to abandon San Giovanni, La Torre, and Villaro, that several geographers, who were ignorant of the true divisions of the country, have spoken of the valley of Angrogna as the principal district of the community. The Marquess de Fleuri, in the cruel persecution of the middle of the seventeenth century, met with so many warm receptions from the peasants of Angrogna, that he declared he would never attack the heretics in this quarter again, with less than 10,000 men.

The weather was favourable to our excursion, which could be made on foot only; for there is no approaching these higher regions in any sort of vehicle; and saddle-horses for a large party cannot easily be procured. There is a road from San Giovanni to the village of Angrogna, which is practicable for small "chars à bœuf;" but nobody would think of riding in such awkward machines as these. It was the first time of our ascending the mountains, and of penetrating into the heart of those seclusions, which have such charms for the imagination; and we set out in high spirits upon the expedition. Pomaretto is much less out of the common track of travellers, than Angrogna; and may be seen from the road to France from Pinerolo; but nothing less than a visit to the spot itself, is likely to conduct to the retired habitations of which we were now in search.

Upon leaving La Torre and the vale of the Pelice, we came to a smooth and level piece of grass-land, at the foot of a chain of heights, which divides two valleys; and there we crossed the torrent, and took the direction of the valley to the right. The ascent soon became more and more abrupt; and the path-way at one time wound up the mountain in the midst of chesnut and walnut trees, whose aged trunks and branching arms have perhaps afforded shelter to many a persecuted fugitive. At other times we suddenly emerged from gigantic fragments of rock, that had rolled from the steeps above, and covered whole tracts of ground with their ruins, and found ourselves walking over well cultivated plots of corn-land, which extended to the brink of precipices, and made us wonder what industrious hand could have made grain to spring up on such repulsive soil.

Ridges of wheat were seen, where every inch of earth on which it grew, was brought by hand from a distance, and spread upon the stony surface.

Rousseau's beautiful and almost poetical image of the sudden change from the bare and barren, to the smiling and productive, was brought before our eyes in frequent succession during this delightful walk; and what *he* fancied, *we* really saw. "Quelque-fois en sortant d'un gouffre une agréable prairie rejouissoit tout à coup mes regards. Un mélange étonnant de la nature sauvage, et de la nature cultivée montroit par-tout la main des hommes, où l'on eût cru qu'ils n'avoient jamais pénetré: à côté d'une caverne on trouvoit des maisons; on voyait des pampres secs où l'on n'eût cherché que des ronces, des vignes dans des terres éboulées, et des champs dans des précipices."

Nothing however added more to the cheerfulness of the landscape than the streams of water, that ran gently down the slopes, or rushed impetuously from the heights; some of them murmuring in cascades, which sparkled in the sun; and others roaring and foaming in cataracts. There were two or three water-courses of a very novel appearance; at first sight they looked as if they were artificial; but, upon inspection, we discovered, that they had made a sort of natural channel for themselves in the sides of the mountain, and were winding their way like our path, and flowing into the valley. A rich foliage was all that was requisite to complete the beauty of the scenery; but as a substitute for this, we had the fringy particles of frost, that hung upon many of the trees. The melody of the Sabbath bell of Angrogna, above us, answered by that of La Torre below, was re-echoed from one side of the ridge of mountains to the other, and produced a very pleasing and solemn effect.

In the summer, when these pastoral people are tending their cattle at a distance from the villages, and occupying their *châlets,* or temporary cabins, upon the summits of the mountain, the clearness of the atmosphere allows the sound of the same Sabbath bells to reach them, calling them to the worship of the Creator beneath the canopy of heaven. It must be a most gratifying and impressive sight to see them hastening from different quarters, and assembling in a convenient place on the green turf, to listen to the exhortations of their ministers, who follow them on every seventh day to their remotest pasturages. They generally select a sort of natural amphitheatre, where they may be shaded from the rays of the sun, and hear their pastor the more distinctly. A congregation, collected on such spots as these, must give rise to some of the most sublime feelings, which man is capable of entertaining. The simple and amiable character of the people, their patriarchal occupation of watching their flocks, their temporary migration, and change of settlement, their contentment and tranquil enjoyment, without any thing to vary their pleasures, the grand and stupendous scenery by which they are surrounded, and the pure air that they breathe in these elevated regions, offer endless subjects for meditation. If pure happiness can be said to exist on earth, it must be amongst these people, whose wishes are limited by their powers of acquirement, and who know of no pleasures but those which are to be found amongst their mountains. Poets and romancers have imagined, that the nearer we approach the ethereal atmosphere, the farther we are removed from the tyranny of those grosser sentiments, which binds us down to earth : and perhaps not without justice. The mountaineer is more virtuous, not only as he is removed from the vices of society, but as he is brought more closely in contact with nature, and, in that to the adoration of the Deity ; the still voice of religion is but faintly heard amidst the crowds of life, but it is loud upon the mountains, where the grandeur of the work bears a visible and continued testimony to the grandeur of the Creator.

Happily for the Vaudois, this feeling is with them in its

greatest purity; and we may find a sufficient reason for their contented happiness, in the sincerity of their religion. All their pastors agree in enforcing the same belief and hopes, and the same duties. Their faith is without fanaticism, and their religious opinions are maintained without strife or division. The end of Christian teaching with them, "is charity out of a pure heart, and of a good conscience, and of faith unfeigned."

Upon our arrival at the village of Angrogna, which is picturesquely situated on the slope of the mountain, we went directly to the presbytery of M. Paul Goante, to whom we were introduced by our friend, M. Vertu. He had but just finished his dinner, after performing service at two churches, at Angrogna, and at a hamlet two miles farther up among the mountains. The house is a long narrow building, constructed in the humble style of Alpine habitations, and not unlike the Swiss cottages, with two galleries in front, which open into the different apartments. It is formed of wood and stone, the materials which the country furnishes, and these arranged without any regard to beauty. For the general purposes of comfort and accommodation, it is but very little better than the presbytery of M. Rodolphe Peyrani, at Pomaretto. The worthy pastor, whose age appeared to be about fifty-five, was sitting, with his wife, in a small bed-room, where there was no fire, and received us with that kindness and entire freedom from restraint, so peculiar to this simple race. There were no apologies for the want of better articles of furniture, or for not having the means of giving the strangers a warmer reception. Poverty is not a subject upon which the Vaudois feel they have need to be ashamed.

M. Goante has not that vivacity of manner, and depth of understanding, which were so imposing in M. Peyrani; but his habits are mild and retired, and he is in all respects fully competent to the duties of his situation. His resources are insufficient for the acquisition of a library; he has but few books, and finds employment enough among his flock, who amount to as many as two thousand souls, dispersed over a surface of several miles. Madame Goante is a woman of superior information and acquirements, to the generality of the females in these secluded corners. She was formerly governess in a family in Holland; but now submits to the quiet uniformity of her life with cheerful good humour. The company of strangers is evidently gratifying to her; and she puts questions to them about the great world, which she has left for ever, with the curiosity, rather than the regret of one who will never see it again. She spoke with much interest and affection of the Hon. Mrs. Fortescue, an English lady, whose richly endowed mind enabled her to find enjoyment, in exchanging for a while the brilliant circles, in which her rank and accomplishments entitled her to move, for the humbler but interesting society of these amiable mountaineers, among whom human nature may be studied in its purest character. Mrs. Fortescue spent some days among the romantic solitudes of Angrogna, and amused herself with taking many sketches of the scenery, several of which she presented to Madame Goante, who exhibited them to us with infinite pride. They were beautifully executed.

We were pressed to take refreshments; and our hospitable hostess would not suffer us to quit her roof before we had tasted of her cakes and wine. Upon our offering to take leave, M. Goante insisted upon accompanying us through the village and higher up the mountain; and, as he walked by our side, the greetings and smiling salutations of the rustics told us, that the pastor of Angrogna was the object of universal affection. Old and young accosted him in the same tone of respectful regard; and for every one he had a word of kindness or enquiry. The greatest monarch on his throne might be jealous of homage so offered, and so received.

Children driving cows or goats to be milked, and mules

and asses to be watered, and cattle seen grazing above our heads, in the upper parts of the mountain, or slowly finding their way home, added life and freshness to the beauty of the scenery about us. The hamlet itself too attracted our attention by the novelty of its appearance, and we became anxious to have a closer view of the cottages which adorned it. One of these was built very high up upon the side of the mountain: constructed of coarse stone, uncemented for the most part, but having a little clay or mud to keep together the loose materials, and exclude the wind on the side most exposed to the weather. There was neither chimney, nor glazed window; and the upper chambers were entered by a ladder and gallery. The eaves, or roof, projected all round so as to form a sort of shelter on the outside. This cottage was one of the best and most substantial, and we were not a little curious to see the interior.

As we approached we heard the voices of children, and upon opening the door of the lower part, a strange medley discovered itself. Immediately to our right, as we entered, was an infant in a cradle, near it a circle of half-a-dozen children, neatly dressed, and of cleanly appearance, who were repeating their catechism to a young girl, of about twelve years of age. To our left were seen a cow, a calf, two goats, and four sheep: and the motley groupe of living creatures helped to keep each other warm. It was the common sleeping chamber of them all. Leaves and straw generally compose the beds of these simple peasants.

The elder girl held in her hand Ostervald's Catechism, in French, from which she was instructing her young companions, for though a patois of Italian is still the common dialect of the province, all the children of the Vaudois are taught French, because their books of instruction are in that language. Until I witnessed this most interesting scene, I confess I thought there was some exaggeration in the account, which Thuanus gave of the Vaudois about two hundred and fifty years ago. "Their houses," says he, "are constructed of flint-stone, with a flat roof, covered with mud, which being spoilt, or loosened by rain, they smooth again, with a roller. *In these they live with their cattle,* separated from them, however, by a fence: they have besides two caves, set apart for particular purposes, in one of which they conceal their cattle, in the other themselves, when hunted by their enemies. Poor as they are, they are content, and live separate from the rest of mankind. One thing is astonishing, that persons externally so savage and rude should have so much moral cultivation. They can all read and write. They understand French, so far as is needful for the understanding of the Bible, and the singing of psalms. You can scarcely find a boy among them, who cannot give you an intelligible account of the faith which they profess [k]."

To this day the same laudable practice is continued, and nothing is so common among the Protestant inhabitants of these valleys as the cry for books. Ask them of what they stand most in need, and the universal reply is, books. One of their ministers, M. Bert, of La Torre, put the following note in my hands. It was a memorandum, that if any were inclined to assist the Waldenses, I might state to such friends their want of books of religious instruction beyond all other necessaries.

"Les Eglises Vaudoises du Piemont de plus en plus pourvues de Bibles et de N. Testaments par la munificence Chretienne de nos Benefacteurs, notamment des Anglais, éprouvent encore besoin journalier de Livres de pieté. Les plus genéralement demandés sont,

"1. Des Catechismes d'Ostervald.

"2. Des Psaumes de David avec musique. (Soit avec les Cantiques de Pictet, soit separés.)

"3. Des Cantiques de Pictet en un volume apart.

"4. Des nourritures de l'Ame, par Ostervald.

[k] Thuanus, B. xxvii. p. 16.

" 5. Des livres de priere de Pictet, ou autres.

" N.B. Les Psaumes usités parmi nous sont eux qui s'impriment à Genève et à Lausanne ou Vevay.

" Le Pasteur de la Tour en particulier desire de petits traites (non en feuille) pour encourager et recompenser ses elèves de l'Ecole du Dimanche."

After we had listened a few minutes to the instruction, which the young peasant girl was giving to her little brothers and sisters, we mounted to the upper part of the cottage, in which we found their father and mother. The apartment was about twenty feet square, and offered as curious a sight as that below. Here was a variety of articles of household use, not lying carelessly about, but sorted and disposed each in its proper place; there were cleanly and well scoured vessels for milk, cheese-presses and churns, and a few wooden platters and bowls. We also observed several implements of husbandry, spinning-wheels, and a large frame for weaving; for almost every thing that is worn by these rustics is made at home. On a crate, suspended from the ceiling, we counted fourteen large black loaves. Bread is an unusual luxury among them, but the owner of this cottage was of a condition something above the generality. He had a few acres of his own, and his industry and good management had enabled him to provide a winter supply of bacon and flour. M. Goante spoke of him afterwards in very high terms, as a steady and honest man, and *above all, a pious Christian*, and lamented that the father of a family, with the best inclination, could not procure religious books for the education of his children. The Ostervald's Catechism, which his eldest daughter had in her hand, was borrowed from another person, and the worthy minister of Angrogna assured us, that elementary and other books of useful instruction were so scarce in his parish, that his poor flock were obliged to separate the leaves of those which they had, and so to pass the detached portions from hand to hand.

The other cottages we entered were of a very inferior order, and had but few of those little comforts, with which in England we desire to see the poorest supplied, and it was quite astonishing to compare the very rude and insufficient accommodations of these people, with their civility and information. In their mode of living, or I might almost say, herding together, under a roof, which is barely weather proof, they are far behind our own peasantry, but in mental advancement they are just as far beyond them. Most of them have a few roods of land, which they can call their own property, varying in extent, from about a quarter of an acre and upwards, and they have the means of providing themselves with fuel, from the abundance of wood upon the mountains.

The tenure, upon which land is hired, requires that the occupier should pay to the proprietor half the produce of corn and wine in kind, and half the *value* of the hay. The indifferent corn-land yields about five-fold, and the best twelve-fold. They seldom suffer the ground to lie fallow, and the most general course is, wheat for two years, and maize the third. The land is well manured from time to time, and the corn is usually sown in August or September, and cut in June. In the vale of San Giovanni, and in a few other productive spots, hay is cut three times in the year. They have sheep, goats, and cattle, but not many horses; the ploughing is done with the assistance of oxen, where the plough can be used, but in the upper regions, and in the rocky soil, where the plots of corn-land are very confined and bordering upon the precipices, they are obliged to do every thing with the spade and hoe. Carts and waggons are rarely seen: the charcoal, which is carried from the valleys to Pinerolo, is conveyed on the backs of mules and asses, and even the corn is carried home in the same way.

Every head of cattle, (pigs and sheep as well as bullocks, &c.) pays a small duty to the government when it is killed, and in the great towns of his Sardinian majesty's dominions, we saw carcases exposed to sale with a stamp of the Royal arms upon them.

Upon taking leave of M. Goante, we varied our course, and did not return to La Torre through Angrogna, nor by the same path by which we mounted these majestic heights, but were disappointed by the snow lying so deep in the higher grounds, as not to permit us to find our way to the celebrated Barricade, the mountain called La Vachera, and the impregnable Pre Du Tour, or Pra del Torno. La Vachera is nearly the centre of the three valleys, and it used to form a retreat, from which neither force nor artifice ever succeeded in dislodging the refugees, when they took shelter there from the rage of their persecutors. The Pre du Tour is situated a little to the south of La Vachera, in the bosom of such inaccessible mountains, that in several places there is no approach to it, but by narrow pathways cut in the rocks.

It was here, in this sanctuary of the brave and the pious, that the ancient college of Angrogna stood, from which the intrepid preachers used to sally upon their sacred missions, and disseminate those lessons, upon which were afterwards founded the doctrines of the Reformation.

On this spot also the invading army of Duke Emanuel Philibert, under the command of the Count de la Trinité, experienced one of the most signal defeats, that regular troops ever received from a body of undisciplined mountaineers. The Count had previously attacked the village of Angrogna, with twelve hundred men, but met with so warm a reception from about two hundred peasants, that he was obliged to retreat, and wait for reinforcements. Irritated by the disgrace, he advanced a second time, and was again repulsed by a little band of heroes, who charged him with loud shouts of "Viva Jesu Christo!" Nothing could equal the fury of the Count upon this second defeat; he wreaked his vengeance upon the defenceless inhabitants of the vale of San Giovanni, and after having recruited his forces with a large detachment of Spanish veterans, he once more tried his fortune against Angrogna.

The royal army now amounted to seven thousand men, and the peasants finding that their first position was no longer tenable, in the face of such superior numbers, abandoned their villages, and retired with the whole population to the Pre du Tour. The Count followed them, and for four days made every effort to get possession of the defiles. Two colonels, eight captains, and four hundred men, fell in these desperate assaults, without an inch of ground being gained. On the fifth day a fresh attack was made in three different quarters, with the reserve, composed of some Spanish companies, but the post was not carried; and upon the general commanding his troops to return again to the charge, they refused to obey. At the moment when they began to waver, the Vaudois saw the opportunity, and made a sortie, which produced a universal panic and rout among the assailants. The pursuit continued beyond Angrogna, and the enemy was so dispirited, that hostilities ceased, and favourable terms were granted to the Protestants.

This exploit took place in 1560, and about a hundred years afterwards, the persecuted inhabitants of the valley were obliged to fly for safety to the same asylums, and La Vachera became the scene of a conflict equally memorable. The mountaineers were commanded on this occasion by the pastor and historian, John Leger, who directed such as were unarmed to climb the rocks which overhung the defile, and to roll down stones upon the assailants. This manœuvre was executed so effectually, that the enemy gave ground; the Vaudois rushed from behind their ramparts, sword in hand, and the rout and slaughter were so complete, that it was said upon this occasion, "Altre volte li lupi mangiavano li Barbetti, ma hore li Barbetti mangiano li lupi." Barbetti, or dogs, was the term of reproach by which the Protestants were then called. "*Hitherto the wolves have devoured the dogs, but now the dogs devour the wolves.*"

The prospects, as we descended from Angrogna, were even more interesting than those in our ascent; for from the stupendous masses which surrounded us, as we were climbing the eminences, the elevation did not appear so great as when we were receding from them. The effect of height and depth is widely different: if you look up to an object, the altitude is by no means so striking, as the profundity when you look down from it. Some of the precipices were frightful; and in several places, the path was so icy and slippery, that all our precaution was necessary; for a single false step would have been irrecoverable. We had told M. Vertu that we wanted to see some narrow mountain passes, and he indulged us. The beauties and the sublimities which this delightful excursion brought before our eyes, were beyond all imagination; and if I had not since been in the higher Alps of Switzerland, where the eternal winter, which reigns on the summits of the Jungfrau, the Wetterhorn, and the Schreckhorn, may be compared even in July, with the bright summer landscape of the Wengern Alp, from which there is a fine survey of their never-melting snows, I should have said that a wintry view from the heights of Angrogna is unrivalled.

But the tourist loses much, unless his excursion is made in the summer; he then finds that perfection of the sublime and beautiful in mountain scenery, which is not to be found in any other part of nature; and that variety of prospect and objects, of lights and shades, of gloom and sunshine, which keeps the eye and mind perpetually in action. Before him is a white mantle of snow, which never disappears; he turns to the right or to the left, and there he beholds all the brightest colours of fruit and foliage, and all the varieties of rock and meadow. Now he is enveloped in cloud, and now a gentle breeze disperses the misty veil, and a bright world seems stretched at his feet. At one moment he is in a solitude, at another in a cheerful hamlet: silence, uninterrupted but by his own voice or steps, reigns in the glen he has just entered; he passes into another, and is greeted with the lowing of cattle, and the music of their bells. In one valley the soft murmurings of cascades and rills persuade him to rest; in another, the roar of torrents and cataracts, admonish him to hasten from the danger of falling fragments of rocks, that are shaken down by their violence. The dark pine forest is succeeded by a blooming orchard; the glacier, by a vineyard; and the angle of a mountain ridge will show the astonished traveller a corn-field on one side, and on the other a dark and barren rock, that towers to the skies.

But I must again have recourse to one of the most eloquent and descriptive of French writers, to help me with my picture. "La nature sembloit encore prendre plaisir à s'y mettre en opposition avec elle-même, tant on la trouvoit différente en un même lieu sous divers aspects. Au levant les fleurs du printems, au midi les fruits de l'automne, au nord les glaces de l'hiver: elle réunissoit toutes les saisons dans le même instant, tous les climats dans le même lieu, des terrains contraires sur le même sol, et formoit l'accord inconnu par-tout ailleurs des productions des plaines, et de celles des Alps. Ajoutez à tout cela les illusions de l'optique, les points des monts différemment éclairées, le clair-obscur du soleil et des ombres, et tous les accidents de lumière, qui en résultoient le matin, et le soir; vous aurez quelque idée des scénes continuelles qui ne cessèrent d'attirer mon admiration, et qui sembloient m'être offertes en un vrai théâtre: car la perspective des monts étant verticale frappe les yeux tout-à-la-fois, et bien plus puissamment que celle des plaines, qui ne se voit qu'obliquement, en fuyant, et dont chaque objet vous en cache un autre."

Although we kept a constant look-out, we did not see

any of the white hares, or large grey pheasants and partridges, which are frequently found in these parts: nor were we favoured with a sight of the chamois, or of the extraordinary animal called bouquetin, which, like the chamois, is neither goat nor deer, but is between the two, and surpasses the chamois itself in fleetness, strength, and agility. Leger's account of this strange creature, and of the still stranger properties of its blood, though containing no absolute impossibility, yet hardly comes within the bounds of rational belief; I allude only to the latter part of his story, the beginning is credible enough. He says, that when a person is afflicted with a violent cold, he has nothing to do, but to mix a few drops with a little wine or soup, to drink it off, and then cover himself up warmly, and lie down. A profuse perspiration will soon relieve him. The historian adds, that he himself tried an experiment, which may serve to throw some light upon the effect which the blood of the bouquetin has upon the human body. He took a small quantity of this blood congealed, and diluted it in wine: he then poured the liquid so mixed, into a basin full of congealed blood, and it had the effect of liquefying the whole, and reducing it to the same consistency, as if it had just been taken from the body of the animal. Query: will this help to solve the mystery of the liquefaction of the blood of St. Januarius?

The same author's account of the *jumarre,* is equally puzzling to the incredulous, who have to set their own conviction with the veracious character of Leger. He observes: " This animal is the issue of an union between a bull and a mare, or a bull and an ass; the former, which is the larger of the two, is called *baf;* and the latter, *bif.* The upper jaw of the baf is longer than the lower, like a pig's; and the upper teeth are more separated from each other than the lower. On the contrary, the lower jaw of the bif is the longest, like that of a hare or rabbit; but the teeth project more. Neither the one nor the other can graze, except where the grass is very long. The head and tail resemble those of a bull; the rest of the body is like that of a horse, or an ass. Their strength is inconceivable: they are less in size than mules; eat but little, and travel with uncommon speed. I myself took a journey of eighteen leagues over the mountains, on the 13th of September, on one of these jumarres, and with much more ease than if I had been on horseback [1]."

Before we left the scenery of Angrogna, and took a last view of its matchless beauties, we looked down upon a vale, the sweetest I ever saw, and which to this moment, after having seen the most lovely spots in Switzerland and Italy, I remember rather as a delightful vision, than a real prospect. It lay in the midst of a circular chain of mountains, so sheltered and protected, that it looked as if no rough winds could ever visit it. The declivities which sloped down to it were clothed with trees of every description, among which were abundance of walnuts, mulberries, chesnuts, cherry and other fruit trees. Its surface was as smooth and level as a village green in England, and retained much of its verdure, even at this season of the year. A clear stream ran gurgling through it, and one small cottage stood upon its margin. If ever there was a place calculated to realize the dreams of happiness in solitude, it is this, where nature appears under the most favourable circumstances. Peace seems amidst these rocks, and health in the air; the ills of society are excluded; but then the barrier which shuts out those evils, is equally effective in shutting out its benefits. The man who has been used to cities is seldom qualified for the happiness of retirement; as long as his imagination is excited by the new aspect of nature, it is well; but that which we see every day we soon cease to admire, and habit dulls enthusiasm, without reconciling us to the solitude which has produced it. The in-

[1] Leger, p. 7.

habitants of remote valleys are not much alive to the attractions of local beauty; they do not borrow their notions of happiness from romance and sentiment; and those who do, and who fancy they could leave the bustle of life to dwell amidst rocks and valleys, will soon sigh to return to the world, and talk about the charms of seclusion. We may sometimes amuse ourselves with the idea, that the serenity which cannot be found in cities, may be discovered in solitudes. But to those who have once lived in society, it is change of scene which contributes to enjoyment.

Upon recrossing the torrent, or Fiume d'Angrogna, we passed very near the dismantled and ruined fortress of La Torre, *il forte de la Torre.* The remains of the old tower, and its dilapidated walls, standing upon a bushy knoll, and shaded by a few venerable trees, is now regarded only as a picturesque object, where it was formerly the terror of the neighbourhood. The government always contrived to have it garrisoned by choice troops, and many a bloody fight, for its capture or recovery, has dyed the waters of the stream beneath it, which is now so limpid and transparent. The tower itself, and the ground upon which it stands, are the property of M. Vertu, who will most probably sacrifice the picturesque to the politic, and take care that not one stone shall remain above another, to be put into a state of repair, lest a new fortress should rise up at some future time, and once more become the terror of the people.

Upon our return to La Torre we took up our quarters at our comfortable inn, and fared and reposed as well as we could have done in one of the best hotels at Turin.

CHAPTER VII.

Fall of snow—Valley of San Martino—M. Bert—Vaudois soldier—The Pelice Torrent—Game on the mountains—Anecdote—Traditionary tales—Le Bric Casteluzzo—Immense cavern—Industry of the Vaudois—The witness of the wilderness—Shrines—Le Pilori Taviere—Villaro—Inquisitors—Church of Villaro—Pastors of the Vaudois—Their ministerial labours—Attempts to seduce the Vaudois from their faith—Unsuccessful—The confessional—Popish rituals—The young penitent—Pope Braschi, Pius VI.—Anecdotes—Dominican monk—Testimonies in favour of the Vaudois—M. Gay, pastor of Villaro.

On the morning when we meant to extend our excursions to some of the more distant villages of the Vaudois, we found, to our great disappointment, that a heavy fall of snow had rendered a visit to the valley of San Martino quite impracticable. Until we arrived at the country itself, we were not aware of its very formidable aspect, but we now learnt that the valley of San Martino can only be entered by the passes over the lofty mountains which encircle it, or by Le Pont de la Tour. For eight or nine months in the year the snow blocks up the mountain passes, and Le Pont de la Tour is a defile between two natural walls of rock, barely wide enough to admit the waters of the Germanasca torrent. High above the bed of the river, one of those frightful Alpine bridges is flung across the chasm, consisting of the trunks of pine trees, supported at each end by the projecting crags of rock, which is merely intended to answer temporary purposes, and may be cut away, or tumbled into the abyss below at the shortest notice. In times of danger the bridge used to be destroyed, and then every access to the valley in this quarter was rendered impassable. These accounts of the valley of San Martino, and its impenetrable bulwarks, excited our curiosity, at the same time that they removed every hope of visiting them at this unseasonable period.

We were even informed that a walk to Villaro and Bobbio would be attended with some difficulty, if the snow continued. It fell in great flakes till past nine o'clock, but our anxiety to proceed induced M. Vertu the elder to offer to accompany us, and with his usual disinterested kindness, he gave up another day to our service. It snowed fast when we set out, and as M. Bert's house lay on our way, we were glad to take shelter for a few minutes under his roof. He has a small property, independent of his income as a pastor of the Vaudois church, and does not reside in the presbytery of La Torre, but in a good substantial dwelling of his own. The rooms are of an ample size, and are well fortified against the admission of cold, but the furniture and decorations, if indeed any thing there could admit of the latter designation, were of that humble kind, which corresponded with the general simplicity of the Vaudois. I do not recollect observing a single article but what was indispensable; neither elegance nor luxury was studied in any one respect; whitewashed walls, plain unpainted wainscot, uncarpeted floors, and uncurtained windows, must appear sadly comfortless to the strangers, who visit this learned and respectable clergyman, who, if I am rightly informed, will succeed M. Peyrani, as the primate or moderator of the Waldenses [m].

To our surprize two English faces presented themselves at M. Bert's, and we most cordially shook by the hand two very fine boys, the one twelve years of age, and the other nine, the sons of Captain Humphreys, of Stockport, who are receiving their education under the paternal care of the pastor of La Torre. The joy of these lads, at being accosted

[m] I have lately been favoured with a letter from M. Bert, in which he informs me, that the synod has elected him to fill the chair of the lamented Peyrani.

by their contrymen, exceeded all description: because we came from England they took it for granted that we must come also from their native county, and be acquainted with their families. We answered their questions as satisfactorily as we could, and lamented that we could not give a better account of Stockport, and the dear objects of their inquiry. The younger of the two had almost forgotten his own language, but the elder, a very intelligent lad, although he spoke it with a foreign accent, was not at any loss for expressions, but addressed us as fluently as if he had but lately left home. They had been three or four years at La Torre.

We pursued our walk from La Torre, and after a while the day cleared up, and the sun shone so brightly that we were glad to leave our great coats at a cottage by the way. It was situated about a hundred and fifty yards up the slope of the mountain, in the midst of a groupe of ancient chesnut trees, some of which might vie with those on Mount Ætna in size and height. The brother of the peasant, who occupied the cabin, served in the French army during the Russian campaign, and rose to the command of a company. He was pointed out to us at La Torre, as having received eleven wounds from the Cossacks, before Leipsic, and is now in the enjoyment of a pension of seven hundred and fifty francs a-year. With this pittance, small as it is, he calls himself happy, associates with the humblest of his former companions, and considers himself as loyal a subject of the king of Sardinia, as if he had never fought under the banners of the conqueror, who obliged his sovereign to take refuge amidst the rocks of Cagliari.

Our road lay due west from La Torre, upon the northern bank of the Pelice. The mountains sloped or broke down to it, and the river was rushing violently along a rocky channel, which encroaches so much upon the valley, as frequently to rob the cultivator of half his labours. The torrents sometimes swell this stream to such a height that the whole of the lower grounds are flooded; and, in that case, the losses of the peasantry are quite ruinous. M. Vertu assured us, that he had three times seen every building swept away before the waters that poured from the heights. He did not mean the habitations of man, but the stone barns for hay and corn, which are erected within reach of these tremendous inundations.

The beauties of the landscape between La Torre and Villaro are not upon the same magnificent scale as those of Angrogna, but there was what could not fail to please. Vineyards extending up to the summits of the hills, gigantic trees shading the road, and dark brushwood contrasting with ridges and patches of snow that glistened above, offered every variety of tint and colouring; while the numerous cottages that spotted the sides of the mountains, imparted an air of cheerfulness to the scene, which never can be recognized unless the hand of man is visible. The woods and coppices which were seen from the road, made us inquisitive upon the subject of game. Partridges, grouse, and woodcocks, and particularly the latter, may be found in great abundance by the sportsman, who will encounter the fatigue of walking up the mountains; but he must have a keen taste for the chase, who will follow a dog under a burning sun in August and September, and climb the rugged acclivities which overhang these romantic vales.

When a traveller speaks of the game which is to be found in these countries, he is not to be understood, as if the mountains produced any thing like the quantity, which is to be seen within the same space upon preserved manors in England.

The lynx and the wolf are not unfrequently discovered; and when parties are made in pursuit of these terrors of the sheep-fold, it is indeed a royal sport; but it must be a very staunch hound which will persevere in the chase of a wolf. Whether it is from fear, from disinclination to hunt down an animal which is so allied to their own species, or from the coldness of the scent, it requires the utmost attention of the hunter to follow up, and urge on his dogs. When he can depend upon the breed and keenness of his hounds, and has vigour and fleetness to keep at no great distance from them, it is said the sport is exceedingly animating.

A year ago a young Englishman took up his abode at the little inn at La Torre, where we pitched our tent, and there remained for several days. We were curious to know what were his researches. Did he enquire much into the condition of the people? No. Did he ramble about the mountains, and admire the scenery? No. Did he sketch, and amuse himself with taking views? No. Did he come here for the purpose of study? No. Then he must have been very fond of the chase, or passed his time in shooting? No, he never left the yard of the auberge. Then what did he do, and how did he employ his time? "*Oh, he was very wicked,*" said one of the daughters of the landlady, "and wanted to do a great deal of mischief." The attraction, it seems, was in doors, and not abroad; he was brought by accident to these innocent seclusions, and wanted to leave guilt and wretchedness behind him; but, happily, the object of his pursuit was too well fortified against his persuasion, repulsed his attentions, and escaped the net which was set for her.

The virtue of the Vaudois females is beyond all praise; their modesty of manner is so striking, that none but a thorough profligate could think of making improper advances. The young girls have such excellent patterns before them in their mothers, and in the married women in general, and such vigilant guardians over their morals, that the observation of a French writer, who well understood human nature, is strictly applicable to this virtuous race. "Quand les femmes feront leur devoir, soyez sur que les filles ne manqueront point au leur."

As we walked along, M. Vertu recounted many little interesting circumstances, connected with the history of the country: the inundations that overwhelmed the valley, the avalanches, or ecroulements, that had changed the face of the mountains; the chasms that had been filled up by sudden convulsions of nature, the battles that had been fought, and the deep recesses, amidst the rocks and forests, which had served as hiding-places in the days of persecution. On one spot the brave soldiers of a Protestant detachment had been hard pressed by a very superior number of assailants, and were upon the point of being obliged to retreat, when a thick fog covered the combatants, and occasioned a temporary cessation of the conflict. The Vaudois were so well acquainted with every pass, that they took advantage of the obscurity, made an unexpected detour, and attacked the enemy in the rear. The battle then recommenced, upon the edge of a yawning precipice. The Popish party supposed that fresh troops were brought against them: their commander (Saquet) was hurled down the abyss, in the confusion of the fight, and the peasants remained masters of the field. The chasm, which, in consequence of this event, went by the name of Saquet, was filled up by a quantity of earth and stones, that rolled down from the mountains more than two hundred years ago; but the tradition still lingers over the spot, and the tale never fails the passing stranger, who seeks from his Vaudois guide the story of these mountains.

But of all the objects to which a legend is attached, none is more conspicuous or remarkable than the stupendous crag, which rears its misshapen head above all the contiguous rocks and peaks, and is seen overhanging Villaro and La Torre, at the distance of several leagues. Whoever has once seen Le Bric Casteluzzo[n] can never forget it; and to hear, as we did, of the fearful deeds, which have been done under its dark brow, narrated by one of the descendants of the sufferers, leaves an impression, which the mere

[n] The word *bric*, seems to be a corruption of the Italian word *bricca*, a steep craggy place.

reader of such details can hardly fancy. But there is neither pleasure nor profit to the reader, in dwelling on the barbarities of other times ; barbarities which are not likely to recur in an age like the present. It will be enough to state generally, that thousands were massacred, and many put to death with tortures of a more horrid and revolting nature than any recorded of the Spanish Inquisition; and that the most barbarous cruelty was united to indecency the most brutal and profligate. The very recital of these scenes would be sufficient to make the book that contained it, a scorn and a horror to society.

To escape from such dreadful treatment, the terrified inhabitants of the commune of La Torre contrived to make a secure hiding-place, into which they might retreat from the pursuit of their tormentors. Near the lofty and projecting crag which soars above Mount Vaudelin, there was a natural cavern, which, it was found, might be hollowed out to answer their purpose. It was difficult of access, and capacious before they began to work upon it; but when it was completed, it became a safe receptacle, in which between three and four hundred persons might conceal themselves, and at the same time lay in a supply of provisions for many days' consumption. This cavern was vaulted, and shaped not unlike an oven, with clefts in the rock, which served for windows, and even for loop-holes ; and prepared with recesses which answered the purpose of watch-houses, from whence they might observe the motions of their assailants. There were also several chambers within this vast cave, accommodations for cooking meat, and a large fountain, well supplied with water. It was impossible to enter it, except by one hole at the top; and those who were in the secret, could only let themselves down one at a time, and by a very slow and gradual process, with the assistance of steps, or foot-holes, cut in the rock. In fact, it was like descending into a mine; and one or two resolute men might easily defend the entrance against the assault of any force that could be brought against them. Such was the cavern of Vaudelin, or Casteluzzo: but we could not explore the spot, for the quantity of snow that had accumulated in the passes that led to it; nor am I able to say what is the present state of a retreat, which was once so often resorted to.

But though we were unable to satisfy ourselves as to the ingenuity of the former inhabitants of this region, in an examination of their asylum in the rocks, we saw enough to judge of the industry, and clever expedients, with which the present natives appropriate to their use tracts of land stolen from the rocks and the torrents. Where the sides of the mountain would be likely to fall in, they form terrace upon terrace, in many places not exceeding ten feet in breadth, and wall them up with huge piles of stone. Upon these terraces they sow their grain, or plant vines. In the same manner they rob the Pelice of part of his bed; and when they have brought a small spot of ground to bear, they surround it with an inclosure of stones, and protect it from the violence of the waters. Amidst the ruins of former labours, among black masses of rock, on projecting ridges of the mountain, on the brink of precipices, and on the margin of the torrent, these indefatigable mountaineers hazard their hopes; and in every possible place, and on the smallest spots where a blade of corn can be made to grow, there they raise a little wheat.

It is this extraordinary and indefatigable industry of the Vaudois, which has partly saved them from being dispossessed of the sterile land, which they are yet suffered to occupy. If they had been driven out of the country, none would have been found to cultivate such an unprofitable soil, and the great landlords would have gone without their rents, and the government without its taxes. It not unfrequently happens, that the bad weather sets in before they have carried home the little corn that can be made to grow, or that the frost and snow cover the ground before they can put in the seed for another crop. In these cases, says

Leger, the men are obliged to leave what little provisions are spared for the women and children, and to abandon their homes in search of work and subsistence. They return about Easter, with the scanty pittance they have earned, to satisfy the demands of the tax-gatherer, and to save their cattle or furniture, which would otherwise be seized.

At other times, the women themselves, that they may be able to purchase a small quantity of salt, which is very dear in these valleys, are forced to undertake long journeys of twenty or twenty-four miles, to Pinerolo, reckoning the distance there and back again, with immense loads upon their shoulders, *(vont porter des longues perches de melese;)* for which they do not receive above a livre. A stranger would be moved with compassion to see these poor creatures tottering under their burdens, and often sinking with exhaustion before they can reach their journey's end. Even in those places where the soil is more fertile, the labour is toilsome and disheartening. Carts and waggons cannot be used, except in very few of the hamlets in the vales; horses and mules are beyond the purchase of most of the peasants; and the only way which many of them have of transporting their hay, corn, and wood to places of security, or of carrying manure on the land, is by means of large baskets and crates, placed upon their own shoulders. Almost all the vineyards of the higher districts are made on rocky soil, where the earth, in which the vines take root, is brought in the first instance from a distant quarter, and afterwards retained in its place, in spite of the torrents and rains that threaten to wash it away, by expedients which require the constant labour and watchfulness of the vine-dresser.

Some ecclesiastical writers have taken occasion to argue, from the barrenness of the soil, and the providential preservation of this little remnant of the true flock, that it is the church predicted in the book of Revelations, under the representation of the woman who fled into the wilderness from the fury of the dragon. "And the woman fled into the wilderness, where she hath a place prepared of God, that they should feed her there a thousand two hundred and threescore years. And to the woman were given two wings of a great eagle, that she might flee into the wilderness, into her place, where she is nourished for a time and times and half a time, from the face of the serpent. And the dragon was wroth with the woman, and went to make war with the remnant of her seed, which kept the commandments of God and have the testimony of Jesus Christ." Revelations xii. 6. 14. 17.

Others say, that the prophecy of the eleventh chapter, and eleventh verse, relates to the restoration of the Vaudois, in the year 1690, after they had been banished from their country three years and a half. "And after three days and an half the Spirit of life from God entered into them, and they stood upon their feet; and great fear fell upon them which saw them." These three days and a half are thought to be prophetical days, and every day must be taken for a year.

The following extract, from Bishop Newton's Dissertations on the Prophecies, will be read with satisfaction by those who agree with that learned prelate; and the concluding anecdote will be considered one of the most extraordinary of the kind that ever was recorded.

"Bishop Lloyd, and after him Mr. Whiston, apply this prophecy to the poor Protestants in the valley of Piedmont, who, by a cruel edict of their sovereign, the Duke of Savoy, instigated by the French king, were imprisoned, or murdered, or banished, and totally dissipated at the latter end of the year 1686. They were kindly received and succoured by the Protestant states; and, after awhile, secretly entering Savoy with their swords in their hands, they regained their ancient possessions, with great slaughter of their enemies; and the duke himself, having then left the French interest, granted them a full pardon, and re-established them by another edict, signed June 4, 1690; just three years and a half after their total dissipation. Bishop Lloyd not only understood the prophecy in this manner; but, what is very remarkable, made the application even before the event took place, as Mr. Whiston relates; *and upon this ground encouraged a refugee minister of the Vaudois, whose name was Jordan, to return home; and returning, he heard the joyful news of the deliverance and restitution of his country.*" P. 614.

The same kind of scenery, with groves waving on the summits, and patches of green interspersed among dark masses of rock, or white banks of snow, continued as far as Villaro. The sound of the woodman's axe among the trees, and of the huge limbs or trunks of the felled chesnut, which are rolled down the slopes, and come thundering and re-echoing into the valley, was a new sort of music to our ears; and at first we mistook the loud reports, when they dashed against the hollow sides of the mountain, for the discharge of guns. A little before we entered Villaro, we passed by one of those Madonnas, or small shrines, erected in honour of the Virgin, so common in Italy, where the pious are often seen kneeling and offering up their supplications to the *mother of God.*

These idolatrous objects are offensive enough to the Protestants; but few as the Papists of these communes are in number, they preserve all their accustomed superstitions; and the former sometimes indulge in a little harmless humour, which reconciles them to such eye-sores. This shrine they call *Le Pilori Taviere,* or Taviere's Pillory, in ridicule of a gallant Piemontese commandant, who thought it better to be raising his hands in prayer to the Virgin for success, than to mix in the fight with his troops, when they were opposing the march of the French into Villaro. During the revolutionary war, the invaders from France crossed the frontiers, to the amount of 5000 men, and attacked Villaro. The Vaudois defended it most resolutely, but the noble Taviere remained in security behind the stone walls of the

Madonna, and from it despatched his aid-de-camp, to report how the engagement was going on. His head was seen occasionally peeping out of the shrine, and thence the joke of *Le Pilori*.

Villaro has nothing in its immediate vicinity either of the softer or more majestic beauties, which we had noticed in other parts of La Valle di Luzerna; and the painful sight of those shocking protuberances, the goitres, in the necks of many of the women and children, made us consider it the least inviting village of any that we had yet seen. Next to Angrogna, the population of Villaro is greater than either of the other communes; and as the extent of land in the parish is not equally large, there is every reason to believe that more poverty prevails here than elsewhere. The church was open; to arrive at it, we had to go through the greater part of the village, and up a narrow lane, by the side of the burial-ground. We found M. Gay, the pastor, catechizing some of the children of his flock. There were present forty-two boys, and twenty-eight girls; and they answered the questions which were put to them, with great readiness and correctness.

Upon this and all other occasions, when there was an opportunity of investigating the proficiency of the children, the result satisfied us, that their acquaintance with the sacred lessons of the Old and New Testament are not less extraordinary at the present time, than at those terrible periods of the history of the Waldenses, when inquisitors and commissioners were sent to make enquiries, which, it was hoped, would criminate these persecuted people. In most cases, they returned ashamed of the cruel business upon which they had been despatched, and made reports most creditable to the reputation of the accused. One declared that he had found persons who could repeat the whole of the New Testament by heart; another confessed that he had never heard so much of the Scriptures as during his conferences with these heretics: but the most remarkable testimony was delivered by a young disputant in theology, who made a journey on purpose to have the honour of confuting the erroneous opinions of these incorrigible schismatics, as he called them. Expectation was raised by the well-known character of the confident polemic; but what was the astonishment of his friends, when he came back, and in a public oration avowed, that he had learnt more of the doctrine of salvation, from the answers of little Vaudois children in their catechism, than in all his previous readings or disputations!

The church of Villaro is large and airy, but by no means handsome. Most of the churches of the Vaudois have bells, and towers or steeples, some of them certainly very small; and in appearance and character they bear every resemblance to what we consider to be the church construction. All the churches are opened for some kind of service four times in the week. On Sundays, for the Sabbath-day duties, on Mondays and Wednesdays for catechetical instructions, which commence and end with prayers; and on Thursdays, for prayers and a sermon. The parochial duties of the ministers are accordingly extremely heavy°, and scarcely allow them any respite whatever; for the old and the sick, as well as the young, have the benefit of their unremitting attentions, and the composition of their sermons takes up no small share of their weekly time. These sermons are not delivered extempore, but are written out, learnt by heart, and preached from memory.

Several of the clergy have been forced to submit to daily labour for their subsistence. This has happened lately; and was made a matter of serious charge against their community, about three hundred years ago, when it was said, among other false accusations, that they *compelled* their

° "Not a day passed during the writer's residence with M. Bert, that he did not see that most excellent and admirable Pastor return from the performance of his duties in a state of exhaustion, scarcely known by our common labourers."—See Mr. Acland's Sketch of the History and Present Condition of the Vaudois.

pastors to follow some occupation, inconsistent with their sacred calling. The answer then made would apply to their present condition. "We do not hold that our pastors ought to work for their bread. They might be better qualified to instruct us, if we could maintain them without their own labour, but our poverty has no remedy."

Knowing the very limited incomes of these excellent men, I asked why the pastors did not unite the office of school-master in their own persons, as there is a regular provision for the school-masters, which would be a material addition to their salaries. The reply was, that the ministers have labours too complicated already to allow of their undertaking any more; and the wife of one of them assured me, that her husband sometimes returned from his walks in a state of the most alarming exhaustion: that his flock was so scattered about the mountains, and put him in such constant requisition, that it was impossible his health could stand the fatigue and agitation, which his pastoral visits occasioned. These good shepherds are summoned upon all matters where their assistance and advice can be of service,—to console the afflicted, to confirm the wavering, to refute the arguments of Roman Catholic missionaries, and to administer an antidote to the poison instilled by them; to reconcile differences, and prevent disputes. It is thus that they obey the Apostle's injunction, and "*warn them that are unruly, comfort the feeble-minded, and support the weak.*" The least relaxation, in their vigilance or exertions, would hazard not only their own reputation, but the safety of the fold; the wolf would get in and seize his prey.

It is quite wonderful that so small a remnant as 20,000, who have but thirteen spiritual guides, should have preserved their integrity, and continue to adhere to the faith of their ancestors, amidst all the arts and bribes and terrors, which have been constantly held out to induce them to enter within the pale of the Roman Church. Offers of the most tempting nature, sums of money, pensions for life, public employments, rank in the army, and grants of land are notoriously proffered to those who will change their religion; but poor and destitute as many of the objects are, to whom these tempting proposals are made, it rarely happens that an apostate can be found. Hitherto a variety of circumstances has operated in favour of keeping the Vaudois a detached people, and in giving force to the exhortations of the clergy. Active persecution is always a stimulus: intolerance exasperates and hardens the heart in its predilections and prejudices, instead of subduing it. The little intercourse, which these mountaineers had formerly with the world, also assisted in the preservation of their faith; they acquired no taste for the different sort of life which a change of religion held forth, but now it is to be feared, lest a long communication with the French, and enlistment in their armies, may have given them a desire for what is not attainable in the solitudes of the Alps. Add to this, they were for a long time like a cherished spot, which their brethren, of the Protestant faith in other countries, would not suffer to be blotted out from the face of the earth, and they took pride in knowing that the eyes of men were upon them.

But at present they are more neglected and overlooked: they have been placed in a condition which they would like to resume; they have been in the enjoyment of privileges which they sigh to have restored, and their pastors, instead of being pensioned and supported, as they used to be, are left to struggle with difficulties and deprivations, which the spirit of man is sometimes too feeble to bear. Under all these circumstances, it never was so much an imperative duty to give a helping hand to the Vaudois clergy, as at present, and to promote the circulation of Christian knowledge among their flocks, by a more regular and liberal supply of books. Elementary instruction is already imparted, in a manner which does credit to the pastors and school-masters, but food must be provided for the minds of the children, beyond the common hours of instruction, that they may be fortified against the seductive means, which are actively employed to separate them from their families, and induce them to apostatize.

None but those who have intermixed a great deal with Roman Catholics, and in countries, where the imposing services of the Roman Church are performed with theatrical attention to effect, can have any idea of the influence, which the Popish priesthood holds over weak understandings. Whatever can affect a lively imagination, a romantic turn of mind, a warm temperament, a nervous constitution, or a sensitive heart, is employed in the public rites, and in the secret practices of the clergy. There is nothing of simplicity in the character of the Romish religion: it is all mysticism, symbol, and delusion. The avowal has been made by one of its most eloquent advocates. "In the regions of the south, where the sky is bright, and nature bountiful, where the heart is warm, and the imagination active, external demonstrations have ever been employed to express feelings too big for utterance, and external shews introduced to convey impressions, and excite sentiments, grand and sublime beyond the reach of ordinary language [p]."

But such external shews and external demonstrations only serve to heat the fancy, and substitute a dangerous enthusiasm, in the place of that genuine and rational adoration, which, springing from the mind, can only perish with the mind. Confessions, breathed into the ear of an indulgent confessor [q], and secret inclinations confided to one, who

[p] Eustace, Vol. II. p. 529.

[q] Read what Mr. Blanco White says, the author of Doblado's Letters, who was educated abroad, in a Roman Catholic college, and ordained a priest of the Roman Catholic church, but afterwards renounced the errors of Rome, and became a minister of the church of England.

"The necessity of confession, seen at a distance, is lighter than a feather in the balance of desire, while at a subsequent period it becomes a punishment on delicacy—an instrument to blunt the moral sense, by multiplying the subjects

is expected to whisper assurances of absolution, but seldom

of remorse, and directing its greatest terrors against imaginary crimes. These evils affect nearly equally the two sexes; but there are some that fall peculiarly to the lot of the softer. Yet the remotest of all, at least as long as the Inquisition shall exist, is the danger of direct seduction from the priest. The formidable powers of that odious tribunal have been so skilfully arrayed against the abuse of sacramental trust, that few are found base and blind enough to make the confessional a *direct* instrument of debauch. The strictest delicacy however is, I believe, inadequate fully to oppose the demoralizing tendency of auricular confession. Without the slightest responsibility, and not unfrequently, in the conscientious discharge of what he believes his duty, the confessor conveys to the female mind the first foul breath, which dims its virgin purity. He undoubtedly has a right to interrogate upon subjects, which are justly deemed awkward even for maternal confidence; and it would require more than common simplicity to suppose, that a discretionary power of this nature, left in the hands of thousands, men beset with more than common temptations to abuse it, will generally be exercised with proper caution *."

It is notorious, and will be attested by all who have seen them, that the books of religious instruction, which are put into the hands of young Romanists, particularly those touching auricular confession, are indecent, gross, and filthy, beyond all conception.

* In corroboration of Mr. White's observations, the reader is referred to the following extract from the *Constitutionnel*, May 2, 1825.—" We have received a little book, printed at Lyons, with the approbation of the Vicar-General, and circulated by the missionaries. It is entitled, ' Examination of the Conscience. Rule of Life. Remedies against Sin. Abridgment of our Faith;' and is distributed among the young people of both sexes at school. We have looked into this book, and found to our surprise, at the 9th page, appropriated to the 6th and 9th Commandments, obscene expressions, impure details, a complete exposé of the most monstrous combinations of licentiousness; in short, a treatise to teach debauchery and corruption; and this at a time when the Jesuits are making such an outcry about religion and morality. The reader may judge of its improper nature, when we say that it is so bad that we cannot, dare not copy it; and we are sure the *Etoile* and *Drapeau Blanc* dare not insert any portion of it in their pages, though it is approved by Vicars Generals, and circulated by the missionaries. The book has been printed at various places, and in a short time will be distributed through the whole of France, and our youth will be instructed by a book to which the cases of conscience of Dr. Sanchez were pure. In looking at this gross abuse, we must ask why the *Procureurs du Roi*, so sensible on other occasions, have no power when morality is thus outraged, and justice violated? Are they not fathers? Have they no daughters at boarding schools? and are they contented with this mode of insinuating into their minds a knowledge of debauchery, and acquainting them with the nomenclature of a series of vices, of which, in ordinary circumstances, women remain ignorant their whole lives? Are these magistrates deaf to the wishes of fathers? and must parents not attempt to save the honour of their families, and the future honour of their country? Is there not a commission to examine books of devotion? Does not the ministry talk incessantly of morality, and has it not extended its cares to the purity of the Opera, and can it allow corruption to be in this manner carried into the heart of every family? Is it not time to overlook the Theatre, and examine what is taught at Church, to set *Tartuffe* at liberty, and put the *Examen* under restraint?"—*Note to Second Edition.*

produce amendment. It happens to me, at this moment, to know a young Roman Catholic female, whose mind is agonized by a sentiment of more than spiritual affection, which she entertains for her confessor. What she calls his graceful performance of the sacerdotal functions, and his majestic appearance before the altar, clad in the splendid robes of his sacred office, compared with his mild and persuasive gentleness, when he assists her private devotions, have inspired this fatal passion; not because she is more susceptible than the rest of her sex, or that he takes undue advantage of her sensibility, but because the pomp and ceremonies of the Roman Church, and the relation between the priest, and the youthful members of a family, where he is venerated as a being of superior intelligence, are calculated to produce such impressions.

There is an anecdote told of Pope Braschi, who assumed the name of Pius the Sixth, which shews, that the Roman Catholic clergy set no little value upon the assistance, that may be derived from personal appearance. Upon an occasion when that pontiff was passing through a street of Rome, and was carried along in his papal chair, with a splendour suitable to his dignity, a voice was heard from one of the windows which was crowded with admiring spectators. It was that of a young lady of rank. *Quanto è bello—quanto è bello. How handsome he is,* cried she, in a moment of enthusiasm. An old woman, in haste to correct any thing that might appear too profane in this exclamation, replied, with her hands joined, and her eyes lifted up to heaven, *Tanto è bello, quanto è santo. He is holy as he is handsome.* It is said, that such a compliment gave Pius the Sixth more secret satisfaction, than all the incense lavished upon him by the prelates at the altar, and all the genuflexions of the sacred college [r].

Several English ladies have acknowledged, in my hear-

[r] Annual Register, 1799.

ing, that they have more *pleasure* in attending the service of the Roman Church than their own, but pleasure surely is not the aim of any form of worship; if it be, I should conceive, that such an aim might be more certainly reached, with most people, by means of the ball-room or the theatre, than by any religious paraphernalia, however strongly such adjuncts might appeal to the senses. "The grand spectacle of an illuminated cathedral," and "the music of psalms tuned to the modulation of Greek chorusses," may be more pleasing to the fancy than the "dull services" of a parish church in England, or of a lowly temple at the foot of the Alps; but until the morals of the votaries, who kneel before the burning cross of St. Peter's, on the solemn vigil of the resurrection, are believed to be as pure as those of the peasantry of my own country, or of the Protestant inhabitants of the valleys of Piemont, I shall continue to feel persuaded, that simplicity of worship is the best promoter of active and efficient religion.

All that I heard and saw gave me the gratifying assurance, that the Vaudois of the present day are not unworthy of the character, which was wrung, in times past, from some of their bitterest enemies, even when employed in endeavouring to detect a subject for criminal accusations. "I wish," said one of these inquisitors, in a moment of remorse, for having been instrumental in persecuting the Waldenses of Frassiniere, when that valley was inhabited by the professors of the Protestant faith, "I wish that I were as good a Christian, as the worst of them!" This man was constrained, by the force of truth, to make such a report to Lewis the Twelfth of France, that he at once silenced the importunities of his advisers, exclaiming in a force of indignation, which put an end to their importunities, "By the holy mother of God, these heretics, whom you urge me to destroy, are better men than you, or myself, or any of my subjects."

"I allow," said a furious Dominican monk, whose zeal

was not much less furious than that of the inhuman Dominic, the founder of his order, and the firebrand who kindled the flames of the inquisition, "I allow, in morals and life, they are good, true in words, and unanimous in brotherly love, but their faith is incorrigible and vile[a]." The observation of the author from whom I have taken this anecdote is unanswerable; "How could the Romanist suppose that the faith of men could be bad, whose fruits were so excellent; could he shew such fruits in the Roman church in general at that time?"

When the Protestant Vaudois extended into the province of Saluzzo, or Marquisate of Saluches, then under the French sovereignty, the governor, Birague, received orders from his court, to commence an active search after all such as refused to attend the celebration of mass, and to put them to death. The governor communicated the orders to his council. A Roman Catholic archdeacon who was present, rose, and made the following bold and honest remonstrance, in favour of these proscribed victims. "Assuredly his majesty the King of France must have received some very false, and malicious information, concerning these poor people. We must delay the execution of this edict, until his majesty can be made acquainted with the real character of this portion of his Italian subjects, who are good and honourable men, well disposed, and faithful in his service, and live peaceably with their Roman Catholic neighbours." This manly and candid testimony, so honourable both to the Protestants and their amiable advocate, was the means of saving their lives, for that time at least. The murderous intention was at first suspended, and afterwards abandoned till another opportunity.

But a still more affecting proof of the high estimation, in which the moral character of the Vaudois was held, even by those who would have gladly seen their extermination,

[a] Milner.

occurred at La Torre, about the year 1560. Emanuel Philibert, the reigning Duke of Savoy at that period, was favourably inclined towards his Protestant subjects, and, for a length of time, resisted all the importunities, which were made to every new sovereign to give a proof of his zeal for the Roman Catholic faith, by publishing fresh penal laws against heretics. The perseverance of the bigoted Philip II. of Spain, at length prevailed over the Duke's scruples of humanity, and a lighted torch was once more thrown into these devoted valleys. A sanguinary army carried fire and sword into every village; and no other expedient was left, but for the Vaudois to abandon the low country, and take refuge among the mountains, while the enemy occupied San Giovanni, La Torre, and Villaro. The Roman Catholic families would have remained; but the licentious conduct of the soldiery was such, that all the young females of La Torre put themselves under the protection of the Protestants, who had retired behind the fastnesses of Angrogna, rather than be exposed to the brutality of men, who came to extirpate heresy, and vindicate the honour of the Roman Catholic religion[t].

Two hundred years ago, in the midst of the bitterest animosities, the honesty and attachment of Vaudois servants were so generally acknowledged, that, it was well known, none of the Popish nobility of the provinces would hire persons of their own faith, as long as they could persuade

[t] This anecdote is confirmed by Thuanus, an historian who hated the Vaudois, but was too candid to withhold the truth. His words are these: "Præcipue castitatis cura et honos inter Valdenses, adeo ut Vicini, qui alioqui ab eorum religione alieni erant, ut filiarum suarum pudicitiæ consulerent, vim a licentioso milite veriti, eas Valdensium curæ et fidelitati committebant."

"The chastity of the Waldenses is so well known, and held in such high repute, that their neighbours, who were at variance with them on subjects of religion, entrusted the honour of their daughters to their protection and fidelity, when they were fearful of the consequences that might result from the presence of a licentious soldiery."

the Protestants to enter their service [u]. It is the same at the present day; and I was repeatedly assured, both at Turin and Genoa, that the Vaudois servants are preferred before all others.

M. Gay, the pastor of Villaro, was so deeply engaged with his pastoral duties, that we had the benefit of very little of his conversation. His parish is considered the least healthy of any in the valley of Luzerna; and we observed that his countenance and voice indicated illness. He is about thirty-six, or thirty-seven years of age, has a young family to add to his anxieties, and seems well qualified to give them an education above the humble sphere of their probable destination. The manners and acquirements of M. Gay are of a degree beyond what is expected at a place like Villaro, which reminded me very much of some of our small fishing towns in England. The presbytery of this parish, which stands close to the church, is a good sized house, with some airy rooms; but it is not fitted up, or furnished, with any attention to comfort, much less to taste or appearance. The furniture was scarcely sufficient for the wants of a family. As we entered by a door, the window-frame of which was unglazed, and is left open in the summer, we observed that paper was pasted on, as a substitute for glass. This paper was torn from a copy-book, or exercise book, and contained the conjugation of a French and English verb. M. Gay understands English, and is teaching it to his children.

[u] Les Gentils-hommes, Seigneurs des lieux, et autres Catholiques aiment mieux encore des serviteurs et des servantes d'entre les notres, que les leurs propres. *Vigneuax.*

CHAPTER VIII.

Bobbio—Magnificent scenery—Breakwater or rampart of Bobbio—Anecdote—Humanity of the Vaudois—Catechetical instruction—Church of Bobbio—M. Muston, pastor of Bobbio—Repast at the Presbytery—Papists and the second Commandment—Infant baptism—Vaudois, not fanatics—Anecdote—A rural sketch—Retrospect—Henri Arnaud—Enterprizing achievement—March of the exiles—La Roche Blanche—The pass of Salabertrand forced—Martial enthusiasm—Anecdote of Arnaud—Intrepidity of the Vaudois—Fastnesses of San Martino—Guerilla warfare—Fortress of Barceglia—Tremendous pass—Sanguinary conflicts—Affecting anecdote—Termination of the contest—Boyer's narrative.

FROM Villaro to Bobbio (Bobi) the road still pursues a due westerly direction, up the banks of the Pelice. The defile opens a little as you advance; and when Bobbio first breaks upon the view, the prospect is one of the most magnificent that mountain scenery presents. The mountains themselves seem to retire, and at the same time to rise in height by irregular swells and gradations, in order to form an amphitheatre of such vastness and beauty, that the traveller must pause, and contemplate the awful picture in front of him, before he approaches to make a nearer examination. To the right the Col d'Aliries lifts up his head far above a succession of ridges, which rise majestically from their rocky basement; and, to the left, the gigantic peak of Mount Viso is seen glistening at one moment in the sun, and at another half enveloped in passing clouds. The enormous masses soar one above another, summit above summit, and crag above crag; each appears at times to be the loftiest of the chain, until a current of wind blows away the misty veil, which conceals the still more elevated eminence in its rear.

Such was the back ground of this grand picture; the fore ground was equally glorious. We had been ascending ever since we left La Torre, a distance of about six miles, and were still on the ascent; but the environs of Bobbio form a vale at the foot of a semicircular range of mountains, which look as if they only now begin to soar. The face of this vale had much variety of aspect and colouring, even after a fall of snow; and there were yet a few green spots left, in sheltered nooks, or on sunny banks, whose cheerful verdure took away from the gloom, which gray rocks and dark pines, intermixed with long tracts of snow or masses of ice, would otherwise have thrown over the landscape. Every kind of tree and shrub, that the soil of this region produces, from the stately walnut to the drooping fruit tree, clothed the banks of the innumerable streamlets that pour into the Pelice, and stand so thick, that when seen at a distance, they look like a grove in front of the village, to protect it from the keen east winds, that blow up the valley of Luzerna. Of this valley, Bobbio is the extreme commune, for it is here that the higher chain of Cottian Alps lock in the valley, and form its barrier between France and Piemont. There is a pass which traverses the Col de la Croix, by which the traveller may reach the frontier in one day.

As you approach Bobbio, the Roman Catholic church, and vicarage, are the two first objects that attract attention. The Protestant church is nearly in the centre of the village, and is discovered by the three windows which appear at the east end. The tower, or belfry, is separated from the church by the burial ground, and is built upon a rock. The presbytery stands very near.

It is impossible to take a first view of this most picturesque village, without fancying that it is capable of providing a secure retreat against all the storms of life. But its vicinity to the frontiers of France, and its exposure to the first brunt of border warfare, with its position under mountains, which pour their torrents with such violence into its bosom, as to threaten a general inundation, will soon shew the enquiring visitor, that it is far from being the sheltered corner of his imagination. In fact there are few of the Protestant communes which have suffered more than this, both from the aggressions of man, and the fury of the elements.

Twice Bobbio has been entirely destroyed by inundations: hundreds of the inhabitants, with almost all their cattle, and every cottage in the vale, have been washed away, by the tremendous force of the waters, which rush like a deluge from the steeps, when the snows melt with more than common rapidity. A rampart, or breakwater, was erected with the assistance of a subscription, raised in Holland, about a hundred and twenty years ago, to protect the village from such fearful visitations. We walked to look at this breakwater, and such a spectacle is beheld at its extreme point, as makes the whole frame shudder. A foaming torrent is seen rolling from the mountains, rushing with impetuous haste, and menacing the very piers on which you stand; then precipitating itself over fragments of rock, dashing blocks of stone against the wall, which is built to check its violence, and roaring as if a hundred battering rams were in motion against the jetty. Nature's horrors, and man's resolute perseverance in the endeavour to counteract them, were finely displayed on this spot; and we could judge, from the state of the torrent at this time of the year, what the Pelice must be in the season when it is swelled by continual rains, and the melting of the snows.

But Bobbio has obtained a still more imperishable reputation from its deeds of humanity, than even from its grand work of industry, the breakwater of the Pelice. In the terrible conflicts between the French and the allied armies in 1799, the sick and the wounded of the contending forces received attentions, which were acknowledged in general orders by the commanders-in-chief of the French, Russians, and Austrians. But the resources of the villagers were at length so much exhausted, that the means of rendering further assistance were denied them; and in this destitute condition, their Christian charity hit upon a scheme, which perhaps never before entered the head of persons so situated. "We cannot relieve you any longer," they said to a French party then quartered on them, "our poverty has nothing left; but since our homes can be no asylum to you, we will carry you to your own." The thing seemed impossible: how could men who were suffering under the intolerable anguish of dangerous wounds, be transported over the mountains? They could not walk, and their maimed limbs would not allow them to ride. "We will convey you on our own shoulders," was the reply of these good Samaritans of Bobbio: and they did so. They prepared litters, which answered their benevolent purpose; and in this way, upwards of three hundred wounded French soldiers were carried over the Alps, and safely set down in their own country.

It is said that M. Rostain, the late pastor of Bobbio, suggested this most humane scheme, after having expended all he was worth in the world in aid of the sufferers, whom the evils of war had recommended to his humanity, without regard to national prejudices, or enquiring whether the objects of his pity were friends or foes.

This good man toiled afterwards as a day labourer, to put bread into the mouths of his children, and soon fell a victim to his exertions. Poverty and oppression broke his heart, and the necessaries of life were not to be procured at a period of his existence, when he had no longer strength to bear up against deprivations: but his charity did not meet with charity.

At the restoration of the legitimate dynasty, two clergymen's widows were turned out of their habitation, in the middle of winter, to make way for a Catholic priest, who had a small hamlet assigned to him for a benefice, where himself, and his woman servant were the only two belonging to the Roman church. I have reason to fear that the widow of the unfortunate and ill-requited Rostain, was one of these widows, who were so cruelly dispossessed.

We found M. Muston, the present pastor of Bobbio, in his church engaged in the same duty as M. Gay had been at Villaro, that is, in giving instruction to his young flock, fifty-six boys, and thirty-two girls. He had almost finished when we entered, and was then occupied in delivering the customary address which follows the catechism. He did it with much judgment, and considerable effect; and as I noticed his earnest manner and paternal anxiety to impress upon his youthful hearers the importance of what he had been explaining, I could not but feel pain under the recollection of the imperfect mode, in which we too commonly discharge this duty in England.

The Bishop of London's late impressive Charge[x] upon this subject occurred to my mind, and I saw before me a

[x] "The general disuse into which this practice has fallen, I consider as calamitous to the interests of piety in the highest degree, not only by removing one of the strongest incitements to the parents to teach, and to the children to learn, the doctrines and laws of their Christian profession, but still more by its fatal effects in frustrating the purpose, which it was the principal object of the ordinances relating to these points to attain. If at the age when the mind is susceptible of the strongest impressions, the young are regularly brought into personal intercourse with their minister, and accustomed to receive their instructions from his lips, they will naturally imbibe a respect for his person, and a reverence to the sacred character of his office, which will prove the strongest of barriers against immorality and vice, as well as dissent and infidelity. They will regard with deep veneration the truths which they have received upon his authority, and will feel, what reasoning can hardly make clear to the ignorant, the danger no less of guilt than of error, in deserting the appointed guide of their youth for intrusive and unknown teachers. The discontinuance of this salutary practice is imputable, neither to the neglect of the ecclesiastical governors,—for they have constantly remonstrated against it—nor to the indolence of

most forcible illustration of the arguments used by that excellent prelate, when he drew a picture of the affecting relation, which must exist between a parish-priest and the younger part of his flock, if catechetical lessons are regularly and zealously imparted. In fact, the very greatest of all opportunities is lost, when a clergyman is unable, or unwilling to give up a stated portion of his time to the children of his parish. He loses an influence over the minds, and a hold upon the affections, which might be turned to the best advantage. The Papists are not blind to this truth: they catechise with strict punctuality; and in several places where I witnessed this service, it was performed with the same patience, good humour, and earnestness, which we noticed in the Waldensian pastors.

The church of Bobbio is an old building, large, cold, and undecorated. Our feet were wet when we entered it, we were warm with walking, and before we came out again, we were trembling with cold. Opposite to the pulpit was an inscription expressive of the moderation, charity, piety, and *loyalty* of the oppressed and slandered Vaudois. "Honour all men. Love the brotherhood. Fear God. Honour the king." I do not remember ever having seen a village church, which bears any resemblance to this. Its walls are strengthened by enormous buttresses, which arch up towards the roof in a very singular manner. The roof itself is constructed with large rafters, and beams stretched across from one side to the other, so that there is altogether a peculiarity of architectural design, and a studied air of massiveness, which looks as if those, who built this church, were apprehensive, lest nothing short of very uncommon precaution could protect it against the inundations, which so frequently threaten the valley.

the parochial clergy; but was a concession most reluctantly yielded to the fastidious impatience of their congregations." *See a Charge delivered to the Clergy of the Diocese of London, at the Visitation in July* 1822, *by William, Lord Bishop of London.*

As soon as we left the church, M. Muston accosted us in that frank and unreserved tone, which distinguishes these kind-hearted people, and gave us a cordial invitation to his house, where we were introduced to his wife and young family. There were no fires when we first went in, but he saw that we were shivering with cold, and a blazing hearth was soon ready to comfort us. Small pans, or vessels of charcoal, were brought for us to put our feet upon, and our hospitable host never ceased to replenish the fuel in the fire-place, "Ligna super foco large reponens," until he saw that we were relieved from the excessive chilliness, which we brought with us out of his cold damp church. The apartment, in which M. Muston welcomed us to his presbytery, was spacious and more comfortably furnished than any we had yet seen. It had the unusual luxury of a sofa, and stuffed chairs, and the walls, or rather wainscoting, of walnut wood, was hung with drawings from M. Muston's own pencil. They were principally sketches of scenery in Switzerland.

The manners of the pastor of Bobbio were simple and agreeable, and had all that warmth and openness which make the stranger feel at home: they were those of the plain good man, whose only wish seemed to be to live and die among his own people. He insisted upon our partaking of his family-dinner, and his kind-hearted wife, an engaging young woman of about twenty-six years of age, busied herself to prepare the repast, while he himself answered all our questions, interrogated us in his turn, and appeared as contented and happy, as if he were in undisturbed possession of the whole valley, where he is but the minister of a secluded parish.

At last the cloth was laid, the table prepared, and the banquet spread, and never did a party sit down with better appetite to a meal, or with a warmer welcome. It was all the produce of the presbytery and of the presbyter's land, for happily the present pastor of Bobbio, unlike his ill-fated predecessor, has a few acres which he can call his own. He has his little vineyard, and garden, and orchard. He has his pasture for his cows and goats, a moderate extent of arable ground, and a stream of water to irrigate them. From this snug farm, as he was proud in giving us to understand, the bread was home-baked, the butter and cheese home-made, and the wine home-pressed. The sausages were of pork fatted in his own sty, and the filberts, chesnuts, and white pippins were gathered from his own trees. Nor did he omit to tell us that his wife had prepared the sausages, the apple fritters, and the baked pears. In truth they did credit to her housewifery; and when he expressed a wish that he had known of our coming, in time to provide something better, we told him with perfect truth, that it was impossible to sit down to a dinner, which we could have enjoyed more than this pastoral feast.

> Dapes inemptas apparet,
> Non me Lucrina juverint conchylia,
> Magisve rhombus aut scari—
> Non Afra avis descendat in ventrem meum,
> Non attagen Ionicus
> Jucundior.———— *Hor. Epod.* ii.

Clean table-linen is an article as abundant perhaps, in these Alpine retirements, as in the most frequented villages in England. It was therefore nothing new to see a napkin placed by the side of each of our plates; but there were things that did not correspond with this luxury. The knives and forks were of the very coarsest workmanship: the spoons were of iron, and the plates and dishes of very ordinary brown ware. But, can the kind welcome, the simple fare, and the unaffected hospitality of the amiable minister of Bobbio, ever pass from my grateful recollection?

The duty in which M. Muston was engaged when we entered his church, gave the principal turn to our conversation, and it was satisfactory to find, how deeply sensible the Vaudois Protestants have ever been of the necessity of giving a spiritual interpretation to the commandments, and of applying their injunctions to the desires of the heart, as well as to the government of the body. We were shewn several comments of this tendency, on which the Pastors are expected to build their own expositions. On the subject of the second commandment these comments dwell with all that force, and nicety of explanation, which were required, in the early period of their church, to shew how heartily they abhorred the unscriptural and dangerous errors, into which the Papists had fallen, in the very face of some of the plainest denunciations, both in the Old and New Testament. The Catechisms in use among the Vaudois have every article of the decalogue verbatim, as we recite it ourselves, and of course the second commandment [y], with each of its clauses, is among the number.

Every thinking Protestant knows, that the Roman Catholic clergy cannot reconcile their practice of adoring the saints, and prostrating themselves before images, with the positive mandate against such acts; and that they therefore leave it out entirely, and divide the tenth into two, to make up the number. A Popish spelling-book, which was shewn to me during my visit to the valleys, and entitled, "Correttissima santa croce per istruzione de' fanciulli," or "A corrected *Christ's cross row* for the instruction of infants," contains the following curious version of the decalogue, in which the second and fourth commandments are both omitted, and an injunction for the observing of *festival days* is substituted for the command, that we should sanctify the Sabbath.

1. I am the Lord thy God, thou shalt not have another God before me.

2. Take not God's name in vain.

[y] In a very old manuscript, in which is found a copious exposition of the doctrines of the Vaudois, the sixth *Echantillon* quotes the words of the second commandment, as they are now learnt by the young catechumens of the present day.

3. Remember to keep the festivals holy.
4. Honour thy father and mother.
5. Do not kill.
6. Do not commit adultery.
7. Do not steal.
8. Do not bear false witness.
9. Do not covet another's goods.
10. Do not covet another's wife.

From infant instruction we came to the discussion of infant baptism, and nothing can be more false than the calumny, that the Vaudois object to infant baptism. One of the arguments used by the petitioners of the commune of San Giovanni, when they implored permission to reopen their new church, was, that in the winter time their poor infants suffered dreadfully from the severity of the cold, in being carried to such a distance as Angrogna to be publicly baptized. They have even a formulary of baptism, very much like that in use by the Church of England, and the service begins thus.

"You present *this infant* to be baptized?"

The ninth Echantillon of the old manuscript exposition, to which I before alluded, gives this explanation of the baptismal ceremony, and leaves it to the discretion of the parties, to have the rite performed by sprinkling or immersion.

"The first sacrament is called baptism, or in our language, the washing by water, either from a river or fountain: and it should be administered in the name of the Father, and of the Son, and of the Holy Ghost, signifying that by the grace of God, and a participation of the benefits of his Son Jesus Christ, who has redeemed us, and by the regeneration of the Holy Ghost, who imprints a living faith in our hearts, the sins of those who are baptized will be pardoned, and they will be received in grace."

The exposition afterwards proceeds to set forth, "The mere visible and material baptism does not make a person either good or bad, but baptism is administered in the full congregation of the faithful, in order that he, who is thus received in the church, may be reputed, and held by all as a brother and a Christian, and that all may pray for his becoming a Christian in heart, as much as he is one outwardly. It is for this purpose that *infants* are presented for baptism."

In some articles of faith, subsequently drawn up by the Waldensian clergy, there are many such strong declarations as these.

"We maintain, that infants must be baptized unto salvation, and consecrated to Jesus Christ, according to Christ's command, 'Suffer little children to come unto me.'"

"We maintain, that the ministers of the church ought to be legitimately ordained, and confirmed in the congregation to that office, by the laying on of hands."

"We maintain, that the ministers of the word of God ought not to be transferred from one place to another, such a practice not being for the good of the church."

These, it will be confessed, are not the doctrines of fanatical schismatics.

The more serious topics, of the doctrine and discipline of the Vaudois church, were succeeded by little anecdotes of the history of Bobbio. Old achievements, and obstinate defences, were recounted by our kind and entertaining host; the scenes where they took place were minutely described, and the humblest martyr, who had suffered in the cause of truth, or whose fidelity had been proof against temptation, had honourable record from the pastor. Most of his tales related to those gloomy times, which, it is to be hoped and believed, will never return: and he told us of one poor rustic, who displayed as much shrewdness as courage, in baffling the missionaries, who were formerly armed with temporal as well as spiritual weapons. After many proclamations had been made, commanding the Protestants to attend mass, several recusants were summoned before the tribunal of a judge, named De St. Julien, to answer for their contumacy. Among the rest, a peasant was ordered to take his infant to a Roman Catholic priest to be rebaptized. "I will obey the order," said the man, "if the president of the court will give me a discharge, signed by his own hand, and taking upon himself and posterity the sin of this act." De St. Julien was alarmed at the proposition, and suffered the peasant to depart in peace.

The mind dwells with uncommon pleasure upon hours such as those, which we passed by the side of the minister's blazing faggot, in this Alpine hamlet. No sketch of rural contentment that ever was drawn, could have more charms for the imagination, than the true picture which we had this opportunity of contemplating. We were regaled under the hospitable roof of a man, who farmed his own few acres[z], and was satisfied with their produce, who had his little stream to fertilize his ground, and his little grove of trees to shade it, and rendered daily thanks to his Maker for shielding him from the ills of poverty. We had left behind us the proud palaces of Turin, the lofty dome of the Superga, and the luxuries of cities, and were literally enjoying the frugal repast of an humble dwelling, where cleanliness was the principal decoration[a]. What poets dream of was before our eyes; the retreats which they affect to love, where innocence dwells, and a little suffices to its contentment. The very characters, which they employ the melody of words and the harmony of verse to describe, were here acting their parts in unassuming simplicity. Grand scenery, similar to that by which we were surrounded, might be found else-

[z] Puræ rivus aquæ, silvaque jugerum
Paucorum, et segetis certa fides meæ,
Importuna tamen pauperies abest.
Hor. B. iii. Od. 16.

[a] Mundæque parvo sub lare pauperum
Cœnæ, sine aulæis et ostro,
Sollicitam explicuere frontem.
Hor. B. iii. Od. 29.

where, but its moral ornament, a Christian minister, faithful to his duty, contented with his limited means, and cheerful in his obscure seclusion, is not to be found in many other parts of Italy.

Within gun-shot of Bobbio, and on a very picturesque hill, which overhangs the Subiasco torrent, there are still seen a few cabins to remind the tourist of the hamlet of Sibaud, from whence Arnaud and his gallant band made their memorable attack upon Bobbio, after forcing the passage of the Col di Giuliano, whose peaks are also seen from this delightful vale. Henri Arnaud is a name so dear to the Vaudois, that it would be injustice to these intrepid mountaineers, and especially to the memory of that singular man, not to give a few particulars of his extraordinary and successful enterprize.

After the perfidy of Victor Amadeus the Second had triumphed over his Protestant subjects, and the Vaudois were driven out of their country in the year 1686, the three valleys were repeopled by Savoyards and Piemontese of the Roman Catholic persuasion. The forts which guarded the passes were garrisoned in part by Piemontese, and in part by French troops. The exiles themselves were dispersed among the Swiss cantons, and in the Protestant German states. Some of them had even taken refuge in Holland, and others in the duchy of Brandenburgh, where the elector had received them with marked attention. Under these circumstances nothing could be more remote from all probability, than that this scattered remnant should rally under a leader of their own, and march sword in hand for the recovery of their possessions. The success of such an enterprize must have appeared still more improbable.

Henri Arnaud thought otherwise. Patriotic, ardent, and enthusiastic, his love for his native valleys would not suffer him to be happy in a foreign land, his courage would hear of no obstacles, and his warm imagination represented the arm of God, as lifted up to succour the holy undertaking.

Lux lucet in tenebris, or *the light shineth in darkness*, was the motto of his community, and the words which were ever in his mouth. He thought he saw the cloud, which was to go before him by day, and the pillar of fire, which was to give him light by night, and he was incessant in his importunities, until he had communicated his own martial spirit to a few faithful friends, and had girt on, what he called, the sword of the Lord and of Gideon, which he solemnly swore never to resign, until the crucifix should be torn down from the altars of the thirteen sanctuaries, which, until this fatal epoch, had never been so idolatrously decorated. In a short time his little troop was increased to upwards of eight hundred daring adventurers, whom he had persuaded to join his standard, from different parts of Germany and Switzerland.

They were obliged to meet in secret, and their nocturnal assemblies were held in the dark retreats of a forest, which then spread over a long tract of country between Nion and Rolle, and extended down to the edge of the lake of Geneva. What was then a forest is now but a wood, and there remains scarcely enough to mark the spot, where one of the boldest exploits was planned, which ever entered into the heart of man to conceive. I have passed through the supposed scene of rendezvous; and the celebrated forest of Soigne, through which the traveller drives from Brussels to Waterloo, has scarcely more interest than this memorable place.

On the night of Friday, the 16th of August, 1689, Arnaud had completed all his preparations; and, putting himself at the head of his men, he seized some boats on the coast, and crossed the lake. Yvoire, in Savoy, was their place of landing, and they would have had to encounter an enemy at the first village, through which they passed, if they had not wisely taken two persons of some distinction, as hostages for their safe conduct through this part of the country. The route, for the first two or three days, was by passes to which they were perfect strangers, but their hostages were answerable for the fidelity of the guides. On the second day, however, they were nearly betrayed, in spite of all their precautions. The inhabitants of Cluses, on the Arve, at first refused to give them a passage through the town, and afterwards despatched a messenger to Sallanches, with instructions for the people of that city to attack the Vaudois in the narrow defile of Maglan, while they themselves would assail them in the rear. Most providentially the treacherous scheme was discovered in time, and no other vengeance was taken than to carry off two more hostages from Cluses. The tremendous pass of Maglan, where a few peasants, armed with stones, might stop the progress of a whole army, was cleared before the troops of Sallanches had notice of this extraordinary march; and though it rained torrents the whole day, the eight hundred reached Cablau before they halted for the night.

It took them two days only to surmount the difficulties of the Montagne de Haut Luce, and that of the Bon Homme. The latter is a chain of the Allée Blanche, and forms part of the Graian Alps. After descending from these snow-covered heights, they followed the course of the mountain torrent called Reclus, and penetrated through a woody ravine, into the plain of Scez, where they encamped on the fourth evening. It was on this day's march that they passed by the large rock of gypsum, which stands at the entrance of the defile that leads to Scez, and is well known as La Roche Blanche, which is supposed to be the celebrated white rock, on which Hannibal spent the night, after the furious attack which was made upon him by the barbarians [b].

[b] "The position of the Roche Blanche was eminently calculated for the defence of their march. From hence Hannibal commanded the whole plain of Scez, and was able to act against the enemy on the heights above St. Germain, as well as upon those on the flanks of the Roman road. General Melville and M. de Luc attach great importance to the fact of the existence of a white rock on the exact spot on which, according to Polybius, it ought to be found. The expression

On the 21st of August the Protestant heroes traversed the valley of the Isere; and though they expected to find this one of the most perilous of their journeys, yet they arrived at Laval in safety. Nothing can be more fertile, or better cultivated, than this lovely valley, which presents some of the finest Alpine scenery to the eye, that is to be met with in Savoy: it was not therefore from the difficulty of the passes or the scarcity of provisions, that Arnaud's troop apprehended interruption; but from the hostility of the inhabitants. The population is numerous on each side of the river; and it was never satisfactorily explained, why the eight hundred were permitted, not only to traverse the valley of the Isere, but also to cross Mont Iseran, and the still more formidable Mont Cenis, without any well ordered attempt to stop their progress; for by this time the object of their march was well known at Turin. A few skirmishes were all they had to encounter; and it was not before the eighth day of their enterprise, that they first came in conflict with any large body of regular troops.

To avoid the garrison of Susa, it was determined to pro-

itself occurs only twice in Polybius, and I am not aware that it is to be found in any other author. Literally translated, λευκόπετρον means a white rock, but in the 10th book, chapter 27, where the word again occurs, it must be taken in the sense of a naked rock. M. de Luc has given a very animated description of General Melville's passage over this ground, and of his discovery of the Roche Blanche, while he had his Polybius in his hand. It is quite certain that the rock in question is called universally by this name, and that there is a tradition among the inhabitants, that a great battle had been fought at the foot of it. Our guide, who was a very respectable inhabitant of Sillar, talked as a matter of every day conversation of Hannibal, and of his march through the country at the time of the *Saracens*. He assured us also, that he had himself seen and handled very large bones of beasts, which had been taken out of the little stream that flows through the ravine up which the Roman road passed. These bones he said were larger than those of oxen, and when the little stream overflowed, and washed away the soil, some of these bones were sometimes found. He himself made no mention of elephants, and seemed ignorant what the bones were; some of them, he said, had been preserved, but we were unable to discover where."—*See Dissertation on the Passage of Hannibal over the Alps*, p. 56.

N

ceed along the banks of the Doire, or Dora, at the foot of the Col d'Albin, which closes in upon the river, and leaves a pass, which is barely practicable at places even for troops, who have no enemy in front. The narrowest part of the defile is near Salabertrand, where a bridge is thrown over the Dora. At this point the Vaudois found their passage disputed by 2,500 French, who summoned them to surrender at discretion. The superiority of numbers against them was fearfully great, the garrison at Susa were prepared to act against them, if they retreated, and hemmed in by the rocks on one side, and the river on the other, the little band had no alternative but to advance. The charge was sounded; and after a most singular conflict, the combatants became so intermixed, that it was hard to know friends from foes. The heat of the fight was maintained at the entrance of the bridge; and, at the most critical part of the engagement, a heavy mist added to the general confusion. Of this the Vaudois took advantage, they shouted the name of their leader, pressed forward, stood firmly by one another, reformed their ranks, and passed the river, with the loss of only fifteen killed, and twelve wounded. The French were so astonished by the rapidity of this movement, and discouraged by the prodigious slaughter made among their own men, that they did not pursue; and in three days more, after unheard of exertions and fatigue, the Protestant exiles found themselves once again in their own valleys.

The following extract from Arnaud's own account of this extraordinary encounter, will strongly remind the classical reader of some of the passages in *Xenophon's Retreat of the ten thousand Greeks;* and the Christian chieftain and historian will not suffer from the comparison, whether we consider his talents as a commander, or the modesty with which he touches upon his own share in the transactions of the day.

" Having first reconnoitred, to discover if there was any

ambuscade, the Vaudois advanced towards the bridge. Some of the enemy, who were entrenched on the other side, called out, *Qui vive?* to which the Vaudois replied, very sincerely, *Amis;* intending to remain so, if they had been suffered to pass without interruption. But the French did not desire to be friends upon these terms; and shouted, Kill them, kill them. A firing then commenced, which lasted a quarter of an hour, during which more than two thousand shots were discharged; but M. de la Tour (Arnaud spoke of himself under this name) having ordered his men to lie down flat upon their faces, there was but one of them wounded. A Savoyard gentleman, one of the hostages, declared that he had never seen so terrible a firing take such little effect: and what was more remarkable, M. de la Tour, Captain Mondon, of Bobi, and two other refugees, were not only obliged to expose themselves to it, but held in check two companies, who attempted to charge the Vaudois in the rear. Our people, finding themselves thus placed between two fires, saw that no time was to be lost, and that every thing would depend upon the promptitude of the moment. At this critical juncture, a voice exclaimed, 'Courage, the bridge is gained!' In an instant, the men rose up, and rushed forward, some sword in hand, and others with bayonets fixed. The bridge was carried; and with such impetuosity did the assailants advance to force the entrenchments, that they were at the very muzzles of the guns, and cut many of the enemy down, before they could fire at them. Never was so violent a shock. The sabres of the Vaudois shivered the swords of the French in pieces, *et se faisoit craindre au feu qui en sortoit, lorsqu'il donnoit sur les fusils, dont les ennemis ne se servoit plus, que pour parer les coups.*

"The victory was so glorious and decisive, that Monsieur the Marquess de Larrey, who commanded, and was dangerously wounded in the arm, cried out, blaspheming in the usual French style, 'Is it possible that I have lost the battle, and my own honour!' Seeing that there was no remedy, he added, *Sauve qui peut,* and then fled with several wounded officers, to Briançon; but not considering himself safe even there, he was conveyed, in a litter, to Embrun.

"The conflict lasted two hours; and the enemy were so completely routed, that many of them, finding themselves intermixed pell-mell among the Vaudois, hoped to escape, by being mistaken for them; but they were all put to the sword: the field of battle was covered with the dead: several companies were reduced to seven or eight men, without any officers. All the baggage and ammunition fell into the hands of the Vaudois; and when the moon rose that evening, not an enemy was to be seen."

The exiles might have re-established themselves at once among the fastnesses of the valley of San Martino, but these brave men were not satisfied with a secure retreat; they resolved to dispossess the Roman Catholics, and to restore their brethren to their lands and habitations, or to perish in the attempt. The valley of Luzerna was occupied in great force by French and Piemontese troops, a detachment of whom was ordered to seize the passes of the Col di Giuliano, and to prevent Arnaud's approach on that side of the valley. But nothing could check his impetuous attack. The heights were carried with scarcely any loss on the part of the Vaudois; and the enemy were pursued from one summit to another, till they retreated into the vale of Bobbio, and took shelter in that village. Bobbio was, at this time, in the hands of the Papists, to whom the confiscated property of the Protestants had been assigned. It was taken by storm, and pillaged by the exasperated exiles, who, upon this occasion, lost sight of the moderation by which they had hitherto been governed.

After these successes, the gallant patriots took an oath of fidelity to each other, and celebrated divine service in one of their own churches, for the first time since their banishment. The enthusiasm of the moment was irrepressible;

they chaunted the 74th Psalm to the clash of arms; and Henri Arnaud mounting the pulpit with a sword in one hand, and a Bible in the other, preached from the 129th Psalm; and once more declared, in the face of Heaven, that he would never resume his pastoral office in patience and peace, until he should witness the restoration of his brethren to their ancient and rightful settlements. Arnaud and his undaunted band have been blamed for giving, what have been considered, too many proofs of this warlike spirit, and for forgetting what belonged to their evangelical character; but the circumstances of the case, and the necessity of keeping their minds worked up to the highest pitch of martial enthusiasm, might well justify them.

Another memorable anecdote is preserved of the intrepid Arnaud. He was so often in front of his troop, and the first in the fight, that his comrades found themselves obliged to remonstrate with him upon this fearless exposure of his life. "I best know," was his reply, "what the cause and occasion require of me: while I advance, follow me; and, when I fall, revenge me!"

Encouraged by their success at Bobbio, the Vaudois marched against Villaro, where there was a strong garrison, and pressed the enemy so hard, as to force them to retire within the walls of a convent; but while they were investing the convent, a strong reinforcement arrived from Pinerolo, relieved the blockade, and obliged the Protestants to abandon the valley of Luzerna, and to retire among the strong holds of the valley of San Martino. This was on the twenty-second day after their landing at Yvoire; and the detachments, both of French and Piemontese, who were sent in pursuit, carried such devastation with them, that, for a time, all supplies of provisions were cut off; and, for several days, they had nothing to subsist upon but fruit and vegetables. The warfare now assumed a more extraordinary turn than ever. The eight hundred had to maintain their ground against brigades sent against them, by the

French King on one side, and the Duke of Savoy on the other: it was no longer a detached force, but a well appointed army, with which they had now to contend. The rocky and barren district of San Martino afforded them no resources; the defiles that led into the more fertile valleys were in the hands of the enemy; famine, fire, and sword, menaced them in every direction, and yet they refused to surrender. Even the fastnesses, which, in former persecutions, protected their fathers, were untenable for any length of time, from want of provisions. Scarcely had they taken up a position, before they were obliged to abandon it, in search of supplies, and it is an extraordinary fact, that for several weeks they had neither food nor ammunition, but what they took from the enemy.

Under these circumstances, it was impossible that the little band should concentrate its force, or remain together. It was obliged to separate, and to act in detached parties. Engagements were therefore taking place almost every day, in different quarters of the valley, the enemy never knew where they would be attacked next, and at length were so intimidated that a whole company would fly at the sound of a single Waldensian fusil. The Vaudois have always been good marksmen, and, upon this occasion, they exercised their skill most successfully. From the summit of a mountain, from the top of a crag, or, from behind a rock, or tree, a marksman would frequently take his stand, and deliberately fire several shots before he could be dislodged: or, knowing every pass and defile, a few of them would make a detour, and pour in a volley upon a bivouacing party of their adversaries, which never failed of causing dreadful slaughter and consternation.

One great thing in favour of this intrepid force was, that they had no women or children to encumber them, for these were still in Switzerland; there was nothing to check the most perfect freedom of their movements, no strong places to attack or defend, for what were strong places to them?

They could fall upon their enemy as they pleased, and when they pleased, and if too hardly pressed, they had a secure retreat in their mountains, from which they could sally forth, at a more favourable opportunity. They were neither to be beaten by force nor baffled by cunning; the enemy would, as they thought, surround them; every possible means of escape seemed cut off, but their intimate knowledge of the mountains and fearless habits, would enable them to march off by paths, which were either unsuspected by the enemy, or considered as utterly impracticable.

As the winter set in, the hardships and deprivations of these poor men encreased; without any shelter, for several nights together, worn down by constant fatigue, and half famished for want of food, it is wonderful how they supported their courage. We find them one day at Prali, on the second taking Perrero by storm, and the day afterwards surprising Pomaretto. We read of them as being at the last-mentioned place on the 26th day of the month, and on the 29th attacking and defeating 500 of the Piemontese, at Angrogna. A view of the map, with the relative distances, and the nature of the country, will shew the extraordinary exertions, which must have been made, to combine these movements with the general plan of defence and aggression; for though they may have been made by different detachments, yet it was no easy matter to keep up communication with each other, so as to render the operations effective.

It was in the neighbourhood of Prali, Villa-Secca, and Rodoretto, in the centre of the valley of San Martino, and on the rocky banks of the Germanasca torrent, that the principal actions were fought, and the history which Arnaud himself has written of the affair, will give a good idea of the stand which may be made in a mountainous country, against any number of regular troops, when the invaded are determined to keep their weapons in their hands, and are firmly united.

There was one fortress which was deemed quite impregnable, and this the Vaudois succeeded in supplying with provisions. It was that of Balsille, or Baceglia, situated in front of one of the defiles, that conduct into the valley of San Martino, and near the source of a mountain stream, which flows into the Germanasca. Just at the point where the craggy sides of the Guignivert, the highest ridge of this chain of Alps, slope down towards the foot of the Col del Pis, (a lofty mountain, which prevents all access from the side of Pragelato,) a rampart of rock stands at the entrance of the pass, and forms of itself a barrier, which requires but little art to render it secure against any force, that can be brought against it. The highest part of this rock rises as steep as a wall, and has three stages, or terraces, surmounted by a sort of natural platform. Upon this platform stood a tower, and in the sides of the rock which rose above each terrace, caverns were hollowed out to serve for barracks. Three fountains supplied the fortress with water, and there was no approaching it with any probability of success, but from the side, where the stream, which I before mentioned, gushes from the mountain. Numberless assaults were made by the enemy upon this position, but nothing could dislodge the little garrison, to whose charge it was confided. When they were most pressed, a messenger from the fort was despatched to Prali, and a detachment from their comrades made an unexpected attack upon the French, in the rear, while they themselves sallied from their bulwarks, and caused an incredible slaughter.

Upon occasions of necessity, there was no mountain path so dangerous, as to deter these gallant men from attempting it; and, in many cases, they succeeded in transporting themselves across glaciers, and by precipices, which had never before been trodden by the foot of man. When the eight hundred were first obliged to abandon the valley of Luzerna, and to retire into that of San Martino, they had no means of securing their retreat, but by a path so exceedingly difficult, that the whole of their baggage was lost; and so perilous, that men, accustomed to climb the most frightful rocks, trembled when they returned to the spot afterwards, and saw the danger they had escaped. The march was conducted by night, and only one man could proceed along the path at a time. "He who has not seen such paths as these," says Arnaud, in his narrative of this nocturnal retreat, "cannot conceive the danger of them, and will be inclined to consider my account of the march a mere fiction. But it is strictly true; and, I must add, the place is so frightful, that even some of the Vaudois themselves were terror-struck, when they saw, by day-light, the nature of the spot which they had passed in the dark."

The most shocking tale, relating to this extraordinary war, remains to be told. The Vaudois had no means of providing for the safe hold of prisoners. No prisoners, therefore, were to be taken; no quarter was given in the fight, and no mercy shewn afterwards. It was literally a war of extermination. The Duke of Savoy, and the King of France, would make no terms with the rebels, as they termed them; and they, in their turn, had no alternative but to destroy every man, who was found in arms against them. Some circumstances, attending this dreadful system, were particularly lamentable.

The French and Piemontese troops were often thrown into confusion at the first onset, unless their numbers were very superior. They would turn their backs, throw away their arms, and fly by the first road that presented itself. In many cases, their ignorance of the country led them to take the most narrow passes; and, not unfrequently, they strayed into rugged tracks, which proved to have no outlets. The Vaudois pressed upon their rear, the wretched fugitives were crowded together, and a fearful massacre took place, to the regret of those, who, in self-defence, were compelled to such severity. The grief of Arnaud, and of his compatriots, for this cruel necessity of shedding blood, is feelingly expressed in the narrative, and oftentimes mercy was shown to their defenceless persecutors, when it was hardly consistent with a due regard to their own safety. One anecdote will explain the emergency to which these poor people were driven; and will shew that even their adversaries were willing to admit, that they were justifiable in refusing quarter.

Several of the French officers were well known to have expressed their dissatisfaction at the inglorious service, in which they were engaged, and their commiseration for the victims whom they were commanded, by their bigotted sovereign, Louis XIV., to hunt down. Among these was the colonel of a regiment of infantry. After a very sharp action, this colonel was left upon the field of battle, dangerously wounded. He was found by the Vaudois, who knew his humane character, and endeavoured to save his life; but they had no experienced surgeon, and none of those necessaries which the wounded man required. Some sort of communication was made with the French general; and the colonel's own surgeon, and a chest, containing several articles of apparel and provision, were sent for his accommodation. He recovered, and was detained by the Vaudois, and treated with all the tenderness which their situation permitted. Some more officers fell into their hands, and they too were spared.

Unhappily, an attack was shortly afterwards made upon the Protestants, which was partly successful, and they were obliged to retreat with great precipitation. "Should we be surrounded," said the commander of the Vaudois to his French prisoners, "we shall want the men who guard you, and your lives must be sacrificed."—"I acknowledge and submit to the necessity," replied the colonel, "and I shall forgive you my death. My blood will be upon the head of none, but the authors of this horrible war." It happened as they had feared: the Vaudois were hard pressed on all sides. At first they presented the French officers to the volleys of the enemy, under the hope that their countrymen would not continue to fire at their risk: but the combat thickened, the prisoners all fell by the hands of their captors, and not till then could the exiles succeed, in cutting their way through the enemy's ranks [c].

Such was the nature of the conflict between the eight hundred, and the allied forces of France and Savoy. It was a murderous system of warfare, in which the regular troops suffered in proportion of twenty to one, at the least; for they never could succeed in alluring the mountaineers from their fastnesses, or in bringing them to action, except where the nature of the ground made up for the inferiority of numbers. The contest continued through the whole of the winter, and until April in the following year, 1690; and was then concluded in favour of the Vaudois, by one of those strange vicissitudes [d] in the affairs of kingdoms, which sometimes produce the most unexpected results.

A rupture took place between Louis XIV. and Victor Amadeus: each was anxious to conciliate the Vaudois, and to secure the services of the gallant band, who had maintained their ground so manfully in the valley of San Martino, and great offers were made by both parties. Always loyal, the Protestants turned a deaf ear to every proposal, but that which came from their own sovereign: a treaty

[c] It will be a subject of congratulation to the friends of the Waldensian cause to know, that Henri Arnaud's History of this singular conflict will shortly appear, under an English form, in a translation by H. D. Acland, Esq. the Author of the "History and present Condition of the Vaudois."—*Note to Third Edition.*

[d] Allix, in his Remarks upon the Ecclesiastical History of the ancient Churches of Piemont, professes to despair of their restoration. He wrote in the reign of King William III. and dedicated his work to that prince. "It is very true," says he, "that the wretched remains of these ancient churches appear too contemptible to attract the eyes of the princes of the earth towards them, their present desolation seeming so universal, that the world looks upon them no otherwise than irrecoverably lost, and finally destroyed."

was effected, a general amnesty was proclaimed, the exiles and their families were invited to return home, and an order published, that their lands and houses should be immediately restored, and their churches reopened for Protestant worship.

The quaint style in which Boyer's[e] translator relates the termination of the war, and his reflections upon the subject, will not be considered uninteresting. "The Duke of Savoy being forced to break with France, by reason of the hardships that were imposed upon him, this rupture was the cause of the liberty and deliverance of the Vaudois: for having understood that the king of France did solicit them to embrace his part, with offers of re-establishing them in the valleys, and giving them liberty of conscience, with free and public exercise of their religion, which would have been very prejudicial to his interest; for instead of one enemy, he would have had two upon his back, and would have been deprived of the succours that the Protestant princes promised the Vaudois, and of the considerable service that they might do him, in keeping the passes, and in hindering the communication of the troops that were in the Delphinate, with the army, commanded by Monsieur Catinat; this prince resolved to draw them to his own party. And, to this effect, he set at liberty all the Vaudois that were in prison, as well ministers as others: he sent an act of oblivion to all those that were in arms in the valleys; and gave to those that were in foreign countries, leave to come home, with necessary passports, with orders to all to turn their arms against the French, whom they must look upon as their true persecutors, and the cause of all their miseries[f].

"He made be brought before him all those that were

[e] Boyer's and Arnaud's accounts were published soon after the events took place and were never contradicted.

[f] See page 56.

prisoners at Turin, and told them, that he was touched with a deep sense of their miseries; and commanded them in his presence, to be clothed, and to be furnished with all things necessary. He excused himself that he had handled them so roughly; and cast all upon the King of France, as the true author of all that had befallen them: and because the number of the Vaudois was so much diminished, that there were scarce two thousand left, after the last persecution, the Duke of Savoy made proclamation, that all those Protestants that were fled out of France, that would come, and dwell in the valleys, and join themselves with the Vaudois, might do it, and be safe under his protection, and have necessary passports. He ordered likewise that at their entrance into Savoy, both the Vaudois and the French should be furnished with arms, and all things necessary for to pass into the valleys, which was punctually put into execution.

"The return of the Vaudois into their country, their entrance into their valleys, and their subsisting there for eight months, are so many wonders and miracles. Is it not a miracle, that eight or nine hundred should undertake to cross an enemy's country of fourteen or fifteen days journey, where they must climb up high mountains, force divers strait passes, where an hundred might not only stop, but beat three thousand? And, that which is most astonishing is, that these passes were guarded with great numbers, and more expert soldiers than the Vaudois: they notwithstanding forced all those passes with their swords in their hands, and routed them that guarded them, killing a great number in gaining them, with very little loss on their side.

"It is likewise another miracle, that they got into the valleys, the entrances being so difficult, being peopled with Roman Catholics, who might have hindered their entrance, being more innumber than they; or at least they might have possessed themselves of the most advantageous posts, which were in the mountains, and defend themselves easily, till the succours from France and Savoy, which were in readiness, could come and second them; but a dreadful fright from God fell upon them, so that they had no courage nor conduct to defend themselves against the Vaudois, who, without any trouble or resistance, chased them out of the valleys.

"Is it not likewise a great miracle, that a handful of people, without any commanders experienced in warlike affairs, should subsist eight months in the valleys, and fight nine or ten battles against the army of France and Savoy, who were sometimes twenty, but oftener thirty against one, without being able to drive them out of their fastnesses, having killed more than two thousand of their enemies? So many happy successes make it clear the God of battles inspired them with the generous courage of returning into their own country, to kindle again the candle of his word, that the emissaries of Satan had extinguished there, that he marched before them, and fought for them, without which it had been impossible to have forced so many difficult passes, and gained such signal victories.

"The conduct of God in the re-establishment of the Vaudois is admirable, and makes it evident that his divine Providence has judgment and ways incomprehensible, surpassing all human understanding. The King of France in the year 1686, pushed on the Duke of Savoy to compel the Vaudois to forsake their religion, and to take the same measures he had taken against the Protestants of France: they joined their arms together to force them, and to compass their design, they violated not only the treaty made with the predecessors of the duke, but also treaties, oaths, and promises made by their generals, took them prisoners, killed and massacred them, violated their wives and daughters, killed their little children, and made use of all sorts of cruelty against these innocent people, after they had laid down their arms: and in the year 1690 God sent a spirit of division between the King of France and the Duke of Savoy, insomuch that they strove who should first gain the Vaudois to their party, and by this division the Duke of Savoy was forced to re-establish the Vaudois in their rights and privileges, and to set all at liberty that had been imprisoned, and to recal all those that were dispersed in foreign countries. And so the king of France, who had been the principal cause of their ruin, became, against his will, the cause of their re-establishment, by forcing the Duke of Savoy to join with the allies: this shews that God mocks and derides the designs and councils of princes when they are levelled against Jesus Christ and his church [g]."

[g] See Boyer's History of the Vaudois, p. 226.

CHAPTER IX.

Rora—Its secluded situation—Retrospect—Gratitude of Victor Amadeus II.—Exploits of Gianavello—Treachery of the Marquess di Pianezza—Heroic defence of Rora—Massacre at Rora—Last achievements of Gianavello—Sufferings of Giovanni Pallias, Paoli Clementi, and Gianavello's sister—Affecting tale—Traits of character—Juvenile disinterestedness—Comparative mendicity in Protestant and Catholic countries—Blasphemy unknown among the Vaudois—Temperate and manly remonstrance.

It was our intention to have crossed the Pelice from Bobbio, and to have found our way over the mountains to Rora, or Rorata, but we were assured that it was quite impracticable in consequence of the late fall of snow. The parish, or communautè of Rora, is the smallest of the Protestant parishes; its population is about seven hundred. It is also situated farther to the south than any of the rest, and may be said to stand almost entirely separated from the other villages of the Vaudois. The craggy tops of the lofty Sea Bianca seem to rise just above it, and Mount Viso itself is distinguished among the towering summits, at the basements of which the little village is built. Mount Friolant separates it from the valley of the Po, and its hamlets are picturesquely suspended over the torrent of Luzerna, which takes its rise from that mountain. Locked up, as it is, in a very narrow valley, its soil is for the most part rocky and unproductive: but in the intervals between the rocks it is fertile, and, like the other districts of the Vaudois, extremely well cultivated. Prodigious chesnut-trees decorate the slopes of the mountains, and for eight or ten weeks in the summer time, the rich pasturages of the higher regions tempt the inhabitants to leave their dwellings in the vale, and to drive their cattle thither.

Unfortunately for Rora, its sequestered situation rendered it an easy prey in the days of persecution, and nearly the whole population have been more than once put to the sword, before their brethren on the north of the Pelice could send them any succours. But Rora, as well as Bobbio and Angrogna, has had its heroes, and its fastnesses have been the secure retreat not only of persecuted Protestants, but also of royal fugitives, when they could find none so loyal and faithful as their Vaudois subjects. The hiding-places of Victor Amadeus are still shewn to the tourist, and the name of Durand will be as little forgotten as the gratitude of his sovereign, in return for the protection which he had afforded. "I grant you," said the Duke of Savoy, "I grant you and your family, for ever, the privilege of using your garden as a burying-ground!!!"

The exploits of Gianavello[h], and his comrades, during the dreadful persecution of 1655, did not fall short of those of Henri Arnaud, and his band of eight hundred, although they were not crowned with equal success in the end. After the bloody havoc that was made by the Marquess di Pianezza[i], at San Giovanni, La Torre, and Villaro, the Count Christophel resolved to display similar devotion to his prince, by doing something at Rora, which should rival those achievements; he therefore sent three hundred soldiers from Villaro, to surprize Rora, and pillage the houses. The inhabitants were too well aware of what had been going on, on the other side of the Pelice, not to be on their guard, and their forces were divided in such a manner, as to watch all the approaches from the quarters occupied by the enemy.

Christophel's detachment had crossed the river, and were espied by Gianavello, just as they were ascending the little

[h] See distinguished mention of this hero in the order of council, referred to in p. 88.

[i] See Appendix, No. 4.

hill of Rumer, behind which he was posted, with seven or eight capital marksmen. Long before the troops were expecting to be received by an armed force, and even before they deemed it requisite to march in any regular order, they were saluted with a rapid fire of musquetry from various directions, for Gianavello had disposed of his men so judiciously, in ambuscade, that it did not seem to come from one point only, but from the right and left, as well as the front. The enemy were thrown into confusion in an instant, and fled amain to Villaro: in their way back they had to traverse a wood, which lies between the mountains and the Pelice. Gianavello and his men pursued, but in such a manner as to keep out of sight, and being concealed, as they advanced, by the trees and shrubs, poured in a murderous fire upon the fugitives.

The commander of the royal army, Di Pianezza, affected to disclaim the whole proceeding, and as Rora had hitherto made no resistance to the soldiers, who were over-running the country, he declared that the three hundred had acted without his orders, and that Rora should have no occasion to fear any thing for the future. But upon the principle that no faith is to be kept with heretics, five hundred men were despatched the next day, to accomplish what the other detachment had failed in doing. Gianavello was again fortunate in his choice of a place, where he remained in ambush with eleven musqueteers, and six slingers, and this small force was sufficient to defeat an enemy, who were already half conquered by their own terrors. The tale of the previous day had filled their minds with a dread, which made them feel more like victims hurried to slaughter, than soldiers marching to battle. The first volley put them to flight, and Rora was once more delivered.

A third enterprise, of the same sort, was projected, but upon this occasion, Gianavello, instead of waiting for the attack, put himself at the head of his little band, and fell upon the vanguard of the Roman Catholics, at Ramasiero. The result of this bold exploit was the third retreat of the invaders to Villaro, and the capture of all their cattle and baggage.

The Marquess di Pianezza now threw off the mask, and under pretence that the people of Rora had been the aggressors, declared that he would take vengeance for the slaughter of his men, and openly made preparations for the destruction of this devoted village. A simultaneous attack was ordered to be made with all the royal forces from Cavour, Bagnol, Barges, Bubbiana, Luzerna, and Villaro. By some accident the orders were misunderstood, and one troop only, that from Bagnol, under the command of an officer named Mario, advanced to the assault. Previous to the attack, these men, among whom were a great many Irish, had dispersed themselves in quest of plunder, and when they were marching to Rora, their ranks were in such disorder, and they were so encumbered by their booty, that it was no difficult matter to put them to the rout. They were pursued as far as a rock called Peyro Capello, which overhangs the torrent, and so precipitate was their flight, that instead of taking the right path, they found themselves cut off from every hope of escape, except by letting themselves down from the precipice into the water. This they endeavoured to effect by tying cords to the nearest shrubs; but the greatest part of them were either drowned in the torrent, or dashed to pieces by falling from the rock. Sixty-five men perished in the action and in the flight, and to add to the success of the Protestants, as they were returning from the pursuit of the troops from Bagnol, they fell in with another party, who were advancing from Villaro, and gained a second victory on the same day.

This, however, was the last day of triumph for the intrepid inhabitants of Rora. Pianezza put his whole army in motion soon afterwards, and while Gianavello and his brave comrades were nobly defending a pass in the mountains, against one of the enemy's detachment, the main body marched against the village, and found no difficulty in making themselves master of it. Men, women, and children, were indiscriminately put to the sword, the few who were not massacred were carried prisoners to Turin, and not a Protestant was left in Rora to tell the tale of its calamities.

The heroic Gianavello, when he found that his arm could no longer be raised in defence of his native hamlet, effected his retreat to the mountains of Angrogna, where, with a few gallant followers, he long continued to be the terror of his persecutors. Upon one occasion he fell upon a convoy, as they were entering the fort of Mirabouc, and did terrible execution; upon another, he carried off a thousand head of cattle from Crusol, and soon after destroyed the bridge of Luzerna. His vigilance was incessant, his courage undaunted, and at last he died, as a brave man should die, with his sword in his hand, and for the welfare of his country. A noble answer is recorded of this brave man, when Pianezza threatened to burn his wife and children, unless he should surrender himself, and change his religion. "There is no torment so violent, nor any death so cruel, which I would not prefer to the abjuration of my religion, and all the threats of the Marquess do but fortify my faith. He has my wife and children in his power, but he can do no more than kill their bodies. As to their souls, I commend them and my own to the protection of God, whose servant I am, and will remain, to the last hour of my life."

The little community of Rora not only enjoyed the honourable distinction of producing heroes in the field, who avenged her injuries, but of exhibiting her martyrs, whose undaunted resolution, in the hour of death, extorted expressions of admiration, even from their persecutors. The Marquess di Pianezza, who signalized himself at the executions, as much as at the massacres of the Vaudois, made use of all his rhetoric, upon one occasion, to persuade a poor peasant, of the name of Giovanni Pallias, to embrace the Roman Catholic faith. He ordered him to be placed upon the ladder of a gallows, and there proposed tempting rewards, or immediate death. " I am proud," said the resigned victim, " to be accounted worthy to suffer for the cross of Christ." He was urged to remember his wife and little ones. " I do remember them, and I pray God that my children may follow their father's steps, and die like myself," was his answer, which so exasperated the monks, and the noble commander, who presided at the execution, that they took upon themselves the hangman's office, and helped to turn the victim off the ladder.

Another man, called Paolo Clementi, was brought to the same place, and shewn the body of Pallias, suspended from the gallows. The sight could not move him. " They may kill my body," said he, " but they can do no harm to the soul of a true believer."

Gianavello's sister, Marguerita, the wife of Giuseppe Garniero, possessed a spirit worthy of her undaunted brother. When Rora was attacked, as she was exhorting her husband to assist in defending the place to the last, she received a shot in her bosom. " Do not be shaken by this," she exclaimed to her husband, " but endure the cross with patience, and hold out to the end." Such courage might almost ennoble guilt, but it hallows the victim of persecution.

A most affecting tale was told me of a young girl, I forget whether of this village or of another, which proves that the fine feelings, and exemplary virtue, of the Vaudois females, are by no means on the decline. She was more beautiful than the generality of mountaineers, but equally simple and unsuspecting. Her brother had been a soldier, and served in several of the campaigns of Napoleon. After his return to the valleys of his native province, he received a visit from a comrade in arms, who was soon attracted by the charms of his lovely sister. His attentions were received with pleasure; he secured the affections of the innocent girl, and betrayed them. The base seducer abandoned the object of his perfidy, and she never lifted up her head afterwards.

How he succeeded was never perfectly understood; for the poor victim was scarcely known to open her lips, when she found herself deserted; and never accused her betrayer. A deviation from the strictest laws of modesty, both in the married and unmarried women of the Protestant valleys, is an event so extremely rare, that it is scarcely credited when it does happen; and, in this case, all were willing to exculpate her; but she could not forgive herself. At church, she stood alone during the whole service, and never approached any of the rest of the congregation. When the sacrament was administered, she never went up to the table, till every one else had participated. It was clear, that she looked upon her offence in so heinous a light, as to feel unwilling to contaminate others by her presence. Within less than a year she died, penitent and broken-hearted; and her last request was, that her remains might be deposited in some retired corner of the church-yard, where they might not lie contiguous to, or pollute the ashes of those, who had gone down to the grave without dishonour.

Tales such as these whiled away our time during our mountain walks, or in the long evenings, which we employed in collecting all the information we could gather from our Vaudois friends, illustrative of the character, manners, and morals, of this primitive race. They live together in such undisturbed harmony, that, during the whole time I passed in their valleys, I observed no symptoms whatever of broils or quarrels. I heard no angry disputes, and saw no rudeness among the children, or lower sorts of the population; but, on the contrary, witnessed two or three instances of forbearance, and disinterestedness, which were uncommonly gratifying. At Pomaretto there was a group of very poor-looking children, who were evidently astonished at the sight of strangers, but there was no rudeness mixed with their wonder, nor did they attempt to follow us. We went up to them, with the intention of dividing some money among the little party. Instead of shewing eagerness, or impatience to share the gift, they all drew back, seeming to refuse what we proffered; and when we pressed it upon them, they pointed out one or two, who, they said, were in greatest want of assistance.

At Angrogna, a small piece of silver was presented to a girl, who was instructing her younger brothers and sisters in the Catechism: it was a long time before she could be persuaded to take it, and not till her father gave her to understand, that she ought not to decline its acceptance.

We were not once importuned by beggars in the Waldensian district. Not only here, but in Switzerland and Germany, we observed, very particularly, that mendicity was scarcely seen in any of the Protestant towns and villages, while it prevailed in the Roman Catholic. The truth of this was so glaring, that, in passing from one canton, or state, to another, we used to know that we had arrived in a Roman Catholic community, from the number of beggars, by whom we were sure to be infested. In the canton of Ury, which is Popish, we communicated our observations to our guide; he acknowledged their justice, but attributed the fact to the Protestant cantons being richer than those of the Roman Catholic. The former, he added, were generally better situated for commerce than the latter. Even if this be true in general, it cannot hold good in regard to the Vaudois, who inhabit the least fertile region in Piemont, and are grievously oppressed by excessive taxes, and unjust restrictions, that disqualify them for any but pastoral occupations.

In speaking of the manners and morals of the Vaudois, I must not omit to mention, that blasphemy, and profane swearing, are held in such abhorrence, as to be the subject of especial punishment: the laws amongst themselves are extremely rigid in this respect; but the execution of them is so seldom called for, that a minister who had been twenty-five years pastor of a parish, declared that he had never known a single example of any of his own flock having been convicted of blasphemy.

Out of a great mass of petitions and remonstrances, which the persecuted Vaudois have addressed to their sovereigns, from time to time, expostulating with them on their cruelty, and imploring their clemency, I have selected the following, to shew with what manly firmness, tempered with mildness, and Christian meekness, they used to touch upon the subject of their wrongs.

"[k] A supplication of the poor Waldenses, to the most serene, and most high prince, Philibert Emanuel, Duke of Savoy, Prince of Piemont, our most gracious lord.

"Festus, governor of Judea, being required by the chief priests and elders of the people, to put to death the Apostle Paul, answered no less wisely than justly, that the Romans were not wont to put any to death, before they had brought his accusers face to face, and given him time to answer for himself. We are not ignorant, most gracious prince, that many accusations are laid against us, and that many calumnies are cast upon us, to make us objects of abomination to all the Christians, and monarchs in the Christian world. But if the Roman people, though Pagans, were so equitable, as not to condemn any man before they knew and understood his reasons; and if the law condemns no man, (as it is testified by Nicodemus, John vii.) before he hath been heard, and before it is known what he hath done, the matter now in question being of so great concernment, namely, the glory of the most high God, and the salvation of so many souls, we do implore your clemency, most gracious prince, that you will be pleased to lend a willing ear to your poor subjects, in so just and righteous a cause.

"First, we do protest, before the almighty, and all-just God, before whose tribunal we must all one day appear, that we intend to live and die in the holy faith, piety, and religion of our Lord Jesus Christ; and that we do abhor all heresies, that have been, and are condemned, by the word of God.

[k] Morland, p. 227.

"We do embrace the most holy doctrine of the Prophets and Apostles, as likewise of the Nicene and Athanasian Creeds: we subscribe to the four councils, and to all the ancient fathers, in all such things as are not repugnant to the analogy of faith.

"We do most willingly yield obedience to our superiors; we ever endeavour to live peaceably with our neighbours: we have wronged no man, though provoked; nor do we fear that any can, with reason, complain against us.

"Finally, we never were obstinate in our opinions; but rather tractable, and always ready to receive all holy and pious admonitions, as appears by our confessions of faith.

"And we are so far from refusing a discussion, or rather a free council, wherein all things may be established by the word of God, that we rather desire the same with all our hearts.

"We likewise beseech your highness to consider, that this religion we profess, is not ours only, nor hath it been invented by man of late years, as it is falsely reported; but it is the religion of our fathers, grandfathers, and great grandfathers, and other yet more ancient predecessors of ours, and of the blessed martyrs, confessors, prophets, and apostles; and if any can prove the contrary, we are ready to subscribe, and yield thereunto. The word of God shall not perish, but remain for ever; therefore, if our religion be the true word of God, as we are persuaded, and not the invention of men, no human force shall be able to extinguish the same.

"Your highness knows, that this very same religion hath, for many ages past, been most grievously persecuted in all places; but so far from being abolished, and rooted out thereby, that it hath rather increased daily, which is a certain argument, that this work and counsel is not the work and counsel of men, but of God, and therefore cannot be destroyed by any violence. Therefore, we beseech your most serene highness to consider, what it is to undertake any thing against God, that so you may not embue your hands in innocent blood! Jesus is our Saviour: we will religiously obey all your highness' edicts, as far as conscience will permit; but when conscience says nay, your highness knows, we must rather obey God than man: we unfeignedly confess, that we ought to give Cæsar, that which belongs to Cæsar, provided we give also to God, what is due to him.

"There want not those, who will endeavour to incite the generous mind and courage of your highness, to persecute our religion by force of arms. But, O magnanimous prince, you may easily conjecture to what end they do it, that it is not out of zeal to God's glory, but rather to preserve their own worldly dignities, pomp and riches; wherefore, we beseech your highness, not to regard, or countenance, their sayings.

"The Turks, Jews, Saracens, and other nations, though never so barbarous, are suffered to enjoy their own religion, and are constrained by no man, to change their manner of living and worship: and we, who serve, and worship in faith the true and almighty God, and one true and only sovereign, the Lord Jesus, and confessing one God, and one baptism, shall not we be suffered to enjoy the same privileges?

"We humbly implore your highness' goodness, and that for our only Lord and Saviour Jesus Christ's sake, to allow unto us, your most humble subjects, the most holy Gospel of the Lord our God, in its purity; and that we may not be forced to do things against our consciences; for which we shall, with all our hearts, beseech our almighty, and all good God, to preserve your highness in prosperity."

This pathetic and strong appeal had no effect. Four hundred men surprised the first Vaudois village of the valley of Luzerna, San Giovanni, in the night; and were followed by a regular army, who dealt most mercilessly with the unhappy Protestants.

CHAPTER X.

Evening at the pastor's house—M. Bert—Liturgy of the Vaudois —Interment of the dead—Roman Catholic obsequies—Funeral ceremony at Geneva—English burial service—Synod of Waldensian church—Solemnities of the holy Sacrament—Parochial schools—Names of Vaudois villages—Village pastor's—Population—Traits of character—Anecdote—Jean Leger's work—Retrospect—The attestation of Du Petit Bourg—Remonstrance of foreign states—Oliver Cromwell—His protection of the Vaudois—Recommends a general collection in England—Writes letters to the Protestant powers, in behalf of the Vaudois —Expostulates with the King of France—Louis the Fourteenth —Cromwell sends an envoy to Turin—Morland's bold and memorable speech to the Duke of Savoy—Shameful treaty of Pinerolo—Its baneful effects—Protest of Swiss Ambassador—Cromwell's spirited conduct—Charles the Second—His letter of intercession to the Duke of Savoy—Compact of blood—Milton's ode on this subject.

Upon our return to La Torre, from Villaro and Bobbio, we found an invitation from one of the principal proprietors of this communauté, to join a young party at his house, which had been kindly formed, in compliment to the strangers. M. Bert had also been several times at the little inn, during our absence, to invite us to sup with him. The evening had closed in before we got back; and the good pastor, supposing we should have some difficulty in finding our way in the dark, came himself with a lanthorn to escort us. The distance to his house was more than half a mile from our quarters.

My companions wished to go early to the dance, and did not accompany me to M. Bert's. They lost a most interesting conversation. The pastor of La Torre, learned as he is, has not, perhaps, all the deep erudition, and lively talent which distinguished the late moderator, Peyrani; nor were his observations so piquant; but there is a seriousness in his manner, an impressive earnestness in his tone, and such an air and aspect of Christian mildness in his general deportment, that it is impossible not to venerate him. He takes an intense interest in the concerns of his sacred profession; his whole soul is with the holy cause, which he supports by his life and conversation; and no topics of discourse appear so pleasing to him, as those which relate to the true Christian character of his people. M. Bert is engaged in a history of the Vaudois, which will be a most valuable production; and it is earnestly to be hoped, that the restrictions upon the press, and the jealousy, with which every literary work, that proceeds from a Protestant, is regarded by the Sardinian government, will not shackle his performance.

If ever sovereign had a faithful and loyal subject, the King of Sardinia has such in M. Bert. His sentiments upon the subject of loyalty, are founded upon those principles of obedience and expediency, which his religion inculcates; and in all our conversations, not a word dropped from his lips, which could be construed in a sense injurious to the constituted authorities of his country. The same tribute may justly be paid to the Vertus, and to every other Vaudois with whom I conversed. These amiable people may suffer wrongs, and feel them deeply; but they have too much Christian spirit, or they are too discreet, to express themselves in any manner, that the ingenuity of the most ill-natured, or suspicious, could represent to their disadvantage [1].

[1] Since my excursion to the valleys, the Reverend B. Bridge, Fellow of St. Peter's College, Cambridge, has visited them, and has printed a brief narrative of

The three or four hours, which I spent with M. Bert, were passed in discussing matters connected with the church

his visit. I am proud to find, that this gentleman has borne favourable testimony to the accuracy of my statements, and the following extract from his interesting pages will place the character of the Vaudois, and of their present excellent moderator, M. Bert, in the very highest point of view.

"I travelled," says Mr. Bridge, "with M. Bert from Turin to La Tour, and spent three or four days with him and his family. During my stay our conversation turned chiefly upon the present state of the Vaudois population, and the relation in which they stand to the Sardinian government. M. Bert often directed my attention to the mountainous and confined situation of the district which they inhabit: a situation which precludes them from all possibility of bettering their condition by making any great progress or improvement in agriculture, manufactures, or commerce. He occasionally adverted to the restrictions under which they laboured, and to the privileges of which they were debarred by the Sardinian government; but I think it right to state, that upon every occasion of this kind, his observations were always accompanied by expressions of pious resignation to the dispensations of Providence, and of thankfulness for the inestimable blessing enjoyed by the Vaudois, in the free and unrestrained exercise of the religion of their ancestors.

"I had but few opportunities of making any observations upon the present state of religion among the Vaudois, except such as occurred to me during my short residence in M. Bert's family, and in a few transient visits to his more immediate friends and relations. But I think I ought not to omit to mention that I attended M. Bert in the public service of his Church, in the examination of his Catechumens, and in his family devotions; and that upon all these occasions, the same spirit of rational piety, the same cheerfulness, the same calmness and resignation, were uniformly displayed in the conduct and manner both of himself and his hearers." P. 3—5.

"In common conversation the Vaudois display a remarkable cheerfulness, and a particular abstinence from querulousness. Of this I had a very striking instance in M. Bert and his friends. M. Bert himself is a person of great natural quickness; M. Meille, the pastor of the adjoining parish of St. Jean, is a person of rather a solemn turn of mind; with these two gentlemen I had long and close conversations, and I had occasional intercourse with two or three other of M. Bert's friends. On all these occasions frequent opportunities were given them, if they had been so disposed, of inveighing against the Sardinian government; but during the whole of our communications not a syllable to this effect ever escaped them. In the course of our conversation some of them, (but more especially M. Meille,) occasionally shewed great anxiety of mind both in countenance and manner: but they always gave vent to their feelings by saying, '*We will wait with patience the appointed time,*' or by using words to that effect. I did not particularly inquire into the meaning of this expression, but I have reason to think that they sometimes alluded to the expected charities from Eng-

history of the Vaudois, and the pecuniary condition of the clergy. It grieved me to find that an unsuccessful appeal had been made to England on the subject of the royal pension, which was first withdrawn in the year 1797[m], and that the memorial, signed by himself and other pastors, had produced no favourable result. But the fears, which this excellent man mildly expressed, lest the humble church of the valleys, had been overlooked by the English hierarchy, were ungrounded, for the unwearied attempts of the Society for promoting Christian Knowledge, and the Society for the Propagation of the Gospel, to obtain the restoration of the pension, have been warmly supported from time to time by the episcopal bench. The anxiety which the Bishop of London, in particular, has displayed upon this subject, and his repeated applications to government, entitle him to the warmest gratitude of the Vaudois. His lordship is still their advocate with his Majesty's Ministers, and it is impossible, that the representations from so high a quarter can fail of ultimate success.

M. Bert expressed himself as explicitly as M. Peyrani on the advantages, which he conceived would result, if the ancient discipline of the Waldensian church could be restored, in its pure episcopal form, but he saw no chance of this, unless they could be enabled to educate their youth at home[n]. The restoration of the college of Angrogna offers the only probable means, of promoting a return to their original uniformity of ecclesiastical practice and ritual. At present, either the Liturgy of Geneva, or Neufchatel, is

land, and sometimes to the part which the Waldenses (and their descendants, the Vaudois) have borne, and which *they still expect them to bear*, in the grand scheme for the propagation of true Christianity among mankind." P. 15.

Note to Second Edition.

[m] See Postscript to Second Edition.

[n] "Ubi enim aut jucundius morarentur quam in patria, aut jucundius continerentur quam sub oculis parentum? aut minore sumptu quam domi?" *Plinius.* Lib. iv. Epist. 13.

read in the churches, according to the discretion of the pastor, but that of Geneva, which is a beautiful production°, is principally followed. It is certain that the ancient Vaudois had a Liturgy of their own, and that it was in use in the sixteenth century, for in a confession of faith, dated 1535, the thirteenth article, speaking of the Lord's Supper, has this expression, " Les terms de *nôtre Liturgie,*" &c. The rituals which are adopted, in conformity to their intercourse with Switzerland, have a service for the communion, and different forms for certain days and seasons. There is also a marriage service, and a baptismal service, but no burial service, unless it be one short prayer. For many years the Protestants of Piemont were not permitted to bury their own dead, or to follow as mourners, but now that this law is remitted, and that *six* of the family, or friends, are graciously allowed, by the government, to follow their friends to the grave, it is extraordinary that they should adhere to the cold and heartless customs of the Swiss, instead of making one of the most awful duties as impressive, as it is melancholy.

England seems to be the only country, where the remains of the dead are consigned to their last home with becoming decency and feeling. In Popish countries upon the Continent, those who loved the deceased most dearly in life, are the first to abandon his remains. They confide to strangers the entire care of the funeral, and hired followers, or confraternities, who take upon themselves this duty, are left to see it discharged. The consequence is, that nothing can be more thoroughly disgusting than a funeral ceremony. At first the body is fantastically decorated and dressed, and placed upon a gorgeous bier; in this state it is borne through the streets, with the head nodding to the motion of the bearers, in hideous inanity. A frightful-looking procession of men, covered from head to foot by a dress worn only upon

° See Appendix, No. 6.

these occasions, accompanies the bier. Each member of the fraternity, who looks more like a demon, guarding his prey, than a human mourner over the dead, walks with a torch, or taper, in his hand, with a peaked cap upon his head, covering his whole face, and provided with two eye-holes, that he may see his way. A few priests march before, yelling out a death-chaunt with indifference that is even more offensive than its discord. The procession arrives at the place of burial; which in cities, is generally a vault within the church, while without the walls is a succession of caverns, each of which is appropriated to its particular day of the year; and in this vault or cavern the dead are deposited, not with decorum and tenderness, but in a way that shews all the previous ceremonies of decoration and attendance, to have been but mockery. The body is cast naked into the charnel-house, and tumbled among the deceased of the day with total disregard to decency. I looked into one of these horrible caverns at Naples, and saw men, women, and children, young and old, heaped together, and upon one another, in one shocking mass of corruption.

In the Protestant cantons of Switzerland the funeral obsequies are performed with becoming solemnity, but are not concluded with that affecting religious service, which is required to dismiss the mourners in comfort and resignation. I followed a corpse to its grave, at Geneva. It was that of a soldier. About one hundred of his companions in arms, fifty of the principal townsmen, and about two hundred of the working orders formed the procession. The brothers and children of the deceased, and a few others of his family, walked next to the coffin, with their heads bare. In serious and silent array the party arrived at the grave, which was about three feet deep; the coffin was lowered into it, and immediately covered with earth. No prayer commended the soul of the dead to mercy, or spoke comfort and consolation to the living. Their thoughts seemed to sink deep into the earth, with the coffin of their relation, and they stood by, weeping bitterly, while the callous sexton heaped in the soil, till the barrier was complete that divided the friends from the friend, the brothers from the brother, and the children from their parent. But the example of the English has not been lost upon the people of Lausanne, and this cold, this heartless separation of life from death, is likely to be superseded by a form more suited to human frailty, and certainly more consonant with religion.

When poor Kemble was buried, last year, at Lausanne, most of the respectable inhabitants attended his funeral; and they were so gratified and moved, by the fine burial-service of the English Liturgy, and by the touching solemnity with which it was performed, that a general desire was expressed of adopting some ritual in conformity to it. The clergy were particularly affected, and it is believed that a form will soon be composed, and authorised by the synod.

Another strong testimony to the beauty and impressiveness of this part of our Liturgy was given by a free-thinker, who took upon himself to amend our Book of Common Prayer. He proceeded through the whole with his alterations and erasements, until he came to the Burial-Service, and *this* he declared to be so noble a composition, that he would not attempt to improve it.

M. Bert expressed himself strongly in admiration of this part of our Liturgy, which, if it be adopted at Lausanne, will most probably find its way into the three valleys.

The general affairs of the Waldensian church are regulated by a synod, which cannot be held but with consent of the government, and consists of the thirteen pastors, and one elder from each parish. The moderator, who presides at the synod, and is the primate of the church, is elected by this venerable assembly, but he must be formally approved by the king, before he can enter upon his office [o]. It is the

[o] The author has learnt that this statement is not exactly correct. The government does not interfere in any of the ecclesiastical transactions of the synod,

synod also, which appoints a pastor to a vacant charge. The parish, which has lost its minister, nominates two or three candidates, and the general assembly chuses the most worthy.

It was affecting to hear the amiable pastor [p] of La Torre explain the solemnities, which precede and accompany the administration of the Holy Sacrament. Young people consider their first celebration of this sacred rite as an epoch in their lives, and the preparations beforehand are long, and of the most serious nature. There is a great number of Protestant families at Turin, and it frequently happens, that young persons of each sex are sent from the capital to the most retired villages among the mountains, that they may have the full benefit of a parochial minister's instruction, and may have their minds effectually impressed with the awful responsibility, which they are about to take upon themselves. There is even a formulary, or catechism, in

nor in the election of the moderator. It is true that the intendant of the province is present at the sittings of the synod: but he has no voice there, and attends merely to see that nothing passes in the synod contrary to law.—*Note to Second Edition.*

p Extract of a letter from a gentleman travelling in Italy, dated from the Valleys, 16th, 17th, and 18th Nov. 1825.—" When we arrived at *La Tour*, Madame Bert told us her husband was just then engaged in his *examin de quartier*. We went to meet him, and found him at a short distance from his house. He was surrounded by his flock. M. Bert received us with much kindness, and we begged him not to interrupt the course of business. M. Bert divides his flock into ten districts, each containing several families, consisting of all ages. The intention of this annual visitation is to ascertain the religious and moral state of each parish, and to make a general report to the assembly of the Clergy. During the short time we remained, M. Bert asked his people if any of them were without a Bible, or if any wished for an explanation of any particular passages of Scripture, which they had not clearly understood. After having addressed himself to almost every one in particular, he concluded by a most affectionate exhortation and a solemn prayer. A psalm was then sung, and we all then retired. We paid a visit to the Hospital, the situation of which pleased us much."

I am delighted at having this opportunity of giving an additional testimony to the merits of M. Bert, and of the Waldensian Pastors in general.—*Note to Third Edition.*

which they are expected to be perfect, before they are admitted to the Lord's table. For this purpose they attend the minister at first privately, and afterwards appear collectively, at church, a few days before the Sacrament is administered, to give an account of their studies and meditations.

There are four seasons in the year at which the Holy Supper is commemorated, and as the greater proportion of the population regularly attends upon these occasions, two successive Sundays are employed in administering the consecrated elements. On the Sunday before the administration of the quarter, particular prayers are introduced in the service, and appropriate psalms and lessons, to prepare the congregation for the duties of the following Sabbath.

Schools are no new institutions in these retreats of pure Christianity; each parish has its schoolmaster, and the objection to educating the lower orders, which is so frequently heard, viz. that those who are taught to read make bad servants, and despise the labours of industry, has long met with a practical answer in the Protestant valleys of Piemont. All the children, as I have observed before, are instructed in the elements of common knowledge; the whole population is pastoral; and the Vaudois servants are the best in his Sardinian majesty's dominions.

M. Bert favoured me with the following corrected statement of the thirteen churches [q], or parishes of the Vaudois;

q By the word *church*, the Vaudois understand a congregation in its ancient acceptation. They speak of the churches of the Vaudois, in the plural, to signify so many *cures*, for benefices they cannot be called. Communautè is the civil division, and comprises the whole population resident within certain limits, whether Catholic or Protestant.

Anciently, a church, or parish, signified the same thing, namely, a Christian minister's charge. In Eusebius, we read of the parish of Alexandria, the parish of Ephesus, &c. &c. Thus

Τῆς ἐν Ἀλεξανδρείᾳ παροικίας. Lib. ii. c. 24.

with the Protestant and Catholic population of the several communes in round numbers. The numeral figures, in the last column, denote the comparative condition, or resources, of the pastors; number 1 denotes the class which is in most easy circumstances; and number 4, the poorest. Some parishes consist of several hamlets, and have two or three churches: in those, the duty of the minister is extremely laborious.

Names of Parishes.	In what valley.	Protestants.	Catholics.	Total.	Names of Pastors.	Comparative income.
						Class
San Giovanni [r] ..	Valley of Luzerna	1700	40	1740	D. Mondon	2
Augrogna	Ditto	2000	150	2150	Paul Goante........	2
La Torre [r]	Ditto	1800	200	2000	Pierre Bert, moderator	1
Villaro	Ditto	2000	200	2200	François Gay	2
Bobbio [r]	Ditto	1700	20	1720	George Muston, secretray to the synod........	1
Rora	Ditto	700	30	730	—— Peyrot......	2
Pomaretto with Envers Pinache....	Valley of Perosa, or Clusone	1100	100	1200	J. Jalla	2
Prali, and Rodoretto	Valley of San Martino	1200	80	1280	Jaques Peyrani	3
Maneglia, Massel, Sabya, and Chabrant ..	Ditto	1200	200	1400	Rostaing, fils	3
Villa Secca, Richaretto, Faetto Bovilla, San Martino, Traversa	Ditto	1200	450	1650	Alexander Rostaing, moderator adjoint....	4
Paramolo	Valley of Perosa	1200	30	1230	—— Vinçon......	3
San Germano....	Ditto	1000	150	1150	Jean Monet	3
Rocca-piatta Parostino, Inversa Porta	Ditto	1800	60	1860	—— Monastier	3
		18,600	1710	20,310		

Τῆς ἐν Ἐφέσῳ παροικίας. Lib. iii. c. 4.

Τῆς Κορινθίων παροικίας. Lib. iii. c. 4.

Τῆς Ἀθηναίων παροικίας. Lib. iv. c. 23.

Τῆς κατὰ Καρχηδόνα παροικίας. Lib. vii. c. 3.

[r] San Giovanni, La Torre, and Bobbio, are frequently called by the French names, St. Jean, La Tour, and Bobi. Several of the other villages have also a French termination.

This table will shew how very small is the proportion of Catholics to Protestants, in the three valleys of Luzerna, Perosa, and San Martino; and though the few lord it over the many, yet in all my conversations with the Vaudois it was delightful to remark, how little bitterness of feeling exists, on their part, towards those who differ from them on points of faith. I never could detect a shade of intolerance in any of their observations. They never aggravated their grievances, or seemed to take any pains to exasperate our minds against those, who had been the cause of their oppression; nor could I learn that, during the short period, in which they were put upon a level with those who professed the religion of the state, they took any opportunity of acting with animosity towards such as had formerly pressed hard upon them. In no part of their history have they displayed a spirit of fanaticism, and, much as they have suffered from the bigotry of others, it does not appear that they have ever allowed their zeal to betray them into acts of religious phrenzy. A most affecting proof of the Christian meekness and forbearance, which distinguish this inoffensive race above every other community professing the faith of Christ, that I ever heard of, came under my own immediate notice. I must not mention the name of the person to whom I allude; because the book, of which I am going to speak, is prohibited by the Sardinian government.

The second part of Jean Leger's very scarce work contains a history of the dreadful persecutions of 1655, and is embellished with plates, representing the tortures inflicted upon the Vaudois. The sight of these horrors, thus depicted, is enough to curdle the blood in the veins of any one, who is not hardened by fanaticism against humanity, and the plates are accompanied by attestations of the facts, which place the truth of them beyond all question. This book was shewn to me by one of my excellent Vaudois friends, who observed the impression it made, and then said, "That volume I never saw till I was twenty-four years of age, although it was in my father's and grandfather's possession; nor have I ever permitted either of my own children to open a page of it. It is one of our principles not to say or do any thing, which shall have the effect of exasperating the minds of our youth against their Roman Catholic brethren."

Can there be a nobler sentiment of forbearance than this, or a more practical lesson upon the Gospel doctrine of charity! "CHARITY SUFFERETH LONG AND IS KIND: IS NOT EASILY PROVOKED: THINKETH NO EVIL, BEARETH ALL THINGS, ENDURETH ALL THINGS. CHARITY NEVER FAILETH."

In the course of this narrative, I have forborne to mention many a tale of the cruelties exercised upon the Vaudois; but as it is requisite to establish the fact of their having been subject to such torture and oppression, I will now proceed to a few details, and shew how literally they have suffered the very things of which the Apostle speaks. "THEY WERE STONED, THEY WERE SAWN ASUNDER, WERE TEMPTED, WERE SLAIN WITH THE SWORD: THEY WANDERED ABOUT IN SHEEP SKINS AND GOAT SKINS: BEING DESTITUTE, AFFLICTED, TORMENTED, (OF WHOM THE WORLD WAS NOT WORTHY:) THEY WANDERED IN DESERTS, AND IN MOUNTAINS, AND IN DENS AND CAVES OF THE EARTH."

The following is the declaration of an eye witness, and a party concerned in the atrocities described. The original was signed by himself, and attested by two credible persons, and is still to be seen in the public library of the University of Cambridge, where it is preserved with many other valuable MSS. of the same sort. A fac simile of the hand-writing will not be unacceptable to my readers. The annexed plate gives the concluding passage and signature of Du Petit Bourg, and his comrades. The declaration alludes to events that took place, while the Marquess di

Pianezza commanded the army which ravaged the valleys, in 1655, and was made in consequence of a state-paper, published by the court of Savoy, under the title of a *Factum*[s], or "Narrative of the several Transactions in the Valley of Luzerna, in the year 1655," in which the Signor du Petit Bourg was called upon, in one of the articles, to contradict the reports that had gone abroad. "He who commanded the said regiment," says the Factum, "was the Signor du Petit Bourg, a professor of the pretended reformed religion, as was the Adjutant, who caused all the orders that were given to be put in execution. Now the Marquess di Pianezza gave command to him, and recommended to his especial care to see that the people of Angrogna should be treated in the mildest manner possible. This Signor du Petit Bourg hath the reputation of a person of so much honour, that there is no doubt he will speedily attest the truth hereof, and that he will never say, he received any order to the contrary." Du Petit Bourg, however, made a very different attestation to what was required of him.

"I, the Signor du Petit Bourg, first captain of the regiment of Gransè, and commander of the same, having received instructions from Prince Thomas, to go and join the Marquess di Pianezza, and to act under his orders, which Marquess was then at La Torre, just as I was ready to set out, the ambassador sent for me, and desired me to speak to M. di Pianezza, and to use my efforts to accommodate the troubles, which were then existing in the Protestant valleys of Piemont: in order whereunto I did then address myself to the said Marquess, and entreated him, with great earnestness, that he would permit me to undertake the said accommodation, which I supposed I should be able to effect. But he refused this my request, notwithstanding the endeavours I used to persuade him, and instead of the least mitigation

[s] See Appendix, No. 4.

of affairs, that this or any other consideration was likely to produce, I was witness to many great violences and cruelties exercised by the banditti and soldiers of Piemont, upon all of every age, sex and condition, whom I myself saw massacred, dismembered, hung up and ravished, with many horrid circumstances of barbarity. And so far is it from truth, that this was done by virtue of orders issued by me, (as it is falsely alleged in a certain relation printed in French and Italian,) that I beheld the same with horror and regret. And whereas it is said, in the same relation, that the Marquess di Pianezza commanded me to treat them leniently, and in the best manner I could, the event clearly demonstrated that the orders he gave were quite contrary: and it is certain, that without any distinction of those who did or did not resist, they were treated with every kind of inhumanity, their houses were burnt, and their goods were plundered, and when prisoners were brought before the Marquess, I saw him give orders to grant them no quarter at all, "*Because,*" said he, "*his Highness is resolved to have none of this religion in any of his dominions.*" And as for what he protests in the same declaration, namely, that there was no injury done to any, except during the fight, nor the least outrage committed upon any lunatic or idiot, I will assert, and do maintain, that it was not so, having seen, with mine own eyes, several men killed in cold blood, and even women, aged persons, and young children, miserably murdered. With regard to the manner in which they made themselves masters of Angrogna, to pillage and burn the same, they did it easily enough, for excepting six or seven who made opposition, seeing there could be no mercy shewn, the peasants thought more of flying than fighting the enemy. In short, I absolutely affirm, and protest, before God, that none of those cruelties above mentioned, were executed by my order, but on the contrary, seeing that I could effect no mitigation, I was obliged to retire, and quit the command of the regiment, for fear of being present at more such iniquitous actions.

"*Done at Pinerolo, 25th Nov.* 1655.

(Signed) DU PETIT BOURG."

"We whose names are here subscribed, captains of the regiments of infantry, of Sault and Auvergne, do, under our hands, acknowledge to have seen the present declaration made by the Signor du Petit Bourg, captain of the regiment of infantry of Gransè, in the city of Pinerolo, and by him written and signed with his own hand, in our presence, in witness whereof we have signed this present attestation at Pinerolo, this 26th of November, 1655.

S. HILAIRE, Captain of Auvergne,
DU FAURE, Captain."

The blood, which was shed in the inhuman massacre of this year, cried aloud to heaven for vengeance, and never was felt such a sensation among the Protestant states of Europe, as upon this occasion, nor perhaps is there any example in history, of so many foreign governments having taken up the cause of a people, making so inconsiderable an appearance upon the chart of the earth. The inhabitants of the three Protestant valleys do not occupy more than sixteen miles square of territory, and this in one of the most secluded spots of the civilized world; yet such was the justice of their cause, the barbarity of their oppressors, and the horror excited by their sufferings, that envoys were despatched for the express purpose, or urgent letters of intercession and remonstrance were sent from the Protector Cromwell, the kings of France, Sweden, and Denmark, the States-General of the United Provinces, the Swiss cantons, the city of Frankfort, the Duke of Wirtemberg, the Prince Elector Palatine, and the Landgrave of Hesse, to represent to the Duke of Savoy the strong indignation, which was felt at such iniquitous proceedings. "Persecutions and butcheries," was the language of the Landgrave of Hesse, " are not the means to suppress our religion, but rather to preserve it, and to spread it abroad." The cantons of Switzerland, from their proximity to the scene of bloodshed, were the first to hear of it, and to address Charles Emanuel upon the subject. The Duke returned a cold and formal answer, in justification; upon which the Protestant cantons commanded a day of public humiliation, recommended a general collection for the relief of the sufferers, and again exerted themselves in behalf of their afflicted brethren in Piemont, by sending M. Gabriel Weis, the Captain-General of Bern, with the commission of negotiator between the Duke of Savoy and his Protestant subjects.

In justice to the memory of Oliver Cromwell, in whom it is a satisfaction to find some redeeming virtue, no foreign power took so active and spirited a part in behalf of the Vaudois, as England at this fatal crisis: but, it should be added, that the poet Milton was the person to whom the Vaudois were principally indebted; and whose great influence with Cromwell was constantly employed, in urging him to espouse their cause. The Protector, immediately that he was informed of what was going on in the valleys, addressed a Latin letter, of which the following is a translation, to the Duke of Savoy:

" Most serene Prince,

" We are informed by letters received from several places in the vicinity of your dominions, that the subjects of your royal highness, professing the reformed religion, have been commanded by an edict, published by your authority, to quit their habitations and lands, within three days after the promulgation of the said edict, under pain of death, and the confiscation of their property, unless they shall enter into an engagement to abjure their own, and to embrace the Roman Catholic faith, before the end of twenty days. We have learnt also, that regardless of their humble petitions to your highness, praying that you would be pleased to revoke the said edict, and to grant the same privileges, which were anciently conceded by your serene ancestors, your army fell upon them, cruelly slaughtered great numbers, imprisoned others, and drove the rest to fly for refuge to desolate places, and to mountains covered with snow, where hundreds of families are reduced to such extremity, that, it is to be feared, they will all shortly perish with cold and hunger. Upon receiving intelligence of the melancholy condition of this most oppressed people, it was impossible not to feel the greatest commiseration and grief; for we not only consider ourselves united to them by common ties of humanity, but by those of the same religion. Feeling, therefore, that we are invoked by the sacred voice of brotherly love, we declare that we should fail in our duty to ourselves, to God, to our brethren, and to the religion we profess, if we were not deeply moved by a sense of their calamities, and if we did not employ every means in our power, to obtain an alleviation of their unparalleled sufferings. It is on this account that we most earnestly entreat, and conjure your highness, in the first place, to call to mind the enactments of your serene ancestors, and the concessions which they made and confirmed from time to time in favour of the Waldenses: which concessions were granted, no doubt, in obedience to the will of God, who desires that liberty of conscience should be the inviolable right of every man, and in consideration of the merits of these their subjects, who have ever been found valiant and faithful in war, and obedient in time of peace. And as your serene highness has graciously and nobly trodden in the steps of your predecessors in all other things, we again and again beseech you, that you will not depart from them in this instance, but that you will revoke this edict, and any other that is oppressive to your subjects, in consequence of their professing the reformed religion; that you will restore them to their paternal habitations and property; that you will confirm their ancient rights and privileges; that you will cause reparation to be made for their injuries; and order an end to be put to all vexatious proceedings against them. If your highness will comply with this request, you will do what is most acceptable to God; you will comfort and support the minds of those unhappy sufferers, and you will be conferring a favour upon the neighbouring Protestant states, and especially upon us, who will ever consider such clemency as the effect of our intercession; which will constrain us to do every kind office in return, and will be the means not only of strengthening, but of renewing and increasing the relations and friendship, which have subsisted between this commonwealth and your dominions. Promising ourselves much from your justice and moderation, we heartily pray God to direct your mind and thoughts, and so to grant you and your people the blessings of peace and truth, and to prosper all your undertakings.

"Given at our court at Westminster, the 25th day of May, 1655.

"OLIVER, PROTECTOR [t]."

[t] The following, and the other Latin letters of Cromwell, were the composition of Milton. The originals, in the hand writing of the Poet's second daughter, Mary Milton, are preserved in the State Paper Office.

"Serenissime Princeps,

"Redditæ sunt nobis multis ex locis ditioni vestræ finitimis literæ, quibus certiores facti sumus, regalis vestræ celsitudinis subditis Reformatam Religionem profitentibus, vestro edicto atque auctoritate imperatum nuper esse, uti triduo quum hoc edictum promulgatum erit, suis sedibus atque agris excedant, pœna capitis et fortunarum omnium amissione proposita, nisi fidem fecerint, se, derelicta religióne sua, intra dies viginti Catholicam religionem complexuros: cumque se supplices ad celsitudinem vestram contulissent, petentes uti edictum illud revocetur, utque ipsi pristinam in gratiam recepti, concessæ a serenissimis majoribus vestris libertati restituantur; partem tamen exercitus vestri in eos impetum fecisse, multos crudelissimè trucidasse, alios vinculis mandasse, reliquos in deserta loca, montesque nivibus coopertos expulisse, ubi familiarum aliquot centuriæ eo loci rediguntur, ut sit metuendum ne frigore, et fame brevi sunt misere omnes periture. Hæc cùm ad nos perlata essent, haud sanè potuimus quin hujus afflictissimi populi tanta calamitate audita, summo dolore ac miseratione commoveremur. Cùm autem non humanitatis modo sed ejusdem religionis communione, adeoque fraterna penitus necessitudine cum iis conjunctos nos esse fa-

He next ordered a general fast, and had a narrative printed, and dispersed through England and Wales, setting forth the distress of the Waldensian church, and recommending a general subscription [u]. He himself set the example of liberality, by contributing 2000*l.* from the privy purse, and a sum was shortly raised, amounting to 38,241*l.* 10*s.* 6*d.* Another measure was to address letters of urgent recommendation to the Protestant sovereigns and states, that they should come forward in support of the Pro-

teamur, satisfieri, à nobis, neque nostro erga Deum officio, neque fraternæ caritati, neque religionis ejusdem professioni posse existimavimus, si in hac fratrum nostrorum calamitate ac miseria, sub sensu doloris afficeremur, nisi etiam ad sublevanda eorum tot mala inopinata, quantum in nobis est situm, omnem operam nostram conferamus; itaq; a vestra imprimis celsitudine majorem in modum enixè petimus et obtestamur, ut ad instituta serenissimorum majorum suorum, concessamque ab iis omni tempore et confirmatam subditis suis vallensibus libertatem velit animum referre; in qua concedenda atque confirmanda, quemadmodum id præstiterunt, quod Deo per se gratissimum procul dubio est, qui conscientiæ jus inviolabile, ac potestatem penes se unum esse voluit, ita dubium non est quin subditorum etiam suorum meritam rationem habuerint, quos et in bello strenuos ac fidelissimos, et in pace dicto semper audientes experti fuissent; utque serenitas vestra in cæteris omnibus et benignè et gloriosè factis avorum suorum vestigiis optimè insistit, ita in hoc nolit ab iisdem discedere, etiam atque etiam obsecramus; sed et hoc edictum, et si quod aliud in quietandis reformatæ religionis causa subditis suis rogatum sit, uti abroget; ipsos patriis sedibus atque bonis restituat, concessa jura, ac libertatem pristinam ratam iis faciat, accepta damni sarciri, et eorum vexationibus finem imponi jubeat; quod si fecerit regalis celsitudo vestra, et rem Deo acceptissimam fecerit; miseros illos et calamitosos erexerit et recreaverit, et a suis omnibus vicinis, quotquot Reformatam Religionem colunt, maximam gratiam inierit, nobisque potissimum, qui vestram in illos benignitatem atque clementiam obtestationis nostræ fructum arbitrabimur. Quod et ad omnes officiorum reddendas vices nos obligaverit, nec stabiliendæ solùm, verùm etiam augendæ inter hanc rempublicam vestramque ditionem necessitudinis et amicitiæ fundamenta firmissima jecerit, neque verò hoc minus ab justitia vestra et moderatione animi nobis pollicemur. Quam in partem Deum opt. max. oramus uti mentem vestram et cogitationes flectat, vobisque adeò vestroque populo pacem ac veritatem, et successus rerum omnium felices ex animo precamur. Dat. ex aula nostra Westmonasterii, 25 Maii, anno 1655.

"OLIVER, P."

[u] See Appendix, No. 10.

testant interest. To the King of Sweden he represented the noble conduct which his royal progenitors had pursued, when the reformed religion was menaced in Germany. In a strain of equal eloquence he explained to the King of Denmark the motives of policy, which should induce all Protestant princes to make a common cause with those, who were defending such as were persecuted for the reformed faith. "We proclaim," said he, in a tone which was likely to fix the resolution of the wavering, "that we are prepared, in conjunction with your majesty, and our other allies of the reformed religion, to use every means in our power to relieve the wants, and secure the safety and liberty of the unhappy sufferers."

In a letter to the States-General, he reminds their High Mightinesses of the effectual struggles, which they themselves had happily made, in the adverse times of the Protestant church in their own country, and declares his readiness to take any measures, in conjunction with them, for the preservation of the same faith in the valleys of Piemont. The Protector's negotiation with the King of France was still more honourable to his character, because he had the difficult undertaking of persuading one Roman Catholic prince to act against another. His first letter to his most Christian Majesty boldly touched upon a very delicate topic, and intimated that the troops of France had been concerned in the cruelties in Piemont.

"Most serene King,

"The groans of those wretched men, the Protestant inhabitants of Luzerna and Angrogna, and other Alpine valleys, within the dominions of the Duke of Savoy, who were lately most cruelly murdered, and the lamentable tidings of the despoliation and the banishment of the survivors of this massacre, which have reached our ears, have constrained us to write this letter to your Majesty: more particularly as it has been reported to us (with what truth has not yet been ascertained,) that this carnage has been committed by some of your own troops, conjointly with those of the Duke of Savoy. It is scarcely possible to believe that such proceedings have been resorted to, for they are neither consistent with the principles of good government, nor with those of your majesty's wise ancestors, who judged that they were best consulting their own interests, and the peace not only of their own kingdom, but of all Christendom, by permitting their subjects of the reformed religion to live securely and quietly under their protecting sceptre: in return for which indulgence, those grateful men did often perform the most eminent services for their sovereigns, both in peace and war. The Dukes of Savoy, in like manner, were wont to treat their subjects of the Alpine valleys with the same benignity, who, on their side, also displayed the most devoted loyalty, and never spared either their lives or their fortunes in the service of their princes. We feel confident, that your majesty's influence and authority with the Duke of Savoy are such, that if you would only employ your mediation, and express your good wishes, you would obtain indemnity for these poor people, and their restoration to their country and former privileges. Such an act would not only be worthy of your majesty, and of the wise example of your ancestors, but would reassure your own subjects, who would then feel that they need entertain no fears on their own account; and it would conciliate your Protestant confederates and allies, and bind them to your majesty by the strongest ties of respect and affection. With regard to ourselves, whatever indulgence shall be conceded to your own subjects of the reformed religion, or obtained by your intercession for the subjects of others, will be received not only with the same, but even with greater gratitude than we could express, for any personal favour that we hope to derive from your majesty's friendship.

"Given at our court at Westminster, the 25th of May, 1655.

"OLIVER, PROTECTOR [x]."

In his second letter, Cromwell gave the king of France to understand, that he expected him, not only to employ his mediation with the Duke of Savoy, in behalf of the Vaudois, but to afford shelter and protection to such as should fly for refuge into the French dominions.

[x] "Serenissime Rex,

"Perlati ad nos gemitus miserrimorum hominum Lucernam, Angrognam, nec non alias in ditione Ducis Saubaudiæ valles incolentium, et reformatam religionem profitentium, quorum factæ cædes cruentissimæ nuper sunt, deque cæterorum direptione atque exilio tristissimi crebrò nuntii, has ad majestatem vestram literas à nobis expresserunt; presertim cùm nunciatum quoque nobis sit (quàm verè nondum satis cognovimus) partim à cohortibus quibusdam vestris quæ cum aliis Allobrogum ducis copiis se conjunxerant, stragem hanc esse editam. Quod tamen haud temerè crediderimus, cùm neque bonorum principum, nec prudentissimorum majestatis vestræ majorum institutis consentaneum esse videatur, qui et sua in primis interesse, et ad pacem regni sui, reique totius Christianæ, quàm maximè conducere arbitrati sunt, uti subditos suos eam religionem colentes sub imperio suo ac patrocinio inviolatos, atque incolumes esse sinerent; qua illi clementia regum suorum permoti præclaram sæpe operam, et pace et bello suis regibus navarunt. Quod idem Allobrogum quoque ducibus persuasit, uti subjectos sibi Alpinarum vallium incolas eadem benignitate tractarent, qui et vicissim sui principis ad obsequium promptissimi, neque vitæ, neque fortunis propriis unquam pepercere. Nobis autem dubium non est, quin majestati vestræ ea necessitudo cum Sabaudiæ Duce intercedat, eaque auctoritas apud eum sit, ut intercessione vestra, ac propensæ voluntatis significatione, pax istis miseris, reditusq; in patriam, et libertas pristina impetrari facillimè possit. Quod factum et majestate vestra dignum erit, et à prudentia atque exemplo serenissimorum majorum vestrorum non alienum, neque solùm animos vestrorum subditorum, nequid sibi unquam ejusmodi metuant, magnopere confirmaverit, sed fæderatos etiam vestros atque socios, qui eandem religionem sequuntur, observantia longè majore ac benevolentia majestati vestræ devinxerit. Ad nos quod attinet, quicquid in hoc genere, vel vestris concedetur, vel aliorum subditis vestra causa impetrabitur, id nobis non minùs gratum, imo gratius profecto erit emolumento quovis alio atque commodo, ex iis quæ ab amicitia majestatis vestræ haud pauca nobis pollicemur. Dat. ex aula nostra Westmonasterii 25 Maii, 1655.

"OLIVER, P."

"Most serene and most potent King,

"I am happy to understand, from your majesty's letter in answer to mine of the 25th of May last, that I was not wrong in the opinion, that those most cruel murders, and barbarous massacre committed by certain troops of yours upon the professors of the reformed religion in Savoy, had neither your command nor authority. I am also extremely rejoiced to find, that your majesty has signified your strong disapprobation to your military commanders, who took upon themselves to perpetrate such atrocities without your orders; and that you have remonstrated with the Duke of Savoy upon the subject of such monstrous cruelty, and have interposed your influence and good offices with so much humanity and earnestness, for the restoration of those unhappy exiles. I did hope that that prince would have conceded something to the intercession of your majesty: but since neither your mediation, nor that of the other sovereigns and states, have been of any avail in their favour, I have thought it my imperative duty to send an ambassador extraordinary to the duke, to give a full explanation of my sentiments, in regard to his excessive cruelty towards the professors of the same religion with ourselves, on no other account but their religion. And in order to promote the success of this mission, I trust your majesty will be pleased to renew your remonstrances, and to give them greater weight than before: and as your majesty has already declared yourself responsible for the fidelity of these poor people to their prince, so you will now take upon yourself to guarantee their security and protection, that a repetition of such inhuman cruelty may not be inflicted upon them again. We cannot but expect this from your majesty, as being nothing but a just and royal proceeding, and perfectly consistent with the benignity and clemency, with which you have watched over the safety and welfare of so many of your subjects, who profess the same religion. By such an act, you will conciliate the affections of all the Protestants throughout your kingdom, who have given you so many proofs of their loyalty and attachment ; and you will satisfy those of foreign nations, that you are not implicated in this iniquity, however much your ministers of state, and commanders may be: more especially if your majesty will punish those ministers and commanders, who have presumed, upon their own authority, and out of their own malignity, to commit such monstrous atrocities. In the mean time, since your majesty disavows this most inhuman and detestable policy, I am confident you will give shelter and protection to such of the distressed refugees, as shall fly into your dominions for an asylum, and will not suffer any of your own subjects to assist the Duke of Savoy against them. It remains for me to assure your majesty of the value I set upon your friendship, and of my readiness, at all times, to give proof of the sincerity of my respect.

"Given at our court at Westminster, July 31, 1655 [y]."

[y] "Serenissime potentissimeque Rex,

"Ex literis majestatis vestræ, quibus illa ad meas quinto et vigesimo Maii proximi datas rescribit, facile intelligo nequaquam fefellisse me eam opinionem, quâ mihi quidem persuasum erat, cædes illas immanissimas, barbaramque eorum hominum stragem, qui religionem reformatam in Sabaudia profitentur, à cohortibus quibusdam vestris factam, neque jussu vestro neque mandato accidisse. Quæ quantum majestati vestræ displicuerit, id vos, et vestris militum tribunis, qui hæc tam inhumana suo solo impetu injussi perpetraverant, ita mature significasse, deque tanta crudelitate Ducem ipsum Sabaudiæ monuisse, pro reducendis denique istis miseris exulibus unde pulsi sunt, vestram omnem gratiam, necessitudinem, authoritatem tanta cum fide atque humanitate interposuisse, majorem equidem in modum sum lætatus. Ea nempe spes erat, illum principem voluntati ac precibus majestatis vestræ aliquid saltem hac in re fuisse concessurum. Verùm cùm neque vestro, neque aliorum principum rogatu atque instantia in miserorum causa quicquam esse impetratum perspiciam, haud alienum ab officio meo duxi, ut hunc nobilem virum extraordinarii nostri commissarii munere instructum ad Allobrogum Ducem mitterem; qui tantæ crudelitatis in ejusdem nobiscum religionis cultores, idque ipsius religionis odio adhibitæ quo sensu afficiar, uberiùs eidem exponat. Atque hujus quidem legationis eo feliciorem exitum speravero,

Three years afterwards, Cromwell proceeded still greater lengths with France, and gave instructions to his ambassador, Lord Lockhart, to urge the expediency of exchange of territory, in order that the Vaudois might be placed for ever beyond the reach of the iron grasp of the Dukes of Savoy. "One of the most effectual remedies," said these instructions, "which we conceive the fittest to be applied at present, is, that the King of France would be pleased to make an exchange with the Duke of Savoy, for those valleys, resigning over to him some other parts of his dominions in lieu thereof, as in the reign of Henry IV. the Marquisate of Saluces was exchanged with the Duke, for La Bresse, which certainly could not but be of great advantage to his majesty, as well for the safety of Pinerolo, as for the opening a passage for his forces into Italy, which, if under the dominion, and in the hands of so powerful a prince, joined with the natural strength of those places, by

si adhibere denuò et adhuc majore cum instantia suam auctoritatem atque operam majestati vestræ placuerit; et quemadmodum fideles fore illos inopes dictoque audientes principi suo ipsa in se recepit, ita velit eorundem incolumitati atque saluti cavere, ne quid iis hujusmodi injuriæ et calamitatis atrocissimæ innocentibus et pacatis deinceps inferatur. Hoc, cùm in se justum ac verè regium sit, nec non benignitati vestræ atque clementiæ, quæ tot subditos vestros eandem illam religionem sequentes ubique salvos et incolumes præstat, summè consentaneum, à majestate vestra, ut par est, non possumus quin expectemus. Quæ hâc simul operâ, cùm universos per suâ regna Protestantes, quorum studium erga vos summaque fides maximis in rebus perspecta jam sæpe et cognita est, arctiùs sibi devinxerit, tum exteris etiam omnibus persuasum reddiderit, nihil ad hoc facinus contulisse regis consilium, quicquid ministri regii atque prefecti contulerunt. Præsertim si majestas vestra pænas ab iis ducibus ac ministris debitas repetiverit, qui auctoritate propriâ, suâque pro libidine, tam immania patrare scelera sunt ausi. Interea cùm majestas vestra factum hoc inhumanissimum, quo dignum est odio, aversari se testetur, non dubito quin miseris illis atque ærumnosis ad vos confugientibus, tutissimum in regno suo receptum atque perfugium sit præbitura; nec subditorum suorum cuiquam, ut contra eos Duci Allobrogum auxilio adsit, permissura. Extremum illud est, ut majestatem vestram, quanti apud me sua amicitia sit, certiorem faciam: cujus rei neque fidem neque fructum ullo tempore defuturum confirmo.

"Dat. ex aula Westmonasterii, 31 Julii, 1655."

reason of their situation, must needs be rendered impregnable."

This scheme and the answer of the King of France, Louis XIV., will excite no small degree of astonishment, when it is remembered, that it was the same monarch, who revoked the edict of Nantz, and urged Victor Amadeus to repeat in 1686, the enormities against which he now affected to protest, in 1655. "I am very glad, Monsieur le Protecteur," wrote Louis XIV. "that you are touched with the calamities of these poor people, and I have anticipated your wishes by continuing my intercessions with the Duke of Savoy, for their comfort and relief, and for their establishment in the respective places of his dominions, which they enjoyed, by concession, from the Dukes, his predecessors. As to what remains, you have judged well, in not believing that I had given any orders to my troops to do such execution among them: in truth there should be no suspicion that I should contribute to the chastisement of any of the Duke of Savoy's subjects of the pretended reformed religion, at the same time that I was giving so many marks of my good will to those of my own subjects of the same profession, *having had cause to applaud their fidelity and zeal for my service, since they have not omitted any opportunity of giving me proof thereof, even beyond all that can be imagined, and have contributed in all things to the welfare and advantage of my affairs.*"

When the Protector Cromwell had taken these preliminary measures, he sent Sir Samuel Morland upon a special mission to the court of Turin, to present letters of strong remonstrance to the Duke of Savoy himself, and to demand an audience, for the purpose of making a public declaration of the indignation, which the proceedings against the Vaudois had excited in England. Cromwell could not have chosen a man better qualified to discharge the duties of such an embassy than Morland. Young, ardent, full of courage, and conscious of the dignity of the character which he had to sustain, as the representative of the commonwealth of England, he procured an audience at Rivoli, where the royal family of Savoy were then residing, and in the presence of Madame Royale, and the whole court, he addressed the Duke in a Latin oration, which, after a few customary expressions of courtesy, contained truths that none but a stern republican could think of sounding in royal ears. It was the pride, and perhaps the policy of Cromwell, to transact all his negotiations with foreign powers in the language of ancient Rome. He would not condescend to hold intercourse in any but his own, or a learned tongue, and he considered that by this means neither himself, nor his ministers, could be made the dupes of equivocal and ambiguous phrases. Milton was the secretary whom he employed to put his own expressions into a correct and classical form, and his Latin letters form some of the most curious scraps of history.

I give the whole of Morland's speech to the Duke of Savoy, in the quaint words of his own translation; and it will serve as an attestation of many of the facts, to which allusion has been made in the course of this work.

"May it please your most serene and royal highness,

"I am sent by the most serene prince Oliver, lord protector of the commonwealth of England, Scotland, and Ireland, unto your royal highness, whom he heartily saluteth, and with a very high and singular affection of mind towards the person of your serene highness, wishing you life, a long reign, and prosperous successes in all your affairs, together with the love and affections of your people. And this respect doubtless is due to your merit, whether a man consider the most noble inclination, and royal extraction, of your highness, together with the high expectation, which the world hath from so many eminent virtues, or whether from perusing the monuments of time past, he call to mind the ancient alliance of our kings with the royal family of Savoy. As for myself, though I be a young man, I confess, and have not much experience in affairs, yet it pleased my most serene and most gracious master, to send me, being one that is very much devoted to your royal highness, and a great lover of all the people of Italy, to negotiate matters of great importance, for so those affairs are to be called, wherein the safety of many poor distressed people, and all their hope is comprehended, which indeed consisteth wholly in this, if so be that by all their loyalty, obedience, and most humble petitions, they may be able to mollify and appease the mind of your royal highness, which hath been provoked against them.

"In behalf of these poor people whose cause truly, even commiseration itself may seem to make the more excusable, the most serene protector of England is also become an intercessor; and he most earnestly entreateth and beseecheth your royal highness, that you would be pleased to extend your mercy to these your very poor subjects, and most disconsolate outcasts: I mean those, who inhabiting beneath the Alps, and certain valleys under your dominion, are professors of the Protestant religion. For he hath been informed, (which no man can say was done by the will of your royal highness,) that part of these most miserable people have been cruelly massacred by your forces, part driven out by violence, and forced to leave their native habitations; and so, without house or shelter, poor and destitute of all relief, do wander up and down, with their wives and children, in craggy and uninhabitable places, and mountains covered with snow. Oh! the fired houses which are yet smoking, the torn limbs, and ground defiled with blood [z]!

* * * * * * * * *

"Some men, an hundred years old, decrepit with age and bedrid, have been burnt in their beds. Some infants

[z] Fumantia passim tecta, et laceri artus, et cruenta humus. Virgines post stupra differto lapillis ac ruderibus utero, miserè efflarunt animas.

have been dashed against the rocks, others have had their throats cut, whose brains have, with more than Cyclopean cruelty, been boiled and eaten by the murderers! What need I mention more, although I could reckon up very many cruelties of the same kind, if I were not astonished at the very thought of them. If all the tyrants of all times and ages were alive again, (which I would speak without any offence to your highness, seeing we believe none of these things were done through any default of yours,) certainly they would be ashamed when they should find, that they had contrived nothing in comparison with these things, that might be reputed barbarous and inhuman [a].

"In the mean time, the angels are surprised with horror; men are amazed; heaven itself seems to be astonished with the cries of dying men; and the very earth to blush, being discoloured with the gore blood of so many innocent persons! Do not thou, oh thou most high God, do not thou take that revenge, which is due to so great wickednesses, and horrible villainies! Let thy blood, oh Christ, wash away this blood!

"But it is not my business to make a narrative of these things, in order as they were done, or to insist any longer upon them; and that which my most serene master desireth of your royal highness, you will better understand by his own letters, which letters I am commanded, with all observance and due respect, to deliver unto your royal highness; to which, if your royal highness shall, as we very much hope, be pleased to vouchsafe a speedy answer, you will thereby very highly oblige my lord protector, who hath laid this thing deeply to heart, and the whole commonwealth of England. You will also, by an act of compas-

[a] If it should be thought that this language was too strong on the part of an Envoy, upon his first audience at Court, let the reader turn to pages, 61, 92 and 253, and see what effect the language of mild remonstrance, and of *gentle* intercession is likely to have upon similar occasions.

sion, most worthy of your royal highness, restore life, safety, and spirit, country and estates, to many thousands of afflicted people, who depend upon your pleasure; and me you will dismiss back to my native country with exceeding joy, and with a report of your eminent virtues, the most happy proclaimer of your princely clemency, and one for ever most obliged to your royal highness."

The result of these negotiations was, that the Duke of Savoy returned an answer to Cromwell, promising to proclaim a general act of indemnity, to restore the Vaudois to their possessions, and to concede the same privileges and immunities, which his ancestors had granted; and he concluded, by referring all differences to the mediation of the King of France. England, and the rest of the Protestant powers, were completely thrown off their guard by these promises: the courts of France and Savoy took advantage of the satisfaction, which was expressed, the matter having been left to be so arranged, and huddled up a treaty, called the treaty of Pinerolo, which left the poor Vaudois at the mercy of their oppressors, under the mask of establishing their security. This shameful treaty, by which the Protestant states were duped, and the Waldensian churches left in the same unprotected condition as ever, was very appositely compared to a leper, arrayed in rich clothing and gay attire; and to Ezekiel's roll, "written within and without, in the mouth as honey for sweetness, but within there were written lamentations, and mourning, and woe!"

The baneful effects of this conclusion of the affair were soon felt by the poor Vaudois themselves, who, in their pathetic appeal for redress, used some of the most affecting expressions in Scripture, to signify their distress. We have *no grapes in the vineyard*, said they; *no cattle in the fields; no herds in the stalls; no corn in the garners; no meal in the barrel;* and *no oil in the cruse. The tongue of the suckling cleaves to the roof of his mouth, and the young children ask bread, and no man gives it to them*[b].

To the French king, whom they justly considered the author of their grievances, since it was he who patched up the perfidious treaty of Pinerolo, they addressed an humble petition, imploring his interposition, and urging him to see justice done to them. But their only answers were some angry letters, written by the French Ambassador (Servient), who had himself assisted in framing the treaty; and who sharply rebuked them, for their presumption and discontent. One of these letters even reproached them for accepting supplies and money from foreigners. This money was the contribution received from England. "Alas!" said the poor sufferers, "was it ever known before that miserable men, after losing the whole of their estates, after having had their houses burnt, and their goods plundered, should have it objected to them, that they had received the charity of those, who had pity on them, to prevent their perishing of hunger!"

One of the Swiss Ambassadors was so dissatisfied with the terms of the treaty, in the first instance, even before it was concluded, that he strongly remonstrated with his colleagues, and urged them not to consent to it: and afterwards subscribed to a protest, the original attestation of

[b] Extract from the translation of a letter, written by the ministers and elders of the valleys of Piemont to their brethren of Geneva, dated Pinache, 14th February, 1657, preserved, among many other Waldensian records, in the State Paper Office:

"Our poor people are in extreme necessitie, the greatest part of our families being destitute of houses, moveables, cattel, or any thing else whereby to subsist.—If you did but know, Sirs, the greatnesse of our miseries, you would certainly have compassion on us, and pitie our sad condition. God is now in good earnest chastizing us for our sins and iniquities, to which wee most willinglie submitt, kissing the rod, and confessing that hee is still just and righteous."

The author cannot sufficiently express the sense of his obligations to Mr. Lemon, the Deputy Keeper of the State Papers, who has, upon all occasions, afforded him the most kind and ready assistance in his researches.—*Note to Second Edition.*

which is among the manuscripts in the university library at Cambridge. A fac-simile is given in the annexed plate, and the following is a translation of it.

"I, who have subscribed my name, do declare by this attestation, that M. Stockar, Ambassador from the city and canton of Schaffhausen to his Royal Highness the Duke of Savoy, during the Treaty of Pinerolo, did earnestly request Messieurs, the Ambassadors his colleagues, not to hasten the said treaty, but rather to defer the conclusion of it, until the arrival of the Ambassadors from England and Holland; and that he urged every remonstrance, and shewed how dangerous and prejudicial this proceeding would be, not only to the inhabitants of the valleys, but also to the common cause of all the Protestants. And when he found that his expostulations were of no avail, and that he was not listened to, he protested that he would not be responsible for the consequences.

(Signed)

"ANDREW SCHMIDT,

"Secretary to the Embassy."

"*Done at Geneva,* 17-27*th Sept.* 1655."

Cromwell was furious upon finding how completely the Protestant states had been over-reached, in their negotiation with the Duke of Savoy, and in the faith they placed in the mediation of the King of France. He wrote to Louis XIV. in a high tone of indignant remonstrance:

"Most serene and potent King,

"Your majesty may remember, that at the time when the negotiation began between us, for the renewal of the alliance, which has proved so beneficial to the two nations, and so detrimental to our common enemies, the cruel massacre of the Vaudois took place; and that we earnestly and pathetically commended the cause of that unhappy people, who appeared to be oppressed and abandoned by all, to your pity and protection. We cannot believe that your majesty neglected to make use of your authority and influence with the Duke of Savoy, when it was so incumbent upon you to exert yourself in the pious and humane character of a mediator: as for ourselves, and many other princes and states, we interposed all that we could, by embassies, letters, and entreaties. The result was, that after a most barbarous slaughter of persons of both sexes, and of all ages, a treaty of peace was concluded, or rather secret acts of hostility were committed, the more securely under the name of a pacification. The conditions of the treaty were determined in your town of Pinerolo: hard conditions enough, but such as these poor people would gladly have agreed to, after the horrible outrages to which they had been exposed, provided that they had been faithfully observed. But they were not observed: the meaning of the treaty is evaded and violated, by putting a false interpretation upon some of the articles, and by straining others: many of the complainants have been deprived of their patrimonies; and many have been forbidden the exercise of their religion: new payments have been exacted; and a new fort has been built, to keep them in check; from whence a disorderly soldiery make frequent sallies, and plunder or murder all they meet. In addition to these things, fresh levies of troops are clandestinely preparing to march against them; and those among them, who profess the Roman Catholic religion, have been advised to retire in time; so that every thing threatens the speedy destruction of such as escaped the former massacre. I do therefore beseech and conjure your majesty not to suffer such enormities, and not to permit (I will not say any prince, for surely such barbarity never could enter into the heart of a prince, much less of one of the duke's tender age, or into the mind of his mother,) those accursed murderers to indulge in such savage ferocity, who, while they profess to be the servants and followers of Christ, who came into the world to save sinners, do blaspheme his name, and transgress his mild precepts, by the slaughter of innocent men. Oh that your majesty, who has the power, and who ought to be inclined to use it, may deliver so many supplicants from the hands of murderers, who are already drunk with blood, and thirst for it again, and who take pleasure in throwing the odium of their cruelty upon princes. I implore your majesty not to suffer the borders of your kingdom to be polluted by such monstrous wickedness. Remember that this very race of people threw themselves upon the protection of your grandfather, King Henry IV. who was most friendly disposed towards the Protestants, when the Duke of Lediguieres passed victoriously through their country, as affording the most commodious passage into Italy, at the time he pursued the Duke of Savoy in his retreat across the Alps. The act or instrument of that submission is still extant among the public records of your kingdom, in which it is provided that the Vaudois shall not be transferred to any other government, but upon the same condition, that they were received under the protection of your invincible grandfather. As supplicants of his grandson, they now implore the fulfilment of this compact: they would rather be your subjects than the duke's, and hope that it may be effected by some mode of exchange, if possible, and if not, that at least they may be taken under your patronage and protection. There are other reasons of state which might induce your majesty not to neglect the Vaudois, but I would not wish so great a king to be influenced by any thing, but his regard to the faith pledged by his ancestors, and by his own piety, and royal benevolence and magnanimity. Thus the honour and praise of so glorious an act will be entirely your own, and your majesty will propitiate the grace and favour of the Father of Mercies, and our Lord Jesus Christ, whose name and doctrine you will vindicate against such nefarious and inhuman proceedings.

"Given at our court at Westminster, this 26th of May, 1658[c].

[c] *Copy of the original Latin Letter.*

"Serenissime potentissimeque Rex,

"Meminisse potest majestas vestra quo tempore inter nos de renovando fœdere agebatur, quod optimis auspiciis initum multa utriusque populi commoda, multa hostium communium exinde mala testantur, accidisse miseram illam convallensium occisionem; quorum causam undique desertam atque afflictam vestræ misericordiæ atque tutelæ summo cum ardore animi ac miseratione commendavimus. Nec defuisse per se arbitramur majestatem vestram officio tam pio, immo verò tam humano pro ea qua apud Ducem Sabaudiæ valere debuit, vel auctoritate, vel gratia: nos certè aliique multi principes ac civitates, legationibus, literis, precibus interpositis, non defuimus. Post cruentissimam utriusq; sexus omnis ætatis trucidationem, pax tandem data est, vel potius inducta pacis nomine hostilitas quædam tectior: conditiones pacis vestro in oppido Pinerolii sunt latæ; duræ quidem illæ; sed quibus miseri atque inopes, dira omnia atque immania perpessi, facilè acquiescerent, modò iis, duræ et iniquæ ut sint, staretur; non statur; sed enim earum quoque singularum falsâ interpretatione variisque diverticulis fides eluditur ac violatur; antiquis sedibus multi dejiciuntur, religio patria multis interdicitur, tributa nova exiguntur, arx nova cervicibus imponitur, unde milites crebrò erumpentes obvios quosque vel diripiunt vel trucidant: ad hæc nuper novæ copiæ clanculum contra eos parantur; quique inter eos Romanam religionem colunt, migrare ad tempus jubentur; ut omnia nunc rursus videantur ad illorum internecionem miserrimorum spectare, quos illa prior laniena reliquos fecit. Quod ego majestatem vestram obsecro atque obtestor, fieri ne siverit: nec tantam sæviendi licentiam, non dico principi cuiquam (neque enim in ullum principem, multo minus in ætatem illius principis teneram, aut in muliebrem matris animum tanta sævitia cadere potest) sed sacerrimis illis sicariis ne permiserit; qui cùm Christi Servatoris nostri servos atque imitatores sese profiteantur, qui venit in hunc mundum ut peccatores servaret, ejus mitissimo nomine atque institutis ad innocentium crudelissimas cædes abutuntur: eripiat majestas vestra, quæ potest, quæque in tanto fastigio digna est posse, tot supplices suos homicidarum ex manibus, qui cruore nuper ebrii, sanguinem rursus sitiunt, suæque invidiam crudelitatis in principes derivare consultissimum sibi ducunt. Vestra verò majestas regni sui fines ista crudelitate fœdare ne patiatur. Meminerit hos ipsos avi sui Henrici protestantibus amicissimi dedititios fuisse, cùm Diguierius per ea loca, quà etiam commodissimus in Italiam transitus est, Ducem Sabaudiæ trans Alpes cedentem victor est insecutus; deditionis illius instrumentum in actis regni vestri publicis etiamnum extat; in quo exceptum atque cautum inter alia est, ne cui postea convallenses traderentur, nisi iisdem conditionibus quibus eos majestatis vestræ avus invictissimus in fidem recepit. Hanc fidem nunc implorant avitam à nepote supplices requirunt; vestri esse quàm cujus nunc sunt, vel permutatione aliqua, si fieri possit, malint atque optarint; id si non licet, patrocinio saltem miseratione atque perfugio. Sunt et rationes regni quæ hortari possint ut majestas

Cromwell also despatched a letter to the Swiss cantons, plainly signifying his own readiness to go all lengths, in conjunction with them, for the benefit of the Vaudois; and warning them that they were bound, by every consideration, of interest, as well as feeling, to see that the most ancient stock of the reformed religion be not destroyed, in the remains of its old faithful professors, lest the next blow should fall upon themselves.

Unfortunately for the Vaudois, Oliver Cromwell did not live to render them farther assistance; he died in the same year that these last letters were written; and, in him, they lost their most zealous and powerful protector. Charles the Second suspended the annual pension, arising from that part of the collection made in England, in 1655, which Cromwell had put out to interest, and did not protest against the continued persecutions of their sovereign, with that earnestness and spirit, which might have enforced attention. But even this prince, attached, as he was, to the Roman Catholic faith, could not entirely forget what was due from the king of a Protestant nation, to the Waldensian sufferers; and the copy of a letter is preserved, which he addressed to the Swiss cantons, in answer to their request that he would use his intercession in favour of their brethren in the valleys. This letter is a curious specimen of the effect, which a just and righteous cause, supported by public opinion, could have, even upon the thoughtless and unsteady mind of Charles the Second.

"Mighty, respected, and noble sirs, our right good friends,

"It is with great pleasure that we have received your

vestra convallenses ne rejiciat; sed nolim aliis rationibus ad defensionem calamitosorum quàm fide à majoribus data, pietate, regiaque animi benignitate ac magnitudine tantum regem permoveri. Ita pulcherrimi facti laus atque gloria illibata atque integra vestra erit, et ipsum patrem misericordiæ ejusque filium Christum regem, majestas vestra, cujus nomen atque doctrinam ab immanitate nefaria vindicaverit, eo magis faventem sibi atque propitium per omnem vitam experietur. Westmonasterio ex aula nostra Maii die 26, anno Domini 1658."

letters of the 11th of June past; and as we have nothing more deeply at heart, or more agreeable to our minds, than to re-establish and renew the ancient affection, which the reformed churches entertained for ourselves and our ancestors, and to deserve a continuance of it, we will do all in our power, and upon every occasion, as you have recommended us, to soften the calamities, and prevent, by our intercession with the Duke of Savoy, the dangers which threaten them. For this reason, as soon as we shall send our minister to that court, we will not fail to make use of our intreaties and interest with the duke, our cousin, in their favour and for their relief, to the end, that in future he may treat them with the mildness they hope for; and that they may exercise their religion with security and confidence. In the mean time, if any opportunity shall offer to promote their views, we shall, from our heart, do all we can towards the preservation and safety of those, who are so closely united to us by the sacred ties of a common faith.

"Given at our court at Hampton, the 14th of July, 1662, and in the fourteenth year of our reign.

(Signed)

"Your good Friend,

"CAROLUS REX [d]."

In 1664 and 1665, the council of extirpation, at Turin, was proceeding so openly in its designs, for the total destruction of the Protestant families in the three valleys, that memorials were again and again presented to the French king, by the different Protestant ambassadors at that monarch's court, and the name of the English minister, *Hollis*, appears at the foot of several documents of this nature. But they were not worded in the strong and indignant language which distinguished the remonstrances of Cromwell, and they were treated with the contempt which feeble ma-

[d] Translated from the copy preserved in Leger's work.

nifestoes deserve to receive. France and Savoy had a perfect understanding upon the subject, and the fiat went forth for blotting the name of the Vaudois from the face of the valleys of Luzerna, Perosa, and San Martino, as it had already been effaced from that of Frassinière, and from the Marquisate of Saluzzo. Most providentially the compact of blood was dissolved in the year 1690, and the Vaudois are still bearing witness to the truth, in the settlements of its first professors.

It was during the dreadful persecution, of which I have been speaking, that Milton wrote the following sonnet.

" Avenge, O Lord, thy slaughtered saints, whose bones
Lie scattered on the Alpine mountains cold:
E'en them, who kept thy truth so pure of old,
When all our fathers worshipped stocks and stones,
Forget not; in thy book record their groans,
Who were thy sheep, and in their ancient fold
Slain by the bloody Piemontese, that roll'd
Mother with infant down the rocks. Their moans
The vales redoubled to the hills, and they
To Heaven. Their martyr'd blood and ashes sow
O'er all the Italian fields, where still doth sway
The triple tyrant; that from these may grow
An hundred fold, who, having learnt thy way,
Early may fly the Babylonian woe!"

SONNET 18.

CHAPTER XI.

A festive party—Alpine dance—Rustic beauty—Return to Turin—Delightful recollections of the Vaudois—General observations—Loyalty of the Protestants of Piemont—Gratitude of the Sardinian government—Ancient Waldensian church—Gradual advance of Romish corruptions—Christianity as it was in the primitive church—Progressive departure from it—Steady resistance and integrity of the Waldenses.

THE time passed so imperceptibly with the good pastor of La Torre, that it was late before we remembered, that we were engaged to look in upon the little festive party, which was collected at the house of one of the family of the Vertus. M. Bert's son and daughter, and one of his English pupils, had set out long before us, and I began to fear, lest I should have the appearance of forgetting the early habits of these simple mountaineers. My venerable friend quieted my scruples, by assuring me, that upon occasions like the present, amusements were extended till long past midnight.

We found the house to which we were invited, as full as it would hold. All the principal families of La Torre were assembled together, young and old, and the largest room was set apart for the use of the dancers. One or two adjoining apartments were employed as rooms, to which the company might adjourn for refreshments, or conversation. In the most complete sense of the word, it was a rustic assembly, where all was good humour, cheerfulness, and frankness. The music consisted of a flute, and a couple of violins: the dances were those of the country; the refreshments were a thin wine, and cakes; and the dress was principally the costume of the Alps. Two or three young girls, and among them the charming girl to whom the younger

M. Vertu[*] was engaged, were dressed in white; but colours, and chiefly red, were conspicuous. The young men were attired without any regard to the fashions of Turin; and the movements of their steps were regulated by nature, and a good ear; and not by the studied lessons of a ballet-master. The elder personages looked on with unfeigned satisfaction; and the youthful actors in this happy scene, performed their parts with all that gaiety of heart, and simplicity of manners, which distinguish the inhabitants of remote villages. It was, indeed, a genuine, unmingled delight to witness the innocent happiness of the hour: for if the sight of pain be itself pain; the sight of pleasure is no less pleasure, where the heart is pure, and the mind is uncorrupted.

I was interested in observing how much M. Bert entered into the spirit of the amusements of the evening. Austerity forms no part of the religious character of the Vaudois; and this worthy minister thought it not at all inconsistent with his sacred profession, to be present at an assemblage of his flock, where music and dancing were admitted. "I love," said he, "to see cheerfulness and happiness under every form; and where can be the harm of young persons thus recreating themselves under their parents' eyes, where nothing indecorous is done; or of my being the spectator of their innocent revels?" Formerly, dancing was prohibited among the Vaudois; but it was in those dark and dismal times, when these poor people were scarcely ever secure of their lives, and when any indication of merriment agreed but ill with their miserable condition. In days of active persecution, piety will naturally assume something of the gloomy tincture of the period; and when the heart ought to be sad, every movement of levity is ill-timed, and unbecoming. Upon this occasion, every body had a smile, or a salutation, or an expression of affection for their bene-

[*] The author has heard that this amiable couple are now married. May their union be attended with every happiness!—*Note to Second Edition.*

volent pastor, and seemed to derive additional pleasure from his presence. The domestics of the family, and several of the peasantry, were in the room where the dancing was going on, or at the door; and though they did not dance, they entered into familiar conversation with all. One of these, a female servant of the house, had a countenance of rather striking beauty: the brilliancy of her eyes was Italian, but there was a modesty, and sweetness of expression, peculiar to the Vaudois. In general, and it may be mentioned as a remark extending to all mountaineers, personal beauty is not a distinction to which the peasantry of the Alps can lay any claim; nor have I observed in any country but in England, that lovely features or fine symmetry, prevail among the lower orders. In Italy, it has been said, that beauty rises with rank. The Swiss peasants cannot be thought handsome; and the dress of the female peasant, in many of the French provinces, is enough to disguise and deform the most perfect figures.

At about half past twelve at night, I returned to my inn: M. Bert accompanied me to the door, and there took his leave. It was done so feelingly, that it will be long before I shall forget the fervent benediction of my pious friend, the pastor of La Torre. He raised his hat gently from his head, pressed my hand in his, and with uplifted eyes, and a solemn tone of voice, prayed God to bless me, and to grant me a safe return to my happy and favoured country.

The next day we returned to Turin; and with the same young friends who accompanied me to these romantic and interesting valleys, I afterwards made the Tour of Italy and Switzerland. We visited all that was most worth seeing in both these enchanting countries; but neither the classic scenes of the one, nor the lovely vales of the other, had charms for our minds superior to those, which I have attempted to describe in this volume. Often did the companions of my journey thank me for bringing them to these picturesque retreats, which are too commonly overlooked by tourists; and after having found our way to spots, which are consecrated to every delightful recollection of poetry and history, one [f] of them, who never left me, assured me, that no remembrance he could carry home with him would be more grateful, than that of the days he had spent in the mountains of the Vaudois.

Much as I was prejudiced in favour of this extraordinary race, before I became personally acquainted with their character, that acquaintance has increased my admiration of them. If innocence, and pure religion, can be said to reign any where, it is here; and all my enquiries and researches have had the effect of bringing the firm conviction to my mind, that they are one of those favoured people, whom the arm of the Almighty has providentially shielded, for purposes best known to his inscrutable wisdom. Their morals correspond with their faith; and their lives and conversation testify, that the doctrines they profess, are those of the truth; for nothing short of a firm persuasion, that they are burning and shining lights, which are not to be put out, could have given them courage and perseverance, sufficient to withstand the temptations, to which their spiritual integrity has been exposed, or to resist the strong hand which has been lifted up against them for more than ten centuries. I had opportunities of observing the conduct of individuals of this little community, at different times, and under various circumstances, at home and abroad, in the transactions of business, and the kindly courtesies of life, and in their hours of devotion and festivity, and I am impressed with the belief that there is nothing exaggerated, either in the favourable representations made by their own historians, or in the eulogies of strangers [g].

[f] Mr. John Hallifax.

[g] A late publication contains the following characteristic and beautiful anecdote: "Five years ago the writer of these pages travelled in the south of France, and met accidentally with an old recruiting serjeant who was from Piemont, and professed the Roman Catholic faith. This man took great pleasure in telling a cir-

There must be something uncommonly striking in the merits of a people, who, from age to age, have excited so much interest as the Vaudois. Almost all Europe has testified its concern for them, at one period or another, and though but a speck on the face of the earth, and of no political consequence whatever, the three valleys have been more the object of general attention than many a kingdom, which, from size and situation, might seem to challenge a far deeper interest. Since their restoration to their native settlements, at the latter end of the seventeenth century, they have enjoyed a comparative calm, which has brought them less into notice than before, but they still have to struggle with difficulties, which should induce every good Protestant to keep a jealous eye upon their Roman Catholic masters. As long as Victor Amadeus found them useful in his wars with France, the Vaudois were caressed, and flattered with promises, but in 1721, when every thing was tranquil upon the frontiers, the Sardinian government began to think it had been too indulgent to them [h]. Edicts of

cumstance which is here related nearly in his own words;—' I was once,' said he, ' entrusted by my captain with an important and difficult commission, which compelled me to pass through one of the Waldensian valleys of Piemont. I reached it on a Sunday morning, loaded with a tolerably heavy burden, and exhausted by heat and fatigue.—Covered with perspiration I entered a house for the purpose of requesting some refreshment.—A widow received me in a welcome and friendly manner, and at the same time intimated to me that it was Sunday, and the time of divine service; but, added she, though I cannot myself stop to give you what you stand in need of, take my keys and help yourself to whatever you want, and afterwards you can rest here in my absence.' This mixture of compassion, simplicity, devoutness, and trust, had made a deep impression on the old soldier, and will, no doubt, produce a similar effect upon the reader."—See " Notice Historique sur les Vaudois."—*Note to Second Edition.*

[h] In the treaty made in the year 1704, between Queen Anne, and Victor Amadeus, Duke of Savoy, the third article bound the parties to the following engagements.

" Her Britannic Majesty engages to make every effort to put his Royal Highness in possession of the valley of Pragela, and to render Mount Genevre the barrier between France and the dominions of his Royal Highness the Duke of Savoy.

restriction followed, in contempt of former engagements, and in 1768 their lamentable situation called once more for

" His Royal Highness the Duke of Savoy engages reciprocally on his part, to permit such of the Protestant inhabitants of the valley of Pragela, as have been obliged to leave their country on account of their religion, to return to their houses, to enjoy the possession of their estates, and the free exercise of their religion; and to grant the same privileges to all others professing the same faith, who may wish to establish themselves in the said valley."

Again, on the 13th of March, 1709, Victor Amadeus addressed a letter to Queen Anne, from which the following is an extract.

" Nothing can give me greater satisfaction than to meet the wishes of your Majesty; not only from feelings of inclination and zeal, but out of regard to the engagements of the treaty. I therefore most humbly entreat your Majesty to rest persuaded, that every attention will be paid to your royal pleasure upon the subject of the inhabitants of the valleys of Pragela and Cyane."

In spite of this solemn treaty, and still more solemn protestations, the ministers and schoolmasters of the Protestant religion were banished from the valley of Pragela, and a royal edict was published by Victor Amadeus, in the year 1721, forbidding more than ten persons to assemble together in the said valley for any purpose whatever, under the severest penalties, and commanding all the inhabitants to take their children to a Romish priest to be baptized, within twenty-four hours after their birth. These, and other oppressive enactments against the Protestant subjects of his Sardinian Majesty, became at length so intolerable, that they were obliged to have recourse to the interposition of foreign ambassadors at the Court of Turin. Mr. Hedges, the British minister, made several applications in their favour in the year 1727, and the subjoined copies of letters from that excellent man, will shew the perfidy of Victor Amadeus and his advisers, and the hostility which they never ceased to feel and exercise against the professors of the reformed religion.

" *Turin, June* 7, *N. S.* 1727.

" Having lately received several complaints from the inhabitants of the valley of Pragela of the new hardships and vexations laid upon them, notwithstanding the remonstrance I had made by his Majesty's orders on that subject—I went on Sunday last to the Marquis del Borgo, to acquaint him with them, and to let him know at the same time the concern I am under, that the representations I had made should have so contrary an effect to what I had hoped from them. I shewed him at the same time the article in their favour, in the treaty concluded in the year 1704, wherein it was expressly mentioned that the inhabitants of this valley should enjoy the free exercise of their religion. I likewise shewed him a copy of a letter wrote by the King of Sardinia, then Duke of Savoy, to Queen Anne, promising her to shew them all manner of indulgence in that respect. To this he answered, *that the promise was conditional, in case the Queen obtained that valley and other places mentioned in it for them, but they had not obtained it by our means, but by exchange of the valley of Barcelonette with the French, and* the pecuniary succour of their friends in England. The French revolution again rendered their services valuable to their sovereign, and none were so faithful or loyal, as the Protestant inhabitants of Luzerna and San Martino. Public orders were full of praises of their valour and fidelity, and royal acknowledgments were naturally expected to be followed by generous concessions. The lawful dynasty was suspended by a new order of things, in 1800, which none were so earnest in their endeavours to prevent as the Vaudois: but the intrusive government, instead of resenting the zeal which had been displayed against foreign invasion, placed this long neglected race upon a footing with its other subjects. Religious disqualifications were taken

were obliged by that exchange to use them in the manner the French did, when that exchange was made, which was in suffering the exercise of no religion there but the Roman Catholic. I used many arguments to him, to endeavour to shew him the wrong way of reasoning he was in, but with which I will not trouble your Grace, but finding him immoveable, I asked him if this were the answer I should send to his Majesty. He told me he had not yet received the King of Sardinia's last orders on this head, and therefore spoke this as his own opinion, but gave me no hopes of my obtaining a more favourable answer, as to the inhabitants of this valley. As to the Vaudois, he said, their case was different, and whatever just grievances they had should be relieved. I purposely abstain from mentioning any thing of this to the King of Sardinia himself, unless I have your Grace's orders to do so, perceiving how ungrateful a subject it is to him; but if some relief be not obtained for this valley, it is certain that the Protestants will be entirely rooted out of it."—*Extract from a Letter to his Grace the Duke of Newcastle.*

" *Turin, Nov.* 5, 1727.

" I can assure you that nothing but great steadiness on our side, and insisting strongly on our treaties, and the King of Sardinia's promises, can preserve the Protestants of the valleys from sure and immediate destruction. The inveteracy against our religion is incredible, and if it be not supported with some warmth, since it is attacked with so much, it must give way to superior force. I have received a memorial from M. de St. Thomas, in justification of their proceedings against the Protestants, whereby he endeavours to prove, *that by their treaties with France, they are obliged to persecute them, and to tolerate no appearance of that religion in those particular valleys, yielded to them by France at the treaty of Utrect.*"—*Extract from a Letter to Horace Walpole, Esq.—Note to Second Edition.*

off, and Protestants and Catholics were rendered equal in the balance of the state.

But, again, the scene changes. By a sudden revolution, the house of Savoy finds itself elevated to that state amongst nations, to which its own unassisted feebleness could never have attained; the principal agent in the work of its restoration, is England, a Protestant power, and yet its first use of revived authority, is to deprive its Protestant subjects of privileges, which they had enjoyed for fourteen years, and to throw the Vaudois once more upon the protection and pity of foreigners. The spirit of the age is too repugnant to any thing like persecution to render it probable, that former modes of enforcing conformity to the Roman Catholic faith will ever be resorted to again; but oppression, mortifying distinctions, petty grievances, and vexatious suits, may do more than open violence; and the Vaudois have now as many claims upon us as at any period of their history, since the sword was raised against them, in 1686. The most ready, and the most useful assistance, may be rendered from England; but should they not receive it from the quarter, to which they naturally look for aid, they may, as at former periods, be thrown upon other states; should this be the case, the purity of their faith may not long continue: abuses may gradually creep in, overthrowing parts, and assimilating themselves with the main body of their ecclesiastical institutions, till the original fabric shall have completely lost its form. What the Vaudois are to gain by such a change, is not very evident, but what they will lose, is sufficiently clear to any one, who compares their moral conduct, and steady religious opinions, with those of the neighbouring people.

For many reasons, it is to be regretted, that causes[i], over which the Vaudois could have no controul, and among the rest, the plague of 1630, which cut off all their minis-

[i] See p. 76.

ters, but two of the most aged; the destruction of their college at Angrogna [k], and the edict, prohibiting the education of their youth at San Giovanni, should have obliged them to have recourse to the Calvinistic clergy of Geneva and Lausanne. Still, the peculiar doctrinal sentiments maintained by Calvin never found any warm advocates in these valleys; on the contrary, I am persuaded, that the Swiss reformer's notions concerning the absolute decrees of God, do not make part of the theology of the Vaudois pastors, but the long established regulations of the Vaudois church were infringed by the new ministers from Switzerland. It is in vain, that we now look for the correct lines and lineaments of the ancient discipline and ritual, which prevailed at the foot of the Alps for so many centuries. The title of moderator was most probably substituted for that of bishop, after the year 1630, and with it the Presbyterian for the Episcopal hierarchy; and new liturgies were introduced in place of the venerable service, to which neither history nor tradition could assign any positive date. According to the direct authority of Leger, the annual visitation of the head of the Waldensian church, which used to contribute so much to the religious purity of this little community, was interrupted, because the new pastors from Geneva were unwilling to submit to his wholesome jurisdiction. If there ever could have been any hope of tracing the forms and discipline of the primitive church, it might have been entertained, as long as the churches of the valleys preserved their ancient discipline and liturgy, inas-

[k] Nothing is more to be desired for the Vaudois, than that they should be furnished with the means of educating their young men, who are intended for holy orders at home. A benevolent family at Bath, (Mr. Frewin Turner's) who have contributed to the fund which is established for the general relief of the Vaudois, and who have generously given 50*l.* for the use of young Peyrani, have written thus to the author of this work. "A college appears most desirable, and after their more pressing wants are attended to, should a further provision be making for that purpose, have the kindness to inform us, and we shall be happy to contribute." *Note to Second Edition.*

much as the corrupt changes which took place in other parts during the sixth, seventh, and eighth centuries, were not likely to reach such remote settlements as these; and indeed tradition, and the authority of credible ecclesiastical writers, assure us, that they did not extend to these secluded spots. But the Swiss innovators did what the corruptions of Rome could not do; and we may not flatter ourselves, that the venerable and perfect monument, which we know was in existence till about two hundred years ago, remains any longer. In points of faith, the integrity of the Vaudois church is as unsullied as ever, but its visible form is no longer that interesting spectacle, that uninjured model of antiquity, which would have been exhibited to the Christian world, if circumstances had not occurred, in which the will of the natives of the three valleys had no concern.

I do not know of any authors, whose writings will assist us in speaking positively of the state of Christianity in these Alpine recesses, for the first four or five centuries, but there is unquestionable evidence, that the whole of the diocese of the north of Italy [1], preserved purity enough, to constitute a true Christian church, though not altogether free from errors and superstitions; and such claims, therefore, cannot be denied to the Vaudois, who formed a portion of that diocese. Even as late as the tenth century, the see of Turin partook, in part only, of the blindness common to other sees, and therefore we may fairly presume, that a pastoral and simple people, whose situation kept them at a distance from the controversies which engender error, and the customs which foster superstition, might remain but little infected by either of these evils. Leger begins his History of the Churches of the Vaudois by a declaration, that they never required any reformation.

Christianity was likely to preserve its primitive purity, as long as it was confined to the retreats of men of plain and

[1] See Allix on the Ancient Churches of Piemont.

simple habits, but when it spread into populous cities, and became the religion of Imperial Rome, it naturally imbibed many of the errors of the people, at the same time that it improved them. Sophistry clogged it with disputable articles, whilst wealth and power thought they could not do less, than load it with some of their own decorations. With splendid services were introduced unnecessary forms, external rites were gradually substituted for spiritual observances; relics, altars, and pilgrimages, diverted the mind from the Creator to the creature, till in time the essence of Christianity grew to be disregarded in the multiplicity of its ceremonies, except in those retired abodes, where the want of costliness and magnificence rendered such forms unimposing, and therefore unacceptable.

It is curious to trace the gradual march of innovation, the introduction of superstition, and the progressive departure of the Christian church from the simplicity of the apostolic age. The refusal of the cup to the laity, the strange doctrine of transubstantiation, the imposition of austerities, the necessity of auricular confession, the worship of the Virgin Mary [m] and of the saints, and the supremacy of the Pope,

[m] But impious and idolatrous as it is, in a Protestant's opinion, to hear the Virgin Mary, and a cloud of saints, invoked in language, which ought to be addressed to the Supreme Being only, and to see religious ceremonies performed in honour not of the Creator, but of creatures, subject to the same infirmities as ourselves, yet it must be allowed, that there is no service in the Roman Catholic Church so impressive, as the evening-service to the Virgin, or *Ave Maria*. Whether it is the shortness, or the simplicity of the service, or the calm and tranquil hour in which it is performed, that hour of sunset which has such inexpressible charms for the imagination, under an Italian sky; or whether it be from a combination of these causes, there in nothing, either of the magnificent or the imposing in Popish solemnities, which can compare with this. " C'était à l'heure de la soirée," says Madame de Staël, in her Corinne, when she is supposing her hero to be in one of his most serious moments, " où l'on entend toutes les cloches de Rome sonner l'Ave-Maria :

——— Sqtilla di lontano
Che paja il giorno pianger che si muore. *Dante.*

et le son de l'airain, dans l'eloignement, paraît plaindre le jour qui se meurt ;" and certainly if the mind cannot be influenced by a solemn call like this, when it

were corruptions that spread by degrees over nearly the whole of Christendom.

There were, however, a few undaunted Christians left, who were scandalized at the assumption of temporal power,

is invited to repose under the security of heavenly protection, during the ensuing hours of gloom and darkness, it never can be religiously affected at all. Rome, however, is not the place, where the impressions of this service are best understood. Who that has been at Venice, and attended vespers at St. Mark's, with feelings that are brought from colder regions, where the name of God alone can warm the heart, has not lamented, that the aspirations of the soul, which seem to be so devoutly offered from the hundreds, who pour into that venerable cathedral for a few moments, before the last glimmer of twilight expires, should be breathed in any other name than that of the most High? Who, as he has beheld the prostrate multitude bending their heads, and humbling their spirits upon the time-worn pavement, which has witnessed the same prostrations for nearly a thousand years, has not been jealous for the King of Ages, and trembled to think, that worshippers should come, in their blindness, to divide their hearts with the Eternal, and to pronounce Sancta Maria, Sancta Dei Genitrix, ora pro nobis, (Holy Mary, Holy Mother of God, pray for us) in the same breath with, Pater de Cœlis, Deus, miserere nobis! (Oh God, the father of Heaven, have mercy upon us!).

Venice is the city of silence. The gondolas, or barges, gliding noiselessly along the water of the canals, are the only things which move, freighted with men or merchandise; not the sound of a wheel, nor the clattering of a hoof ever breaks upon the ear. The hum of human voices is all that is heard, and this seems to cease, when the chimes have pealed for Ave-Maria. St. Mark's, which of all other sanctuaries, from its dark and retiring aisles, its massy pillars, its antiquated construction, its dingy colouring, and imperfect light, is calculated to add to the effect of this evening-service, is completely filled every evening a few minutes after the vesper-bell has tolled. A concourse of people hurry in from all quarters; the merchant ceases from his half-finished bargain, the young and the gay desist from trifling, the porter leaves his burthen upon the steps of the cathedral, and all that happen to be near quit their occupations or amusements, to offer up the prayer of a moment to the Virgin. The organ plays a soft symphony, while the multitude are entering, and dispersing themselves through the church: on a sudden a small bell tinkles, and every knee is bent, and every head bowed in silent adoration. Not a sound from within or without disturbs the spirit of supplication. This lasts for a minute or two. The bell tinkles again: the congregation then rise from their knees, the tapers are extinguished, and the sacred walls are soon left to solitude and darkness. I witnessed this scene several times, and never without an unusual degree of emotion. It was impossible not to honour the feeling of devotion, short-lived as it might be, which brought so many to the foot of the altar, and equally impossible not to condemn the profane system which directs the supplicant to address his prayers to the imaginary *Queen of heaven*, and *Mother of God.*

in the professed servants of Him, whose "kingdom is not of this world," and thought they saw "the image of the beast," and the marks of Antichrist, in such unscriptural arrogance. They protested against the pontifical tyrant, and cast away his chains from them. Anathemas were first fulminated against such daring rebels: and afterwards, the vassals of the Roman church, that is to say, kings and princes, were ordered to be the executioners of Papal vengeance, and to carry fire and sword into the valleys of Piemont, where the seeds of the obnoxious heresy were first spread. But the Vaudois were neither to be convinced nor compelled: for the one, they had too much faith; for the other too much courage: and both faith and courage were only still more excited by the violence adopted for their suppression. Fire and the sword never yet made converts; their appeal is to the flesh, while conviction is of the mind.

Should it then be asked, where was the true church of Christ to be found, after so many heresies were avowed by the Roman Hierachy, at the second council of Nice, in 767, the answer is:—It was to be found in the churches of the Valleys of Piemont; to preside over which Bishop Claude was called from Spain, that he might stem the torrent of idolatry, and oppose further attempts at unscriptural innovations[n].

[n] "It is proved," said the late Rodolph Peyrani, moderator of the Vaudois, in his answer to the pastoral letter of the Romish Bishop of Pignerol, in 1818, in which that prelate accused the Vaudois of heresy and schism, "It is proved by fact, and by the history of the different innovations of well-known date, that the Vaudois do not form a new church—they continue to be what they have ever been since the days of the Apostles. From the apostolic age until the seventh century when no vital errors had as yet been introduced into the Church, we made one with the universal Church. Insensibly errors crept in elsewhere, but the ancestors of the Vaudois would not admit them—and their priests or ministers have not on that account ceased to be the successors of those established by the Apostles. To persevere constantly, and without interruption from the time of the Apostles, in the pure doctrines of the Apostles, cannot surely be schism." *Note to Third Edition.*

CHAPTER XII.

General observations—The Churches which have been planted by the Vaudois—In Calabria, Spain, and France—Persecutions in these countries—The Waldenses of Provence—Their correspondence with Œcolampadius—Francis I.—The cruelties practised at Merindol, at Cabriere—Aymond de la Voye—The Waldenses of Piemont take measures for their own defence—Concessions granted by their Sovereign—Review of their character, conflicts and opinions—Their claims to attention—Concluding observations.

The Waldenses were the first to expose the superstitions of the Roman church, and the monstrous absurdities which its hierarchy introduced into the forms of Christian worship. They were the first who engaged to cleanse this Augean stable of corruption: and if we had records that would enable us to follow them, step by step, through their bold and arduous undertaking, we should be able to exhibit one of the most glorious pictures of human perseverance that was ever displayed. They not only succeeded in preserving the pure doctrine and discipline of the primitive ages in their own secluded valleys of Piemont, but they carried them into distant parts; and upon the banks of the Rhine and the Danube, in the remote provinces of Spain and Calabria, and in the plains of France, were witnessed for a time the extraordinary effects produced upon the manners and character of the inhabitants, by Waldensian preachers, whose Alpine retreats gave the name to a church, which has withstood every assault that has been made upon it, on the spot where it was originally founded. And this, it will be observed, is not the least remarkable feature in the history of the Vaudois. They sent forth teachers, who crossed the Alps, the Appenines, and the Pyrenees, making proselytes wherever they went, and establishing the same fundamental truths, and even the same forms of worship, which prevailed among their own community; but no where, save between the Pelice and the Clusone, in Piemont, have those truths been uninterruptedly preserved. The parent stock remains, but most of the branches have been cut off. They were soon put down in Spain; the spirit of the proselytes there was not enough to support them against the strong arm of oppression, although the country presented the same mountain fastnesses, as that from whence the purer faith had reached them. In Calabria, the new church flourished for about two centuries: it was planted in the year 1370; and though the lords, and landed proprietors of that province, were indignant at the idea of being set right upon the vital topics of religion by their vassals, yet they found it to be to their interest to protect a peasantry, who were more industrious in their habits, more quiet in their conduct, and more regular in their payments, than the turbulent inhabitants of the adjoining districts. But when the progress of Lutheranism threatened to hurl the triple tyrant from his throne, the Waldenses of Calabria were thought to be too much in concert with the reformers of the north, and too near the states of the church, to be suffered to remain unmolested. The bull for their extermination went forth, and no mercy was shewn to those who refused to be baptized by a popish priest: the pastors were carried in chains to Rome, some were starved to death in prison, others were tortured in the dungeons of the Inquisition, after witnessing the utter destruction or dispersion of their flock; and two were burnt at the stake, to gratify the malignity of Pope Pius IV. who could not be satisfied, unless he saw, with his own eyes, the expiring agonies of the heretics, who had dared to question his infallibility.

In France, the Waldensian name and faith continued to be upheld for several hundred years; but even there, after extending into Dauphiné, Provence, Languedoc, Guienne, and Picardy, they could not finally make head against persecution, but gradually submitted to the strong hand of power. It is not meant to say, that the spirit of religious reformation has been at any period of history totally subdued in those provinces, where the Albigenses and Waldenses once formed so large a portion of the population. But where religious services are performed as they were there, in secret, and where there is no visible church or congregation, as has been the case at different periods in the history of the French Protestants, there, it must be allowed, you cannot expect to find the faith of the reformers in the same purity as among men, who resolutely persevere in making an open profession of their opinions, who form a community among themselves, and are prepared to assert their right of conscience, sword in hand, whenever it is disputed.

From century to century, the Waldenses of Piemont have composed a distinct people, and have successfully vindicated their religious independence. The churches of the three valleys have remained churches: and whenever it was found that an attempt was making to prevent the free exercise of their religion, in the more habitable and accessible regions that bordered upon the plains, these hardy mountaineers retreated, with their wives and children, to the rocks and forests of the higher Alps, rather than renounce the doctrines of their ancestors. If they could not worship God in their own way in the villages, the whole race of them retired to their strong holds in the mountains, until the fury of persecution had exhausted itself: but they never submitted nor recanted, nor were they ever entirely driven from their ancient settlements. Like the Athenians of old, who declared by retiring to their ships, that Athens consisted not in its walls, or houses, but in its citizens, who would not receive a foreign yoke; so did these intrepid Vaudois shew, that the pure Waldensian church continued to exist, in the faithful adherence of its professors to the creed that had been delivered to them, whether it was in their places of usual habitation and resort, or in the glens and caverns, whither they had fled for shelter.

But the Waldenses of Piemont will not only be honoured by a distinguished mention in history, as having retained their political existence, and original settlements, when other professors of the same faith were unable to do so; but, also, as having preserved their religious opinions in greater purity. Nothing has ever prevailed among them, like the fanatical or compromising principles, which are to be detected in others, who have been known under the same denomination, and the reader of ecclesiastical history should be cautious, in not attributing the wild doctrines of some of the Bohemian and Provençal Waldenses, to the Vaudois of the Cottian Alps. The Waldensian pastors, who held a correspondence with Œcolampadius, the Reformer, and professed their doubts as to the lawfulness of submitting to the civil and constituted authorities[o]; and who even acknowledged that their clergy held it wrong to marry, but frequently broke their vows of celibacy[p]; these, it must be remembered, were Waldenses of Provence. It was to the same persons also, that Œcolampadius had afterwards occasion to write his letter of remonstrance, upon the subject of their timid compliance with the unscriptural practices of their Roman Catholic neighbours. "I have heard," said he, "that, from fear of persecution, you dissemble and conceal your faith; that you communicate with unbelievers;

o "Tertio, an leges civiles, et hujusmodi ab hominibus inventæ, quibus circa temporalia mundus regitur, valeant secundum Deum, quia scribitur, leges populorum vanæ sunt?"—*Gerdesii Historia*, tom. ii. p. 407.

p "Inter nos nemo ducit uxorem, tamen ut verum fatear, tecum enim cum multâ fiduciâ omnia loquor, non semper castè nobiscum agitur."—*Gerdesii Historia*, tom. ii. p. 404.

and that you attend abominable mass. But if you may conscientiously conceal your faith from Antichrist, you may do so with the Turk, or you might worship, with Diocletian, at the altars of Jupiter or Venus[q]."

The perils to which the Protestants of Provence were at this time exposed, will palliate, if they cannot justify, the compliance which is here complained of; and as the persecution of Francis I. which took place shortly afterwards, was the most dreadful, and fatal to its interests, which the Waldensian church in France ever experienced, after that of the Albigenses, by Simon de Montford, I shall not consider it a digression to enter into a short detail of it, particularly as its terrible effects could not fail to reach the valleys of Perosa and Luzerna, part of which were then subject to the French crown.

It must be humiliating to those, who would place dependence in what are called the nobler and more heroic traits of human nature, to reflect that the gallant and chivalrous Francis I. consented to sacrifice some of his most unoffending subjects to the bigotry of his confessor. So far from treading in the steps of his predecessor, Lewis XII. who resisted every attempt that was made to prejudice his mind against men, whose only crime was heresy, and who began his reign with having a gold coin struck with a motto on the reverse, which made the proud Pontiff, Julius II., tremble on his papal chair, "Perdam Babylonis nomen,"—"I will blot out the name of Babylon," so far from displaying a generous spirit like this, Francis submitted to be controlled by the Pope's nuncio, and put his signature to an edict, which threatened the total extinction of the Protestant cause, throughout the whole of his do-

[q] "Audimus quod metu persecutionum fidem vestram ita dissimuletis, et occultam habeatis, ut etiam communicetis cum infidelibus, et accedatis ad abominabiles illorum Missas.—Si licet sub Antichristo fidem occultare, licebit etiam cum Turca, licebit etiam cum Diocletiano ad aras Jovis, vel Veneris adorare."—*Gerdesii Historia*, tom. ii. p. 411, 412.

minions. It enacted that every dissentient from the holy mother church should acknowledge his errors, and obtain reconciliation within a stated period, under the severest penalties in case of disobedience, and because Merindol was considered to be the principal seat of the heresy, that devoted city was ordered to be razed to the ground. With a species of the most refined cruelty, the edict added, that all the caverns, hiding-places, cellars, and vaults, in the vicinity of the town should be carefully examined and destroyed, that the woods should be cut down, and all the gardens and orchards laid waste, and that none who had possessed a house or property in Merindol, or within a certain distance, should ever occupy it again, either in his own person, or in that of any of his name or family, in order that the memory of the excommunicated sect might be utterly wiped away from the province, and the place be made a desert. This horrible decree was put into execution by an armed force, without the least mercy or forbéarance; the wretched inhabitants fled *en masse,* and because they refused to surrender themselves at discretion, the commander of the troops which marched agäinst Merindol, threatened death without trial or appeal, to every one who should render them the least assistance. Nothing ever exceeded the dreadful scenes which followed. Two or three facts will suffice for the whole. An helpless multitude of aged men, women, and children, pursued their flight, rather as chance directed them, than with any certain destination, while such as were armed, and had youth and strength on their side, made a feeble shew of protecting their retreat. Before they could reach the mountain-passes, where there might have been some chance of making a successful defence, the enemy came up, and soon routed this inefficient rear guard. During the conflict, the main body of the fugitives took refuge in a wood: they did not expect to escape observation, but hoped that their defenceless condition would soften the hearts of their pursuers. But what mercy was ever shewn by persons impelled by religious hatred? Not one was left alive of that wretched multitude.

At Cabriere the same atrocities were committed. It was taken by storm, and every living creature was put to the sword. At another place, four hundred women thought to find an asylum, in a building which had been used as a place of worship. It was set on fire, and as the poor creatures endeavoured to escape from the doors and windows, the soldiers butchered, in cold blood, those whom the flames had spared. It was in this manner that plunder, carnage, and violation, were spread from one end of Provence to another; Dauphiné and Languedoc experienced nearly the same horrors, and few were the Protestants who were spared, and fewer those who had the courage to acknowledge that they belonged to the proscribed party. There was, however, one illustrious champion left, whose name ought not to be forgotten, and while others of more questionable merit are suffered to occupy a place among saints and martyrs, Aymond de la Voye ought at least to have honourable mention in these pages. This brave and pious man boldly went from village to village, to confirm the wavering, and reassure the hopeless, until at length he exposed himself to suspicion, and was carried before a tribunal, which was sitting for the condemnation of heretics. The first question that was put to him was intended to draw forth a disclosure, that would lead to the apprehension of others.

Who are your associates?

My associates are those, who know and do the will of my Heavenly Father, whether they be nobles, merchants, peasants, or men of any other condition.

He was asked, Who is the head of the church?

Jesus Christ.

Is not the Pope the head of the church?

No: if he is a good man, he is the minister and primate of the Roman church, but nothing more.

Is not the Pope the successor of St. Peter?

Yes, if he be like St. Peter, but not else.

His persecutors saw that he was not to be moved, and ordered him to be led to execution. As he passed by an image of the Virgin Mary, he refused to salute it; and the execrations of an infuriated mob had no other effect upon him, than to make him pray aloud, "Oh, Lord, I beseech thee, to make it known to these deluded creatures, that it is to thee only they are to bow the head, and offer supplications." As he mounted the scaffold, he cried out with a firm voice, "Be it known that I do not die a heretic, but a Christian." The clamorous multitude insisted that his voice should be stopped; and before the executioner had inflicted the tortures usual upon these occasions, an end was ordered to be put to his existence, because there was no other way of silencing the undaunted Aymond de la Voye, whom even prolonged suffering could not intimidate.

While the Provençal Waldenses were exposed to enormities like these, which were meant to extinguish the light of the Protestant faith on the western side of the Alps, their brethren the Vaudois of Piemont were illustrating the truth of their motto, "Lux lucet in tenebris,"—"The light shines in darkness," in a most extraordinary manner. The sanguinary proceedings in France put them upon their guard; they expected that a similar attack would be made upon themselves, and precautions were taken against it. The passes and defiles that led into their valleys, were put in a state of defence, preparations were made to retire behind their natural fastnesses upon the first alarm: the barbes were more active than ever in fortifying the minds of their flocks, the young people and children were instructed and catechized with the minutest care, and the villages and hamlets bore the aspect of being soon to be deserted. Strange to say, it now became the turn for their tyrants to express dismay. The lords of the soil were apprehensive that their lands would be abandoned by the cultivators;

the princes of the house of Savoy were fearful of losing the taxes and services of a loyal and industrious community: and, for the first time in the history of the Vaudois, their sovereign offered to make certain concessions, which should secure to them the free exercise of their religion, upon the compliance of conditions, which were far from being disadvantageous or dishonourable.

These events took place about the middle of the sixteenth century, and though the concessions which were then granted have been again and again violated, and recourse has been had to arms, from time to time, to secure their liberty of conscience, and political existence, yet have the Vaudois continued to obey the government of their country in all that relates to temporal matters, with the most scrupulous fidelity, but without sacrificing one iota of their spiritual integrity. They present the rare spectacle of a small community maintaining its religious independence in the midst of enemies; and of enemies, according to all human calculation, both able and desirous of compelling them to conform; but, "where is the fury of the oppressor?" They occupy a mountain district, which is scarcely known by name, even to those who take an interest in exploring remote corners, and in making researches among people, whose manners and character have been but imperfectly investigated; and yet, from this secluded spot, have they disseminated doctrines, whose influence is vitally felt over the most refined and civilized part of Europe. They occupy the same villages and hamlets, follow the same pastoral occupations, speak the same language, have the same patriarchal habits, and simple virtues, and retain the same religion, which was known to exist there more than a thousand years ago. They profess to constitute the remains of the pure and primitive Christian church, and those who would question their claims, cannot shew, either by history or tradition, that they ever subscribed to the Popish rituals, or bowed before any of the idols of the

Roman church. Their enemies say of them, that heresy always existed in their valleys, which is the strongest confirmation of their pretensions, and whereas some positive date can be assigned to the period, when other Protestant states became reformed, there is no evidence to prove, that Reformation ever took place among them. They have seldom been free from persecution, or vexatious and intolerant oppression, and yet nothing could ever induce them to conform, even outwardly, with the religion of the state.

There is nothing extravagant in their religious opinions[r]: there is nothing in their institutions, in their intercourse with each other, in their views of Scriptural promises, which is likely to feed or stimulate enthusiasm in such a degree, as to account for their adherence to the faith of their fathers by any common mode of human reasoning. Every thing goes on evenly and quietly among them, the clergy perform their pastoral duty faithfully and zealously, not because celebrity, reward, promotion, or popularity, is likely to recompense their exertions, but because they act from principle, and upon sober and rational grounds of piety.

In short, there is no other way of explaining the political, moral, and religious phenomenon, which the Vaudois have continued to display for so many centuries, than by ascribing it to the manifest interposition of Providence, which has chosen in them "the weak things of this world, to confound the things that are mighty:" and not for all the attractions which any other route could have offered, would I have lost the opportunity of visiting these worthy descendants of the Waldenses, on the spot of their original settlements. The excursion has been rewarded with a higher degree of satisfaction, than even that, which is derived from exploring scenes, that have been hallowed by the footsteps of the good and the brave, and in comparing

[r] See "Confessions of Faith," and "Ancient Catechism" of the Vaudois, in Appendix, No. 12.

the grand localities of a country, where heroic achievements have been wrought, with the magnificent and impregnable mountain fastnesses, that the imagination has depictured. The principal interest consists in having had the means of observing how far the posterity of men, who occupied so eminent a place in history, assimilate with their ancestors in those estimable qualities, which assigned them an imperishable name in the annals of the Reformation. It consists in being able to declare, with perfect truth, after tracing habits, manners, and peculiarities of domestic life, which identify the Vaudois of the present day, with the veritable representatives, in kin and character, of the Waldenses of earliest times, that the Protestant inhabitants of the valleys of Luzerna, San Martino, and Perosa, have the same claims to attention, which distinguished the ancient members of their church, and so often excited the admiration and sympathy of the Protestant states of Europe.

CONCLUSION.

SINCE my return to England, I have had several communications with persons of elevated situation, and high influence, both in the Government, and in the Church, upon the claims of the Vaudois to the pension, which was suspended in the year 1797, in consequence of the occupation of Piemont by the French; and it is in justice to the feelings which are entertained upon this subject, and to the exertions which have been made, by those who might be expected to promote the cause of this injured people, that I make this statement.

In the several interviews, with which I have been honoured by the parties to whom I allude, I have invariably found that kind and patient attention, which promises that the matter will be thoroughly investigated; and for which, I wish I were at liberty to express myself in plainer terms of grateful admiration.

A reference to what has been detailed in these pages, on the subject of the royal pension[s], will shew that the Vaudois do not merely ask the restitution of it, as a benefaction, but as a stipend, to which they think they have the same just and equitable title, as to that which is still paid to them by "the Incorporated Society for the Propagation of the Gospel in Foreign Parts." The one originated in the national collection made in the year 1768, and the other in that of 1655: and though there may be no existing deeds[t]

[s] See pages 87, 88, 89, 221; and Appendix, No. 10.

[t] The author has had the satisfaction of discovering that his apprehensions on this ground are unfounded. The State Paper Office contains documents that explain the nature of the investment of these monies. See p. 89. *Note to Second Edition.*

to shew the particulars of the investment of the monies, which Charles the Second seized; yet the fact of the pension having been renewed in the reign of William and Mary, and continued for more than a hundred years afterwards, must be regarded as some evidence of the existence of a claim [u].

[u] Since the greater part of this work went to press, I have been favoured by the Rev. Anthony Hamilton, Secretary to the Society for the Propagation of the Gospel in Foreign Parts, with the following copy of the minutes of the Society, dated so far back as January 15, 1795. It will correct a mistake made in p. 84, relative to the amount of the stipend paid annually by the Society to each of the Vaudois clergy, and may serve to throw some further light upon the nature of the further claim, which the Vaudois have upon this country. Whether it be founded on the bounty of 500*l.* per annum, left by Queen Mary, or on the surplus of the collection of 1655, "put out to interest in sure hands," their title to the royal pension remains the same, if either of the statements be correct.

"Vaudois Committee.

"It was reported,

"That Queen Mary left a bounty of five hundred pounds per annum, for the maintenance of the Vaudois pastors in Piemont.

"That of this sum, 140*l.* more or less is sent to the Vaudois at Wirtemburgh, in Germany; and that upon an average, the Vaudois of Piemont receive only 266*l.* per annum of that bounty; that formerly they received 385*l.* The cause of the variation is not known to the Committee.

"That from this sum of 266*l.* they deduct 5*l.* for each superannuated minister, generally two or three; and 14*l.* more are deducted for sundry expences of synods, journeys for public affairs, and visitations, by which the sum is reduced to 237*l.* This is equally divided, with some trifling differences, in favour of those parishes which are the worst.

"That it appears from the best calculation that can be made, allowing for exchange from London to Turin, that each minister, being thirteen in number, receives for salary,

From the Royal bounty	18*l.*
From the Society	17*l.*
	35*l.* per ann.

"Some of the parishes may contribute about 120 livres of that country, 6*l.* sterling, towards the maintenance of the minister; but this is not always the case.

"Upon this report, it was agreed to make an addition of 3*l.* sterling per annum to each of the thirteen ministers; and since that period they have regularly

But even allowing that nothing in the shape of a claim can be established by the Vaudois, for the restitution of the royal pension, yet surely it must be acknowledged, that the reasons for renewing it as a benefaction exist in as much force as ever, and that the same motives, which induced the English government to extend pecuniary assistance to the Waldensian clergy, for more than a hundred years, might be permitted to operate in their favour now.

They are as poor and as aggrieved as they were previous to the year in which the pension ceased. They are as quiet and as unoffending, and as submissive to the constituted authorities of their country, as when the King of Sardinia declared, in June 1794, that he had not more loyal subjects than themselves. Be it remembered too, that in the late attempt at revolution, in the Sardinian dominions, the Vaudois took no measures which could excite the slightest jealousy on the part of their sovereign.

They are so far from being apostates, or unfaithful to the cause which recommended their fathers to the protection of England, that they have preserved their integrity, unsullied and unimpaired, in the midst of greater seductions, if not greater perils, than ever threatened the constancy of the ancient Waldenses.

They are esteemed so deserving of notice by other Protestant sovereigns and states, that the Emperor Alexander[x], and the kings of Prussia[y] and of the Netherlands, have very lately exerted their kind offices, and extended their royal bounty, by remonstrances in their behalf, and grants of money for their relief.

It cannot then be apprehended that this country will now

drawn on the treasurer of the Society for the amount of these salaries, and certain annual stipends for the widows of the deceased ministers, to the extent of 32*l.* in addition, making in the whole 292*l.*"

[x] See p. 85.

[y] For a more detailed account of the King of Prussia's benevolence towards the Vaudois see "Postscript to Second Edition."

neglect a community, which has been so supported by us in former years, when the same reasons still exist for holding them in estimation, viz. respect for the cradle of the reformed churches, respect for the descendants of the men, to whom we are indebted for our religious doctrines, and respect for the people themselves, whose faith hath failed not, under persecution, want, or sufferings. There is a solemn bond of justice and gratitude incurred by us, which we cannot be unwilling to redeem; and when it is considered, that there never was a period in English history, when the interests of humanity and true religion were more consulted, than by those who guide the counsels of the nation at this present time, it is not possible to be otherwise than sanguine in expecting, that the claims of the Vaudois, if they are proved to be founded in equity and justice, will be amply recognized[z].

[z] I am happy to find that this Narrative is likely to be followed by a work, which will elucidate still more completely some of the subjects, to which I have endeavoured to attract attention. The Rev. Thomas Sims*, who has been exploring the villages and hamlets of the Vaudois, since my excursion, has brought to England a large and valuable collection of papers, which were committed to his charge, by the family of the late lamented moderator, Rodolphe Peyrani. These manuscripts comprise many unpublished compositions of that learned pastor, which appear to be of the most interesting nature. They are upon various topics, chiefly theological: but some of them contain critiques and observations upon the Greek Drama. Those of which I have been favoured with a sight, more than confirm the high opinion, which my short interview with Peyrani enabled me to form of his extraordinary talents, and variety of information. When a selection can be made, it is proposed to publish them, for the benefit of his destitute family. How melancholy to reflect, that a man of such uncommon erudition and endowments, as the late pastor of Pomaretto, should have left behind him such a mass of valuable materials, which the poverty and obscurity, to which he was consigned, prevented his committing to the press!

* The author is indebted to Mr. Sims for enabling him to correct a mistake in p. 86. Several private benefactions to be distributed among the widows, schoolmasters and poor, have been remitted to the Valleys from England, in addition to those which are there mentioned. Among these, it ought to have been stated, that they received the amount of the profits arising from the sale of "A Brief Memoir respecting the Waldenses," published in 1815.—*Note to Second Edition.*

POSTSCRIPT

TO THE

SECOND EDITION.

THE rapid sale which the first edition has had, and the extracts, which have been reprinted from the work in a variety of daily journals, and other periodical publications, are a sufficient evidence, that the history and cause of the Vaudois required only to be made known to excite universal concern in their behalf. By one of the Reviews I was especially gratified—" Here is a book," says the critic " and the very title of it stirs a tide in the heart—Researches among the Waldenses! among that holy, retired, and delightfully pure and romantic people, who watched over the sacred fire of [religious] liberty when the darkness of superstition and the degradation of tyranny had extinguished it throughout the rest of Europe.—Those fathers of religious liberty! Let us see how nobly they resisted, and how heroically they suffered, when there was none to assist and applaud. In a case like this, as for criticism, that is out of the question, so thankful are we that the book exists."

But even this sort of testimony, expressing that the public are glad to have the history of the ancient and the condition of the present Waldenses brought before them, has been exceeded in value by another of a still more delightful nature. I have received letters after letters, unexpected applications not only from my own friends, but also from perfect strangers, requesting to know in what way the writers of them could make remittances of money, to relieve the wants of this interesting and distressed Protestant community. To two of these I have referred in pages 110, 249.

The venerable bishop of Durham, whose long life (far extended beyond the longest span of man's age) has literally been passed in doing good, no sooner read the narrative of their sufferings, than his Lordship honoured me with a communication, desiring that I would point out the best means of rendering a donation beneficial to these poor Vaudois, and become his almoner.

I have it also in my power to refer to a more illustrious example still; His Majesty himself has been graciously pleased to express the interest which he takes in the Vaudois, by contributing one hundred guineas towards the fund which is raising for their relief.

After such gratifying proofs that the cause of the Vaudois, is not a matter of unconcern in this country, I was sanguine in my expectations of being able to report, before my last sheet goes to press, that the pension, of which so much has been said in the preceding pages, has been restored by the British government; more particularly as liberal donations from several of his majesty's ministers appear on the subscription list, and shew that they are well disposed towards these most deserving petitioners. Hope however is still deferred, but I trust that this hesitation or delay is to be attributed solely to circumstances, which render it necessary that the claim to the restitution of the pension, as a matter of justice, should be fully established, before a grant be renewed, which might lead to embarrassing applications from other quarters, if it appeared to be made merely as an act of benevolence.

Much additional light has been thrown upon the subject, since it was first discussed, and whatever was advanced by way of conjecture, or upon the authority of Morland, Leger, and other historians of the Vaudois, relative to the pension being originally paid out of the interest of monies raised by

Parochial collections in 1655, is fully confirmed by researches, which I have had permission to make in the State Paper Office. Since the first edition was printed, very valuable and interesting information relative to the energetic part, which Cromwell took to relieve and assist the suffering Protestants of Piemont, has been gathered from the original books of the Council of State which were kept during the interregnum, and contain minutes of the daily transactions of the Executive Government, from 1649 to 1659. The greater part of these most curious documents was originally brought to light, and has since been arranged by Mr. Lemon, Deputy Keeper of the State Papers, a gentleman, to whom every body, who has the privilege of making researches in the State Paper Office, cannot but acknowledge himself indebted for able assistance, and for the most kind and ready attention. The following are copies of minutes most essential to the establishment of the fact, that the pensions which the Vaudois enjoyed till the year 1797, and now petition to have restored to them, originated in a public contribution which was raised in their behalf.

" *Committee of Affayres of Piedmont,*
Wednesday, May 6th, 1657.

" Ordered,

" That it be referred to Sir Gilbert Gerard, Sir J. Trevor, Sir Thos. Vyner, Sir C. Pack, Mr. Cresset, Mr. Nye, and Mr. Jenkyn, to take into consideration, and to inform themselves, how the remainder of the moneys paid in upon collection for Protestants of Piemont, and not disposed of, may be let out to further advantage to that work, with respect to securing the principal, and letting it forth, so as to be called in again upon a short warning, and report at next sitting."

" *November* 27, 1657.

" Ordered,

" That the Treasurers dispose of the residue to the best advantage.

"That Sir Thomas Vyner have £5000 of the same moneys at 4 per centum, to be paid in at a month's warning.

"That the Chamberlain of London, have £4000, on the security of himself and son, on like terms.

"That Mr. Backwell have £2000 more on like terms, giving such security as shall be satisfactory to Sir Thomas Vyner and Sir C. Pack."

"*At the Committee for the Valleys of Piemont, Wednesday, ye 11th of May* 1658, 9 *in ye morning.*

"They desire Mr. Secretary to signify to the Council, that they wish £3000 to be sent speedily to enable the poor Protestants to manage the war, with which they are threatened, as occasion may require.

"In regard of their future establishment they desire the remainder of the moneys to be employed as follows:" [The particulars and amount of pensions will be found in a note in p. 88.]

"*Tuesday,* 18*th May,* 1658.

"At the Council of Whitehall, Mr. Serret reports [The report consisted of the resolutions contained in the foregoing extract.]

"His Highness and the Council do approve of the said report, and order that the Treasurers, for the moneys collected for the said poore Protestants, doe accordingly transmit the said several sums unto the said Committee, to be employed and distributed according to the said report.

"Signed,

"W. JESSOP,
Secretary of the Council."

"*By the Committee for the Affayres of the poor people in the Valleys of Piemont.*

"*October* 12, 1658.

"Whereas his late Highness and the Council did by their order bearing date the 18th of May, 1658, settle an annual pension upon the ministers, school-masters, and several others among the said Protestants, and by another order of the 27th of May, 1658, did appoynt the actual remission of the said pensions, that is to say, for one halfe yeare ending the 24th of June next ensuing, amounting to the summe of three hundred and seven pounds: and whereas Mr. Morland has represented to us, that as the time is now approaching that another halfe yeare from the said terme of the 24th of June will bee expired, at least before the said moneys can actually be received.

"Wee doe therefore humblie declare that we doe consent, in case the same bee thought fitt, by his Highness and the Council, that the above-mentioned summe of £307, being the just summe of one halfe yeare's pension, be forthwith payd by the Treasurers, viz. Sir Thomas Vyner and the Lord Pack, to Mr. Morland, and by him remitted as he has done the former summes.

"Signed,

"EDWARD CRESSETT,
"TOBIAS BRIDGE,
"PHILIP NYE,
"WILLIAM JENKYN,
"JOSEPH CARYT."

This last minute proves beyond all question that there was no misapplication of the capital or interest of the Fund established for the Vaudois, out of the Collection raised in 1655, during the Protectorate either of Oliver or Richard Cromwell, and the pensions, which were granted to them by William and Mary[a], were no doubt appointed in lieu of

[a] "King William and Queen Mary had granted all their reign, or at least for many years of it, a pension of 425*l.* to the *Vaudois* in Germany*. But this pension having been struck off when he [Archbishop Sharp,] came to be made the Queen's almoner, he put into her Majesty's hands a memorial of the pensions that had been paid in the late reign, among which he set down this to the Vaudois; but this taking no effect, and the Vaudois ministers pressing for the pension and the arrears, he wrote to my Lord Treasurer as the properest person to be applied to.

* When the Grant was first made, in 1689, the whole Vaudois population were exiles in Germany and Switzerland.

those of which they were most unjustly deprived during the reigns of Charles II. and James II. The continuance of the royal bounty, encreased to £500 annually, which was regularly received till the year 1797, appears like a tacit acknowledgment on the part of the British Government, that the national honour and faith were pledged to the payment of it, in compensation for the capital which Charles II. seized. I have said that the royal bounty was received until the year 1797. In reality it was not intended to be withdrawn previously to the year 1807, and orders were given to the Exchequer to issue the usual payments for the Vau-

" 'Give me leave (says he) to lay a matter before you, which I think I am bound to concern myself in, and your lordship also, who made me the queen's almoner. I have received since I came to York two letters from *the Vaudois ministers* in Germany, wherein they set forth their great necessities, and earnestly petition for the continuance of that pension, which was settled upon them by King William and Queen Mary in 1689. The first of these I have sent up to Dr. Battle, the sub-almoner, and desired him to move the Queen on their behalf. The other I now make bold to send to your Lordship, together with a memorial of the state of these poor people, which I received this last week from Sir John Chardin. I find that those ministers and schoolmasters who are upon the Dutch establishment receive their pensions duly and are well maintained. Sure then, my Lord, those *that the crown of England promised to provide for*, should not be quite abandoned,' &c. He obtained at last a promise from her Majesty, that this matter should be taken care of.

" But when the treaty of peace was on foot in the year 1709, then was the season for doing true service to the foreign Protestants; and he was not wanting to remind either her Majesty or her ministers of it. As, May 1, 1709; '*In the evening at the Queen's appointment, I waited on her Majesty......I pressed heartily, that now, in the treaty of peace that is on foot, her Majesty would order her plenipotentiaries to concern themselves about the Protestant religion both in France, the Palatinate, the Vaudois, Silesia, &c. that we might not be served as we were at the great treaty of Berwick. She saith over and over again, that she will take care of that matter. I recommended to her, that she should send a minister on purpose, who would be content with a very small salary, and such a one as understood the state of the Protestants abroad. And that it should be his business to manage that affair. I prevailed with her, that she would receive a memorial about the state of religion in foreign parts, which Mr. Hales is preparing, and which the Bishop of Ely has promised to present; and to solicit the Queen and my Lord Treasurer about that affair.*' "—See Life of Archbishop Sharp, by the Rev. T. Newcome.

dois till the fifth of July, 1807. Owing to some cause, however, which has not yet been clearly ascertained, the poor pensioners did not receive their stipends after 1797, although for ten years subsequent to that date they were entitled to them. This makes the hardship of the case still greater, and an investigation into this matter is now proceeding, with every assistance that Government can offer to facilitate it.

Whatever reason might have existed in 1807 for suspending the pensions; whether it was done in consequence of Piemont having become part of the French empire, or in consequence of some informality or irregularity in transmitting the claims for the continuance of the grant, which might have been owing either to the difficulties thrown in the way of intercourse with England during the war, or to some defaulter on this side of the water; yet the very fact of the Vaudois losing the benefit of the royal bounty for ten years, while our government meant that they should continue to enjoy it, is a further motive why their cause should be earnestly taken up, now that the circumstance is known.

Every thing hitherto seems to have gone hard with this distressed and unoffending community. In the first place, the war with France occasioned by some means or other the deprivation of the stipends, which their clergy had received from England for more than a century. After a time, compelled to become subjects of France, the complaints which they had to make, in common with others who were obliged to submit to the new order of things, were softened by having all religious disabilities removed, and by being admitted to a share of equal privileges with their Roman Catholic fellow-subjects. This, however, did not last long; at the restoration of the House of Savoy to its ancient dominions, the poor Vaudois found themselves placed in as bad a situation as ever. The edicts which had been rescinded are renewed against them, they return to limitations, restrictions, penal statutes, and oppressive exactions, and the pensions from England, which were formerly granted to their clergy to ameliorate their condition, are withheld at a time when it is more intolerable than before.

It cannot but be the anxious wish of every friend to this sacred cause of humanity and justice, that the British government should give it a favourable consideration, when we find that almost every Protestant State in Europe is at this very crisis testifying its concern for the poverty and distress to which the Vaudois are reduced. In page 85 I have spoken of the assistance which they have received from the Emperor of Russia, and the king of Prussia, towards building an hospital, and repairing their dilapidated churches.

A delegate, M. Appia[b], has lately arrived in England, and is commissioned by his countrymen to make their wants known to the benevolent of this nation. He has previously been visiting many of the Continental States for the same purpose, and nothing can exceed the kind reception which he has received in the progress of his journey. M. Appia has produced the most respectable credentials to verify his mission, and to shew the attention which has been paid to his representations in the Swiss Cantons, in the smaller German States, and the kingdoms of Wurtemburgh, Saxony and Prussia. The following is a correct copy.

Les Officers de la Table, ou Modérateurs représentants le Corps des Eglises Evangéliques Vaudoises, dans les Vallées de Luserne, Pérouse, Saint Martin, et Terres Médiates, faisant partie de la Province de Pignerol en Piémont.

Sa Majesté Charles Félix, Roi de Sardaigne, notre très-gracieux Souverain, ayant daigné condescendre à nos voeux, en permettant dans nos Vallées pauvres, herrissées de montagnes arides, l'établissement d'un Hôpital, qui formera au

[b] An anecdote of M. Appia is well worth recording, as an illustration of the Vaudois character. He was asked if he had been to either of the Theatres. "No," he replied, "it would ill become a delegate, whose commission is to plead the poverty of his community, to be seen at a theatre."

milieu de nous l'unique asile pour la vieillesse et l'infirmité indigentes : nous nous sommes prévalus de l'acte authentique, qui nous a été délivré au nom de *Sa dite Majesté* par Mr. l'Intendant de la Province de Pignerol, pour acquérir dans la commune de la Tour, vallée de Luserne, un local jugé propre à atteindre le but désiré, ainsi que pour nommer la commission, qui devra administrer ce précieux établissement ; mais dénués de moyens suffisans, nous nous fondons sur les consolantes espérances, qui nous ont été données, et nous recourons à la munificence des Ames Bienfaisantes des différentes Communions Chrétiennes, afin que notre pieuse entreprise puisse atteindre le degré de prospérité nécessaire.

Nous supplions le Dieu Consolateur du malheur et de la souffrance, qui tient en ses mains les cœurs des Rois et des Grands de la terre, de les incliner à compassion en faveur de notre projet et nous prions tous les amis de la religion et de l'humanité, qui voudront bien nous tendre une main secourable, de verser leur charitable offrande dans les mains de notre Député-Collecteur Mr. Pierre Appia de la Tour, petit-fils d'un de nos Modérateurs défunts, qui dévoue ses fatigues et ses soins à l'accomplissement de cette bonne œuvre.

Les souscriptions reçues directement par notre délégué seront remises par lui aux différents Comités, qui se sont organisés et s'organiseront dans chaque Etat avec l'approbation de leurs Gouvernements respectifs : dans le but de provoquer et de réunir les secours, que la piété voudra nous destiner.

Nous nous concerterons avec ces Comités pour placer dans chaque Pays de la manière la plus solide et la plus utile les capitaux recueillis et suivrons avec empressement les avis et propositions de ces Réunions respectables dont nous considérons les membres comme nos plus vrais et plus zêlés amis.

Notre digne compatriote Mr. Joseph Malan, Négociant à Turin, qui possédant à juste tître notre pleine confiance a été revêtu par nous et par la Commission administrative de l'Hôpital de la charge de trésorier de cet établissement, tiendra le régistre général des dons confiés aux divers Comités, qui voudront bien lui en donner l'indication et lui faire parvenir les rentes des fonds placés.

Habitans paisibles d'une partie des hautes Alps, qui séparent l'Italie de la France, l'existence actuelle de vingt mille Vaudois est peu connue sans doute, mais notre nom est consigné depuis le 9me siècle, dans les fastes de l'histoire ecclésiastique, et tous les cœurs religieux et sensibles y verront avec satisfaction, que nous avons des titres à l'intérêt général que nous invoquons maintenant.

C'est avec effusion que nous exprimons au nom des Pasteurs et des Eglises de nos Vallées les sentimens de la plus vive gratitude envers nos généreux Donateurs, en priant le Souverain des souverains de verser sur Eux ses plus précieuses bénédictions, selon la promesse de Son Evangile, qu'un verre d'eau même donné pour l'amour de Son Nom ne demeurera pas sans récompense.

La Tour, le trois Mars, Mille huit cent vingt quatre.

(L. S.)
P. Bert, Pasteur à La Tour, et Modérateur.
Alex. Rostaing, Pasteur à Villesèche, et Modérateur Adjoint.
G. Muston, Pasteur à Bobi, et Secrétaire de la Table.

Suivent les légalisations, et les déclarations des Gouvernements, qui ont daigné appuyer l'Appel de bienfaisance énoncé ci-contre.

Sur la demande de messieurs les Pasteurs composant la Modérature des Eglises Vaudoises, je certifie l'authenticité de leurs signatures apposées au bas de la pièce ci-contre.

Turin, le 11 Mai, 1824.

L'Envoyé extraord. et Ministre plénipotent. de S. M. le Roi de Prusse près S. M. Sarde.

(L. S.) *Le Comte de Waldbourg Truchsess.*

The undersigned His Britannic Majesty's Chargé d'Affaires hereby certifies that this copy agrees in every respect with the original document.

Turin, May 20, 1824.

(L. S.) *G. Crawford Antrobus.*

La Chancellerie d'Etat de la République et Canton de Genève certifie, que cet Etat a pris un vif intérêt à la pieuse entreprise, recommandée dans la présente pièce, entreprise à laquelle le gouvernement et les particuliers ont concouru par des souscriptions.

Genève, le 1 Juin, 1824.

(L. S.) *De Roches*, Secrétaire d'Etat.

La Chancellerie d'Etat de la Principauté et Canton de Neuchâtel certifie que cet Etat a pris aussi un vif intérêt à la pieuse entreprise dont il s'agit dans la présente pièce, entreprise à laquelle le Gouvernement et des corporations ont concouru par des souscriptions.

Au Château de Neuchâtel, le 5 Juillet, 1824.

Le Secrétaire du conseil d'Etat,
(L. S.) *Fr. Aug. de Montmollin.*

Le Chancelier de la Ville et République de Berne certifie que cet Etat a pris un grand intérêt aux pieux établissement dont il s'agit dans la présente pièce, et que le gouvernement y a concouru.

Berne, le 12 Juillet, 1824.

Le Chancelier,
(L. S.) *Gruber.*

Le Chancelier de la Confédération Suisse atteste que le Directoire Fédéral a pris un vif intérêt à l'établissement de bienfaisance dont la présente pièce fait mention, et l'a recommandé aux Etats du corps Helvétique professant la

Religion Evangelique, lesquels, pour la plupart, y ont contribué par des dons.

Berne, le 12 Juillet, 1824.

Le Chancelier de la Confédération,

(L. S.) *Mousson.*

La Chancellerie du Canton d'Aargovie atteste, que le Gouvernement de ce Canton s'est beaucoup interessé à l'établissement de bienfaisance, dont il s'agit, et qu'il y a contribué.

Aarau, le 19 Juillet, 1824.

Le Secrétaire d'Etat,

(L. S.) *F. Rothpletz.*

La Chancellerie du Canton de Basle déclare par les présentes, que le Gouvernement de ce Canton s'intéresse beaucoup à l'établissement de bienfaisance dont il s'agit, et qu'il y a également contribué.

Basle, le 31 Juillet, 1824.

pr. le Secrétaire d'Etat, le Secrétaire substitué,

(L. S.) *Lichtenhahn.*

La Chancellerie du Canton de Zurich atteste, que le Gouvernement de ce Canton s'intéresse beaucoup à l'établissement de bienfaisance, dont il s'agit, et qu'il a contribué par un don, en decrêtant aussi, de ne pas s'opposer à ce qu'il soit fait ici publication de l'entreprise.

Zurich, 25 Août, 1824.

Le troisième Secrétaire d'Etat,

(L. S.) *Hottinger.*

La Chancellerie du Canton de Schaffouse atteste, que le Gouvernement de ce Canton s'intéresse beaucoup à l'etablissement de bienfaisance dont il s'agit, et qu'il y a contribué par un don, en ne s'opposant pas non plus, qu'il soit fait ici publication de l'entreprise.

Schaffouse, le 10 Septembre, 1824.

Le Chancelier,

(L. S.) *Fs. de Meyenbourg.*

11

La soussignée certifie, que le Gouvernement de la partie Evangelique de ce Canton prend un vrai intérêt à l'établissement de bienfaisance dont il s'agit dans la présente pièce, et qu'il y a concouru de son côté par un don.

Frauenfeld, le 12 Septembre, 1824.

La Chancellerie du petit Conseil
Evangelique du Canton de Thurgovie,
(L. S.) *Müller*, Chancelier.

Gesehen bei dem Königlich Württembergischen Ministerium des Innern, und wird dem Inhaber gestattet, mittelst öffentlichen Aufrufs an Menschenfreunde freiwillige Beiträge zu dem invermeldeten wohlthätigen Zwecke zu sammeln.

Stuttgart, den 25 Septbr. 1824.

(L. S.) *Schmidlin.*

No. 11678. Gesehen bei dem Grossherzoglich Badischen Ministerium des Innern, und sind sämmtliche Dekane des Grossherzogthums unter Anschluss eines Aufrufs aufgefordert worden, Beiträge zu vorgedachtem Zweck zu sammeln, und solche an die oberste evangelische Kirchenbehörde zur Abgabe an das zum Empfang bevollmächtigte Handelshaus einzusenden.

Carlsruhe, den 2 October, 1624.

In Abwesenheit des Ministers der Ministerial-Director,
(L. S.) *L. Winter.*

Gesehen bei dem Grossherzoglich Hessischen Ministerium des Innern und der Justiz und wird dem Inhaber gestattet, mittelst öffentlichen Aufrufs an Menschenfreunde freiwillige Beiträge zu dem fraglichen wohlthätigen Zweck zu sammeln.

Darmstadt, am 9 Oktober, 1824.

(L. S.) *v. Grolman.*

Die Canzlei der freien Stadt Frankfurt beurkundet andurch, dass durch Beschluss hohen Senats dieser freien

Statd, von 9ten dieses, dem Inhaber anheim gegeben worden, mittelst öffentlichen Aufrufs an Menschenfreunde, freiwillige Beiträge zu dem betreffenden wohlthätigen Zweck zu sammeln.

Frankfurt am Main, den 12 November, 1824.

Canzlei
der freien Stadt Frankfurt.
Der Canzlei-Rath
(L. S.) *Dr. Usener.*

Die Königlich Sächsische Landes-Regierung bezeugt hierdurch, dass sämmtliche Kreis-und Amtshauptleute im Königreiche Sachsen beaufragt worden sind, durch Bekanntmachungen in öffentlichen Blättern das Publicum zu Leistung freiwilliger Beiträge zu dem fraglichen wohlthätigen Zwecke aufzufordern, auch sich der Einsammlung dieser Beiträge und deren Abgabe an das bezeichnete Handelshaus zu unterziehen.

Dresden, am 6 December, 1824.

Königlich Sächsische Landesregierung,
(L. S.) Frhr. *v. Rochow.*

Von Seiten des Königlich Sächsischen Kirchen-Raths und Ober-Consistorii wird, soviel die demselben untergeordnete Behörde und Geistlichkeit anbelangt, zu der vorstehend bemerkten Sammlung die nöthige Ermächtigung hierdurch ebenmässig ertheilt.

Dresden, am 6 December, 1824.

v. Globig,
Königlich Sächsisch. wirklicher Geheimer Rath
(L. S.) und Ober-Consistorial-Präsident.

Von Seiten des Königlich Preussischen Ministerii der Geistlichen-Unterrichts- und Medicinal-Angelegenheiten wird hierdurch attestirt, dass zu dem von der Waldenser-Colonie in den Thälern von Pignerol zu errichtenden Hospitale mit Genehmigung Seiner Majestät des Königs nicht allein eine allgemeine Kollecte in sämmtlichen evangelischen Kirchen des Preussischen Staates angeordnet, sondern dass das Publikum von dem Abgeordneten der Colonie auch noch durch einen hiesigen Verein zu Beiträgen für das gedachte Hospital aufgefordert werden darf.

Berlin, den 12 Januar, 1825.

Der Königlich Preussische wirkliche
Geheime Staats-Minister
(L. S.) *Altenstein.*

When M. Appia was at Berlin, he addressed an humble petition to the King of Prussia, requesting that his Majesty would be pleased to permit a collection to be made for the Vaudois in the Protestant churches of his dominions. That benevolent monarch graciously condescended to return an answer to M. Appia, signed by his own hand, and ordered it to be accompanied by a donation of a hundred ducats, about £50.

The following is a copy of his Majesty's Letter:

A M. Pierre Appia, Délégué des Eglises Vaudoises des Vallées du Piémont.

En réponse à la requête que Vous m'avez adressée en date du 12 de ce mois, je vous informe que j'ai chargé le Ministre Baron d'Altenstein d'examiner l'admissibilité des Collectes dans les Eglises Evangéliques de la Monarchie Prussienne au profit de la fondation d'un hôpital pour les pauvres malades de la Colonie des Vaudois dans les vallées de Pignerol. En attendant la résolution ultérieure que le Baron d'Altenstein vous fera connaître, vous recevez avec la présente la somme *de Cent Ducats* pour la faire employer à la destination mentionnée. Berlin, le 21 Décembre, 1824.

(Signé) FREDERIC GUILLAUME.

Since this gracious act of royal condescension, the King of Prussia has sanctioned the formation of a Committee to raise subscriptions, under his Minister of Finance, and has authorized Collections to be made for the Vaudois in all the Protestant Churches of his kingdom.

I am happy to be able to follow up this intelligence by adding, that a Committee to promote subscriptions for the Vaudois, and to manage the Fund raising for their relief has also been formed in London. A transcript of the first Resolutions, will not, it is hoped, be unacceptable to my readers.

"At a Meeting of some of the principal Subscribers to the Fund, which is now raising in England for the general relief of the distressed Vaudois, held at the house of Sir G. H. Rose, M.P. May 26, 1825,

"The Right Honourable and Right Reverend the LORD BISHOP OF LONDON in the Chair;

"It was unanimously Resolved—That the following persons be requested to form a Committee, for the management of the said fund, and for taking into consideration the best means of applying it, in aid of the Establishment of an Hospital, in the commune of La Tour, in the valley of Luzerne and province of Pignerol, Piedmont; and for such other purposes as may be thought expedient by the Committee, consistently with the objects expressed in the Royal Letters Patent of his late Majesty King George III. bearing date, viz. 1768:—

"To enable the Vaudois to maintain their Ministers, Churches, Schools, and Poor, which they are not able to support in any tolerable manner."

The Earl of CLARENDON
The Earl of St. GERMANS
The Lord Bishop of LONDON
The Lord Bishop of WINCHESTER
The Right Hon. Sir G. H. ROSE, M.P.

Sir T. Dyke ACLAND, Bart. M.P.
Sir Thomas BARING, Bart, M.P.
Sir Robert INGLIS, Bart. M.P.
Archdeacon WRANGHAM
The Rev. Dr. BURROW
The Rev. Dr. PHILLPOTTS
The Rev. Dr. RICHARDS
The Rev. Dr. SCHWABE
The Rev. Dr. SUMNER
H. D. ACLAND, Esq.
Jasper ATKINSON, Esq.
Charles F. BARNWELL, Esq.
Samuel BOSANQUET, Esq.
The Rev. Bewick BRIDGE
William COTTON, Esq.
The Rev. William S. GILLY
W. R. HAMILTON, Esq.
The Rev. Anthony HAMILTON
G. HARRISON, Esq.
Gorges LOWTHER, Esq.
The Rev. I. S. PONS
The Rev. Thomas SIMS
The Rev. Joseph WIGRAM

"With the power of adding to their number, as circumstances may require.

"That of the fore-named Committee, Five shall form a Quorum.

"That, at all such meetings of the Committee as shall be called for the purpose of giving orders for the transmission of money to the Vaudois, the whole of its members shall be summoned by a Circular Letter to attend, and that no money shall be transmitted without the consent of the majority present at such meeting.

"That, for conducting the ordinary business of the Committee, a Sub-Committee be appointed, three of whom shall form a Quorum, and that such Sub-Committee consist of the following members:

The Right Hon. Sir. G. H. Rose. M.P.
Sir Thomas Dyke Acland, Bart. M.P.
W. R. Hamilton, Esq.
The Rev. Dr. Burrow
The Rev. Dr. Richards
H. D. Acland, Esq.
J. Atkinson, Esq.
C. F. Barnwell, Esq.
The Rev. B. Bridge
The Rev. W. S. Gilly
The Rev. I. S. Pons

" With such Bishops as are on the general Committee.

" That George Harrison, Esq. Samuel Bosanquet, Esq. and the Rev. Anthony Hamilton, who have hitherto acted as Trustees to the Vaudois Fund, be requested to continue their services in that capacity.

" That the Rev. Bewick Bridge be requested to undertake the office of Treasurer to the Fund.

" That the Rev. W. S. Gilly be requested to act as Honorary Secretary to the Committee; and that the Rev. I. S. Pons be requested to assist him in conducting the Foreign Correspondence.

" That the following Bankers be requested to receive Subscriptions. viz.—

" Messrs. Glyn, Mills, Halifax, and Co. Lombard-street.

" Messrs. Bosanquet, Pitt, Anderdon, Franks, and Co. Lombard-street.

" Messrs. Masterman, Peters, Mildred, and Co. Nicholas-lane.

" Messrs. Hoare and Co. Fleet-street.

" Messrs. Herries, Farquhar, and Co. St. James's-street.

" Messrs. Drummonds, Charing Cross.

" Messrs. Coutts and Co. Strand."

From the information which I have received from M. Bert, and the Officers of the Table, it will want seven or eight thousand pounds to enable the Vaudois to complete the Hospital, and to maintain it when finished ; and nearly the same sum would be required to enable them to support their schoolmasters and widows of deceased clergy, in any tolerable manner. Many of their long-established schools have been closed for want of funds to continue them. It surely is not too much to hope, that the contributions in this country and on the continent will amount to the sum of which they stand in need, and that the relief which has so often been extended to this suffering community, will not fail them at the present crisis.

After my last page had gone to Press, I had the satisfaction of receiving the following Letter, in intimation of a most handsome collection from a respectable body of Protestant Dissenters, whose generous example and liberal co-operation will no doubt excite a general spirit of emulation.

" *London Vestry, Providence Chapel, Gray's-Inn-Lane, Monday, June 6th,* 1825.

" Sir,

" The present state of the Vaudois must, it is presumed, attract the benevolent interference of every Protestant State, and excite the sympathetic feelings of every individual, who is desirous of evincing his good will to a people, among whom the purity of the Christian faith and worship has been preserved in so remarkable a manner through a succession of ages, and in the midst of difficulties, privations, and persecutions which must long since have exterminated them, but for the evident interposition of Divine Providence in their behalf.

" In accordance with these sentiments, the Trustees of Providence Chapel, Gray's-Inn-Lane, acting for, and in the name of the congregation of Protestant Dissenters late under the pastoral care of the Rev. William Huntington, deceased, felt a strong inclination to aid the proposed subscriptions for the relief of this distressed and suffering branch of the Christian Church, and on intimating their wishes to others their friends, they had the satisfaction of finding that a similar desire pervaded the congregation. A public collection was therefore appointed, which took place at the above Chapel on Sunday, the 24th of April, 1825, last, after suitable sermons in the morning and evening by the Rev. Joseph Chamberlain, and as the effect thereof we feel truly gratified in presenting to this laudable fund the sum of £127 8*s*. 6*d*.[c] including thirteen pounds from several other friends at Staplehurst, in the county of Sussex. We have reason to expect that this sum may be further augmented from two or three branches of the same connection in different parts of the country, but as the final results cannot be ascertained until a few weeks hence, we deem it expedient to make the present communication, and at the same time to express our fervent hopes that, with due publicity, the plan may meet the general concurrence of the Protestant public, in support of the benevolent views implied in the liberal donations of His Majesty and many distinguished characters of this country, and may ultimately terminate in a settled national allowance that shall prove an effectual relief to the oppressed sufferers, and a permanent honour to the British government.

[c] This connection of Protestant Dissenters have since increased their very liberal subscription, and it now amounts to £230 10*s*. 6*d*. The particulars are as follows:

	£.	s.	d.
At Providence Chapel, Grays-Inn-Lane, including 13*l*. from Staplehurst, Sussex	127	8	6
At Salem Chapel, Leicester	31	3	0
At Castlegate Chapel, Grantham	31	0	0
At Providence Chapel, Cranbrook	40	19	0
	230	10	6

Other bodies of Dissenters have followed this good example, to the great increase of the Vaudois Fund. Some generous Roman Catholics, and among them a few Piemontese Nobles, have also contributed their assistance.—*Note to Third Edition.*

"With the most heartfelt wishes that success may attend your future exertions in this excellent cause,

"We have the honour to be,

Sir,

Your most obedient servants,

THOMAS BENSLEY, *Clapham Rise*, }
CHRIST. GOULDING, *Northampton Square*, } TRUSTEES.

"*P. S.* The collection will be made at Leicester on Sunday next, the 12th inst. At Grantham on Sunday the 19th inst."

It gladdens my heart to have such a concluding passage to my work—to be thus assured that Protestants of all parties and denominations are likely to extend the hand of Christian fellowship, and to unite in succouring the descendants of those who transmitted to them their common faith.

POSTSCRIPT

TO THE

THIRD EDITION.

THE cause of the Waldenses continues to excite the compassionate sympathies of almost all the Protestant Communities in Europe. The Reformed Churches in France are making collections in their behalf, and 2500 francs were subscribed in Paris at the beginning of the present year.

The following letter will shew that the King of the Netherlands has followed the gracious example of the King of Great Britain, of the late Emperor Alexander, and the King of Prussia.

Translation of a Letter from the Belgian Secretary of State, to the Rev. P. Appia, in answer to his petition to His Majesty the King of the Netherlands.

" *The Hague, October* 28, 1825.

" SIR,

" The wants of the Churches of the Waldenses, which you represent, have made a strong impression on his Majesty's heart. The King has therefore cheerfully granted the prayer expressed in your address of the 20th inst.— and orders have been issued that the object of your mission, and the interests of your flock should be advocated in all the Protestant Churches of this kingdom.

" His Majesty trusts this measure will increase the favourable disposition of his subjects towards your countrymen, who, as you say, have already had the benefit of their sympathy. In the mean time, and with the hope that fresh success will be added to the already favourable result of your application, His Majesty hastens to manifest the interest he takes in the situation of your Churches, and to present an offering on the altar of charity. I am therefore commanded to enclose the sum of one thousand florins, in the joint names of His Majesty and the Queen, and to assure you that their Majesties feel happy to have this opportunity of shewing to the Waldenses, that they have not forgotten their ancient attachment to their Family, and have been peculiarly pleased with the unanimous concern the Waldenses expressed, on occasion of the late disastrous events which afflicted this country.

"I remain, &c.

(Signed) "H. DE MEY DE STREEFKERK."

The concluding sentence of the above letter alludes to a subscription, for the relief of sufferers from the late inundations, which the Vaudois raised among themselves, amounting to 4800 francs, and *to which the whole population contributed*, in small sums, in gratitude for the many benefactions they had received from time to time from Holland.

The contributions in Holland, reported up to the 7th of March, 1826, amount to 30,000 florins.

The LONDON COMMITTEE have lately published a Report of their proceedings, of which the annexed is an abstract.

"The principal objects which the Committee have in view, are to ESTABLISH AN HOSPITAL, TO ASSIST THE MINISTERS AND THOSE WHO ARE EDUCATING FOR THE MINISTRY, AND TO MAINTAIN SCHOOLS.

"THE HOSPITAL.

"The want of an Hospital of their own, has been deeply felt by the Waldenses, being excluded from the Hospitals of Piedmont by reason of their Religion. The accidents and maladies which assail the poor of a barren mountain district, the greater part of which is covered with snow during eight months in the year, require no explanation, for it is evident that numbers must perish every season for want of medical and surgical assistance. A suitable house and ground are already provided, and Mr. Thomas Coucourde (a native of the Valleys) has been appointed Physician and Steward to the Hospital, with a salary of 500 francs a year, with apartments in the building, and the use of the ground. The Hospital is expected to be opened for the reception of Patients, early in the spring of this year.

" THE MINISTERS.

" The merits and distress of these exemplary men are stated above. Should the Committee succeed in obtaining the restitution of the Royal Grant, a competent provision will be secured for them, but a fund will still be required for those who are educating for the ministry. At present their only opportunity of pursuing studies to qualify them for holy orders, is to accept the offer of small exhibitions at the Universities of Lausanne and Geneva, which are granted by the Swiss Cantons. The inconveniences inseparable from this system need not be detailed, and it would be obviously a great benefit if the means could be afforded them of studying for their sacred profession at home, as they did in former times.

" SCHOOLS.

" The Waldenses stand in great need of aid to enable them to instruct their children in the duties of religion. They require a superior degree of education, first, because the French language must be taught them in addition to their own, as no books of religious instruction or devotion, consistent with their own faith, are permitted to be circulated in Italian; and secondly, because the principles of religion must be fully and systematically explained to a peasantry, who are exposed to all the seductions of sophistry and bribery on the part of their Roman Catholic neighbours. They also require a greater number of schools and teachers, because the children cannot pass from place to place during the perils and severities of a long winter, except at the imminent hazard of their lives, and must therefore be instructed in their own hamlets.

" DISPOSAL OF THE SUBSCRIPTIONS.

" In order that permanent good may result to the Waldenses from the benevolent exertions which are now making for them in England, the Moderator and 'Officers of the Table' (who manage the eleemosynary concerns of the community,) have intimated to the Committee, that it would be most desirable to invest, in the British funds, the amount of the subscriptions raised in England, and to remit the interest of the capital as it may accrue, by yearly or half-yearly payments. In conformity with this intimation, and to introduce a definite system into their accounts, and to be able at all times to appropriate the several sums which shall be received, each to its separate and specific destination, the Committee have adopted the following resolutions.

" I. That the donations for the Hospital and for general purposes be invested in the 3 per cent. consols, as a separate fund.

" II. That the donations for affording pecuniary aid for the young men of the Waldenses intended for the Ministry, be invested in the 3 per cent. reduced, as a separate fund.

" III. That the sums received for Schools, be invested in the 3½ per cents. as a separate fund.

" IV. That the Committee do not, hereafter, take charge of any sums raised for purposes of education in the Valleys of Piedmont, unless they are placed under the direction of the Committee, to be at the disposal and discretion of the 'Officers of the Table,' of the Waldenses.

" The Committee have already been able to act upon

these measures, and to advise the 'Officers of the Table,' that they may immediately draw upon the Treasurer of the Committee for the first half-year's interest of the capital now in hand, a capital which they hope to see increasing every day.

" Summary of the Treasurer's Account, as laid before the Committee, Jan. 31, 1826.

" Dr.	£.	s.	d.	" Cr.	£.	s.	d.
" Amount of Subscriptions for Hospital and general purposes	3872	3	5	" By purchase of Stock in 3 per cent. Consols ..	3245	6	6
For the education of young men intended for the Ministry	531	4	1	Ditto, in 3 per cent. reduced	448	3	9
For Schools	337	18	0	Ditto, in 3½ per cents. ..	181	2	6
				Reported from Lichfield, but not yet placed to Treasurer's account ..	†409	16	0
				Ditto, from Farnham, ditto	36	9	0
				By remittances to the Waldenses, by order of Committee	154	12	0
				By sundry disbursements in advertising, printing, postage, &c.	126	5	10
				Balance in hand	139	10	11
	*£4741	5	6		£4741	5	6

THE publication of this edition has been delayed for several weeks, in expectation of being able to announce the success of the Committee's endeavours to draw the attention of His Majesty's Government to the claims, which the Waldensian Clergy have to the restitution of their former pensions on the Royal Grant. A Deputation of the Committee, consisting of the Earl of St. Germans, Sir Thomas Dyke Acland, Dr. Sumner, Mr. Hamilton, and the Author of this Narrative, were appointed to solicit an interview

* N. B. This account does not include 211*l.* 13*s.* received for the exclusive use of the sons of the late Moderator, nor 100*l.* ditto for the present Moderator.

† Since encreased to 550*l.*

with the first Lord of the Treasury and the Chancellor of the Exchequer, that they might have an opportunity of stating the case fully and satisfactorily. Their request was readily granted, and on Saturday the 25th of March, they were received by Lord Liverpool and Mr. Robinson with a degree of attention to the subject, which does honour to the advisers of a Sovereign, to whom, whether in his own Gracious Person, or through his Ministers, an appeal in a just and righteous cause has rarely been made in vain*. THE RESULT OF THIS INTERVIEW WAS AN ASSURANCE THAT MEASURES SHOULD BE ADOPTED TO RESTORE THE STIPEND TO THE VAUDOIS CLERGY, WHICH THEY FORMERLY ENJOYED FROM THE BOUNTY OF THE BRITISH GOVERNMENT.

I have thus to close my Narrative with the gratifying intelligence, THAT ALL THE OBJECTS OF IT ARE COMPLETELY ATTAINED. The regards of our Protestant Nation and Government have been attracted to the present condition of the Waldenses. The most pressing of the temporal wants of this interesting community will be relieved by a public subscription, and their spiritual welfare will be promoted by a provision for their Ministers and School-masters, IN THE RESTITUTION OF THAT ANNUAL PENSION, WHICH ORIGINATED IN A NATIONAL CONTRIBUTION, AND WAS AFTERWARDS RE-ESTABLISHED BY ROYAL BENEVOLENCE.

March 27, 1826.

* A few hours before this communication was made, the Vaudois lost one of their most zealous friends and generous benefactors, in my venerated Patron the good Bishop of Durham. In addition to his several contributions, amounting in all to 172*l.* 10*s.* the Bishop has bequeathed 500*l.* to the Waldensian Church.

Fac Simile of the Attestation of M. Tronchin taken from the Original M.S. deposited in the Library of the University of Cambridge.

Je sousigné Ministre du Sainct Euangile et Professeur
en Theologie à Geneve atteste que le Sr Jean Paul Perrin estant
vena en cette ville pour y faire imprimer l'histoire
des Vaudois et Albigens par luy composée me commu-
niqua son ouurage et quelques manuscripts originaux
dont il auoit extrait leur doctrine et discipline et
que ie n'ay veu alors. En foy de quoy i'en baille la present
témoignage pour seruir à la verité quand et où besoin
sera fait à Geneue le 19 Novembre 1656

T. Tronchin

Fac Simile of the concluding Sentence of the Declaration of Captain Du Petit Bourg & of the Attestation of the two Witnesses to the same taken from the Original M.S. deposited in the Library of the University of Cambridge.

au cantonatz voyant que
ne pouvoir point y aporter de remede
fu contraint de me retirer a abandonner
conduicte du regiment de pierre dassiette
de sa manaige [illegible] faict a pignerol le
vingt [illegible] novembre 1655

dupetit bourc

Nous Soubsigner Capnes aux Regts dinfanterie de saulx dauvergne
certiffions auoir veu faire La prisante declaration dans cette ville
de pignerol [illegible] la escritte et signee de sa propre main en nostre
presence en foy de quoy nous auons signé La presante a pignerol ce
Novembre 1655 au sieur de petit Bourg Capne au Regt dinfanterie
de France

S. hyllaire Capne dauvergne

Dufaure capitaine de Sault

Fac Simile of the Attestation of M. Schmid taken from the Original M.S. deposited in the Library of the Univers

Je Soubsigne fais foy par la presente, que Mons
bassadeur de la Ville & Canton de Schaffhause
de Savoye, durant le traitté de Pignerolle, a
d'instances aupres Messieurs les Ambassadeurs ses
haster pas ledit traitté, mais plustost d'en differe
jusques à l'arrivée des Mess.rs les Ambassadeurs d'A
lande, leur ayant par toute sorte des raisons rem
dangereuse & prejudiciable cette procedure seroit
habitans des Vallées, mais aussy à la cause commun
testans. & quand non obstant tout cela, il ne vou
escouté, il fit une proteste de ne vouloir pas estre
qui pourroit ensuivre. Fait à Geneve ce $\frac{17}{27}$ Sep

(L.S.)

Andr
tuial

MAP
of PART of
Piemnt & Savoy.
with e Country of the
VAUDOS OR VALDE
and shewing Route over the Alps by Mont C.
Scale of Italian Ml. 60 to the Degree
Note. Torino. Latitude 45 : 4
D M
FRANCIA
PIEMONTE
BRIANCON
M. Dauphin
M. Genevre
Col de la Rou
Col. Albin
Col d. Alenes
Glazier et Mont de la Venoise
S. Michel
Modane
Lanslebourg
Hospital
Susa
Exilles
Oulx
Angliana
Rivoli
Nona
PINEROLO
SALUZZO
VALDESI
Pomarets
Perosa
Bobbio
Villaro
Angrogna
Brickerasio
La Torre
Barge
Cavour
Balma
PO R.

APPENDIX.

APPENDIX.

N°. I.

Notice of Publications relating to the Vaudois during the three last Centuries.

WITH the intention of directing the reader to those sources of information, from which the Author has derived much of his own knowledge of the interesting people, who form the subject of the present Narrative, a list is subjoined, and with it a brief description, of the books, that have been consulted upon the occasion.

A hasty or partial review of some of these authorities, might lead to conclusions, as to the antiquity of the Waldensian church, different from those, which are drawn in the preceding pages; but no fears are entertained in regard to the opinions of such, as have opportunity and patience to pursue the investigation thoroughly.

1. " Histoire Generale des Eglises Evangeliques des Vallées de Piemonte, ou Vaudoises, divisée en deux livres. Dont le premier fait voir incontestablement, quelle a esté de tous tems, tant leur discipline que sur tout leur doctrine, et quelle maniere elles l'ont si constamment conservée en une si grande pureté, dès que Dieu les a tirées des tenebres du Paganisme jusqu' à present, sans interruption, et necessité de Reformation. Et le second traite generalement de toutes les plus considerables persecutions,

qu'elles ont suffertes, pour la soûtenir, sur tout dès que l'inquisition a commencé à regner sur les Chrêtiens, jusqu' à l'an 1664.

" Par Jean Leger, Pasteur et Moderateur des Eglises des Vallées, et depuis la violence de la persecution appellé à l'Eglise Wallone de Leyde. Le tout enrichi de tailles douces.

" A Leyde, chez Jean le Carpentier." 1669.

This work is in folio, and by far the most complete history of the ancient Vaudois, that is extant; but it is very scarce. There are 212 closely printed pages in the first part, and 385 in the second. The map, which accompanies it, is upon a large scale, and very correct, except that some of the places have the Italian, and others the French names, or terminations.

2. " Histoire Ecclesiastique des Eglises Reformées recuillies en quelques Vallées de Piemonte, et circonuoisines, autrefois appellés Eglises Vaudoises, commençant dès l'an 1160 de nostre Seigneur, et finissant en l'an mil six cents quarante trois.

" Par Pierre Gilles, Pasteur de l'Eglise Reformée de la Tour.

" A Geneva, pour Jean de Tournes, imprimeur ordinare de la Republique et Academie." 1664. pp. 569.

This is by no means so valuable a work as that of Leger. Its information, upon the subject of the early history of the Vaudois, is often incorrect. It occupies sixty-one chapters, of which the three first treat of the doctrine and discipline of the Vaudois; the fourth, of the persecution of the fifteenth century; the fifth, of the reformed churches in Germany, and the remainder, of the persecutions of the Vaudois, between the years 1533 and 1642.

It contains scarcely any thing of importance, which is not to be found in Leger's folio volume.

3. " The History of the Evangelical Churches of the Valleys of Piemonte; containing a most exact geographical Description of the place, and a faithful Account of the Doctrine, Life, and Persecutions of the ancient Inhabitants: together with a most naked and punctual Relation of the late bloudy Massacre in 1655, and a Narrative of all the Transactions, to the Year of our Lord 1658. All which are justified partly by divers ancient Manuscripts, written many hundred Years before Calvin and Luther; and

partly by other most authentic Attestations, the true Originals of the great part whereof are to be seen in their proper Languages by all the curious, in the public Library of the famous University of Cambridge.

"Collected and compiled, with much pains and industry, by Samuel Morland, Esquire, during his abode in Geneva, in quality of his Highness Commissioner Extraordinary for the affairs of the said Valleys, and particularly for the distribution of the collected moneys among the remnant of these poor distressed people." London. 1658. Folio. pp. 705.

This work is as valuable as that of Leger, and will supply the English reader with almost all the information contained in the French of the latter. Morland was Envoy from the Protector Cromwell to the court of Savoy, in 1655.

4. "Some Remarks upon the Ecclesiastical History of the ancient Churches of Piedmont. By Peter Allix, D.D." Octavo. pp. 361.

This very recondite work was originally printed in 1690, and reprinted at Oxford in 1821. It contains some most interesting and learned researches into the early history of the Waldensian church; and its authority may generally be relied upon. In fact, it is almost the only volume, which grapples with the subject of the remote antiquity of the Vaudois, in a masterly way.

5. "The History of the Vaudois; wherein is shewn their original: how God has preserved the Christian Religion among them in its Purity, from the time of the Apostles, to our Days: the Wonders he has done for their Preservation, with the signal and miraculous Victories that they have gained over their Enemics: how they were dispersed, and their Churches ruined; and how, at last, they were re-established beyond the Expectation and Hope of all the World.

"By Peter Boyer, a Minister of the Gospel. Dedicated to the King of England; and now translated out of the French, by a Person of Quality." London. 1692.

This is a small volume, of 250 pages, and is principally an abridgment from other works; but it is curious, as being a continuation of Morland's and Leger's Histories, from 1658 to 1691.

6. " Histoire de la Glorieuse Rentrée des Vaudois dans leur Vallées, où l'on voit une troupe de ces gens, qui n'a jamais été jusqu' à mile personnes, soûtenir la Guerre contre le Roi de France, et contre S.A.R. le Duc de Savoye : faire tête à leur armée de 22,000 hommes, s'ovrir le passage par la Savoye, et par le haut Dauphiné, batre plusieurs fois les ennemis, et en fin miraculeusement rentrer dans ses heritages, s'y maintenir les armes à la main, et y retablir le culte de Dieu qui en avoit été interdit depuis trois ans et demi.

" Par Henri Arnaud, Pasteur et Colonel des Vaudois," 1710.

Dedicated to Queen Anne.

The Author has not been able to procure a sight of this very rare, curious, and entertaining work since his return to England, except at the British Museum, notwithstanding some very diligent searches for it in libraries and bookshops, nor does he think a copy of it is to be bought. He was equally unsuccessful in Switzerland, and met with it no where but at the public library at Geneva, the directors of which had the goodness to lend it to him for several days. He took the opportunity of making copious extracts, with which he has enriched his own volume.

7. " Histoire de la Negociation des Ambassadeurs envoyés au Duc de Savoy, par les Cantons Evangeliques, 1686." Geneva, 1690.

For a sight of this little tract, the Author was also indebted to the library of Geneva, and obtained much information from it, relative to the oppressive proceedings of Victor Amadeus the Second, against his Vaudois subjects, in 1686.

A copy of it may be seen at the British Museum.

8. " History of the Waldenses, connected with a Sketch of the Christian Church, from the Birth of Christ to the eighteenth Century. By William Jones." London. 1812. Octavo. pp. 576.

This volume does not enter upon the subject of the Vaudois till the 319th page, and carries their history no farther than the year 1686.

9. "Histoire des Vaudois divisée en trois parties.

"La premiere est de leur origine, pure croyance, et persecutions, qu'ils ont souffert par toute l'Europe, par l'espace de plus de quatre cens cinquante ans.

"La seconde contient l'histoire des Vaudois appellés Albigenses.

"La troisieme est touchant la doctrine, et discipline qu'ils ont eu commune entre eux, et la refutation de la doctrine de leurs adversaires.

"Par Jean Paul Perrin. Lionnois." 1619.

Perrin was a native of Lyons, and as such, anxious to establish the erroneous opinion, that Peter Waldo was the founder of the Waldensian church. His History relates more to the refugee Waldenses, and their descendants, than to the native Vaudois of Piemont.

10. Mosheim is far from being correct in his account of the Church of the Vaudois.

11. Milner's account of the Waldenses, in his third volume of "The History of the Church of Christ," is principally compiled from Perrin and Allix, and forms a correct and interesting relation up to the middle of the sixteenth century.

12. Usher, in the sixth and eighth chapters of his very learned treatise, "De successione et statu Ecclesiarum Christianarum," Newton, in the latter part of his "Dissertations on the Prophecies," and Thuanus the historian, will be found to bear honorable testimony to the undaunted courage, and purity of life and conversation displayed by the Vaudois, at different periods of their history.

13. "Gerdesii Historia Reformationis," (4 vols. 4to.) contains some interesting particulars respecting the Waldenses, and their communications with the early Reformers; but the Author had not an opportunity of consulting it, till after the greater part of his work had gone to press. It was then pointed out to him by the kindness of the Bishop of London, who is deeply read, and warmly interested, in all that relates to this extraordinary community.

The only publications, with which the Author is acquainted, that have brought down the history of the Vaudois to a late period, are,

1. " A brief Memoir respecting the Waldenses, or Vaudois, Inhabitants of the Vallies of Piedmont, the Result of Observations made during a short Residence amongst that interesting People, in the Autumn of 1814. By a Clergyman of the Church of England." London. Hatchard. 1815. pp. 42.

This little treatise is, as it professes to be, very brief, and occupies only forty-two pages, but the information it gives is accurate, and it excites a strong desire to know more of the subjects of the memoir.

2. " Brief Observations on the present State of the Waldenses, and upon their actual Sufferings: made in the Summer of 1820. By Gorges Lowther, Esq." London. 1821.

Mr. Lowther's pamphlet contains about fifty pages, and has been translated by himself into Italian. It is an uncommonly spirited production, to which the Author of this Narrative is indebted for some valuable facts, and he is glad to have this opportunity of acknowledging other assistance, which has been rendered to him by that gentleman, in the progress of his work. The statements, in Mr. Lowther's memoir, form the principal materials of a small French pamphlet of thirty-one pages, published at Paris, in 1822, under the title of

3. " Notice sur l'Etat actuel des Eglises Vaudoises, Protestantes des Vallées du Piemont."

The Editor of this treatise professes to have had some help from " un rapport officiel redige par plusieurs notables Vaudois sur les lieux mêmes, et presenté en Angleterre aux ministres des trois dénominations des dissenters," and published in London, in 1816, as a " Sketch of the past and present State of the Vaudois, or Waldenses, inhabiting the Valleys of Piedmont, translated from the original Italian Manuscript."

The last publication, which it is thought necessary to notice, is,

4. " A Sermon preached to the English Congregation assembled at Rome, on Sunday, April 6, 1823, for the Benefit of the

Primitive Church of the Vaudois, or ancient Albigenses and Waldenses. By the Rev. Lewis Way, A.M. Minister of the Episcopal Protestant Chapel at Nice. Second Edition. With an Appendix." Hatchard. 1823.

The extraordinary feature of this sermon is, that it should have been preached at ROME; the very place from which first issued the bulls and anathemas against the Vaudois; and the fact is a strong argument in confirmation of Mr. Way's favourite hypothesis, that "persecution is on the decline." It would be hailed with transport, if all the Roman Catholic Sovereigns would imitate the enlightened policy of the late most amiable Pope Pius VII. and his liberal-minded and excellent minister, and Cardinal Consalvi: both of whom, *unfortunately* for the States of the Church, are now no more [a].

[a] Since the publication of his first Edition, the Author has consulted the following works, which he recommends to the reader, as throwing additional light upon the past and present history of the Waldenses.

"Histoire des Vaudois, ou des Habitans des Vallées Occidentales du Piémont, qui ont conservé le Christianisme dans toute sa pureté, et à travers plus de trente persécutions, depuis les premiers siècles de son existence jusqu' à nos jours, sans avoir participé à aucune réforme." Utrecht. 1794. pp. 400.

"Notice Historique sur les Vaudois des Vallées du Piémont." Genève. 1824. pp. 19.

"Die Waldenser in den Piemontesischen Thalern." 1824. pp. 8. with a small Map of the Valleys. *Note to Second Edition.*

"History and present Condition of the Vaudois." London. 1826. 2nd. Edition. pp. 56. By H. D. Acland, Esq. This pamphlet contains most valuable and interesting information, collected by the author during an excursion of many weeks in the valleys, made in the summer of 1825.

N°. II.

The Noble Lesson, a treatise on Christian doctrine and practice, is conjectured to have been written in the year 1100, from the purport of the two lines,

Ben ha mile e cent an compli entierement,
Que fo Scripta lora, C son al derier temp.

There are already a thousand and one hundred years accomplished,
Since it was written thus, For we are in the last time.

The language is the ancient Waldensian, a sort of Patois, between French and Italian, and from the corresponding termination of the last syllables, in almost every two or three lines, the treatise appears to have been meant for verse.

It is inferred from the line,

Que tuit li papa que foron de Silvestre en tro en aquest, &c.
All the Popes which have been from Sylvester to this present time, &c.

that the writer of *La Nobla Leyçon* assigns the period of the first opposition of the Waldensian church to the corrupt church of Rome, to the age of Constantine the Great.

We gather from the sentence, "*Illi dicon quel es Vaudés*," "they call such an one a *Vaudois*," that the Protestant congregation in the valleys of Piemont, have been known as such, under the same name, for upwards of 700 years.

A few of the first lines of this curious manuscript are inserted to give some idea of the language in which it was written.

O frayre entendé una nobla leyçon.
Sovent deven velhar e istar en oreson.
C. nos veen aquest mont esser presdel chavon.
Mot curios deorian esser de bonas obras far.
C. nos veen aquest mont de la fin apropiar.
Ben ha mil e cent an compli entierement.

Que fo scripta lora, C. son al derier temp.
Poc deorian cubitar ; C. son al remanent.
Totiorn veen las enseignas venir à compliment.
En acreysament de mal e en amermament de ben.
Ayço son li perilli que l'escriptura di.
L'Avangeli ho recoynta e Sant Paul aesti.
Que neun home que viva non po saber la fin.
Enperço deven mays temer ; C. nos non son certan.
Si la mort nos penté enehoy o deman.
Ma cant venré al jorn del jujament.
Un çascun recebre per entier payament.

TRANSLATION.

Oh brethren, hear a noble lesson.
We ought always to watch and pray,
For we see this world is near its end.
We ought to be earnest in doing good works,
For we see the world is coming to an end.
Eleven hundred years are fully completed,
Since it was written, The end of all things is at hand.
We ought to covet little, for the end is at hand.
We daily see the signs of this accomplishment,
In the increase of evil, and the decrease of good.
These are the perils that the Scripture mentions,
Which the Evangelists have recounted and St. Paul has written,
That no man living knows when the end will come.
Therefore we should tremble, since we cannot be certain
Whether death will seize us to-day or to-morrow,
But when the day of judgment shall arrive,
Every one shall receive his just recompence.

N°. III.

A brief History of Claude, Bishop of the Valleys, between the Years of our Lord 817, *and* 839; *with some Account of his Doctrines and Writings against the Corruptions of the Church of Rome.—Extracted from " Remarks upon the Ecclesiastical History of the Ancient Churches of Piedmont." By Peter Allix, D.D.*

" THIS Claudius was born in Spain; he had been a disciple of Fœlix, Bishop of Urgel; he was for some years in the court of Ludovicus Pius, amongst his chaplains; and being endowed with great talents for a preacher, when Lewis was advanced to the empire, he caused him to be ordained Bishop of Turin. It will probably be imagined, that he had borrowed from Fœlix, Bishop of Urgel, the companion of Elipandus, the opinions of Nestorianism: but whosoever thinks so, will find himself mistaken; for his character of a great preacher, which had procured him the esteem of the emperor, and his long continuance in Lewis's court, during the life of Charles the Great, a court where that opinion, since the condemnation of Fœlix and Elipandus, at Francfort, in 794, was very much had in detestation, are sufficient to purge him from any such suspicion. But over and above all this, his writings upon the Scripture shew him to have been very far from that opinion; for we find, in several passages, unquestionable evidences of his orthodox judgment in this point. What he saith upon the 25th of St. Matthew, ver. 31, is decisive in this matter; and yet he expresseth himself more strongly, if it be possible, on Matt. xxi. ver. 2. Neither is it less easy to purge him of another calumny, which was cast upon him after his death, by Jonas, Bishop of Orleans, who, in his preface to King Charles the Bald, accuseth him for having endeavoured to revive the sect of Arius. I thought at first, that this was only a fault of the transcriber, who had writ Arius for Aërius; but the manner of Jonas's expressing himself, has made me retract my first conjecture: however, it is no less easy to refute this calumny, than it was to clear him from the first suspicion. In a word, we do not find any thing like it in so many books writ by him, and we find that which is contrary to it on Matt. xii. ver. 25. Let them make out to us, that any such thing was found amongst his papers after his death, as Jonas seems to insinuate, and we shall believe that Jonas was not over apt to give credit to those men, whose only aim was to bespatter the reputation of Claudius, and to make it odious and detestable to posterity, because he cried down their superstition and idolatry. Except they perform this, we must still look upon this accusation as a mere calumny.

"As for the works of this great man, we may affirm, there were few in his time who took so much pains to explain the Scripture, or to oppose themselves against the torrent of superstition.

"He wrote three books upon Genesis, in the year 815. He made a commentary on St. Matthew, which he published the same year, dedicating it to Justus, Abbot of Charroux.

"He published a commentary upon the Epistle to the Galatians, in the year 816, and dedicated it to Dructeramnus, a famous abbot, who had exhorted him to write comments upon all St. Paul's Epistles.

"He wrote a commentary on the Epistle to the Ephesians, which he dedicated to Ludovicus Pius, who commanded him to comment upon St. Paul's Epistles; which dedicatory epistle of his has been published by Mabillon.

"He made a commentary upon Exodus, in four books, which he published in the year 821, dedicating them to the Abbot Theodemirus.

"He made also another on Leviticus, which he published in the year 823, and dedicated it to the same abbot. Oudin tells us, he hath seen a commentary of his on the book of Ruth, in a library in Hainault.

"Of all these his works, there is nothing printed but his commentary upon the Epistle to the Galatians. The monks of St. Germain have his commentary upon all the Epistles in MS. in two volumes, which were found in the library of the Abbey of Fleury, near Orleans. They have also his MS. commentaries on Leviticus, which formerly belonged to the library of St. Remy, at Rheims. As for his commentary on St. Matthew, there are several MS. copies of it in England, as well as elsewhere.

"We may judge in what credit and esteem the doctrine of Claudius was at that time, by the earnestness wherewith the Emperor Ludovicus Pius, and the most famous abbots of those times, pressed him to explain the Holy Scripture in his writings. We may also conclude the same, from his being promoted to the episcopal dignity in a place where the superstition, in reference to images, obliged the emperor to provide them with a bishop that was both learned and vigorous; for Jonas of Orleans cannot dissemble, but that it was upon this very consideration, that the emperor made a particular choice of Claudius to be consecrated Bishop of Turin. Moreover, this see was not an ordinary bishopric, but a very considerable metropolis, in the diocese of Italy; but it was not till some time after, that the title of Archbishop was bestowed upon the metropolitans.

"The time wherein he was advanced to the episcopal dignity is not certainly known. Father Le Cointe conjectures, very probably, that it was in the year 817. But whether that be so or no, sure it is, that Claudius, in his illustration of the Scripture, plainly shewed himself to be very free from those errors, which at this day are in vogue in the Romish communion.

"We need only read his commentary upon the Epistle to the Galatians, to assure us, that he every where asserts the equality of all the Apostles with St. Peter, though the occasions seemed naturally to engage him to establish the primacy of St. Peter, and that of his pretended successors. This we find in ten several passages of that commentary; he only declares the primacy of St. Peter to consist in the honour he had of founding the church both amongst the Jews and Gentiles, p. 810. And indeed every where throughout his writings he maintains, that Jesus Christ is the only Head of the Church.

" He overthrows the doctrine of merits in such a manner, as overthrows all the nice distinctions of the Papists on that subject.

" He pronounces anathemas against traditions in matters of religion: so far was he from giving occasion to others to suspect, that he made them a part of the object of his faith, as the Church of Rome at present doth.

" He maintains, that faith alone saves us, which is the point that so extremely provoked the Church of Rome against Luther, who asserted the same thing.

" He holds the church to be subject to error, opposite to what at this day the Romanists pretend in so unreasonable a manner.

" He denies, that prayers after death may be of any use to those that have demanded them.

" He very smartly lashed the superstition and idolatry, which then began to be renewed, being supported by the authority of the Roman see.

" These things we find in his commentary upon the Epistle to the Galatians: but the other writings of this great man, manuscript and printed, shew us yet more of his mind. Indeed, we find him giving very public marks of his zeal for the purity of religion in several points. First, he proposeth the doctrine of the Church, in reference to the Eucharist, in a manner altogether conformable to the judgment of antiquity, following therein the most illustrious doctors of the Christian Church, and shewing that he was, as to that matter, at the farthest distance from the opinions which Paschasius Radbertus advanced eighteen or nineteen years after that Claudius had writ his commentary upon St. Matthew.

" It was worth our while to take notice of these opinions of Claudius, and of the manner of his reforming his diocese, that we might make it appear, that he laid the solid principles of the Reformation in these parts, as to several points. And this was the more necessary, because the Papists, as Genebrard, in his Chronology, and Rorenco, have owned that the valleys of Piedmont, which did belong to the bishopric of Turin, preserved the opinions of Claudius in the ninth and tenth century."

N°. IV.

Factum of the Court of Savoy.

In consequence of the general indignation expressed by the Protestant states of Europe, upon receiving intelligence of the dreadful massacre committed upon the Vaudois in 1655, the Duke of Savoy thought it necessary, in justification of his conduct towards his subjects of the reformed religion, to publish a statement of the transactions, which took place in the valleys of Luzerna, San Martino, and Perosa, in the year 1655.

This narrative was printed in Italian, French, and Latin, under the title of " *The Factum of the Court of Savoy;*" and although it endeavoured to make out a favourable case for the duke's government, and charged the Vaudois with bringing all the mischief upon themselves, yet it acknowledged quite enough to shew, that the atrocities complained of, had really been perpetrated. Never was such a medley of contradictions and improbabilities put together!

The following pages contain extracts from Morland's English translation of this curious state paper. The original is to be found in volume O, of the Cambridge Manuscripts.

" A Narrative of the several Transactions in the Valley of Luzerna, in the Year 1655.

" His Royal Highness, upon the 25th of January, 1655, commanded his subjects of the pretended reformed religion, by virtue of an order of his Auditor Gastaldo, to transport themselves, within three days, upon pain of death, into the valley and confines of Angrogna, the lands of Rorata, Villaro, Bobbio, and the villages thereunto belonging, and to quit their habitations, and the goods which they possessed in other parts of the said valley; nevertheless they had liberty to sell those goods, although they were confiscated, (as having been purchased contrary to express order).

"Their decision was, never to yield obedience to any such order, and that arms should be taken up if they should be forbidden to return to their houses, (which now they had quitted), that the estates by them unlawfully purchased, beyond the prefixed limits, should not be sold to any Catholic whatsoever, and that those should be severely punished, who should openly advise to the contrary, or should shew the least inclination to turn Catholics. For the ratification of which, they all took a solemn oath, and the ministers added an act of excommunication, against all those who should sell their estates to Catholics.

"This being done, they returned upon their own authority into the places prohibited, (notwithstanding, that they still negociated by deputations, as if they had had no intention at all to break out into an open rebellion), and that with such, and so great contempt of his royal highness's authority, as cannot sufficiently be expressed.

"His royal highness did indeed suffer this patiently for several days together, and ordered certain persons of the country of Luzerna, to remonstrate with them on their error, and on the necessity of correcting it. But finding all in vain, his highness resolved to send the Marquess of Pianezza thither, with 500 foot, of the regular troops, some of the militia, and 200 horse, not so much to punish them by quartering upon them the said army, (which was not however very numerous) but to see whether even without the letters of procuration, those affairs might yet be settled with the same deputies, and be brought to such an accommodation as might satisfy both justice and the sovereign.

"The Marquess of Pianezza having arrived within two miles of S. Giovanni, (and not much farther from La Torre), sent only a single person, who was accompanied with a peasant, with written orders from his royal highness to the places above said, to prepare quarters, each of them for about 300 foot, and some horse.

"The houses in S. Giovanni were at this time all uninhabited, all those who were fit to carry arms, with many others of all the other villages, particularly those of San Martino and Perosa, having already transported themselves to La Torre, where they had a very considerable number of musqueteers.

"This order being presented to them at La Torre, their answer was, that the Marquess of Pianezza knew well enough that they were now at La Torre, contrary to the command of his royal highness, and that therefore it was superfluous to send them his said highness' orders for the quartering of soldiers, and with this they threw the said order, in a contemptuous manner, at the messenger who brought it; after which, when the Marquess of Pianezza advanced towards them with his troops, they saluted him with a volley of musquet-shot, and forced him to give the word to those troops, who rendered themselves masters of the place in a very short time, but with the effusion of little or no blood; while the rebels, with the advantage of the night, and the mountains, fled without being at all pursued.

"The soldiers then took up their quarters in the said La Torre, to which they did no other hurt or damage than an army of friends are wont to do, when they come in a great body into a village forsaken by the inhabitants, which was, to make use of what they there found. The neighbouring villages, which continued acts of hostility, and which for several days together sent their musqueteers over the mountains, to assault the head-quarters of the army in La Torre, were taken by assault, and sacked. And the Marquess of Pianezza was also obliged to increase his army, by the addition of some of the French regiments, which were then in Piemont.

"On the other side, in the valley of Pelice, and in the villages of Villaro, and Bobbio, there were some troops who were commanded by the Marquess Galeazzo Villa, and the regiment of Villa, and that of Chamblay, whose major's name is Monsieur di Montafon, and several other officers, who make profession of the pretended reformed religion, are able to attest, whether there were committed, or any orders given, for cruel actions in those places. Those of Villaro and Bobbio made no resistance at all in quartering the troops, but yet they did all of them quit their habitations, and retired with all their provisions into the villages and cantons of the upper parts of the valley, by which means, the soldiers were put to this alternative, either to die with hunger, or else to go and seek for victuals with their muskets in the said villages; where they could never, either by forbearance or remonstrance, obtain an amicable reception, much less persuade them to part with any provisions. Those people chose rather to suffer their houses to be sacked and burnt, one after another, although they had, as examples before their eyes, the few inhabitants of Villaro and Bobbio, who remained there unmolested, and who lived in peace, together with some others, who had at the first withdrawn themselves into the valley of Queiras, and afterwards returned back into their own country, and to whom was given a portion of bread, by the command of his royal highness. At this time, it rained in torrents in the plain, and the tops of the mountains were covered with such deep snow, that many, who seeing the above-said villages thus lost to them, thought to have saved themselves in the valley of Queiras, perished miserably in the snow. Others thinking to escape with their whole families, lost many of their little ones, who being quite tired out, what with their heavy burdens, and what with the badness of the way, were left behind, and were afterwards found dead, and many men and women were overwhelmed by the avalanches that fell from the mountains. As for those young children, who were found alive, they were taken up in a woeful plight almost dead with cold, and used with all the care and charity imaginable, and were afterwards distributed throughout Piemont, and a register was kept, of their names, and of the places where, and the persons to whom they were thus disposed, which may be produced, if occasion require. In like manner, those women who were made prisoners, were with all the care imaginable taken out of the hands of the soldiers, to whom there was given a ransom for them, and set at liberty, or (if they desired it) were placed out at service in Piemont, and of those also there was a roll or register kept. The greatest number of lives that were lost did not exceed two hundred, adding together both those who perished in the snow, those who died with cold, and those who were slain with the sword. By all which it will easily appear, how false the calumnies of the rebels are, who, to render themselves the objects of pity, and those who chastised them, of hatred, publish to the world, that there was exercised all manner of cruelty upon all sorts of persons, of all ages and sexes, which can never be proved or made good.

"The village of Rorata, consisting of about twenty-five families, was not at all assailed before that time. And the Marquess of Pianezza believed that they would not conduct themselves worse than those of Villaro and Bobbio had done, and therefore granted them likewise a *salva guardia*. But Joshua Gianavello resolving that his rebellion should surpass that of all the rest, came with a squadron of soldiers that were the inhabitants of that place, whom he himself commanded, and assaulted several Catholics not far from Luzerna, and set men in ambuscade in several posts near Rorata, although that place had never received any thing but grace and favours. The marquess, finding them altogether so ungrateful, resolved to attack and destroy (as he did) the said squadron of Joshua, of whom some were killed upon the spot, and others made their escape among the precipices of the mountains, and after that he demolished the nest of such assassins, by the destruction of this village of Rorata, which was already uninhabited.

"This is a true relation of what passed in the valley of Luzerna, whereby it may be seen with what impudence those rebels, who have brought destruction upon themselves, do now spread abroad such strange reports, thinking thereby not only to excite the compassion of the world towards them for their deserved chastisement, but also to leave a bad impression against such as have, with much moderation, inflicted the same upon them, who so barbarously and inhumanly conducted themselves against persons over whom they had no authority at all, and took the most extravagant, and most unheard-of manner of revenge that ever was practised against the most innocent of their countrymen and kinsmen, who had not any knowledge or share in the troubles which had taken place."

N°. V.

The subjoined Copies of Edicts and Concessions, which have been granted, at different Periods of History, in Favour of the Vaudois, by their Sovereigns, will shew how little has at any time been conceded to them, how moderate have been their Demands, and how frequently their Enemies have violated the most solemn Engagements.

---

1. EDICT OF PHILIP EMANUEL, DUKE OF SAVOY, DATED JUNE 5, 1561.

[The original is in volume O, of the Cambridge Manuscripts.]

In the name of God,

HIS Highness issues out these his letters patent, by which it will appear, in what manner his highness grants an indemnity to the people of the valleys of Angrogna, Bobbio, Villaro, Valguicchiardo, Rora, Tagliaretto, La Rica di Boneti, La Torre, San Martino, Perosa, Roccapiatta, and S. Bartolomeo, and every one of these, as also to all such as shall be found to have assisted them, for all offences by them committed, whether they be damages, deaths, or fines; as well in particular, as in general, either against his highness, their immediate lords, or other particular persons within his highness' dominions, restoring them to his favour as if they had never done any thing against his highness; and receiving them under his gracious protection.

1. It shall be permitted to those of Angrogna, Bobbio, Villaro, Valguicchiardo, and Rora, being districts of the valley of Luzerna, and likewise to those of Parlibece, Roderet, Masel, Maneglia, and Salea, districts of the valley of San Martino, to have preaching

assemblies, and other ministerial offices, according to their religion, in their wonted places.

2. It shall be permitted them to have the same at Villaro, which is a district of the valley of Luzerna; and this shall be until such time as his highness shall make a fort in the said place; for after that such a fort is erected, it shall not be permitted to the people of the said place to have preaching, or congregations, within the bounds of the said place: but it shall be lawful for them to erect a place convenient for such like services, in some adjacent place towards Bobbio, as they shall find most convenient. Nevertheless it shall be permitted to the ministers to come within the said bounds, to visit the sick, and perform other necessary duties of their religion, provided that they neither preach, nor gather together any suspected congregation. At Tagliaretto and Rua de Boneti, which are the confines of their lands, it shall be permitted them to have preaching, and congregations in the wonted places; provided, that they do not enter into the other confines of their lands, to do the same.

3. It shall not be permitted to the inhabitants of the abovementioned districts of the valleys of Luzerna, and San Martino above said, to come within the other bounds of the said valleys, or the rest of his highness' dominions, passing the bounds of their prescribed limits there, to have preaching congregations, or disputations, but only to do this within their own bounds. And if by chance they shall be questioned touching their faith, it shall be lawful for them to make answer, without incurring thereby any punishment, either real or personal.

4. It shall be permitted to those of the parish which is on the other side of Perosa, who are at present fugitives for the sake of the said religion, to have preaching, and congregations, and other ministerial offices, according to their said religion, only in the place nominated, and not in any other place within the bounds of the said parish.

5. It shall be permitted to those of the parish of Pinachia, in the valley of Perosa, and to those of Roccapiatta, who are at present fugitives for the cause of their said religion, and do adhere

to it, to have one minister only, who shall have liberty one day to administer and preach in the place of San Germano, called Adurmiglioso, and the other day at Roccapiatta, in the place called Goadini, and not in any part of the said parishes.

6. It shall be permitted to all persons of the said valleys, who are at present fugitives, and do adhere to their said religion (notwithstanding any promise or abjuration made against their religion before this war), to return and live in their houses with their families, according to their religion; and to go, and return, from the sermons and congregations which shall be made in the said places, and other services of their religion; provided, that they observe what they engage to observe. And forasmuch as many of the above-said will be found in the lands of the said valleys, at a great distance from such places, and will thereby necessarily stand in need of visitations, and other ministerial functions, according to their religion: it shall be permitted to their ministers, (such as dwell within their limits, without any prejudice to such limits), to visit and perform their ministerial duties, according as they shall have occasion; only they shall not have public preaching, or such as may afford the least suspicion.

7. To all the inhabitants of the said valleys above mentioned, and to all the fore-named fugitives, and those who persist in their religion, as well as those of the territories of the said valleys, as those of Roccapiatta, S. Bartolomeo, and Miana, their goods that have been confiscated shall be restored to them; provided, they be not confiscated for any other cause than that of religion, and the present or past war.

8. It shall be permitted to all the fore-named, to recover, by course of law, their moveables and their cattle, whereof they have been robbed, and which shall be found to have been sold by their neighbours, provided they be not soldiers; and the same is permitted to their neighbours against the above mentioned.

9. All the freedom, immunities, and privileges, (as well general as particular) which have been granted either by his

highness' most illustrious predecessors, his highness himself, or other immediate lords, shall be confirmed to the afore-named; provided they prove the truth thereof, by authentic acts and instruments.

10. Those of the said valleys shall be obliged to write down the names and surnames of all such as belong to the territories of the afore-said valleys, who have fled on account of the persecution of their religion, as well such as have abjured, as others who have remained with their goods and families, that so they may enjoy the favour and benefits that their prince and lord shall be pleased to bestow upon them.

11. Because it is lawful for a prince, in his own country, to cause forts to be made, according to his pleasure, without being controlled, or opposed, by any of his vassals, or subjects, to remove any cause of suspicion which might be entertained in the minds of the afore-named of the said valleys, it is declared, That from this time forward, within some few days, his highness may peradventure cause a fort to be made in the commune of Villaro; nevertheless it shall be without any cost of those of the valley, except in what it shall seem good to them to contribute lovingly to their prince: which being done, by God's permission, it shall be provided with a governor, and a captain, who shall attend only for the service of his highness; nevertheless, this shall be without the least prejudice to any man's conscience, or his goods.

12. It shall be lawful for the afore-named, before those ministers be dismissed (whom it shall please his highness to order to be sent away) to have others in their places; provided they do not retain Signor Martino, of Pragella; nor may they change or shift their abodes from one place to another of the said valleys, otherwise than it shall be permitted to them.

13. In the parishes of the said valleys, where preaching is held, and congregations are instituted, or the ministries of the said valley exercised, mass shall be celebrated, and other offices, according to the custom of the Roman Church; but the afore-named shall not be constrained to go thereunto, or to give any help or assistance to any that officiate in that service; and if any

shall be pleased to go thither, no disturbance shall be given him by the afore-named.

14. His highness shall make a free gift, and irrevocable remission of all the expences which he hath been at in this war, and of the 8000 crowns which the afore-named did owe unto his highness, upon account of the 16,000 crowns agreed to be paid in the former war.

15. All the prisoners who may be found in the soldiers' hands, shall be restored and set at liberty, provided they pay a reasonable ransom according to their means, leaving the judgment and ransom to the discretion of the Lord de Raconisi, and to the Lord della Trinita: and all those whom the said lords shall judge to be no lawful prisoners, shall be released without any ransom, who shall also cause to be released, without any payment, all those of the said valleys who shall be found in the galleys for cause of their religion, and not for any other offence.

16. Finally, his highness shall permit all the afore-said of the said valleys, and the afore-said of Miana, Roccapiatta, and S. Bartholomeo, of what state and condition soever they be (provided they be not ministers) to be included in the common society and intercourse with his other subjects, to stay, go, and come, in all places and countries of his highness' territories; and likewise to buy, sell, and traffic in all sorts of merchandizes, provided they refrain from preaching, from drawing together assemblies, and from disputation, as is above-said: and those that are in the limits, who have not a settled residence without their own limits, nor any within the territory of the said valleys, without their own territory, and the confines thereof, and those of Miana, Roccapiatta, S. Bartholomeo, shall not encroach beyond their own confines: and these things being punctually observed on their parts, no disturbance or molestation, whether real or personal, shall be offered unto them, but they shall remain under the protection and safeguard of his highness.

17. Moreover, orders shall be issued out by his highness, wherein there shall be sufficient provisions made against all disturbances, inconveniences, or plots of malignant spirits, to the

end that the above-named may peaceably and quietly enjoy their own religion.

18. For the observance of all the conditions, and that no inconvenience may arise about the performance and execution of the above-written articles, Georgio Monastieri of Angrogna, sent by the said valleys, and Syndic of S. Constance, and of Ateszani; and Rambaudo Syndic of Bobbio; Michele Ramondetti, sent by the commonalty of Tagliaretti, and Rua di Bonetti to La Torre; Giovanni Mala-notte, sent particularly by those of S. Giovanni; Pietro Pasquale, sent by the commonalty of the valley of S. Martino; Thomasso Romano, of S. Germano, sent by the said commonalty, and by the whole valley of Perosa, do promise for their commonalties respectively, that the contents of the above-said articles shall be inviolably observed; and in case of non-observance, they do submit to such punishment as it shall please his highness to inflict on them; promising in like manner, to cause this their engagement to be approved and confirmed *(per capita domorum)* by the heads of families.

The most illustrious Lord de Raconisi doth promise that his highness shall ratify and approve the above-written articles to the under-written, in particular, and in general, granted by the intercession of her most serene highness, Madame, as a pure act of her special grace: in witness whereof, the afore-said lord hath subscribed these presents with his own hand; and the ministers, in the name of all the afore-said commonalties, have under-written their names *in quor. fid.* this 5th of June, 1561.

Phillippo di Savoya.
(Signed)
Francisco Valle, Minister of Villaro in Luzerna.
Claudius Bergio, Minister of Tagliaretto.
Georgio Monastieri, of Angrogna.
Michele Ramondetti, of Tagliaretti.

2. PETITION OF THE VAUDOIS, AND CONCESSIONS GRANTED TO THEM, BY CHARLES EMANUEL, DUKE OF SAVOY, APRIL 9, 1603.

[The original is in volume K, of the Cambridge Manuscripts.]

Translation.

Most serene lord,

The most faithful subjects and servants of your most serene highness, who make profession of the reformed religion, according to the gospel of Jesus Christ, in the valleys of Luzerna, Perosa, and San Martino, Roccapiatta, San Bartholomeo, Talluco, Miana, Matis, and the Marquisate of Saluzzo, making up one body in Christ, declare and represent to your most serene highness, their natural and lawful prince, that being troubled, questioned, and molested, upon the account of their afore-said religion, after they have frequently presented their petitions to your highness for securing them from such troubles, molestations, and inquisitions, without having obtained any relief, but rather experiencing from bad to worse, and seeing even an indication to execute the penalties contained in certain edicts, and considering that this would bring upon them a total and deplorable ruin; they therefore think it expedient to declare to you, the extreme grief of heart which they are feeling, and to implore your bounty, that they may enjoy that gracious tranquillity, which they have enjoyed, by the mercy of God, under the good pleasure of their good princes of happy memory, and of your most serene highness, which tranquillity your above-said petitioners desire may be established and made perpetual; and therefore they cast themselves once more, in all humility, at your highness' feet, beseeching you that you will vouchsafe to grant unto them the particulars under-written, to the end that they may live in quiet, and they will employ both their lives and estates for the service of your most serene highness.

Petitions.	Answers.
First, that your highness would be pleased to abolish and declare null all restrictions whatsoever, upon the account of religion, together with all the proceedings and confiscations which have been made, and especially the illegal confiscation of the goods of Signora Beatrice Solara, and her children, (she having dwelt in the said valley of Luzerna now above thirty years, and her children being born in the said valley), and that they may be all restored into a peaceable condition.	His highness doth not intend that they should be molested for their pretended religion, so that they abstain from exercising it, out of the places of the valleys of Luzerna, San Martino, and Perosa.
Moreover, to grant them the free preaching and exercise of their religion in all the valleys of Luzerna, Perosa, San Martino, Roccapiatta, San Bartholomeo, Talluco, Mina, Matis, and the Marquisate of Saluzzo, in the places accustomed, and usual, until this present time.	Provided, they do it only in the limits tolerated in the said three valleys, they shall not be molested.
Moreover, that all those of this religion of these valleys may return and abide in their houses, live in liberty of conscience, and use the exercise of their religion in the places accustomed.	As to the natives of the said three valleys, they may return, his highness suspending, as to them, the order which hath been made for those who have property without the limits designed.
Moreover, that those of the said religion may exercise, and	His highness, in what concerns the exercise of public

may be admitted to all kind of public offices in the abovesaid valleys, and that they may traffic through all the states of his most serene highness, and make their harvest, and thresh their corn, without molestation or inquisition, because of the said religion, as also that those who shall lodge and entertain them for assistants, may not be molested; and, in like manner, that those who dwell in the said valleys, shall have confirmed to them all the privileges and concessions usual until this present time.

offices, doth grant it in the said three valleys, and permits that they may go and make their harvest, and thresh their corn, upon condition, notwithstanding, that they abstain from publishing their doctrine.

Moreover, to restore to liberty of conscience all those who have renounced their religion.

It is not a thing which belongs to his highness to meddle with.

Moreover, that none upon account of religion may be chased away, or prohibited to dwell in the valleys and places petitioned for, nor hindered from exercising public offices.

Provision is made in the answer given to the third and fourth head.

Moreover, that poor Cupini, detained in Asti now above two years past, and only for the said religion, may be released.

His highness will write about him to the Bishop of Asti, that he may be set free.

Moreover, his most serene highness is most humbly implored, that he will be pleased to grant, according to his wonted goodness and clemency,

His highness, at the request of the count of Luzerna, knight of his own order, is pleased to pardon the Banditti petitioned for. Except, notwithstanding, that those men who are honest may live quietly in the said valleys, and, for public quietness' sake, to grant pardon and favour to those who were described or named Banditti, in the publication made in the valleys of that edict, published by the illustrious lord the chief justice, by order of his most serene highness, and to all their coadjutors, abettors, counsellors, and adherents, for the faults, excesses, and crimes by them said to be committed and perpetrated in the tumults hitherto, for matters of religion or otherwise, together with a prohibition of all real or personal molestation of them.

PIETRO BRUNO, for the commonalty of Bubiana and Champiglione.

CHIABERTO BODETTI, for Villaro, Bobbio, and La Torre.

GIRARDO MALANO, for Angrogna.

those that are written down and noted in the edict made last by the lieutenant of justice Bergera, &c. *(illegible)* detained now in Pinerolo, and of *(illegible)* of Angrogna, upon this condition, notwithstanding, namely, that they restore the churches, and repair the damages done to them. Provided also, that should the said outlaws return, or others who may hereafter be banished by justice, they do then take them prisoners, living or dead, and keep the said valleys clear from such heinous malefactors, under the penalty of making good all damages which shall be sustained from such persons, and of other punishment at pleasure.

Given in Cunio, the 9th of April, 1603.

(Signed)

CAROLO EMANUEL.

V. F. MILLET.

3. PETITION OF THE VAUDOIS, AND CONCESSIONS GRANTED, JUNE 20, 1620.

[The original is in volume K, of the Cambridge Manuscripts.]

Translation.

Most serene lord,

The most faithful and most humble subjects of your most serene highness of the religion of the valleys of Luzerna, Perosa, and San Martino, and of the other places contiguous to them, having in times past obtained through the clemency of your highness, and also of your most serene father, of glorious memory, certain favourable grants concerning the exercise of their said religion, have always endeavoured to live conformably to them, in a Christian manner, under the protection and obedience of your highness, in which they desire they may always quietly continue; but now finding themselves molested in consequence of the edicts, contrary to their grants aforesaid, which are said to be published in certain places of the said valley of Luzerna, and proceedings being made to put in execution the penalties contained in the said edicts, with threatenings of greater damage, they, assuring themselves that this doth not proceed from the intention of your highness, from whom alone, next under God, they expect, as from their natural and most gracious prince, a deliverance so necessary, they think fit to cast themselves at your feet, humbly beseeching that you will be pleased, according to your wonted goodness, to forbid all molestation of your said petitioners for matters of religion, restoring them into a peaceable condition; and, for this purpose, to confirm and grant them the humble petitions following.

Petitions.	Answers.
First, that you would be pleased to confirm all the gra-	As to the first, his highness confirms it, and commands that

cious grants made to them, as well by your most serene highness, as by your most serene father of happy memory, so that they may continue in the free exercise of their religion in the places hitherto tolerated and used, notwithstanding any order published, made or to be made to the contrary, and that you will annul all the proceedings, confiscations, declarations of penalties, fines and inquisitions made upon occasion of the said orders, restoring all those who have been disquieted or molested, so that they may hereafter live peaceably under the dominion of your highness, and that you will command that the said petitions may be granted and registered for them gratis, freeing them from the payment of the quos, decima, albergo, sigillo, signattura, and other charges whatsoever, which they hope to obtain, and they shall pray to the Lord for the happiness of yourself, and of the most serene princess. Registered 3, 170 register. First 245. I say 245. Registered in the chamber.

the grants made unto the petitioners upon the 9th of April, 14th of May, and last day but one of September, 1603, shall be observed as to the valleys of Luzerna, San Martino, and Perosa, together with Roccapiatta, San Bartholomeo, Prarostino, and the other places in the grants, as is petitioned, and within the limits graciously tolerated, notwithstanding any other order unto the contrary, and also he gives unto them pardon and remission of all the penalties incurred for breaking his orders, and for other faults and excesses committed before the general pardon, notwithstanding the sentences of the captain of justice and the senate, derogating in this respect from that which the said pardon expresseth, and all this his highness hath done and doth of special favour, upon condition of payment of six thousand ducatoons, to be paid at the rate and according as usual, by the said three valleys; moreover, that those of San Giovanni shall stop up the gate of the church newly made, and not otherwise, nor in other manner.

The second and last his highness grants. Given in Turin, the 20th of June, 1620.

(Signed)

CARLO EMANUEL,
ARGENTERO,
CERNUSCO, Carron.
ARNALDO MAGALLI, Secretary.

These very concessions were confirmed by Madame Royale, in the year 1638. And again, by his royal highness then reigning, upon the 30th of June, 1649, and the 2d of June, and the 29th of December, in the year 1653. Upon which very day, those of the reformed religion, having reiterated their supplications to his royal highness, to the end that the abovesaid confirmation of the said concessions might be "Senza alcuna restrittione, ne alteratione, non ostante qual si voglia ordine fatto, ò da farsi, ò qual si voglia altra cosa in contrario," i. e. Without any restriction or alteration, notwithstanding any order made or to be made, or any other thing whatsoever to the contrary. His royal highness made them answer at the end of their supplications, in the following terms: "Dichiara sua Altezza Royale non esser di mente sua, cher per le risposte date al memoriale e capi delli 2 Giugno, 1653, s'intendino ampliate ne diminuite le concessione debitamente spedite, le quali hanno li supplicanti rapportate del fu Duca Carlo Emanuel avo suo, et de' alteri suoi serenissimi predecessori. In Torino li 29 Decembre, 1653," i. e. His royal highness declares, that it is not his intention that the concessions which have been granted in due form, which the petitioners have obtained of the late Duke Charles Emanuel, his uncle, and of others his most serene predecessors, should be altered, enlarged, or diminished. In Turin, the 29th of September, 1653.

After these declarations followed the massacres of 1655 and 1686 !!!

N°. VI.

The Liturgy of Geneva.

As this formulary is principally used in the Protestant valleys of Piemont, the Author is desirous of laying the Table of Contents before his readers, that some idea may be formed of its design and tendency.

TABLE OF CONTENTS.

N°. VII.

Translation of the Letter of Scipio Lentulus, a Neapolitan, giving an Account of the Persecution in the Protestant Valleys of Piemont, under the Count de la Trinité, in the Year 1561. *From Morland's History, p.* 230.

[The original is in volume P, of the Cambridge Manuscripts.]

" Most honoured Sir,

" SEEING you have given me to understand, that it is your desire to know what things have fallen out among us in Piemont, to the end that I might the more conveniently answer your expectation in this particular, I have determined to give an account of those things by letter, rather than by word of mouth: forasmuch as it will be of some use also to serve the purpose of those men, who desire to have the same things committed to writing, and are able to set them forth much more exactly.

" There is a certain valley in the county of Piemont, within five or six miles of Mount Vesulo, which from the town Luzerna, is called the valley of Luzerna; and in it there is a little valley, which from Angrogna, a small river running through it, is called the valley of Angrogna. Next adjoining to this there are two other valleys, that is to say, the valley of Perosa, so called from the town of that name, and the valley of S. Martino. In these there lie divers little towns and villages, whose inhabitants, assisted by the ministers of God's word, do make open profession of the Gospel.

" Moreover, I suppose that there are near eight thousand faithful souls (as I may call them) inhabiting in this place. But among the men, who are bred up to endure labour, seeing they have from their childhood been inured to husbandry, you will find very few that know how to engage in combat with any. From hence it comes to pass, that very few of them are ready, upon any urgent occasion, to defend themselves against public injuries. Yea and the valleys themselves lie so remote from each other, that they cannot help one another till it be too late. And although these towns and villages have their counts or lords (as they call them) yet the Duke of Savoy is lord over them all.

"This duke, before he came from Nice into Piemont, diligently took order with those counts and lords of places, that they should admonish the inhabitants of the valleys to submit to him and the Pope; that is, that casting off their ministers, they should admit Popish preachers, and the abominable mass. Whereupon our people sent a certain messenger to Nice, together with their confession of faith, and petitions unto the prince, beseeching him that he would take it in good part, if they were resolved rather to die than lose the true religion of Jesus Christ, forasmuch as they had received it, through a very ancient tract of time, as it were by hand, from their ancestors; and that he would not doubt but they shall be ready to amend their errors, if any there were, in case it should be manifested to them out of the word of God, to which alone they are to submit in this business; and as to what concerneth them in matters of behaviour, and tributes, and other things due both to him and to their other lords, that he would send persons to make diligent enquiry whether they have at any time committed any offence, that so due punishment may be inflicted on them, because he should assuredly know they will endeavour, that he may understand they are willing to approve themselves, with due reverence, most obedient to him in all these things.

"These petitions came to the hand of the prince, but availed nothing with him, who was become a sworn enemy with Antichrist against Christ. Thereupon, he sent forth edicts, declaring that those who should be present at the sermons of the ministers of the valleys, if but once, should be fined at one hundred crowns;

and if a second time, then they should be condemned to the galleys for ever. Orders also were given to a certain judge, to ride circuit up and down to put the penalties in execution, and to bind Christians and imprison them. The lords also, and magistrates of places, had the same power given them, and at length the godly were, by this most impotent prince, utterly given up to be plundered by all sorts of villains, and afflicted with most grievous calamities.

" He sent also a certain collateral judge of his own, first to Carignan, there to act inhuman butchery upon the faithful ones of Christ; whereupon he caused one Marcellinus, and Joan his wife, he being a Frenchman, but she a woman of Carignan, to be burnt alive with fire, four days after they had been apprehended. But in this woman God was pleased to manifest an admirable example of constancy: for, as she was led to execution, she exhorted her husband, saying, Well done, my brother, be of good courage; this day, doubtless, we shall enter together into the joys of heaven. Some few days after this, there was apprehended also one John Carthignan, an honest plain man, and truly religious, who, after three days' imprisonment, endured the torments of fire with very great constancy. Who is able to reckon up the several incursions, slaughters, plunders, and innumerable miseries wherewith this most savage generation of men did daily afflict all pious men, because being exhorted by their ministers to patience, they took no course to defend themselves against injuries? Not long after also they apprehended one John, a Frenchman and a minister, at a town called St. Germano, and carrying him to a certain abbey near Pinerolo, there burnt him alive, who left behind him a noble example of Christian constancy. The like was done also to the minister of the town of Maine, who was put to death at Susa, by a slow fire, while he, in the mean time, stood as it were immoveable, and not being touched with any sense of so incredible a cruelty, having his eyes fixed upon heaven, breathed out his happy soul.

" Therefore, when things were come to this pass, and these miseries were encreased every day more and more, and seeing that the patience and extreme misery of our people, could not in any measure allay the fury and rage of these most merciless brutes, they at length resolved by force, as well as they could, to free themselves, and their wives and children, from that barbarous usage. And although some of our ministers declared it was not well done, yet no admonitions could keep the people from resolving to defend themselves by arms. Hereupon it came to pass, that several encounters falling out, within a few days, there fell about sixty of the plunderers. When news hereof was brought to the tyrant, he commanded his men to forbear, and sent two of his noblemen, principal persons, to wit, the Lord Raconisi, and the Lord de la Trinité (whom I shall for discourse sake, more aptly call the Lord de la Tyrannitie) that so they might bring matters to an accommodation with our people: but when it was perceived, that all their drift was, that our ministers might be cast out, and the pope received, the people would by no means yield to it; and so they departed *re infectâ*.

" Wherefore, when the prince came into Piemont, and resided at Versello, about the kalends of November, in the year 1560; with intent to destroy all in the valleys by fire and sword, he sent an army of above 4000 foot and 200 horse, under the command of the Duke de la Tyrannitie. And the next day, in the morning, they fell upon Angrogna, which lay first in their way. But there being in a steep place of a mountain some men of ours, which kept guard there, (who were not above fifty in number) they with slings, wherewith most of them were armed, sustained the first assault made by 1200 men: but afterwards, others coming in several ways to the assistance of ours (though the whole number hardly amounted to 200) they not only put the enemy to flight, but slew seventy of them, with the loss of no more than three of our own; and the next day, when they attempted to come up to us out of another part of the valley, hard by Villaro and Taillaretto, a small number of ours put a very great body of the enemy to flight, and slew of them about thirty. For these causes then, that most crafty fox, the Lord de la Tyrannitie, understandeth that to be a very difficult business, which he conceived otherwise most easy, forasmuch as our men, who, he supposed, would have been frightened with the bare name of an army, fought stoutly and most valiantly, although they were but ill armed, a small number, and without experience of military affairs; wherefore he thought it requisite to have recourse (as his manner is) unto deceitful practices. To this end, he employed persons to give hopes of peace, if they would lay down their arms; whereupon certain false brethren, in design to serve their own private ends (as experience hath made manifest) persuaded the people, though almost all the ministers cried out against it, that, too easily giving credit to the most false promises of their enemies, laying down their arms, and sending deputies to the prince to promise obedience, and beg pardon in the name of all the people, they might for 16,000 crowns redeem both themselves and their religion. As soon as all these things were yielded to, and promised by the too credulous people (with whom some men consented that ought not to have done it) through a vain hope of obtaining peace and religion; and when our deputies arrived at Versello, they were from thence carried, by the Lord de la Tyrannitie, to a certain cloister, there to abide for two months space (to the end there might be time for collecting the monies,) and at length casting themselves down at the feet of the prince, and of the pope's legate (who were both there, attended by a great number of the nobility and men of inferior rank) they were constrained to supplicate the prince first, then the pope's legate, that they would take pity on the people from whom they were sent, and to promise them by an oath, that they would be ready to all things that should be commanded by them.

"The prince, therefore, growing confident upon this most solemn promise, immediately sent persons to command our people to receive and embrace that horrid idol of the mass: whereupon considering the inconstancy of their deputies, and the deceit, or rather extreme perfidiousness of the tyrant's being discovered, they plainly refused to yield that those things should be ratified which their deputies had unadvisedly transacted, through their own levity, not with the consent of the people; for, they had been sent upon such terms, that they should do all those things in the name of the whole people, which might conduce to peace, with the safety of religion. Then the tyrant, as soon as he came to understand this, was much more inflamed than ever before with anger, or rather outrageous fury against our people; and collecting a rabble of an army, he gave command to the Lord de la Tyrannitie to waste and destroy all by fire and sword, without any regard either of sex or age. Hereupon houses were every where set on fire, goods plundered, nor is there any kind of mischief which was not acted by those most wretched villains: by which means they forced our people, with their wives and children, to have recourse to the more craggy places of the mountains: a thing indeed very lamentable to be seen! For, at the very first assault, they were in a manner astonished, because being spoiled both of their arms and goods, living in extreme want of all things, they did not see by what means they might be able to undergo so great and troublesome a war.

"But at length taking heart, and trusting in the mercy and help of God, and the goodness of their cause, and being confident because of the impiety and treachery of their adversaries, they resolved once again to defend themselves. To this end they appointed their guards and garrisons, fortified several places, blocked up passages, and were wholly resolute upon this point, to die, rather than they would in any measure obey a perfidious and wicked prince in so abominable a matter. But what need many words? Things were come to such a pass, that in several fights, above 900 of the enemy were slain; whereas, on our side, hardly fifteen were wanting.

"But I must not omit also to inform you, that at that time there fell eight of those leaders, whom the prince held in highest esteem, because of their extraordinary valour and skill in military affairs, whereof he had had experience, chiefly in his war against the king of France. Of that number was Charles Trusset, lord of a certain town called Runclaret, a man of great strength, most daring, and not only exercised in arms from his very childhood, but one generally reputed most stout in action. This man, leading two regiments, consisting of about 600 men, on that side where we little imagined any enemy would come, advanced with his men to the top of a mountain, where he overlooked our party: which, as soon as ours beheld, then pouring out prayers before the Lord (for they always have a minister with them) although they were scarce thirty in number, they courageously proceeded against the enemy; who being very jocund, as if they had already gained the victory, came down. They were no sooner engaged; but six slingers of ours, by a passage unknown to the enemy, immediately possessed themselves of the top of the mountain, which the other, fearing nothing, had quitted; and crying out aloud from thence, Let Jesus Christ be glorified, they issued down upon them with so great a force, that the enemy utterly failed both in strength and courage, while ours, in the mean time, became the more active and courageous. And as soon as the enemy perceived about eighty men advancing from the next town, for the succour of our friends, they all presently betook themselves to their heels: whereupon the snow, being then above a cubit deep, and those that fled finding the passages very straight and cumbersome, part of them threw themselves headlong from broken rocks, and part were slaughtered at pleasure by the pursuers. As for Trusset, he being led betwixt two soldiers (because his leg had been broken by a blow with a stone) was with his own sword most miserably slain by a certain plough-boy, after he had levelled another stone at his back from a sling with such a force, that being left by the soldiers, he fell down upon the ground half dead: and in that fight there fell about 200 of the enemy, without any loss of our own. Many more such passages might be related of several encounters, wherein a few of our friends have always worsted a great number of the enemies: of the truth whereof this is a very ample evidence, that so great store of arms came to the hands of ours, that they were not at all troubled for the loss of their own formerly, through treachery, seeing a return made of them in so great abundance.

"These are the occurrences which at this time I could communicate to you concerning this business; and if so be that you think them too few, I promise you I will very diligently take care that within these few days you may receive a more large account: for, I am every day in expectation of a person who was not only present, but a principal man also in those actions. In the mean time, you will (I hope) entertain these which I have by snatches rudely written, to the end that I might (how meanly soever) testify my singular love and respect towards you, who are so worthy a person. Farewell.

(Signed) "Tui studiosissimus,
"Scipio Lentulus, Neapolitanus.
Or,
"Your's most affectionately devoted,
"Scipio Lentulus, Native of Naples."

N°. VIII.

Extracts from a translation of the Bull of Pope Innocent the Eighth, for the Extirpation of the Waldenses, given to Albertus de Capitaneis, Legate and Commissioner, in the Year 1487.

The original was contained in volume G, of the Cambridge Manuscripts, which volume has been stolen from the public library of that University; but a copy is preserved, together with the English translation, in Morland's History of the Evangelical Churches of the Valleys of Piemont.

"Innocentius, bishop, a servant of the servants of God, to our beloved son, Albertus de Capitaneis, archdeacon of the church of Cremona, nuncio of the see apostolic, and our commissioner for the dominions of our beloved son, that noble person, Charles, Duke of Savoy, on this and on the other side of the mountains, through the city and diocese of the Delphinate, Vienne, and Sedun, and the places near adjoining thereunto, greeting and apostolical benediction.

"We have heard, and it is come to our knowledge, not without much displeasure, that certain sons of iniquity, inhabitants of the province of Evreux, followers of that abominable and pernicious sect of malignant men, who are called the poor people of Lyons, or the Waldenses, who have long ago endeavoured in Piemont, and other neighbouring parts, by the instigation of him who is the sower of evil works, through by-ways, purposely sought out, and hidden precipices, to insnare the sheep belonging unto God, and at last to bring them to the perdition of their souls by deadly cunning, are damnably risen up under a feigned pretence of holiness, being led into a reprobate sense, and do greatly err from the way of truth; and following superstitious and heretical ceremonies, do say, act, and commit very many things contrary to the orthodox faith, offensive to the eyes of the Divine Majesty, and which do occasion a very great hazard of souls.

"We therefore having determined to use all our endeavours, and to employ all our care, as we are bound by the duty of our pastoral charge, to root up and extirpate such a detestable sect, and the aforesaid execrable errors, that they may not spread further, and that the hearts of believers may not be damnably perverted from the Catholic church; and to repress such rash undertakings; and having special confidence in the Lord concerning your learning, your ripeness in counsel, your zeal in the faith, and your experience in the management of affairs; and in like manner hoping that you will truly and faithfully execute the things which we shall think good to commit unto you for the extirpating of such errors; we have thought good to constitute you at this time, for this cause of God and the faith, the nuncio commissioner of us, and of the apostolical see, within the dominions of our beloved son, Charles, Duke of Savoy, and the Delphinate, and the cities and diocese of Vienne, and Sedun, and the adjacent provinces, cities, lands, and places whatsoever, to the end you should cause the same inquisitor to be received and admitted to the free exercise of his office, and that you should induce the followers of the most wicked sect of the Waldenses, and all other polluted with any other heretical corruption whatsoever, to abjure their errors, and to obey the commandments of the same inquisitor, and give way to your seasonable remedies; and that you may do this so much the more easily, by how much the greater power and authority is given you by us, to wit, a power, that by yourself, or by some other person or persons, you may admonish and require most urgently all archbishops and bishops seated in the Duchy, Delphinate, and the other forenamed adjacent places, whom the Most High hath called to share with us in our cares, and command them, by virtue of holy obedience, that together with our venerable brethren the ordinaries of the places, or their vicars, or general officials, in whose cities and dioceses you shall think fit to proceed with the orders, and to execute the office which is enjoined you with the forenamed inquisitor, a man no doubt endued with learning and fervent zeal for the salvation of souls, they do assist you in the orders, and together with you be able and willing to proceed to the execution thereof against the forenamed Waldenses, and all other heretics whatsoever, to rise up in arms against them, and by a joint communication of processes, to tread them under foot as venomous adders, and to procure diligently that the people committed to their charge do persist in the confession of the true faith, and be confirmed therein; and that they do with a ready mind, as they are bound, use all their endeavours, and bestow all their care towards so holy and so necessary an extermination and dispersion of the same heretics; and they are to be required to omit nothing which may contribute thereunto.

"And if you shall think it expedient, to cause, exhort, and induce all the faithful in those parts, by fit preachers of God preaching the cross or the crusade, to fight manfully against the same heretics, having taken the saving sign of the cross upon their hearts and garments; and to grant, that such as are signed with the cross, and fight against the said heretics, or such as contribute thereunto, may obtain, according to your appointment, once in their life, and also at the point of death, a plenary indulgence and remission of all their sins.

"In the mean time to choose, depute, and confirm one or more fit generals of war, and captains, for the collecting the crusade army in our name of the church of Rome, and command them that they take this burden upon them, and execute it faithfully for the praise and defence of the faith; and that all others do endeavour jointly to obey him or them; and to enjoin, that all the moveable and immoveable goods of the heretics may be lawfully seized and given away by any body whatsoever; and to make a booty of all goods which the heretics bring, or cause to be brought, unto the territories of the Catholics, or carry, or cause to be carried, out of the same; and to command, that all who are in the service of the same heretics any where, shall depart within the time by you prefixed unto them, under such penalties as you shall see good; and to admonish and require them, and all ecclesiastical and secular persons, of what dignity, age, sex, or order soever they may be, to yield obedience, and give attendance with reverence to the apostolical commands, under the penalties of excommunication, suspension, or interdiction; and that they abstain from all commerce with the foresaid heretics: and to declare, that neither they, nor any others, who, by any contract or otherwise, are in any sort bound unto them to perform or pay any thing, are henceforth at all obliged, or by the same authority can be compelled thereunto."

N°. IX.

Ancient Language of the Vaudois.

The ancient language of the inhabitants of the Cottian Alps, called Valdesi, Waldenses, or Vaudois, was, (as their topographical situation between France and Italy would imply) a mixture of French and Italian. The Patois, as it is now spoken in the Valleys, is nearly the same; and a comparison between the words in the brief vocabulary subjoined, and those in the original of the "Noble Lesson," which will be found in Appendix No. II, will show how little the language of this secluded community has varied, for the last seven hundred years. It will also serve to establish the opinion, that the present inhabitants of the Protestant Valleys of Piemont are of the aboriginal race, and not descendants from any German or other refugees.

English.	Italian.	Vaudois.	French.
Day	Dì, or giórno	Di	Jour.
Morning	Mattina	Matina	Matin.
Evening	Séra	Sera	Soir.
Night	Nótte	Notte	Nuit.
You	Voi, vi	Vous, vi	Vous.
Your	Vostro	Vost	Vôtre.
I	Io	I	Je.
Flock	Gregge	Tropel	Troupeau.
Lamb	Agnello	Jaynel	Agneau.
Cold	Freddo	Fred	Froid.
Warm	Caldo	Caoud	Chaud.
Hunger	Fame	Fam	Faim.

English.	Italian.	Vaudois.	French.
Thirst	Sete	Sè	Soif.
Fatigued	Stanco	Strac	Fatigué.
Time	Tempo	Temp	Temps.
Summer	State	Està	Eté.
Winter	Inverno	Invera	Hiver.
Mountain	Montagna	Montagna	Montagne.
Scripture	Scrittura	Scritura	Ecriture.
Bible	Bibbia	Bibia	Bible.
Festival	Festa	Festa	Fête.
Vigil	Vigilia	Viay	Veille.
Hen	Gallina	Galina	Poule.
Stable	Stalla	Stabi	Ecurie.
Horse	Cavallo	Caval	Cheval.
Arm	Braccio	Bra	Bras.
Leg	Gamba	Gambe	Jambe.
Eye	Occhio	Yeue	Œil.
Head	Testa	Testa	Tête.
Box	Casetta	Cassia	Cassette.
Fire	Foco	Feu	Feu.
Country	Paese	Paiis	Pays.
Soup	Brodo	Breu	Bouillon.

English.	Italian.	Vaudois.	French.
I will go	Ci andrò	I vaou	J'irai.
Rest yourself	Riposi	Repousévé	Reposez-vous.
Let us go away	Andiamocene	Andoumsene	Allons nous en.
Give me	Mi dia	Demme	Donnez-moi.
Are you amused?	Si diverte ella?	Vi demousévé?	Vous amusez-vous?
He is wearied	Egli s'annoja	A sanneuya	Il s'ennuie.
I am cold	Ho freddo	I ai freid	J'ai froid.
I am warm	Ho caldo	I ai caoud	J'ai chaud.
I am hungry—thirsty	Ho fame—sete	I ai fam—sè	J'ai faim—soif.
I am not fatigued	Non sono stanco	I son pa strac	Je ne suis pas fatigué.
Bring the key	Portate qui la chiave	Pourté mé la ciav	Apportez la clef.
Let us get away	Sbrighiamoci	Surtourma	Sortons.
Make haste	Usciamo via	Degagiournese	Depêchons-nous.
Let us see the horse	Vediamo il cavallo	Buccourna el cavall'	Voyons le cheval.
It is very poor	Quanto è magro	Al e ben maire	Il est bien maigre.
It is lame	E' zoppico	A soppio	Il boite.
What age is it?	Quanti anni ha?	Vaire an allou?	Quel âge a-t-il?
It is an old horse	E un cavallo vecchio	Alle un veii caval	C'est un vieux cheval.
What price do you ask for it?	Quanto ne volete	Cosa na voule ou?	Quel prix en voulez-vous?
It is a good saddle horse	E un bel cavalloda sella	Alle un bel caval da sella	C'est un beau cheval de selle.
It is not worth more	Cio non vale di più	Souli val pa de pie	Cela ne vaut pas davantage.
For that price	Per questo prezzo	A coust preci	Pour ce prix.
I will take it	Io la prendero	La pierai	Je la prendrai.
I will not have it	Non ne voglio	Na voui pa ne	Je n'en veux point.
Give me some soup	Datemi il mio brodo	Demme un breu	Donnez moi un bouillon.
Good day, Sir	Buongiórno, Signore	Bon di, Signor	Bon jour, Monsieur.
How do you do?	Come sta?	Com vaila?	Comment vous portez-vous?
Very well	Ottimamente	Drees a drees	Fort bien.

N°. X.

Notice of the parochial Collection made in England, in the Year 1655, for the Relief of the Vaudois.

A VERY explicit and satisfactory account of the manner in which this great collection, amounting to 38,241*l.* 10*s.* 6*d.* was raised, of the mode pursued for dispensing immediate assistance to the sufferers, and of the measures taken for relieving the future necessities of the Vaudois, by establishing a permanent fund, was published by the authority of the Protector Cromwell and the Privy Council. Morland's History contains a copy of this statement, from which it appears that a committee, consisting of part of the Privy Council, the Lords Chief Justices, and twenty-four other persons of known integrity, was appointed to manage the distribution of the money; and that Morland himself, after his unsuccessful mission to Turin, resided a year at Geneva, as "Commissioner extraordinary for the affairs of the valleys."

It will be needless to give the whole account of the receipts and payments, as the following abbreviate will furnish a sufficient idea both of the contributions, and the disposal of them.

RECEIPTS.

Anno, 1655.	£.	s.	d.
Given by the Lord Protector	2000	0	0
Collected within the cities of London and Westminster	9384	6	11
Collected in the other parishes of England and Wales	24977	18	4
Given by particular individuals	1735	2	0
Gained by remission of part of the above	144	3	3
	£38241	10	6

PAYMENTS.

	£.	s.	d.
By cash, corn, bedding, clothes, &c. between June 1655 and Jan. 1658	21908	0	3
Remain in Treasurer's hands, to be put out to interest*	16333	10	3
	£38241	10	6

* Seized at the restoration by Charles II.

N°. XI.

Notice of some of the most distinguished Ministers, or Barbes of the Waldenses.

For want of a regular and well-continued history of the Waldenses, or Vaudois, it is a difficult matter to assign a certain date to the periods, in which some of their most eminent pastors flourished; more particularly as we lose sight of them, when they were obliged to fly from the heat of persecution, or when their records were destroyed by their adversaries. But nothing can be more true, or more important to the cause of truth, than the fact, that for centuries before the age of Luther, and of the other great men, to whom the holy work of the Reformation is attributed, the same doctrines, which they preached, were already established, in their utmost purity, among this little community of mountaineers, who preserved, in their impregnable fastnesses, the faith, and very probably the exact discipline also, of the primitive church of Christ.

Allix, in his "Remarks upon the ancient Churches of Piedmont," contends, that, "if we had such a history, it would be easy to make it appear, that they have always preserved among themselves a church government, and that they distinguished their clergy into three orders, bishops, priests, and deacons."—P. 238.

Raynerus, the inquisitor, who wrote an account of the Vaudois in the year 1250, and who, from being a Waldensian barbe, became a persecutor of his former associates, leaves it upon record, that they had a chief bishop among them, who was always attended by two clergymen, one of whom he called his elder, and the other his younger son; and that to this bishop were made the reports of those, who were spreading their doctrines in foreign parts.

The number of Waldensian barbes, or pastors, was at one time very considerable; and, in an Italian manuscript, preserved in vol. R, of the Cambridge MSS. entitled, "Historia breve degl' Affari dei Valdesi delle Valli," and bearing date A.D. 1587, it is stated, that there were once assembled at a synod held in the Val Clusone, no less than *one hundred and forty barbes.*

The same manuscript informs us, that some of these barbes travelled into distant countries, to preach the Gospel, and to visit the Waldensian churches, established in France, Germany, Lombardy, Calabria, &c. and that those who staid at home attended strictly to their pastoral duties, or instructed the youth in grammar, logic, moral philosophy, and divinity, at the college of Angrogna, and at other places consecrated to study.

Chronological Table of remarkable Persons and Events in the History of the Vaudois.

	A. .D
Sylvester, Bishop of Rome, whose arrogance is said to have occasioned the first protest of the churches of the valleys	314
Ambrose, Bishop of Milan and the north of Italy, protests against the introduction of images into churches, and shews that certain superstitions, prevalent elsewhere, had not extended into the mountainous regions of his diocese	374
Claude, Bishop of Turin, and of the valleys of Piemont ..	817
Claude writes a commentary on Exodus and Leviticus, against Image-worship	823
Date of La Nobla Leyçon, MS. written by a Waldensian barbe, name unknown	1100
Date of a treatise upon Antichrist, MS. written by a Waldensian barbe, name unknown	1120
Arnoldo, a Waldensian barbe, fl.	1150
Esperone, a Waldensian barbe, fl.	1156
Inquisition established against the Waldenses	1204

Date of a treatise on the word of God, MS. written by a Waldensian barbe, name unknown 1230

Belinanza, Waldensian barbe.............................. 1250

Raynerus, the inquisitor, writes against the Waldenses.. 1250

Bull of Pope John XXII, against the Waldenses........ 1332

Walter Lollard, a Waldensian barbe, burnt at Cologne .. 1350

Bull of Pope Clement VII, against the Vaudois, speaks of increase of heresy in the valleys of Luzerna and Perosa 1370

Persecution in the valleys of Pragela and Perosa........ 1400

Stephano, the Waldensian bishop, who ordained the three Bohemian pastors, burnt at Vienna 1470

Bull of Pope Innocent VIII, against the heretics, or Vaudois of Piemont.................................. 1487

Olivetan Robert, a native Vaudois, prints the Bible in French at Neufchatel.............................. 1535

Articles of faith drawn up, and presented by the Waldenses to Francis I. 1544

Persecution of the Vaudois, by Emanuel, Duke of Savoy 1560

Edict published by Emanuel Philibert, Duke of Savoy, in favour of the Vaudois 1561

A second persecution by Emanuel Philibert............ 1565

Edict of Charles Emanuel, in favour of the Vaudois 1582

Persecution of the Vaudois, by Charles Emanuel........ 1602

Second edict, published by Charles Emanuel, in favour of the Vaudois 1608

Second persecution of Charles Emanuel 1622

An ambassador sent from England by Charles I, to intercede for the Vaudois............................ 1627

A second ambassador, Lord Carlisle, sent by Charles I, to intercede for the Vaudois 1629

Edict of Victor Amadeus I, in favour of the Vaudois.... 1635

Persecution of Victor Amadeus I..................... 1636

Edict of Charles Emanuel II, in favour of the Vaudois .. 1653

Terrible persecution of Charles Emanuel II, and great collection in England to relieve the Vaudois 1655

Pietro Gilles, and Jean Leger, historians of the Vaudois.. 1669

Massacre, persecution, and banishment of the Vaudois, by Victor Amadeus II. 1686

March of the exiles, under Arnaud, for the recovery of their country.. 1689

Restoration of the Vaudois to their country............ 1690

Proclamation of Victor Amadeus II, in acknowledgement of the loyalty and services of the Vaudois 1706

Edict of Victor Amadeus II, against the Vaudois 1730

Letters patent by George III, recommending a parochial collection throughout England, in behalf of the distressed Vaudois.................................... 1768

Letter of Victor Amadeus III, acknowledging the loyalty and services of the Vaudois 1794

Edict of the King of Sardinia, annulling the laws of the late government in favour of the Vaudois 1814

N°. XII.

Confessions of Faith and Ancient Catechism of the Vaudois.

THAT the reader may have an opportunity of judging of the religious tenets of the Vaudois, and of the steadiness with which they have adhered to the faith of their ancestors, he is here presented with their most ancient, and their latest Confession extant.

A Confession of Faith of the Waldenses, bearing date A.D. 1120, *taken from the Cambridge MSS.*

"ARTICLE I.—We believe and firmly hold all that which is contained in the twelve Articles of the Symbol, which is called the Apostles' Creed, accounting for heresy whatsoever is disagreeing, and not consonant to the said twelve Articles.

"ARTICLE II.—We do believe that there is one God, Father, Son, and Holy Spirit.

"ARTICLE III.—We acknowledge for the holy canonical Scriptures, the books of the Holy Bible, viz.

The Books of Moses called:
- Genesis
- Exodus
- Leviticus
- Numbers
- Deuteronomy

Joshua
Judges
Ruth
1 Samuel
2 Samuel
1 Kings

2 Kings
1 Chronicles
2 Chronicles
Ezra
Nehemiah
Esther
Job
Psalms
The Proverbs of Solomon
Ecclesiastes, or the Preacher
The Song of Solomon
The Prophecy of { Isaiah / Jeremiah }
The Lamentations of Jeremiah
Ezekiel
Daniel
Hosea
Joel
Amos
Obadiah
Jonas
Micah
Nahum
Habakkuk
Zephaniah
Haggai
Zachariah
Malachi.

Here follow the books Apocryphal, which are not received of the Hebrews. But we read them (as saith St. Jerome in his Prologue to the Proverbs) for the instruction of the people, not to confirm the authority of the doctrine of the church, viz.

Esdras
Tobit

Judith
Wisdom
Ecclesiasticus
Baruch with the Epistle of Jeremiah
Esther from the tenth chapter to the end
The Song of the three Children in the furnace
The History of Susanna
The History of the Dragon
1 Maccabees
2 Maccabees.

Here follow the books of the New Testament.

The Gospel according to St. { Matthew, Mark, Luke, John }
The Acts of the Apostles
The Epistle of St. Paul to the Romans
1 Corinthians
2 Corinthians
Galatians
Ephesians
Philippians
Colossians
1 Thessalonians
2 Thessalonians
1 Timothy
2 Timothy
Titus
Philemon
The Epistle to the Hebrews
The Epistle of St. James
The 1 Epistle of St. Peter
The 2 Epistle of St. Peter
The 1 Epistle of St. John

The 2 Epistle of St. John
The 3 Epistle of St. John
The Epistle of St. Jude
The Revelation of St. John.

" Article iv.—The books above-said teach this, that there is one God, Almighty, all-wise, and all-good, who has made all things by his goodness; for he formed Adam in his own image and likeness, but that by the envy of the Devil, and the disobedience of the said Adam, sin has entered into the world, and that we are sinners in Adam and by Adam.

" Article v.—That Christ was promised to our Fathers who received the law, that so knowing by the law their sin, unrighteousness, and insufficiency, they might desire the coming of Christ, to satisfy for their sins, and accomplish the law by himself.

" Article vi.—That Christ was born in the time appointed by God the Father. That is to say, in the time when all iniquity abounded, and not for the cause of good works, for all were sinners: but that he might shew us grace and mercy, as being faithful.

" Article vii.—That Christ is our life, truth, peace, and righteousness, also our pastor, advocate, sacrifice, and priest, who died for the salvation of all those that believe, and is risen for our justification.

" Article viii.—In like manner, we firmly hold, that there is no other mediator and advocate with God the Father, save only Jesus Christ. And as for the Virgin Mary, that she was holy, humble, and full of grace; and in like manner do we believe concerning all the other Saints, viz. that being in Heaven, they wait for the resurrection of their bodies at the day of judgment.

" Article ix.—*Item*, we believe that after this life, there are only two places, the one for the saved, and the other for the damned, the which two places we call Paradise and Hell, absolutely denying that purgatory invented by antichrist, and forged contrary to the truth.

" ARTICLE X.—*Item,* we have always accounted as an unspeakable abomination before God, all those inventions of men, namely, the feasts and the vigils of Saints, the water which they call holy. As likewise to abstain from flesh upon certain days, and the like: but especially their masses.

" ARTICLE XI.—We esteem for an abomination and as Antichristian, all those human inventions which are a trouble or prejudice to the liberty of the spirit.

" ARTICLE XII.—We do believe that the Sacraments are signs of the holy thing, or visible forms of the invisible grace, accounting it good that the faithful sometimes use the said signs or visible forms, if it may be done. However, we believe and hold, that the above-said faithful may be saved without receiving the signs aforesaid, in case they have no place nor any means to use them.

" ARTICLE XIII.—We acknowledge no other Sacrament but Baptism and the Lord's Supper.

" ARTICLE XIV.—We ought to honour the secular powers by submission, ready obedience, and paying of tributes."

A Confession of Faith published by the Evangelical Churches of Piemont, in 1655.

" Having understood that our adversaries, not contented to have most cruelly persecuted us, and robbed us of all our goods and estates, have yet an intention to render us odious to the world, by spreading abroad many false reports, and so not only to defame our persons, but likewise to asperse with most shameful calumnies that holy and wholesome doctrine which we profess, we look upon ourselves as obliged, for the better information of those, whose minds may perhaps be preoccupied with sinister opinions, to make a short declaration of our faith, such as we have heretofore professed and held, and do at this day profess and hold as conformable to the word of God; and so every one may see the falsity of those their calumnies, and also how unjustly we are hated and persecuted upon the account of our profession.

"*We believe,*

"1. First, that there is one only God, who is a spiritual essence, eternal, infinite, all-wise, merciful, just, and in sum, all-perfect, and that there are three persons in that one only and simple essence, viz. the Father, Son, and Holy Spirit.

"2. That the same God has manifested himself unto us by the works of Creation, and Providence, as also in his word revealed unto us, first by oracles in several manners, and afterwards by those written books which are called the Holy Scriptures.

"3. That we ought to receive those Holy Scriptures (as we do) for sacred and canonical, that is to say, for the constant rule of our faith and life: as also to believe, that the same is fully contained in the Old and New Testament; and that by the Old Testament we must understand only such books as God did intrust the Judaical church with, and which that church always approved and acknowledged to be from God: namely, the five books of *Moses*, *Joshua*, the *Judges*, *Ruth*, 1 and 2 of *Samuel*, 1 and 2 of the *Kings*, 1 and 2 of the *Chronicles*, the 1 of *Ezra*, *Nehemiah*, *Esther*, *Job*, the *Psalms*, the *Proverbs* of *Solomon*, *Ecclesiastes*, the *Song of Songs*, the four great, and the twelve minor Prophets; the New Testament contains only the four Evangelists, the *Acts* of the Apostles, the Epistles of *St. Paul*, 1 to the *Romans*, 2 to the *Corinthians*, 1 to the *Galatians*, 1 to the *Ephesians*, 1 to the *Philippians*, 1 to the *Colossians*, 2 to the *Thessalonians*, 2 to *Timothy*, 1 to *Titus*, 1 to *Philemon*, and his Epistle to the *Hebrews*, one of *St. James*, 2 of *St. Peter*, 3 of *St. John*, 1 of *St. Jude*, and lastly, the *Revelation*.

"4. We acknowledge the divinity of these books, not only from the testimony of the church, but more especially because of the eternal and undoubted truth of the doctrine therein contained, and of that most divine excellency, sublimity, and majesty, which appears therein; besides the testimony of the Holy Spirit, who gives us to receive with reverence the testimony of the church in that point, and opens the eyes of our understanding to discover the beams of that celestial light, which shines in the

Scripture, and prepares our taste to discern the divine favour of that spiritual food.

" 5. That God made all things of nothing by his own free will, and by the infinite power of his word.

" 6. That he governs and rules all by his providence, ordaining and appointing whatsoever happens in this world, without being author or cause of any evil committed by the creatures, so that the defect thereof neither can nor ought to be any ways imputed unto him.

" 7. That the angels were all in the beginning created pure and holy, but that some of them are fallen into irreparable corruption and perdition: and that the rest have persevered in their first purity by an effect of divine goodness, which has upheld and confirmed them.

" 8. That man was created clean and holy, after the image of God, and that, through his own fault, he deprived himself of that happy condition, by giving credit to the deceitful words of the devil.

" 9. That man by his transgression lost that righteousness and holiness which he received, and is thereby obnoxious to the wrath of God, death, and captivity, under the jurisdiction of him who has the power of death, that is, the devil: in so much that our free will is become a servant and a slave to sin: and thus all men, both Jews and Gentiles, are by nature the children of wrath, being all dead in their trespasses and sins, and consequently incapable of the least good motion, or inclination to any thing which concerns their salvation: yea, incapable to think one good thought without God's special grace, all their imaginations being wholly evil, and that continually.

" 10. That all the posterity of Adam is guilty of his disobedience, and infected by his corruption, and fallen into the same calamity with him, even the very infants from their mothers' womb, whence is derived the term original sin.

" 11. That God saves from that corruption and condemnation those whom he has chosen from the foundation of the world, not for any disposition, faith or holiness that he foresaw in them, but of his mere mercy in Jesus Christ his Son; passing by all the rest, according to the irreprehensible reason of his free will and justice.

"12. That Jesus Christ having been ordained by the eternal decree of God, to be the only Saviour, and head of that body which is the Church, he redeemed it with his own blood in the fulness of time, and communicates unto the same all his benefits, together with the Gospel.

"13. That there are two natures in Jesus Christ, viz. divine and human, truly united in one and the same person, without either confusion, separation, division, or alteration; each nature keeping its own distinct proprieties; and that Jesus Christ is both true God and true man.

"14. That God so loved the world, that is to say, those whom he has chosen out of the world, that he gave his own Son to save us by his most perfect obedience, (especially that obedience which he expressed in his suffering the cursed death of the cross) and also by his victory over the devil, sin, and death.

"15. That Jesus Christ having fully expiated our sins by his most perfect sacrifice once offered on the cross, it neither can, nor ought to be reiterated upon any account whatsoever, as they pretend to do in the mass.

"16. That the Lord having fully and absolutely reconciled us unto God, through the blood of his cross, by virtue of his merit only, and not of our works, we are thereby absolved and justified in his sight, neither is there any other purgatory besides his blood, which cleanses us from all sin.

"17. That we are united with Christ, and made partakers of all his benefits by faith, trusting and confiding wholly to those promises of life which are given us in the Gospel.

"18. That that faith is the gracious and efficacious work of the Holy Spirit, which enlightens our souls, and persuades them to lean and rest upon the mercy of God, and so thereby to apply unto themselves the merits of Jesus Christ.

"19. That Jesus Christ is our true and only mediator, not only redeeming us, but also interceding for us, and that by virtue of his merits, and intercession, we have access unto the Father, for to make our supplications unto him, with a holy confidence and assurance that he will grant us our requests, it being needless to have recourse to any other intercessor besides himself.

" 20. That as God has promised us, that we shall be regenerated in Christ; so those that are united unto him by a true faith, ought to apply, and do really apply themselves unto good works.

" 21. That good works are so necessary to the faithful, that they cannot attain the kingdom of Heaven without the same, seeing that God hath prepared them that we should walk therein, and therefore we ought to avoid vice and to apply ourselves to Christian virtues, making use of fasting, and all other means which may conduce to so holy a thing.

" 22. That although our good works cannot merit any thing, yet the Lord will reward or recompense them with eternal life, through the merciful continuation of his grace, and by virtue of the unchangeable constancy of his promises made unto us.

" 23. That those, who are already in the possession of eternal life by their faith and good works, ought to be considered as saints, and as glorified persons, and to be praised for their virtue, and imitated in all good actions of their life, but neither worshipped nor prayed unto, for God only is to be prayed unto, and that through Jesus Christ.

" 24. That God has chosen unto himself one church in the world for the salvation of mankind, and that same church to have only one head and foundation, which is Christ.

" 25. That that church is the company of the faithful, who having been elected before the foundation of the world, and called with an holy calling, come to unite themselves to follow the word of God, believing whatsoever he teaches them, and living in his fear.

" 26. That that church cannot err, nor be annihilated, but must endure for ever, and that all the elect are upheld and preserved by the power of God in such sort, that they all persevere in the faith unto the end, and remain united in the holy church, as so many living members thereof.

"27. That all men ought to join with that church, and to continue in the communion thereof.

"28. That God does not only instruct and teach us by his word, but has also ordained certain Sacraments to be joined with it, as a means to unite us unto Christ, and to make us partakers of his benefits; and that there are only two of them belonging in common to all the members of the church under the New Testament, to wit, Baptism, and the Lord's Supper.

"29. That God has ordained the Sacrament of Baptism to be a testimony of our adoption, and of our being cleansed from our sins, by the blood of Jesus Christ, and renewed in holiness of life.

"30. That the Holy Supper was instituted for the nourishment of our souls, to the end that eating effectually the flesh of Christ, and drinking effectually his blood, by the incomprehensible virtue and power of the Holy Spirit, and through a true and living faith; and so uniting ourselves most closely and inseparably to Christ, we come to enjoy in him and by him the spiritual and eternal life. Now to the end that every one may clearly see what our belief is as to this point, we have here inserted the very expressions of that prayer, which we make use of before the Communion, as they are written in our Liturgy or form of celebrating the Holy Supper, and likewise in our public Catechism, which are to be seen at the end of our Psalms; these are the words of the Prayer.

"Seeing our Lord has not only once offered his body and blood for the remission of our sins, but is willing also to communicate the same unto us as the food of eternal life, we humbly beseech him so to give us of his grace, that in true sincerity of heart, and with an ardent zeal, we may receive of him so great a benefit; that is, that we may be made partakers of his body and blood, or rather of his whole self, by a sure and certain faith.

"The words of the Liturgy are these, Let us then believe first, the promises which Christ, (who is the infallible truth) has pronounced with his own mouth, viz. that he will make us truly partakers of his body and blood, that so we may possess him entirely, and in such sort that he may live in us, and we in him. The words of our Catechism are the same, *Nella Dominica* 53.

" 31. That it is necessary the church should have ministers, known by those who are employed for that purpose, to be learned, and of a good life, as well to preach the word of God, as to administer the Sacraments, and wait upon the flock of Christ, (according to the rules of a good and holy discipline) together with elders and deacons, after the manner of the primitive church.

" 32. That God hath established kings and magistrates to govern the people, and that the people ought to be obedient and subject unto them, by virtue of that ordination, not only for fear, but also for conscience sake, in all things that are conformable to the word of God, who is the King of kings, and the Lord of lords.

" 33. Finally, that we ought to receive the symbol of the Apostles, the Lord's Prayer, and the Decalogue, as fundamentals of our faith, and of our devotion.

" And for a more ample declaration of our faith, we do here reiterate the same protestation which we caused to be printed in 1603, that is to say, that we do agree in sound doctrine with all the reformed churches of France, Great Britain, the Low Countries, Germany, Switzerland, Bohemia, Poland, Hungary, and others, as it is represented by them in their confessions; as also we receive the Confession of Augsbourg, and as it was published by the authors, promising to persevere constantly therein with the help of God both in life and death, and being ready to subscribe to that eternal truth of God, with our own blood, even as our ancestors have done from the days of the Apostles, and especially in these latter ages.

" Therefore we humbly entreat all the Evangelical and Protestant Churches to look upon us as true members of the mystical body of Christ, suffering for his name sake, notwithstanding our poverty and lowness; and to continue unto us the help of their prayers to God, and all other effects of their charity, as we have heretofore abundantly found and felt, for the which we return them our most humble thanks, entreating the Lord with all our heart to be their rewarder, and to pour upon them the most precious blessings of grace and glory, both in this life and that which is to come. *Amen.*"

Catechism of the Ancient Waldenses for the Instruction of their Youth, composed in the 13th century.

Minister. If one should demand of you, who are you, what would you answer?

Child. A creature of God, reasonable, and mortal.

Min. Why has God created you?

Answ. To the end that I might know him and serve him, and be saved by his grace.

Min. Wherein consists your salvation?

Answ. In three substantial virtues, which necessarily belong to salvation.

Min. Which are they?

Answ. Faith, Hope and Charity.

Min. How can you prove that?

Answ. The Apostle writes, 1 Cor. xiii. " Now abideth faith, hope, and charity, these three."

Min. What is faith?

Answ. According to the Apostle, Heb. xi. " It is the substance of things hoped for, and the evidence of things not seen."

Min. How many sorts of faith are there?

Answ. There are two sorts, viz. a living and a dead faith.

Min. What is a living faith?

Answ. It is that which works by charity.

Min. What is a dead faith?

Answ. According to St. James, it is that which without works is dead. Again, faith is null without works; or a dead faith is, to believe that there is a God, and not to believe in him.

Min. What is your faith?

Answ. The true Catholic and Apostolic faith.

Min. What is that?

Answ. It is that which in the result (or symbol) of the Apostles, is divided into twelve articles.

Min. What is that?

Answ. I believe in God the Father Almighty, &c.

Min. By what way can you know that you believe in God?

Answ. By this, that I know and I observe the commandments of God.

Min. How many commandments of God are there?

Answ. Ten, as is manifest in Exodus and Deuteronomy.

Min. Which be they?

Answ. "Hear O Israel, I am the Lord thy God, thou shalt have none other gods before me. Thou shalt not make any graven image, or any likeness of any thing that is in heaven," &c.

Min. What is the sum or drift of these commandments?

Answ. It consists in these two great commandments, viz. Thou shalt love God above all things, and thy neighbour as thyself.

Min. What is that foundation of these commandments, by the which every one may enter into life, and without the which foundation none can do any thing worthily, or fulfil the commandments?

Answ. The Lord Jesus Christ, of whom the Apostle speaks in the 1 Cor. "Other foundation can no man lay, than that is laid, which is Jesus Christ."

Min. By what means may a man come to this foundation?

Answ. By faith, as saith St. Peter, 1 Pet. 2 ch. 6 v. "Behold I lay in Sion a chief corner stone, elect, precious, and he that believeth on him shall not be confounded." And the Lord saith, "He that believeth hath eternal life."

Min. Whereby canst thou know that thou believest?

Answ. By this, that I know him to be true God, and true man, who was born, and who hath suffered, &c. for my redemption, justification, and that I love him, and desire to fulfil his commandments.

Min. By what means may one attain to those essential virtues, faith, hope, and charity?

Answ. By the gifts of the Holy Spirit.

Min. Dost thou believe in the Holy Spirit?

Answ. Yes, I do believe. For the Holy Spirit proceeds from the Father and the Son, and is one person of the Trinity; and according to the Divinity, is equal to the Father and the Son.

Min. Thou believest God the Father, God the Son, and God the Holy Spirit: thou hast therefore three Gods.

Answ. I have not three.

Min. Yea, but thou hast named three.

Answ. That is by reason of the difference of the persons, not by reason of the essence of the divinity. For, although there are three persons, yet notwithstanding there is but one essence.

Min. In what manner dost thou adore and worship that God on whom thou believest?

Answ. I adore him with the adoration of an inward and outward worship. Outwardly, by the bending of the knee, and lifting up the hands, by bowing the body, by hymns and spiritual songs, by fasting and praying, but inwardly, by an holy affection: by a will conformable unto all things, that are well pleasing unto him. And I serve him by faith, hope, and charity, according to his commandments.

Min. Dost thou adore and worship any other thing as God?

Answ. No.

Min. Why?

Answ. Because of his commandment, whereby it is strictly commanded, saying, "Thou shalt worship the Lord thy God, and him only shalt thou serve." And again, "I will not give my glory to another." Again, "As I live, saith the Lord, every knee shall bow before me." And Jesus Christ saith, "There shall come the true worshippers which shall worship the Father in spirit and in truth." And the angel would not be worshipped by St. John, nor St. Peter by Cornelius.

Min. After what manner prayest thou?

Answ. I pray, rehearsing the prayer given me by the Son of God, saying "Our Father which art in Heaven," &c.

Min. What is the other substantial virtue appertaining to salvation?

Answ. It is Charity.

Min. What is Charity?

Answ. It is the gift of the Holy Spirit by which the soul is reformed in the will, being enlightened by faith, whereby I believe all that ought to be believed, and hope all that ought to be hoped.

Min. Dost thou believe in the Holy Church?

Answ. No, for it is a creature, but I believe that there is one.

Min. What is that which thou believest concerning the Holy Church?

Answ. I say, that the church is considered two manner of ways, the one substantially, and the other ministerially. As it is considered substantially, by the Holy Catholic Church is meant all the elect of God, from the beginning of the world to the end, by the grace of God through the merit of Christ, gathered together by the Holy Spirit, and fore-ordained to eternal life; the number and names of whom are known to him alone who has elected them, and in this church remains none who is reprobate; but the church, as it is considered according to the truth of the ministry, is the company of the ministers of Christ, together with the people committed to their charge, using the ministry, by faith, hope, and charity.

Min. Whereby dost thou know the church of Christ?

Answ. By the ministers lawfully called, and by the people participating in truth of the ministry.

Min. But by what marks knowest thou the ministers?

Answ. By the true sense of faith; by sound doctrine; by a life of good example; by the preaching of the gospel, and a due administration of the sacraments.

Min. By what mark knowest thou the false ministers?

Answ. By their fruits, by their blindness, by their evil works, by their perverse doctrine, and by their undue administration of the sacraments.

Min. Whereby knowest thou their blindness?

Answ. When not knowing the truth, which necessarily appertains to salvation, they observe human inventions as ordinances of God. Of whom is verified what Isaiah says, and which is alleged by our Lord Jesus Christ, Matt. xv. "This people honour me with their lips, but their heart is far from me. But in vain they do worship me, teaching for doctrines the commandments of men."

Min. By what marks knowest thou evil works?

Answ. By those manifest sins of which the Apostle speaks, Gal. v. saying, "That they which do such things, shall not inherit the kingdom of God."

Min. By what mark knowest thou perverse doctrine?

Answ. When it teacheth contrary to faith and hope; such is idolatry of several sorts, viz. towards a reasonable, sensible, visible or invisible creature. For, it is the Father alone with his Son and the Holy Spirit, who ought to be worshipped, and not any creature whatsoever. But when on the contrary they attribute to man and to the work of his hands, or to his words, or to his authority in such a manner, that men ignorantly believe that they have satisfied God by a false religion, and by satisfying the covetous symony of the priests.

Min. By what marks is the undue administration of the sacrament known?

Answ. When the priests not knowing the intention of Christ in sacraments, say, that the grace and the truth is included in the external ceremonies, and persuade men to the participation of the sacrament without the truth, and without faith. But the Lord chargeth those that are his to take heed of such false prophets, saying, "Beware of the pharisees," that is to say, "of the leaven of their doctrine." Again, "Believe them not, neither go after them." And David hates the church or the congregation of such persons, saying, "I hate the church of evil men." And the Lord commands to come out from the midst of such people, Numb. xvi. "Depart from the tents of these wicked men, and touch nothing of theirs, lest you be consumed in their sins." And the Apostle 2 Cor. vi. 14. "Be ye not unequally yoked with unbelievers. For what fellowship hath righteousness with unrighteousness, and what communion hath light with darkness, and what concord hath Christ with Belial, or what part hath he that believeth with an infidel? And what agreement hath the temple of God with idols? Wherefore come out from among them, and be ye separate, saith the Lord, and touch not the unclean thing, and I will receive you." Again, 2 Thess. "Now we command you, brethren, that you withdraw yourselves from every brother that walketh disorderly." Again, Rev. xviii. "Come out of her, my people, that ye be not partakers of her sins, and that ye receive not of her plagues."

Min. By what marks are those people known who are not in truth within the church?

Answ. By public sins, and an erroneous faith. For we ought to fly from such persons, lest we be defiled by them.

Min. By what ways oughtest thou to communicate with the Holy Church?

Answ. I ought to communicate with the church in regard of its substance, by faith and charity, as also by observing the commandments, and by a final perseverance in well doing.

Min. How many things are there which are ministerial?

Answ. Two. The word and the sacraments.

Min. How many sacraments are there?

Answ. Two, namely, Baptism, and the Lord's Supper.

Min. What is the third virtue necessary to salvation?

Answ. Hope.

Min. What is hope?

Answ. It is a waiting for grace and glory to come.

Min. How does a man wait (or hope) for grace?

Answ. By the mediator Jesus Christ, of whom St. John saith, "Grace comes by Jesus Christ." Again, "We have seen his glory, who is full of grace and truth, and we all have received of his fulness."

Min. What is that grace?

Answ. It is redemption, remission of sins, justification, adoption, and sanctification.

Min. Upon what account is this grace hoped for in Christ?

Answ. By a living faith, and true repentance, saying, "Repent ye, and believe the Gospel."

Min. Whence proceedeth this hope?

Answ. From the gift of God, and the promises of which the Apostle mentioneth, "He is powerful to perform whatsoever he promiseth." For he hath promised himself, that whosoever shall know him, and repent, and shall hope in him, he will have mercy upon, pardon, and justify, &c.

Min. What are the things that put us beside this hope?

Answ. A dead faith, the seduction of Antichrist to believe in other things beside Christ, that is to say, in Saints, in the power of that Antichrist, in his authority, words, and benedictions, in sacraments, reliques of the dead, in purgatory, which is but forged and contrived, in teaching that faith is obtained by those ways which oppose themselves to the truth, and are against the commandments of God. As is idolatry in divers respects. As also by wickedness and simony, &c. Forsaking the fountain of living water given by grace, and running to broken cisterns, worshipping, honouring, and serving the creature by prayers, by fastings, by sacrifices, by donations, by offerings, by pilgrimages, by invocations, &c. Relying upon themselves for the acquiring of grace, which none can give save only God in Christ. In vain do they labour, and lose their money and their lives, and the truth is, they do not only lose their present life, but also that which is to come; wherefore it is said, that "the hope of fools shall perish."

Min. And what dost thou say of the blessed Virgin Mary? For she is full of grace, as the angel testifies, "I salute thee full of grace."

Answ. The blessed Virgin was and is full of grace, as much as is necessary for her own particular salvation, but not to communicate to others, for her Son alone is full of grace, and can communicate the same as he pleaseth, and "We have all received of his fulness, grace for grace."

Min. Believest thou not the communion of saints?

Answ. I believe that there are two sorts of things wherein the saints communicate, the first substantial, the other ministerial.

As to the substantials, they communicate by the Holy Spirit, in God through the merit of Jesus Christ: as to the ministerials or ecclesiastics, they communicate by the ministry duly performed, namely, by the word, by the sacraments, and by prayer; I believe both the one and the other of these communions of saints. The first only in God, and in Jesus Christ, and in the Holy Ghost by the Holy Spirit. The other in the church of Christ.

Min. Wherein consists eternal life?

Answ. In a living and operating faith, and in perseverance in the same. Our Saviour says, John xvii. "This is life eternal, to know thee the only true God, and Jesus Christ whom thou hast sent." And "he that endures to the end shall be saved."

GENERAL INDEX.

C.

D.

E.

F.

G.

H.

I.

R.

V.

W.

THE END.

www.ingramcontent.com/pod-product-compliance
Lightning Source LLC
LaVergne TN
LVHW020520100826
845148LV00010B/1292

* 9 7 8 1 5 9 7 5 2 2 5 4 0 *